The Microsoft® Guide to

C++ PROGRAMMING

The Microsoft® Guide to

C++ PROGRAMMING

Kaare Christian

PUBLISHED BY
Microsoft Press
A Division of Microsoft Corporation
One Microsoft Way
Redmond, Washington 98052-6399

Library of Congress Cataloging-in-Publication Data
Christian, Kaare, 1954–
The Microsoft guide to C++ programming / Kaare Christian.
p. cm.
Includes index.
ISBN 1-55615-394-5 (softcover) : $27.95 ($37.95 Can.)
1. C++ (Computer program language) I. Title.
QA76.73.C15C5 1992
005.26'2--dc20 92-15668
CIP

Printed and bound in the United States of America.

1 2 3 4 5 6 7 8 9 AGAG 7 6 5 4 3 2

Distributed to the book trade in Canada by Macmillan of Canada, a division of Canada Publishing Corporation.

Distributed to the book trade outside the United States and Canada by Penguin Books Ltd.

Penguin Books Ltd., Harmondsworth, Middlesex, England
Penguin Books Australia Ltd., Ringwood, Victoria, Australia
Penguin Books N.Z. Ltd., 182-190 Wairau Road, Auckland 10, New Zealand

British Cataloging-in-Publication Data available.

Acquisitions Editor: Dean Holmes
Project Editor: Erin O'Connor
Technical Editor: Daniel Lipkie

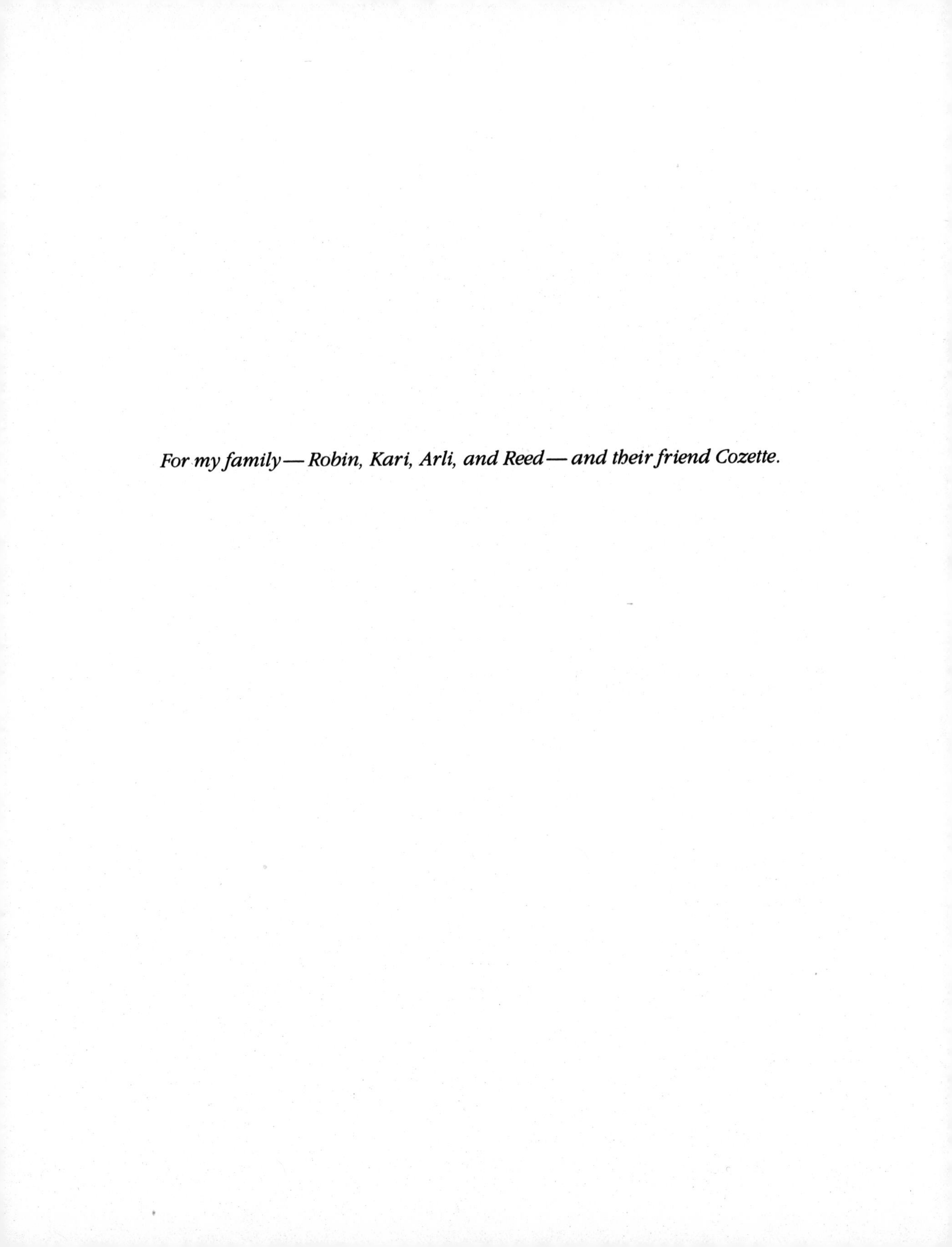

For my family—Robin, Kari, Arli, and Reed—and their friend Cozette.

Contents

Acknowledgments

Everyone working with C++ owes a debt to Bjarne Stroustrup, who skillfully transformed C into an object-oriented language. More personally, I'd like to thank Torsten Wiesel and Charles Gilbert at the Rockefeller University, my editors Dean Holmes and Erin O'Connor at Microsoft Press, Dan Lipkie, and many people at Microsoft, including Keith Rowe, Jeff Harbers, Steve Sinofsky, and Chuck Sphar.

Introduction

An object is data combined with procedures that endow the data with behaviors. An existing object can be reused and can serve as a basis for new objects created by modification or extension. An object is a software machine, a component that can be used in much the same way that physical components can be used in other disciplines. This deceptively simple advance in software technology is a breakthrough because it revolutionizes the way we developers think about software construction.

In essence, object-oriented programming lets us create software objects that correspond to significant elements in the problem domain, and then we create applications by combining those objects. Over time, we are able to assemble complex applications from collections of reliable, reusable objects.

Object-oriented programming thus encourages a new way of thinking about software construction. It is admittedly difficult to change perspective, to look at problems in a new way. Understanding object-oriented programming requires that you dissect the way you think so that you can envision sturdy object-oriented solutions to replace today's aging procedural solutions.

A few years ago, the challenge lay in convincing programmers that they should take object-oriented technology seriously, but today the challenge lies in teaching programmers to apply this technology. More specifically, the challenge lies in identifying problem-domain concepts that can be embodied by objects and in identifying the interfaces for those objects.

C++, a superset of the C language, is the best object-oriented language for delivering efficient, robust applications. Other object-oriented languages are appropriate for various specialized purposes, but only C++ offers the wide range of facilities required by professional developers. C++ is in the process of standardization, it is strongly supported by numerous third-party libraries, and the quality of C++ compilers on the PC is exceptionally high.

Only C++ effectively taps the existing pool of C programmers who are ready to move to more productive realms. C programmers can readily learn C++ object-oriented programming skills, and existing C programs can readily absorb C++ object-oriented features. C++ extends an already rich and productive C tradition instead of forcing a complete break with the past.

Nevertheless, I've felt that existing C++ books focused too much on C++ language features, and that's why I wrote this book. Language features are important, and a professional has an obligation to master his or her tools. But understanding C++ itself is only part of what a professional must do to become a productive object-oriented practitioner. It is equally important to understand the object-oriented paradigm.

In Part 1, I place the principal object-oriented concepts in a C++ framework. If we don't understand the goals and concepts of object-oriented programming, we won't make optimum use of the C++ language features designed to support those concepts.

Part 2 of this book is a guide to the C++ language, organized around language topics. It assumes that you are already proficient in C, and it proceeds at a level of detail appropriate for professional developers. I try to cover the language fairly and completely, and I try with examples to impart lessons gleaned from my own use of C++ over the last five years.

The third part of this book builds on Parts 1 and 2. Another concept that many books on C++ have ignored is the idea that a professional's C++ toolset now extends beyond the language to include class libraries. That's why I think Part 3's consideration of the Microsoft Foundation Class library that comes with the Microsoft C/C++ 7.0 compiler is significant. Yes, Part 3 helps you get a quick start in Windows development, but more important, I've intended its analysis of this elegant library to be an extended lesson in class library design. Part 3's use of the MFC library to create complete Windows applications links the first two parts of the book.

Object-oriented technology has been so hyped that it is tempting to dismiss it as just another fad. But I think object-oriented technology is living up to its hype. When some of us first tried C++ in the mid-80s, old C habits got in the way, the changing C++ specification made us uneasy, the C++ implementations were mediocre, and powerful class libraries seemed to lie far in the future. Today all of this has changed; object-oriented technology is moving us into the next era of software development.

PART 1

OBJECT-ORIENTED PROGRAMMING

A major problem in software development today is a need for sophisticated products that has far outstripped our tools and techniques. Software development has become more efficient and the software we develop more reliable during the past two or three decades, but each success has led to greater expectations. Our current abilities looked at from the perspective of 30 years ago are impressive. Our current abilities looked at from the perspective of today's users anxious for better solutions are inadequate.

Object-oriented development technology is our best hope for meeting the challenge. With object-oriented techniques, we can create software objects that correspond to real-world objects. We can create a software Motor object to control a physical motor. We can create a Vector object to represent a vector. Over time, software objects can become highly reliable and reusable software components. Eventually, we'll construct new applications primarily by reassembling, extending, and modifying existing software objects.

In Part 1 of this book, we'll look at the concepts, terms, and relationships we'll need to understand in order to do object-oriented software development. Chapter 1 places the object-oriented programming paradigm in its historical context among programming models, and then Chapter 2 goes directly into a discussion of objects and classes. Chapters 3, 4, and 5 go into the most important ideas in object-oriented programming, with a strong emphasis on the needs of C++ programmers. Chapter 3 introduces the concepts of encapsulation and abstraction, and Chapter 4 the key ideas inheritance and polymorphism. Chapter 5 ties it all together with its focus on object-oriented design followed by an object-oriented case study. Chapters 3, 4, and 5 don't go into the details of using C++; they focus instead on the underlying principles of object-oriented technology.

Throughout Part 1, you'll find examples of C++ classes that might be hard to follow until you know C++. For the time being, while you acquaint yourself with the principles we'll explore in Part 1, take the example code as it is intended, as mere illustration of the fundamental concepts of object-oriented programming. After you've picked up some proficiency with C++, you can come back to these examples with greater understanding.

1

The Object-Oriented Paradigm

A paradigm is a pattern, a generic blueprint that suggests ways of solving problems. For the past four decades, we've used several similar procedural paradigms to create most of our computer software. We've taken a top-down, or structured, approach to software solutions: The main task was partitioned into subtasks, the subtasks further partitioned, and so on, until the tasks were simple enough to be programmed in the language of choice.

Development from the late 1940s through most of the 1980s saw machine language give way to assembly language, which yielded in turn to higher-level languages such as COBOL, FORTRAN, Basic, Pascal, C, and Ada. These and other HLLs made programming more convenient, but they didn't alter in any fundamental way the procedural programming paradigm that had its roots in machine language. Yes, the HLLs were more expressive and less tied to detail than machine language, but the programming paradigm was the same: to bring about a sequence of operations.

Object-oriented technology, which is poised to dominate programming in the 1990s, is the first fundamental change of paradigm in almost half a century of software development. In object-oriented development, we construct software by combining software objects. In its emphasis on reusable components, object-oriented programming has more in common with the standard paradigms of other engineering disciplines than it has with the procedural software paradigms it supersedes. But the object-oriented approach doesn't repudiate procedural design—it uses procedural methods as appropriate to build objects. An object is an instance of a traditional data type, such as a C struct, plus a set of routines, called "member functions," that endow the object with behaviors.

Object-oriented technology is as big an evolutionary step forward as the top-down approach and the HLLs were. It will change the way software is developed, it will change user expectations about software, it will increase the range and the kinds of applications, and it will mean success for the individuals and the companies who can adapt quickly.

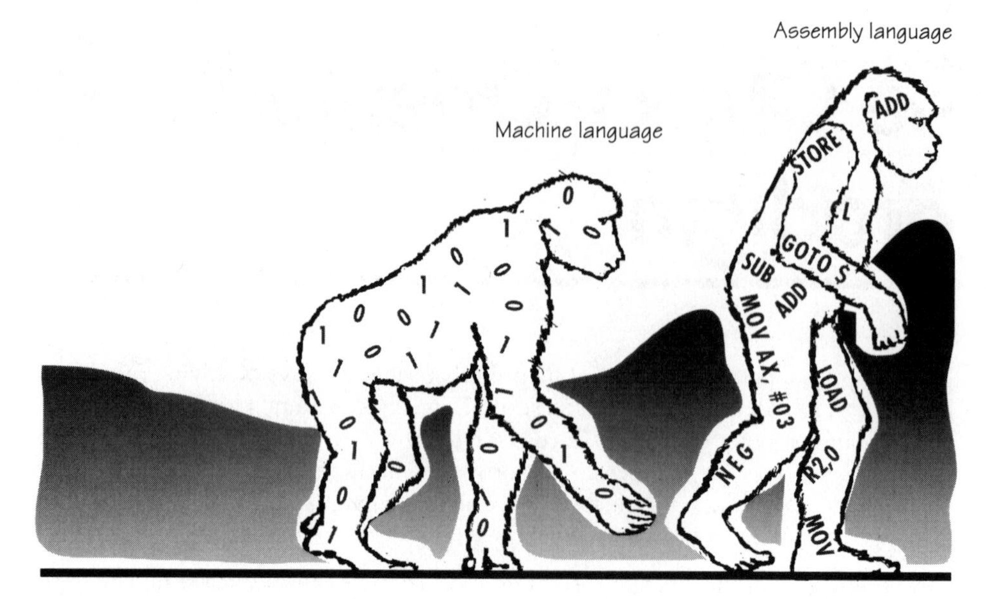

The evolution of programming paradigms.

Object-oriented technology brings these benefits to software development:

- *Reusability.* Objects are designed from the outset for reuse. In any given domain, the first object-oriented application might be more difficult to achieve than a traditionally designed application would be, but subsequent applications will be easier to construct because they can reuse many of the objects created for the first project.

- *Reliability.* Object-oriented applications can be more reliable because they incorporate standard tested parts. Less new code is written for each application as more code is pulled in from highly reliable libraries.

And in C++ programming, there is still another benefit:

- *Continuity.* Object-oriented software development in C++ is compatible with the skills and reflexes of the existing pool of C programmers. An experienced C programmer can learn object-oriented principles in a day or two and can become fluent in a matter of weeks or months. Existing C applications can be upgraded to C++.

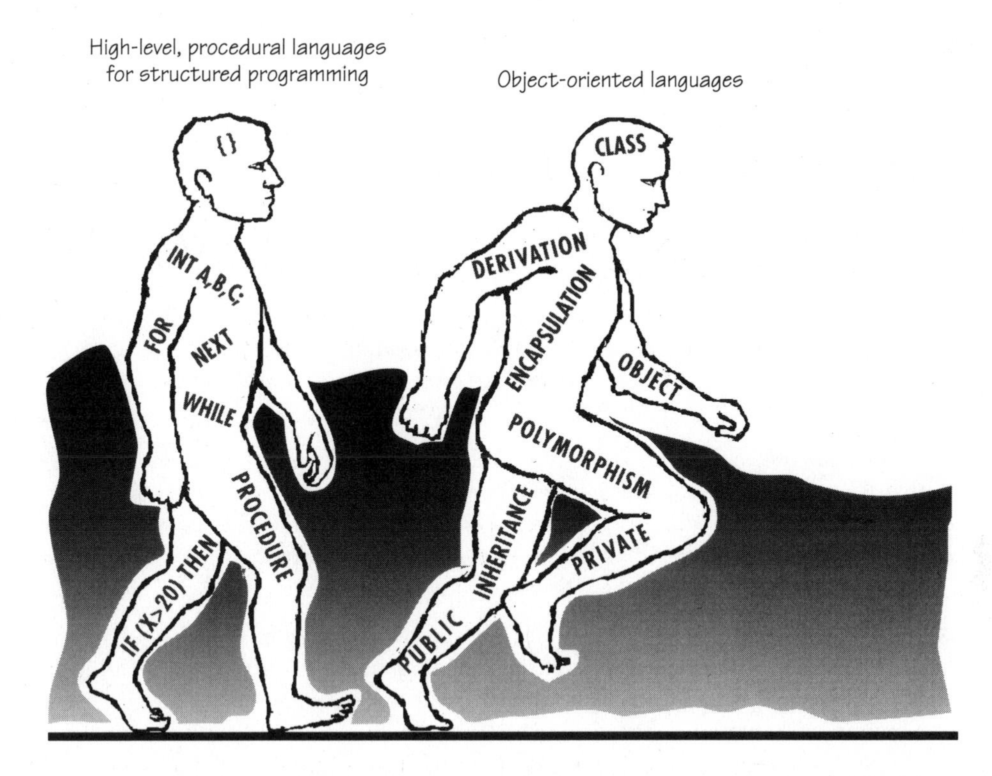

Object-oriented development can be done in many languages; there are innumerable variations on the object-oriented paradigm. But C++ is the only object-oriented language that can take advantage of the massive pool of C programmers and C applications. C++ is not yet a formal standard, but for most practical purposes, C++ is already a multivendor, multiplatform standard. Reusability and reliability gains have moved object-oriented programming into the mainstream, and the concern for continuity has made C++ the most widely used OOP language.

What Is an Object-Oriented Language?

In the closing years of the 1980s, the word "object" joined "structured," "user-friendly," and a few other high-tech holy words. Overuse tends to rob words of their appointed meanings, and in the software industry, we've used the word "object" and the term "object-oriented" in a multitude of ways.

Several vendors sell programming products that they claim are object oriented but that are really just very high-level programming environments. Creating a menu-driven software application by answering questions and filling in a few forms is not object-oriented programming.

Characteristic Features

Programming languages that are generally recognized as object oriented support several features:

- *Objects.* An object is an instance of a data structure that combines data with procedures. Most programmable systems provide for a relationship between data and procedures. In an object-oriented language, data and procedures are fused in an object. In C++, the *class* data type is used to create objects.

- *Programmability.* You can create documents or drawings from objects such as paragraph components or Bézier curve components, but that doesn't constitute object-oriented programming. An object-oriented language is a programmable object-oriented system. C++ is programmable.

- *Access controls.* An object should be able to protect certain of its elements so that they can be reserved for internal use and protected from unwarranted tinkering. Conversely, an object should be able to advertise other elements so that they can be used to manipulate the object. In C++, classes have private, protected, and public access controls.

- *Inheritance.* It should be possible to create new object types, or classes, from existing object types by a combination of adding to and modifying the existing object type's characteristics. You can add data and procedures to an existing class, and you can redefine an existing class's procedures. In most object-oriented languages, including C++, the original class is called the "base class," and classes descended from the base class are called "derived classes." The usual intent in deriving one class from another is to create a more specialized class from the existing class.

- *Polymorphism.* Inheritance in programming, as in living systems, creates a family. Often all classes in a family implement some version of a routine that has the same name in all the classes, such as the *draw()* routine in a family of graphics classes. Polymorphism, which means having many forms, enables you to write programs that invoke the *draw()* routine of any object belonging to one of the family of graphics classes, even if the exact object type isn't known during compilation. C++ implements polymorphism using the new *virtual* keyword.

- *Predictability.* An object must be in a predictable state at all times. And some objects need to perform cleanup chores before they cease to exist. In C++ as in most object-oriented programming languages, these needs are met by constructors and destructors, routines that are invoked when objects are created and destroyed.

In a true object-oriented language, the support for these characteristic features is direct, convenient, and central to the language.

Desirable Capabilities

Several other facilities are of great interest to object-oriented developers. These capabilities have been implemented in many traditional programming environments, but they are particularly desirable in object-oriented environments:

- *Standardization.* If the underlying mechanisms of object-oriented technology were more standardized, it would be possible to create an object in one language (in C++, for example) that would be usable in another language (say, in Visual Basic). Or it would be possible to have an object operating on one type of machine (perhaps on a supercomputer) under the control of a program operating on another machine (on a desktop PC, for instance).
- *Persistence.* Some object-oriented systems allow objects to be stored for later use or transmitted across networks. This facility is often provided by library routines. Microsoft's MFC library implements object persistence.
- *Concurrence.* Some object-oriented systems allow objects to execute concurrently. This facility is often provided by library routines.
- *Automatic garbage collection.* The support of object-oriented languages for inheritance and encapsulation makes the creation of basic objects that can facilitate automatic reclamation of unneeded heap storage somewhat easier.
- *Operator functions.* Although many software objects represent sophisticated ideas whose functionality is best accessed by means of user-defined names, the functionality of some objects, especially numeric objects, is best expressed by algebraic notation. For operations that can sensibly be expressed by means of algebraic notation with object operands, it's desirable for an object-oriented language to contain operator functions. C++ contains operator functions.

The Efficiency Issue

Historically, object-oriented software development has involved a few negatives too. Some of the early object-oriented languages, such as Simula and LISP, were notorious for their inefficiency. C++ stays close to the runtime efficiency of C, paying for a language feature only when it is being used. C++ retains all the C features that let you write lean, mean code, but it also allows you to deliver those features conveniently. And several capabilities that are new in C++, such as inline functions, references, and full procedure prototyping, mean that C++ compilers can sometimes generate more efficient code than C compilers can.

What Took Us So Long?

The key ideas of object-oriented programming have been around since the mid-1960s, but it wasn't until the end of the 1980s that mainstream software developers began to notice and evaluate those ideas. And it wasn't until the early 1990s that object-oriented technology started to be widely used. Why so late?

C++ outstrips the early object-oriented languages, with a runtime efficiency that approaches C's.

In most other disciplines, the idea of working with objects is so basic it goes without saying. If you talked to an electrical engineer, you'd discover that he or she works with components such as integrated circuits, resistors, connectors, capacitors, and the like to design digital circuits. Talking to another electrical engineer, you'd hear about power transistors, transformers, and other heavy-duty components used to build power supplies. It's taken for granted that the digital circuit designer needn't worry much about the power supply. There are many to choose from, all well described in glossy catalogs from multiple vendors.

Until recently, software developers wouldn't have known what you were talking about if you had asked them what objects they used. For a variety of reasons, software developers had become accustomed to building almost everything from scratch. There had been many good books of algorithms and other good books on data structures, but there hadn't been any glossy catalogs to help a developer choose a stack, a balanced binary tree, or an optimized matrix package.

The last milestone in software development before the emergence of the object-oriented paradigm was the development and refinement of structured programming during the 1970s and early 1980s. The concepts that cluster around the idea of structured programming focus on programming in the small—on the development of a correct routine, on the clear expression of an algorithm, and on compilation aids that promote reliability (type checking, array bounds checking). Object-oriented programming doesn't pretend to replace, or to repudiate, structured programming.

Developers still need structured programming to develop software by means of the object-oriented paradigm. The object-oriented paradigm focuses on programming in the large—on how programs should be organized, on how code can be reused and extended, and on how complexity can be managed.

Several factors account for the nearly two decades it has taken to move significantly beyond structured programming. Partly, it's that computers are so important to most organizations that it's hard to take time out to try something new. And many software projects fail, or are late, or are too expensive, or have other major difficulties. This means that risk reduction (conservatism) is a powerful force, an overriding influence on those with the most to say about what languages are to be used for major software projects.

The shift to object-oriented thinking can't be accomplished in a day or two, and C++ is a far more complex language than C. But C++ is now stable, and current implementations of C++ are far more robust than the early versions of C were. The benefits of object-oriented programming are clearly worth the effort. We can bring new ways of thinking to the design process. We can build new applications that take advantage of tried and true components. We can shorten product cycles while improving product performance and reliability.

2

Objects and Classes

A primary goal of object-oriented programming is to make working with software objects as easy and productive as an engineer's work with physical objects. Where an electrical designer uses a motor, a software designer can use a *Motor* object. Where an optical designer uses a prism, a software designer can use a *Prism* object.

In both the physical and the software realms, an easy-to-use, reliable, and powerful parts collection can empower a designer to be more productive. Instead of building from scratch, the designer can take advantage of the work of others, assembling ready-made components. The catalog of parts from which a software designer selects objects is the class library.

But exploiting the availability of ready-made, reusable software building blocks isn't the most profound or innovative use of software classes. The more significant employment of classes is as foundations from which more specialized classes can be derived. The parts in the catalog, the classes in the class library, can sometimes be used as is. More often, they must be customized. In object-oriented programming, the specialization of a class is accomplished by means of derivation. The existing class becomes the "base class" (sometimes called the "parent class"), and the newly minted, specialized class is the "derived class" (the "child class"). The development of families of classes, of class hierarchies, makes for easier coding and, as we'll see, can lead to runtime efficiencies.

Classes

The class is the key to object creation. A class is a data structure that combines traditional data elements with routines for manipulating the data elements. A C++ class is a C struct that has been extended so that in addition to the data elements, it also contains procedures.

View a class as another data type. Like an *int* or a *double*, a class is a blueprint for creating data; it specifies the rules and interpretations that apply to a region of storage. If an *int*, for example, is stored in a memory location, an all-zero bit pattern in that location is usually interpreted as the number *0*, and so on. For *int*, *double*, and the other built-in types, such rules are built into the language. For classes, you make your own rules. Classes are user-defined data types.

Telescope Kit

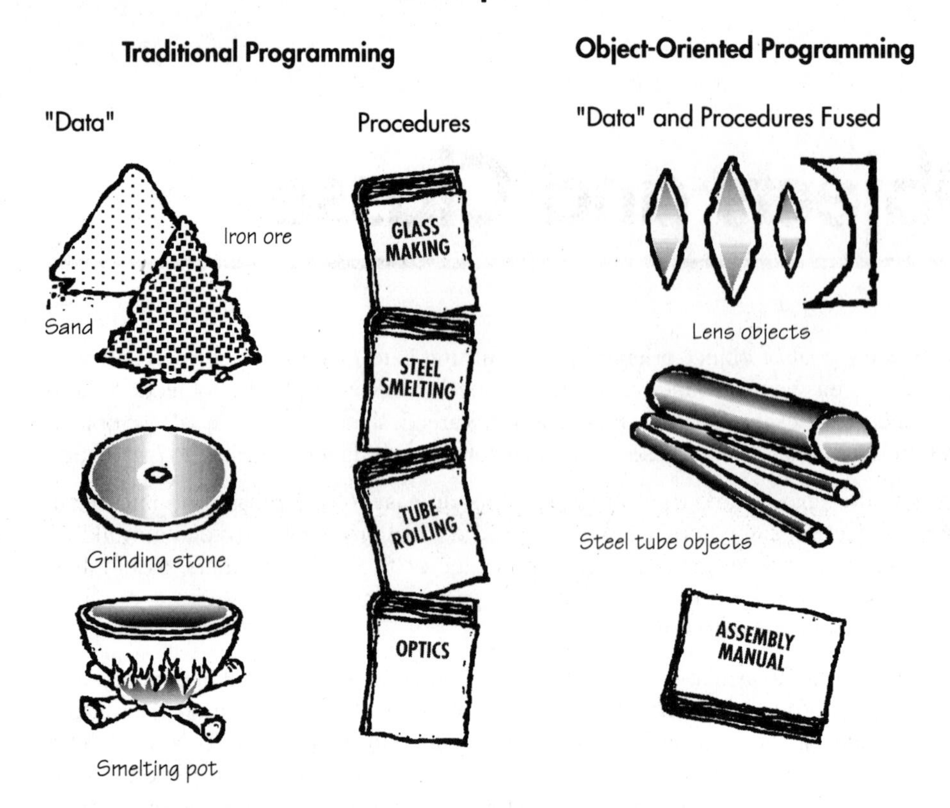

Each of the things that you make from the class blueprint is an instance of the class, an "object." The class is the idea, the ruleset. The object is the realization of the idea, the actual region of storage that is subject to the ruleset.

C++ class notation is based on C's structure notation. A class is declared this way:

```
class Complex {
    /* class member declarations here */
};
```

The key difference between a class and an ordinary data type is that the class can have both data members and procedure members, as in this fleshed-out declaration of class *Complex*, a class containing two data members that store the real and imaginary parts of a complex number, and two member functions that return the magnitude and direction of a complex number:

```
class Complex {
    double realpart;          // data member
    double imagpart;          // data member
    double magnitude();       // procedure member
    double direction();       // procedure member
};
```

(C++ honors both traditional C commenting style and comments that start with a double / that is in effect to the end of the line.)

Declaration vs. Definition

We've just looked at a class declaration. Both C and C++ distinguish between a declaration and a definition. A declaration introduces a name to the compiler and tells the compiler something about that name. The delaration

```
double magnitude();
```

tells the compiler that *magnitude()* is the name of a function that returns a *double* value. The function is defined (implemented) elsewhere. A compiler can "see" a declaration many times. It sees a definition only once.

A definition is the full story on a program element, a complete description. Sometimes a declaration is a definition too, in that it tells the full story, leaving nothing unsaid. Each program element must be defined fully and only once. A definition of a variable or a function reserves space in memory. A definition of a class, a struct, a union, or an enum does not.

Class vs. Object

Keep in mind the difference between a class declaration, such as the declaration for class *Complex* we've just seen, and setting aside space for an object of that class. Here is the declaration of a single *Complex* object and of an array of 50 *Complex* objects:

```
Complex val;
Complex cplx_array[50];
```

Note that there is a single *Complex* class, but that in the declaration above there are 51 *Complex* objects.

Example: The Gilbert Prisms

I put some object-oriented ideas into practice in a recent project in which I worked with Charles Gilbert to develop a device for studying disparity in the human visual system. Disparity refers to the difference between the world view of the left eye and that of the right eye. Disparity, which is an important aspect of our visual perception of depth, increases as objects come closer to us.

For his ongoing studies of the visual system, Charles wanted to be able to change the direction of the gaze of one eye relative to the gaze of the other. The device that Charles designed uses a pair of prisms in front of each eye, as shown in Figure 2-1. Each prism can be rotated to a specified angle by a stepper motor. The rotation of the prism results in a corresponding change in the direction of gaze of the subject. The stepper motors are hooked up to a standard stepper motor controller circuit, which moves the motor one step clockwise or counterclockwise each time a step pulse is applied. Step pulses—that's where the computer comes in. A standard issue PC is hooked up to generate the step pulses for the stepper motor controller circuit.

Before talking about the software, let me make a few comments about the hardware I've just described. First, notice that I described it in only three or four sentences. If you don't know much about stepper motors, elementary optics, and basic electronics, you're probably a bit puzzled, but if you occasionally read *Scientific American* or *Popular Mechanics,* you probably have a pretty good idea of how Charles's disparity control system works. By using standard components in his design, he has made it easy to describe.

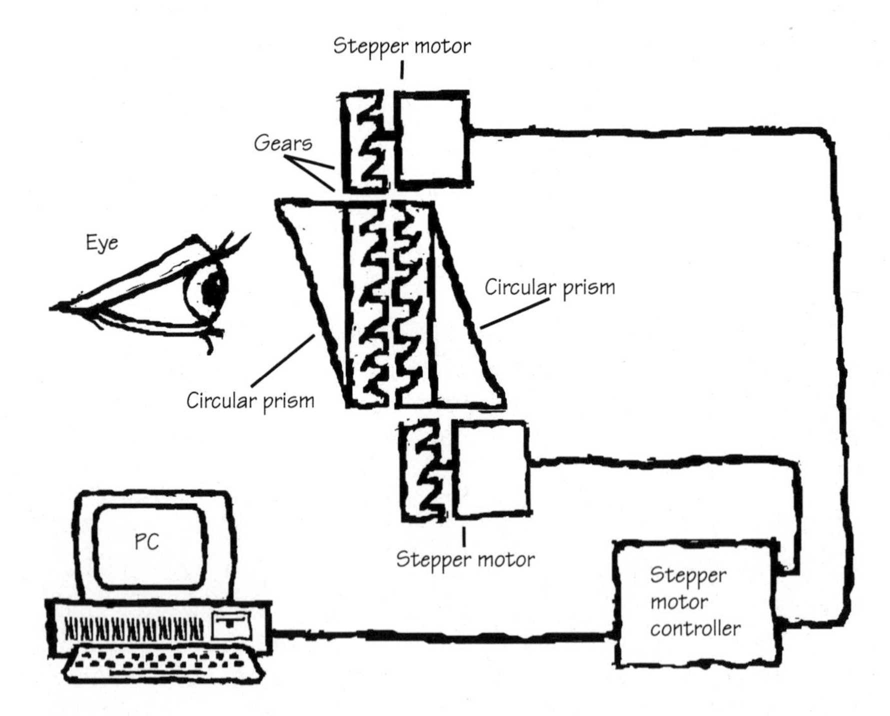

Figure 2-1.
The Gilbert prism system. Each prism is mounted in a geared ring so that it can be rotated by motors.

The second point is that the prism mechanism was designed by Charles Gilbert, who is trained as a neurophysiologist, not as an optical engineer, or as a mechanical engineer, or as a machinist. If Charles had been forced to invent the idea of a prism, or if he had even had to specify how the prism should be ground, or if he had been asked to specify how the motor should be designed, his task would have been far more difficult.

The software that I developed to control Charles's disparity prisms mirrors the mechanical apparatus, as Figure 2-2 suggests. I created a *Motor* object, whose main purpose is to remember the current position of a stepper motor. The *Motor* object can also be given a target rotational position and be asked to move one step toward the target. I also created a *DualPrism* object that is based on a pair of *Motor* objects. The purpose of the *DualPrism* object is to translate a request in the form "Move the left eye gaze 1 degree left and .5 degrees up" into targets for the *Motor* objects. Because the electrical pulses for the stepper motors must be applied at a specific rate, I also used a *Timer* object.

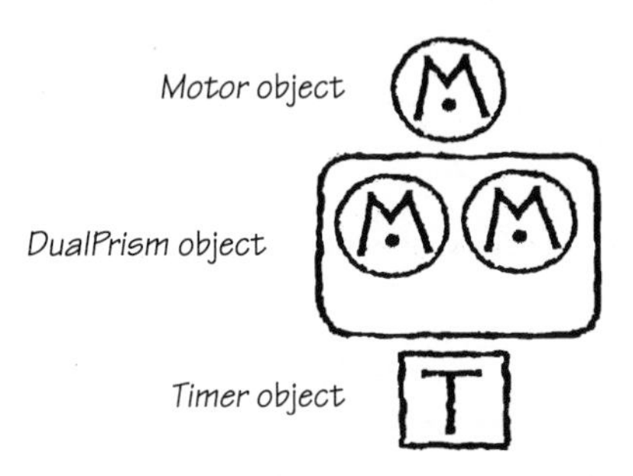

Figure 2-2.
Software objects that manage the Gilbert prisms.

Several aspects of the software design are noteworthy. Largely because the software is organized around software objects that relate directly to physical objects, I can describe its general organization in a few sentences. Had I approached the project from another perspective, I suspect that the software would have been much harder to describe. Because each object has a well-defined role, the software was easily written and worked correctly almost from the first.

Another advantage of designing with software objects is that objects make it easy to create simple interfaces. The *DualPrism* object can be given a target position, can be instructed to move toward that target, and can be queried for completion of the task. I can imagine replacing the *DualPrism* object with my five-year-old son and giving him similar instructions. "Move it up. Is it there yet? No? Keep going." This simple interface makes it easy to embed the prisms software in a simple testing program, or to use it inside other software that is concerned primarily with other tasks.

For some experiments, Charles uses a single prism assembly, but for other experiments he needs two, one for each eye. Because we've taken an object-oriented approach, two *DualPrism* objects are as easy to use as one. In fact, we did all the testing with one prism mechanism, and the first time we needed two, everything worked fine. It is certainly possible to create similar capabilities by means of conventional methods, but it takes extra effort.

Many a programmer would complain here, I suspect, that I'm describing programming in the small. "But what about programming in the large, such as software for controlling the Space Shuttle?" Construction of very large (nonsoftware) systems has always been a hierarchical undertaking. The Space Shuttle itself is a large hierarchical assembly of parts—why shouldn't its software be organized similarly? The shuttle designer who worked on attitude control during reentry certainly never worried about how the lift-off rocketry worked. Shouldn't software designers have the same freedom to focus on manageable aspects of a problem?

Some Object-Oriented Terms

Throughout this book, you'll encounter a specialized language appropriate for object-oriented programming. And C++ has its own lexicon.

Objects

The term "object" actually plays two roles in the discipline of object-oriented programming. Its first is as an organizing principle. The object concept is central to the way we think about "object-oriented" software design and programming. We design and program software objects that correspond to real-world objects. The term's second role is more mundane. An object is a region of storage that contains one copy of the item specified by the class blueprint.

When I was thinking about how to design the software to control Charles's prisms, I realized that I would need an object to manage the motion of the stepper motors, an object to correspond to an entire prism assembly, and an object for timing. At that point in the design phase, I was using the term "object" in the first sense. I was thinking about how things should be organized and deciding on the basic components of the design that would correspond to the real-world objects.

After a bit of work, I had realized my design in a test program. The test program declared a *DualPrism* object, which contained two *Motor* objects. That declaration reserved a region of storage, which is the second sense of the term "object." Another term synonymous with this second meaning of "object" is "instance." My test program created a single instance of the *DualPrism* class. The term "instance-oriented programming" never became popular because "instance" doesn't speak to our first meaning of the term "object."

Names for Members

SmallTalk has established precedence for use of the term "class variable" for a class member shared by all objects of the class. I try to avoid "class variable" because it has a very different meaning from the meaning of the similar sounding "class member." In C++, we often say "static class member" instead of "class variable" because in C++ the keyword *static* is used to declare what SmallTalk calls a class variable.

So I'll say "member" when I am talking about any class member in general—data or procedure. For data members specifically, I'll say "member variable" or "data element," and for procedure members, I'll say "member function." For class variables, I'll say "static class member."

"Call" and "Invoke"

In C, we "call" functions. For example, we can call the *sin()* procedure to calculate the sine of a number. But although we often call functions in C++ too, sometimes the relation between a C++ function and the way it gets activated is more tenuous. For example, it makes more sense to say that a class's constructor function is "invoked" because the constructor function call is performed for us by the compiler. Similarly, we often use the word "invoked" when we refer to the activation of operator functions and virtual functions.

Classes

The inheritance idea raises its own naming issues. In C++, the class you start out with is called the "base class," and the classes you create from the base class are called "derived classes." Synonyms for these terms are "superclass" and "subclasses" and even "parent" and "children." A superclass is a base class, or parent, and a subclass is a derived class, or child. The term "base class" sometimes refers to the ultimate base class in a class hierarchy—that is, to the root of a hierarchy, the only class in a hierarchy that isn't also a derived class. That sense of the term isn't common C++ usage; when we mean "ultimate base class," we generally just say that.

3

Encapsulation and Abstraction

Encapsulation and abstraction are opposite aspects of an object's treatment. "Encapsulation" refers to the ability of an object to have private elements, to hide internal details. Encapsulation establishes boundaries around an object, managing the internal state of the object. "Abstraction" has to do with the external state of an object. It is the process of describing the concept an object embodies, the tasks the object can perform, and the interface used to access the object. Abstraction treats the part of the object that is visible externally. Figure 3-1 on the next page is a real-world illustration of the concepts of encapsulation and abstraction.

Encapsulation entails two prerequisites. The first is that an object be complete. The object must implement an entire concept, address the full problem. This is a matter of design; if you're seeing problems with encapsulation, step back and think about your basic design. An object can't guarantee its own operation if half of its vital mechanism is external.

The second key to encapsulation is privacy. Most objects need to restrict access to certain of their data and procedures so that internal consistency can be maintained. Privatization helps to guarantee the proper operation of an object, but it is also an important aid for debugging. Making some member elements private reduces the number of ways in which they can be manipulated, thereby reducing the number of places you must look when things go awry.

An object's "interface" is the meeting ground of encapsulation and abstraction. In designing the interface, you must consider both ideal and practical needs. Ideally, an object's interface should take a minimalist approach. It should publicize only the essential aspects of an object, those aspects that are needed to use the object, while hiding as much of the object as possible to protect its encapsulation. But pragmatic considerations often carry considerable weight. Even though the preservation of encapsulation calls for the return of information to a client by value, that is, in copies of information, the practical reality is that copying information can involve a performance hit. To increase efficiency, the client is often given access by reference to the

Motor Encapsulation:

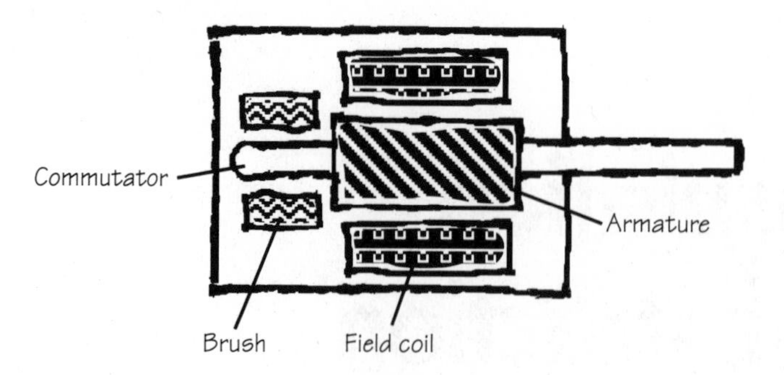

Motor Abstraction:

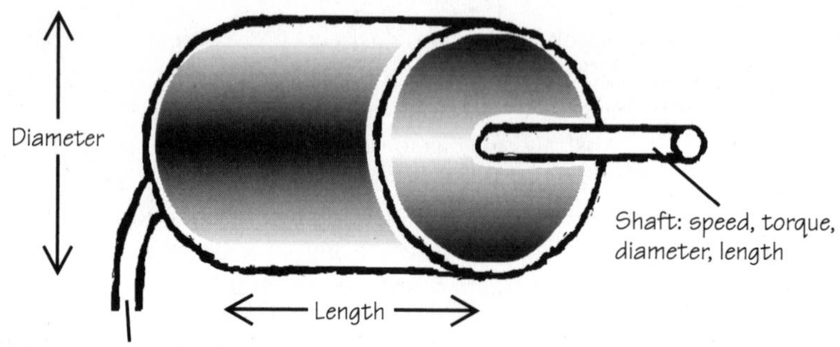

Figure 3-1.
A physical demonstration of encapsulation and abstraction: the internal, hidden elements and the external, visible elements of a motor.

information instead. Yes, private elements should stay private, but sometimes important client needs are easiest to satisfy by relaxing or bypassing the rules.

If you envision an object's interface as a wall, these practical concessions obviously create chinks in the wall. Although some purists will disapprove, I'm not too concerned about a sturdy wall that has a few missing blocks and a few unlocked doors. It's when these practical concessions make the wall start to wobble that you should rethink your design. Your wall might have been put up in the wrong location.

Although C++ contains features that promote encapsulation and abstraction, the primary onus for a design that enables encapsulation and abstraction falls on the software designer. The first step in such a design's process is to create classes and class hierarchies that embody specific, clearly defined concepts. I believe that there is a strong relationship between the precision with which you can informally express the main idea of a class and the successful encapsulation and abstraction of that idea in your design.

Public and Private

In C, you can create a limited form of encapsulation by using the *static* keyword. When a variable is declared as *static* inside a function, the variable has the lifetime of a global (file-scope) variable but is visible only within the function. This facility is useful but limited. The other use of *static* in C is in declarations of free, global variables and procedures, in which it indicates that visibility is limited to the current file. This use of *static* in a variable or procedure declaration lets you use file scope to achieve modularity and to avoid name clashes. Figure 3-2 illustrates these uses of *static* in C.

```
int win_height;      /* the free variable win_height is visible throughout
                        the program */
static int win_x;    /* the free variable win_x is visible only in the
                        current source file */
void movewin(void)   /* movewin() is visible throughout the program */
{ static int win_base;   /* win_base is visible only within the */
    /* . . . */          /*  function movewin() */
}
{  /* . . . */  }
static void drawwin()    /* drawwin() is visible (callable) only in the */
{  /* . . . */  }        /*  current source file */
```

Figure 3-2.
C's use of the keyword static *to limit access.*

The *public* Keyword

C++'s much more powerful support for encapsulation and abstraction is based on the class. Every element of a C++ class is declared as *public*, *private*, or *protected.* It's the *public* class elements that make up the class interface. They are the embodiment of the class's abstraction. Our natural desire for economy, simplicity, and security dictates that we should, on principle, keep the public elements at a minimum. This conflicts with our equally natural desire to have convenient, communicative (often redundant) class interfaces and to allow for powerful interactions that might require more complex and profound interfaces.

The *private* Keyword

The *private* elements of a class are not accessible outside a class except to friend classes (classes that have been declared with the keyword *friend*) or to outside friend functions. This lets a class rely on its private elements because their manipulation and use are completely within the domain of class member functions (plus friends).

The need for a *protected* keyword

Privacy sounds good in theory, but in practice it has proved to be almost too much of a good thing. Private data is so private that even derived classes can't get at it. Sometimes a derived class has a legitimate need to access elements in a parent class that should be otherwise inaccessible, that is, that should be inaccessible to classes outside the family. The solution is a weaker form of *private*, the keyword *protected*. We'll put a full discussion of the concept of protection off until the next section. Figure 3-3 simply illustrates the declarations of a friend class and of *private*, *protected*, and *public* class members.

```
class W {
    friend class Y;      // Y members can access all W members
    private:
        int x;           // x and y are accessible only to W class member
        int y;           //  functions and to friend classes and functions
    protected:
        int win_ht;      // win_ht and win_wid are as accessible as
        int win_wid;     //  private members; plus, they are accessible
                         //  to derived classes
    public:
        void win_draw(); // public members are universally
                         //  accessible
};
```

Figure 3-3.
C++'s use within a class of a friend class and of the private, protected, *and* public *keywords to control access.*

Static Member Variables

The other C++ feature that enables encapsulation and abstraction is the old *static* keyword. When a class member variable is declared as *static*, only one copy of that variable appears in a program—not one copy in each object, which is the norm for an ordinary (non-*static*) class member variable—and it is shared by all objects of the class. In some object-oriented programming languages, C++'s static class data elements are called "class variables," and the ordinary (per object) class data elements are called "instance variables." Figure 3-4 illustrates use of the *static* keyword with a class member variable in C++.

```
class C {
    static int a;        // static data member--one copy in the program
    int b, c, d;         // ordinary data members--one copy in each object
};
C vals[3];               // create an array of three class C objects
```

Figure 3-4.
Class C *member variables— both static and ordinary.*

Static Member Functions

C++ also allows a class member function to be declared as *static*, which means that it can execute even if there are no class objects. A static member function is limited to tasks that can be accomplished without reference to object member variables.

Static member elements—both variables and functions—provide a way for a class to store and manipulate information that pertains to the class as a whole, not to individual objects of the class.

In Figure 3-4, each member of *vals* is a class *C* object, which means that each member of the array *vals* contains *b*, *c*, and *d*. The integer *a*, which is a static member variable of class *C*, exists in the global scope of the program, and there is only one copy of *a*, no matter how many class *C* objects exist. Figure 3-5 diagrams the difference between ordinary member variables and a static member variable.

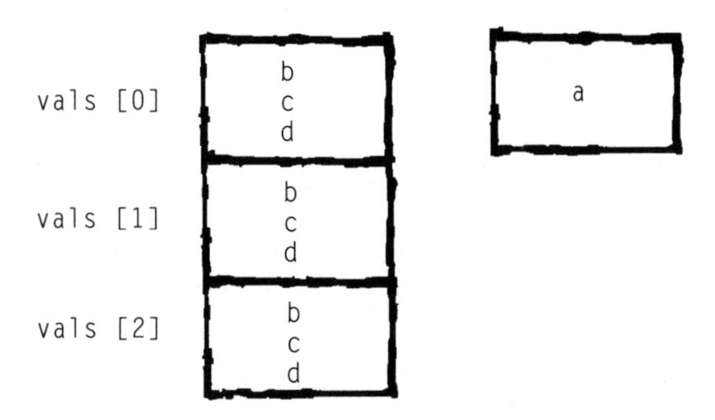

Figure 3-5.
Each object in the array vals *contains the ordinary member variables* b, c, *and* d. *The static member variable,* a, *appears only once in the program.*

Encapsulation, Derivation, and the *protected* Keyword

C++ private class member variables are truly private; they are accessible only to class member functions and to a class's friends. Private member variables are inaccessible to clients of a class—and even to classes that are derived from a class. Yes, a class's private member variables are inaccessible even to a class's offspring.

Making data inaccessible to derived classes is often too severe a restriction because it can limit the flexibility and effectiveness of a base class. C++ therefore features an intermediate keyword, *protected*. Protected class members are hidden from clients of the class, but they are accessible to derived classes. To you as a class designer, the question is this: If someone were to use your class as a foundation (a base class) upon which to build a new class, which of the private members would need to be accessible to the derived class?

The essence of protection can be expressed in a family metaphor. Someone who extends your class is a member of the family, and someone who simply uses your class, a client, is an outsider. A family does have secrets, things parents don't reveal to their offspring—they're *private.* Other things are well known in the family but not known outside—they're *protected.* Figure 3-6 illustrates these access rules.

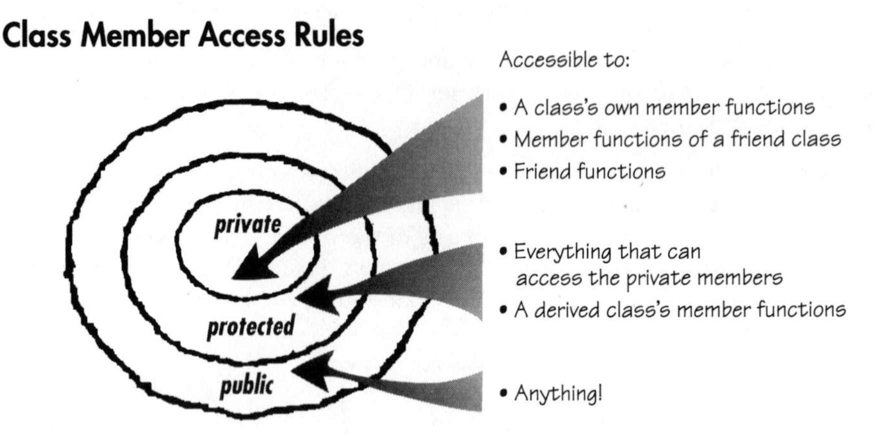

Figure 3-6.
Access rules for the public, protected, *and* private *members of a class.*

There are several motives for differentiating between the access privileges of derived classes and those of ordinary clients. The most obvious is the need to be practical. In order to derive a class from a class, to extend and customize a class, it might be necessary to have access to some of the implementation details that should properly be hidden from a class client.

The other important motive is trust—or lack of it. A class designer should instinctively distrust the clients of the class. He or she should make every effort to create a class that can't be broken or abused by even the most careless of client users. As we will see, several C++ language facilities help achieve this security, but as usual, the most important safeguard is the vigilance of the class designer.

Unfortunately, an extreme distrust of programmers who are deriving classes from your foundation classes doesn't abet the cause of code reuse. Class derivation is practical only if much of the base class's inner workings are accessible. And remember that class derivation is the most important feature of C++ for facilitating code reuse. It can make a great deal of sense to distrust client users of your class. A user might glance at the class's description in the manual and then immediately apply creative abuse. It makes less sense to distrust a programmer who is extending or specializing your class. That person is likely to need to be more careful, thoughtful, and reflective.[1]

---

1. It is, of course, possible that you will encounter an insidious derived class, one that takes advantage of the facilities that you have trustingly publicized. In software, as in life, we have to strike a balance between paranoia and blind trust.

Deciding which parts of a class are to be private and which protected can be a thorny task. Some developers adopt the expedient of making everything protected, arguing that to do otherwise makes class derivation too difficult. They claim that they can't foresee the needs of derived classes and that they therefore shouldn't inhibit the creators of derived classes. Several considerations override this argument. The first is that there are fundamental elements that some classes rely upon, and they can be relied upon only if they are private. The creator of a class should be sparing in deciding that some aspects of a class are so critical as to be completely hidden, but I believe that often there are such elements.

And making certain parts of a class private is a useful tool for constraining those who derive from your classes. Privatization is C++'s only way to control class derivation. It's otherwise impossible to prevent others from deriving from your classes. You can guarantee that objects of a C++ class won't be created, but you can't forbid the derivation of one class from another. Privatization is the next best thing.

Another reason for making elements of a class private is your own design uncertainty. Sometimes you are simply exploring the design of a class and don't yet know whether the member variables and member functions you design will stand the test of time. In the face of uncertainty, it's best to make liberal use of the *private* keyword. If you don't, derived classes will effectively freeze your design by taking advantage of implementation details that you might want to change later. Such use of the *private* keyword does decrease reusability, and that's the whole point. Premature reuse can prematurely harden your design.

Deliberate Attacks

C++'s features for private and protected class members are safeguards that enforce access restrictions during compilation. The safeguards help because they pinpoint violations earlier in the development process—at compile time rather than at runtime. In C, or in any other language with data structures, you can conceptually intend certain parts of a structure to be private and others to be public, but you can't get the compiler to help you maintain the restrictions. In C++, you can say, "Don't let me use these members except in member functions," and the compiler will remember and check your restriction.

It doesn't take much skill to circumvent C++'s access restrictions. They aren't a secure system in the way that data encryption schemes are secure or that password protected computer resources are secure. When full source code is available, anyone with a text editor can simply change all the private and protected members to public members and then recompile. Some people actually use this technique, somewhat refined by means of the *#define* statement, for debugging their own work. Even without full library source code, a programmer can circumvent some restrictions simply by editing the library header files.

In the absence of full library source code and of read/write access to the library header files, there's always the time-tested technique of using pointers and a bit of knowledge to get at something in the library. It's not a good idea, but it's certainly not difficult.

C++ compilers could be developed that took advantage of hardware memory protection capabilities to add some enforcement to the language rules. Some discussion of using hardware assistance to guarantee that *const* data remains unchanged by placing it in read-only memory segments has already gone on. Unfortunately, even the relatively simple enforcement of *const* is difficult to implement and breaks some programs.

Constructor and Destructor Member Functions

An object is the embodiment of an idea. The object implements, in a software system, the promises and relationships that are spelled out in the class, whose declaration can be viewed as a contract. The object is required to faithfully honor the contract at all times.

The C++ mechanism that makes this possible is the "constructor," a special class member function that builds an object from raw storage. The constructor must initialize member variables, allocate any necessary additional storage, and perform any other chores that are required to convert a chunk of memory to an object. The constructor member function has the same name as the class; the constructor for a class named *Vector* is therefore a member function named *Vector()*.

A class can have several constructors, provided each has a different argument list. For example, a class for a vector type can have one constructor that takes a *Vector* parameter, another constructor whose parameter is a single integer, and a third constructor whose parameter is a string. The first constructor might build a duplicate of the original vector, the second might build a vector of the specified size and initialize it to *0*, and the third might use the string as a file name and create a vector to hold the information from that file. Here's a class declaration that shows how the work might be divided:

```
class Vector {
// . . .
public:
    Vector(Vector& v);      // constructor--create new as copy of v
    Vector(int n);          // constructor--build n element Vector
    Vector(char *nm);       // constructor--open nm and read in vector
    ~Vector();              // destructor
// . . .
};
```

The opposite of a constructor is a "destructor," a member function called each time an object goes out of existence. A class can have only one destructor, and its name is the class name with a tilde (~) prepended. The destructor for the *Vector* class is therefore a member function named *~Vector()*. A destructor, like a constructor, doesn't have a return type and can't return values.

Operator Member Functions

Abstraction can be seen as the art of making something appear simple even though it is complex. In many fields, notation is an important aspect of abstraction; using standard notation makes it easier to communicate. Try to imagine an introductory calculus book in which the author is forced to write "Take the integral over the range zero to pi of the sine function" instead of using standard notation:

$$\int_0^\pi \sin(x)dx$$

Notation is also an important aspect of programming. A programming language will have a set of operators that invoke functionality. One of the notable features of C is its large and innovative set of operators.

The major limitation of C's rich set of operators is that it can be applied only to built-in data types. If variables *a* and *b* are *doubles*, you can write

```
a += b
```

but if *a* and *b* are of a user-defined vector type (or a matrix type, string type, or any other user-defined type), operations on *a* and *b* must be expressed as function calls:

```
vecAddTo(a, b);      /* add vector b to a (in C) */
```

C++ extends C's functionality with the addition of "operator member functions," user-written member functions that are called automatically when operators are applied to user-defined data types. For example, if *a* and *b* are *Vector* objects and the *Vector* class includes an *operator+=()* operator member function, you can express the addition of object *b* to object *a* by using this standard notation:

```
a += b;              // add vector b to a (in C++)
```

C++ doesn't allow you to define new operator symbols, and it doesn't let you change the precedence or associativity of the existing operator symbols. Nonetheless, C++'s seemingly modest operator function capability is a significant part of C++'s encapsulation and abstraction toolkit.

Example: A Circular Number Class

As children we learn that numbers are infinite, that for any given number we can always make a bigger number by adding one. Figure 3-7 on the next page shows this whole number continuum extending infinitely in both the positive and negative directions.

But sometimes we want to use a numbering system that wraps around, so that adding one to the last number brings us back to the first number. In geometric software, for instance, we might represent angles as degrees from 0 through 359. Adding 1 to 359 should yield 0, not 360. Figure 3-8 on the next page illustrates such a circular numbering system.

Infinite Whole Numbering System

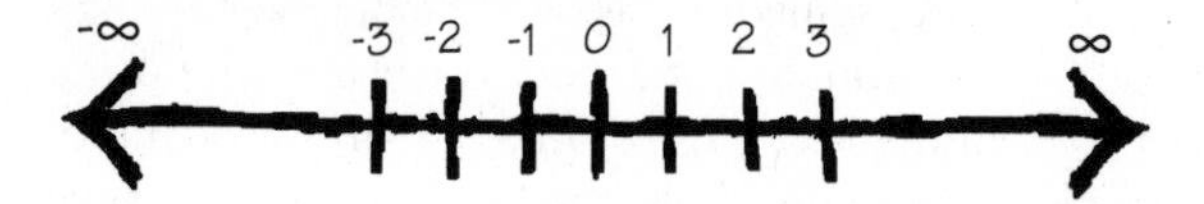

Figure 3-7.
Infinite whole numbers go on forever.

Circular Whole Numbering System

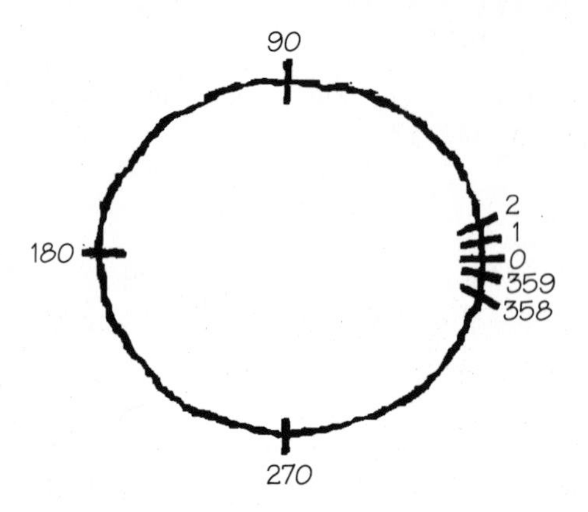

Figure 3-8.
Circular whole numbers return to the first number.

In C++, we can use a class to express the concept of a circular numbering system. The class, which we'll call *Circnum*, should provide a set of operations that allow numbers in the circular system to be added, compared, and so on, and the class should ensure that the value stays within the object's appointed range. Thus, if *c* and *d* are *Circnum* objects, we should be able to write statements that contain expressions like the comparison in this one:

```
if (c < d)
    c++;
```

And the class should have conversion functions so that the circular numbers can be converted to integers and integer values can be converted to circular numbers. Such conversions would allow statements that contain comparative and assignment expressions such as this one:

```
if (c < 180)
    d = 0;      // d is a Circnum, and 0 is an integer
```

To keep things simple, let's consider whole circular numbers only, and let's further stipulate circular numbers that start at *0* and have a positive maximum value. The first choice we must make is the data to be stored in each *Circnum* object. Of course, we have to store the current value; the interesting consideration is whether we also want to store range information in each object. The most flexible solution would be for each circular numbering object to know its range because this would allow us to use several different ranges in a single program. The drawback in this solution is that we would need to decide how to handle mixed operations, such as comparing the value of a variable whose range is *0* through *10* with that of a variable whose range is *0* through *1000.*

For simplicity's sake, let's store the maximum value in a global variable. In C, we would probably create a public global and initialize it to the maximum value:

```
unsigned Circ_MaxVal = 359;
```

and then, in the *Circnum* header file, we would use the statement

```
extern unsigned Circ_MaxVal;
```

so that we could access the value as necessary.

C++ offers ways to improve on this scheme. The first is to put the *Circ_MaxVal* variable into a class, so that it is a class member variable, not a free variable. This makes the ownership of the variable clear, and it makes name collisions much less likely. (In C++, you create a member variable shared by all objects of the class by declaring a member variable as *static*. See the static members discussion in Chapter 8.)

The second advantage C++ offers is that access to the *Circ_MaxVal* variable can be restricted by means of the keyword *private* so that the variable can be accessed only by *Circnum* member functions.

The third C++ option is to make *Circ_MaxVal* a *const* so that its value can't be altered.

The next decision that needs to be made about the *Circnum* class is what operations it should support and how they should be supported. The abstraction should encompass sensible arithmetic operations so that *Circnum* values can be used as other numeric values are. For my application, in which I used a circular numbering system to represent angles in whole degrees, I needed add, subtract, increment, decrement, and compare operations. A more complete abstraction might include multiply operations.

These operations can be supported in several ways. In C, we would write freestanding functions that take *Circnum* parameters and return *Circnum* values. For example, we could write a *CircAdd* function that would, for *Circnum* objects *c*, *d*, and *e*, let us write

```
c = CircAdd(d, e);
```

In C++, it makes more sense to use operator functions, so that the notation used to manipulate *Circnum* variables is the same as that used to manipulate built-in variables. For example, if we create *operator+()* and *operator=()* operator functions for the *Circnum* class, we can write

```
c = d + e;
```

The *operator+()* operator function will be called automatically to perform the addition of *d* and *e*, and the result will be assigned to *c* by means of the *operator=()* operator function.

For *Circnum* values, the operations plus, minus, and assignment are relatively straightforward. The abstraction primarily requires more attention to range checking and overflow than to ordinary whole number arithmetic. But the abstraction for comparison is quite different. For example, the *Circnum 359* (using the range *0..359*) is smaller than the *Circnum 0* because *359* plus *1* is *0*. In a circular numbering system, larger and smaller translate into the concepts counterclockwise and clockwise; $a > b$ means that a is counterclockwise from b (shortest route).

A simplified *Circnum* class declaration is shown in Figure 3-9.

```
//
// circular values
//
class Circnum {
private:
    unsigned val;
    static const int Circ_MaxVal;
public:
    Circnum(int v);                       // integer constructor
    Circnum(const Circnum& c);            // copy constructor
    Circnum();                            // default constructor
    ~Circnum();                           // destructor
    Circnum operator+(const Circnum& r);  // addition
    Circnum operator-(const Circnum& r);  // subtraction
    int operator==(const Circnum& r);     // equality
    int operator<(const Circnum& r);      // less than
    int operator>(const Circnum& r);      // greater than
    Circnum operator++(int);              // post-increment
    Circnum operator--(int);              // post-decrement
    Circnum operator++();                 // pre-increment
    Circnum operator--();                 // pre-decrement
    void operator=(int i);                // assignment of an integer
    void operator=(const Circnum& r);     // assignment of a Circnum
    void operator+=(const Circnum& r);    // assign sum
    void operator-=(const Circnum& r);    // assign difference
    operator int();                       // convert to integer
};
```

Figure 3-9.
The Circnum *class declaration.*

The class declaration lists the members, both variables and functions, of *Circnum* but doesn't show the implementations of the functions. You'll find the complete source code of the *Circnum* class at the end of this chapter. Most of the member function definitions are very simple. Here, for instance, is the definition of the post-increment member function:

```
Circnum::operator++(int) {
    Circnum tmp(*this);
    if (val == Circ_MaxVal)
        val = 0;
    else
        val++;
    return tmp;
}
```

And here is a simple test program that exercises a few of the capabilities of the *Circnum* class:

```
#include <stdio.h>
#include "circnum.h"
const unsigned Circnum::Circ_MaxVal = 359;      // set the range
void main(void)
{
    Circnum c = 270;
    Circnum d = 45;
    Circnum e = 360;
    printf("c, d, e: %d %d %d\n",
        (int)c, (int)d, (int)e);
    printf("c %s d\n", (c < d) ? "<" : ">=");
    c += 45;  printf("c += 45;\n");
    d -= 90;  printf("d -= 90;\n");
    e--;      printf("e--;\n");
    printf("c, d, e: %d %d %d\n",
        (int)c, (int)d, (int)e);
}
```

The example above declares and initializes three *Circnum* objects. Note that *e* will actually be initialized to *0* because *360* is out of range. Here is the output:

```
c, d, e: 270 45 0
c < d
c += 45;
d -= 90;
e--;
c, d, e: 315 315 359
```

When you are designing a class, you need to consider how the class will be used. In designing *Circnum*, I was trying to simplify a program that often used circular values. I designed the *Circnum* class to be somewhat more complete and flexible than was warranted by my immediate needs, but I wasn't trying to design the ultimate circular number abstraction. If someday I come across another application that needs a circular numbering system, I might revise my original solution to be more comprehensive. But even though *Circnum* is a modest effort, it is successful in both its encapsulation and its abstraction. The class is complete and easy to use, performs a useful task, and stands by itself.

The *Circnum* Class

Figure 3-10 is the complete source code for the *Circnum* class.

```
//
// circular values
//
class Circnum {
private:
    unsigned val;
    static const int Circ_MaxVal;
public:
    Circnum(int v) {                                  // integer constructor
        while (v > max) v -= (max+1);
        while (v < 0)   v += (max+1);
        val = v;
    }
    Circnum(const Circnum& c) : val(c.val) {}        // copy constructor
    Circnum() { val = 0; }                           // default constructor
    ~Circnum() { }                                   // destructor
    Circnum operator+(const Circnum& r) const {      // addition
        Circnum tmp(val + r.val);
        return tmp;
    }
    Circnum operator-(const Circnum& r) const {      // subtraction
        Circnum tmp(val - r.val);
        return tmp;
    }
    int operator==(const Circnum& r) const           // equality
        { return (val == r.val); }
    int operator<(const Circnum& r) const            // less than
        { return (*this - r).val >= Circ_MaxVal/2; }
    int operator>(const Circnum& r) const            // greater than
        { return (*this - r).val < Circ_MaxVal/2; }
    Circnum operator++(int) {                        // postfix increment
        Circnum tmp(*this);
        if (val == Circ_MaxVal)
            val = 0;
        else
            val++;
        return tmp;
    }
```

Figure 3-10.
The Circnum *class.*

(continued)

Figure 3-10. *continued*

```
    Circnum operator--(int) {                       // postfix decrement
        Circnum tmp(*this);
        if (val == 0)
            val = Circ_MaxVal;
        else
            val--;
        return tmp;
    }
    Circnum operator++() {                          // prefix increment
        if (val == Circ_MaxVal)
            val = 0;
        else
            val++;
        return *this;
    }
    Circnum operator--() {                          // prefix decrement
        if (val == 0)
            val = Circ_MaxVal;
        else
            val--;
        return *this;
    }
    void operator=(int i) {                         // assignment
                                                       of an integer
        while (i > Circ_MaxVal) i -= (Circ_MaxVal+1);
        while (i < 0) i += (Circ_MaxVal+1);
        val = i;
    }
    void operator=(const Circnum& r)                // assignment
                                                       of a Circnum
        { val = r.val; }
    void operator+=(const Circnum& r)               // assign sum
        { *this = *this + r; }
    void operator-=(const Circnum& r)               // assign difference
        { *this = *this - r; }
    operator int()                                  // cast to integer
        { return (int)val; }
};
const int Circnum::Circ_MaxVal = 359;
```

4

Inheritance and Polymorphism

The idea that a new type of object can be created by having it inherit the characteristics and behaviors of an existing object type is a key contribution of object-oriented design. Inheritance is a natural way to express the hierarchical nature of many problems and is thus a tool for specialization and reuse. We can take a general class *Boat* that encapsulates the essentials of what it is to be a boat and then derive the more specialized classes *Powerboat* and *Sailboat* from that class. The designs for *Powerboat* and *Sailboat* would inherit all the properties of the class *Boat* and add properties that go into the more specialized classes derived from *Boat.* The specialized designs can take advantage of the work that has already gone into the general design and refine it.

By first concentrating on the essentials and then turning our attention to the specifics, we also tackle the complexity of the problem by reducing it, in a natural and meaningful way, into manageable parts.

The real trick in class design is to have the foresight as we solve today's task—the design of a class *Powerboat,* say—to develop the design in such a way that some as yet unanticipated task—the design of a class *Sailboat,* say—can take advantage of the work already done.

Derivation

Traditional programming languages offer poor support for expressing hierarchical layers of specialization. They don't have language-supported ways to express ideas such as "A powerboat is the same as a boat except...." Object-oriented programming languages such as C++ remedy this shortcoming.

Inheritance is used to express what are sometimes called *is a* relationships or "kind of" relationships. Inheritance is not useful for expressing "part of" relationships, and trying to use inheritance to express such relationships is a common mistake among novices. An *is a* relationship is pretty much what it sounds like: A motor *is a* machine, a square *is a* shape, a steel belted radial tire *is a* radial tire, and a radial tire *is a* tire. A set of four tires is not an automobile; rather, the tires are parts of an automobile. Deriving the class *RadialTire* from the class *Tire* makes sense; deriving the class *Tire* from the class *Automobile* is probably a mistake.

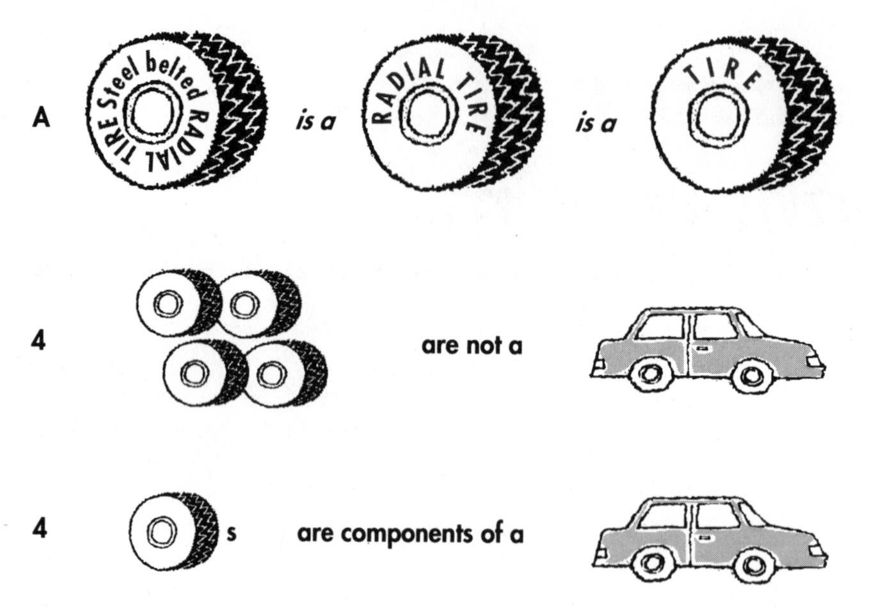

The diagram in Figure 4-1 below shows how a set of zoological classes are related.

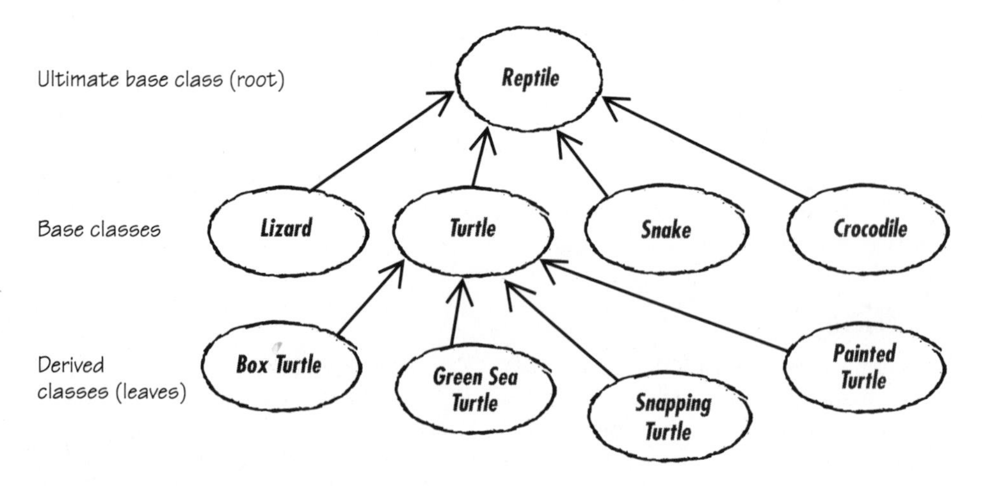

Figure 4-1.
Single inheritance. Derived turtle classes, various reptile base classes, and the ultimate Reptile *base class.*

In class diagrams, an arrow is usually drawn from each derived class to its base class. In Figure 4-1, arrows show that a *Box Turtle* class is derived from a *Turtle* class, which in turn is derived from a *Reptile* class.

When you derive a new class from an existing class, you can make several kinds of changes in the derived class:

- You can add new member variables.
- You can add new member functions.
- You can redefine existing member functions.
- You can adjust the accessibility of existing members.

You might be surprised to learn that the class derivation scheme doesn't make any provision for deleting member variables and member functions.[1] The practical reason for this limitation is that C++ and most other object-oriented programming languages view a derived class as simply an extension of its base class and allow a derived class to be used in any context that calls for the base. If some members of the base class were missing in the derived class, that wouldn't always be possible. And class derivation is an act of specialization, of refinement. The tendency should be toward more and finer tools, not fewer and coarser.

Sometimes a feature of a base class doesn't make much sense in a derived class. Consider a base class for representing shapes that contains member variables for width and height and a member function for computing shape sizes. If you derive a point class from the base shape class, the class members for width, height, and computing size no longer serve a useful purpose. You can improvise, setting height and width to *0*, for instance, or making the irrelevant members inaccessible; or you can rethink your class hierarchy.

Multiple Inheritance

In ordinary inheritance, sometimes called "single inheritance," a class is derived from a single base class. In the derived class, you can add members and redefine member functions in order to create a specialized inheritor of the base class. In Figure 4-1, the set of single inheritance relationships looks like a tree; each base class is a node, and each of its derived classes branches from the node. A class without derived classes is a leaf. In single inheritance, each leaf or node has at most one parent although it can have several ancestors—a grandparent, a great-grandparent, a great-great-grandparent, and so on.

In "multiple inheritance," a leaf or a node can have more than one parent. Multiple base classes enable a derived class to inherit features from more than one base class. Multiple inheritance doesn't change the nature of the *is a* relationship; the derived

---

1. True deletion of members isn't allowed, but you can make members inaccessible, which often is just as good.

class has an *is a* relationship with each of its base classes. The *HouseCat* class shown in Figure 4-2 is derived from both a *Feline* class and a *Pet* class. A *HouseCat is a Feline* and *is a Pet.*

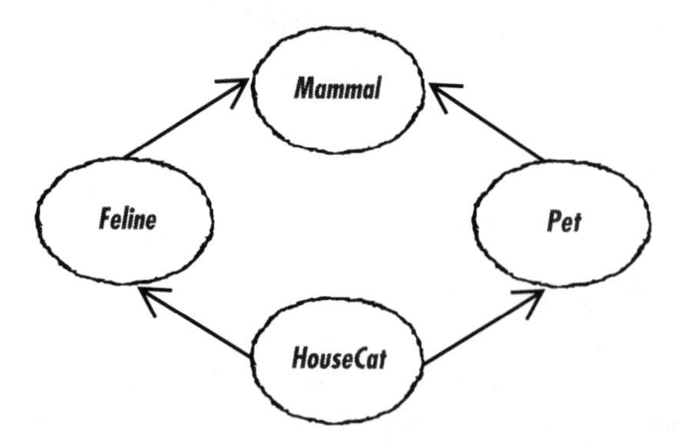

Figure 4-2.
Multiple inheritance. The HouseCat *class is derived from the base class* Feline *and the base class* Pet.

Multiple inheritance relationships are diagrammed as single inheritance relationships are, except that each node can have more than one parent.

Multiple inheritance can become tangled. In Figure 4-2, both the *Feline* class and the *Pet* class are derived from the *Mammal* class. The *HouseCat* class thus has two separate lines of inheritance coming from *Mammal.* This could be the beginning of a confusing thicket of relationships.

For compiler writers, multiple inheritance is an area of great difficulty, with its potential for contradictions, confusing and inefficient duplications, and complex storage layout questions. For language users, subtle rules and consequences of multiple inheritance can be hard to deal with. We'll deal with some of the rules in detail later in this chapter.

The most prominent use of multiple inheritance so far has been in the iostream class library developed at AT&T to replace the C standard I/O library. The role of the iostream library is to provide at least the convenience and functionality of the C standard I/O library while adding type safety and extensibility. We'll look at other aspects of the iostream library in Chapter 12. Right now, we'll focus on the iostream library's use of multiple inheritance.

The base class in the *iostream* hierarchy is *ios.* It provides common status and error facilities used by streams for formatted input and output. The *ios* class is the base class for several derived classes, including *istream* and *ostream.* The *istream* class contains numerous facilities related to input from streams, including the input conversion functions and some buffered input functions. The *ostream* class contains output conversion functions and simple buffered output functions. Roughly, *istream* replaces *fscanf()* and *fread()* from the C standard I/O library, and *ostream* replaces *fprintf()* and *fwrite().*

For some applications, we need both read and write operations on a single file. In the iostream library, the *iostream* class, derived from both *istream* and *ostream*, meets that need. The *iostream* class, whose lineage is shown in Figure 4-3, is a creature of multiple inheritance. It's a stream connection that has all the functionality of both *istream* and *ostream*. An *iostream is an istream*, and it also *is an ostream*.

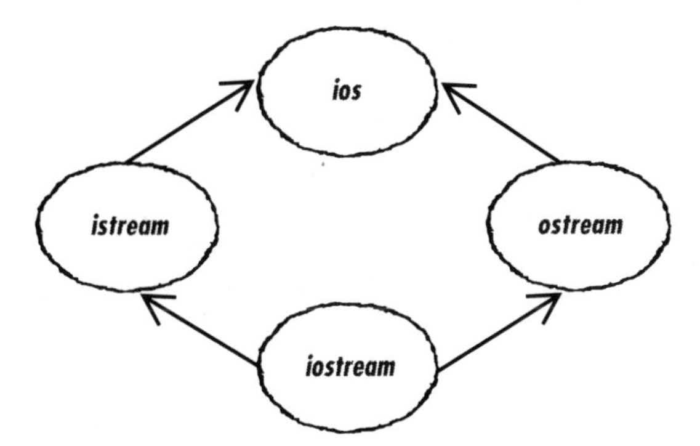

Figure 4-3.
Multiple inheritance. The iostream *class is derived from the base class* istream *and the base class* ostream.

The point of all this is safety. When you create an input stream object, all you can do with that object is input; no output operations are available. A C++ compiler can thus do a "sanity check" of your I/O code during compilation. This is much safer than I/O in C, which lets you open a file for reading and then lets you write, write, write.

Some object-oriented programmers advise against using multiple inheritance. They claim that the gains are offset by the added complexity, and they claim further that most or all code that uses multiple inheritance can be improved by rewriting it without the multiple inheritance. I have some misgivings about multiple inheritance and have not found any use for it in my own work. But I am also convinced that there are hierarchies, such as the iostream library, in which multiple inheritance is profitably employed.

Invariants and Assertions

Class hierarchies can and should be used to create more reliable software through the use of trustworthy base classes. Correct, bulletproof base classes can make it much easier to create correct derived classes. They provide a solid foundation and reduce the complexity of classes derived from them.

Class Invariants

Another opportunity for increasing reliability is to use base classes to express class invariants. An "invariant" is a tautology, a logical expression that should always be true. I say "should" because when things go awry, an invariant can become false.

A "class invariant" is a logical expression that is always true for all objects of the class—and for all objects of all classes that are derived from the class. Of course, there can be brief periods while a class object is being modified during which an invariant might not be true. For example, while a class member function is executing, it might temporarily do something that violates the invariant. However, an invariant should be true on entry to all client-accessible (public) member functions, and it is usually true on entry even to private member functions.

An invariant should also be of a local, testable nature. In a class representing a sorted list, it might be nice to have an invariant of the form "Each element is less than the following," but such an invariant would be too difficult to check, say, on entry to all member functions. A more appropriate invariant would be "If the current element is not first, it is greater than the previous, and if it is not last, it is less than the following." This reduced-strength invariant could be checked on entry to all public member functions.

Testing class invariants

An "assertion" is a mechanism for testing an invariant. Assertions come in a variety of forms. Typically, an assertion subroutine is called with a boolean argument. If the argument is false, some action is taken, such as termination of the program or a simple error message display.

The object-oriented Eiffel programming language offers explicit support for the notion of class invariants. When a class is derived from an existing class, invariants of the new class are *AND*ed with the base class invariants to create even more stringent invariants. Another aspect of Eiffel's support for invariants is its ability to turn invariant checking on and off using command line compilation controls. With Eiffel, you can therefore develop programs using the safety of invariants but deliver applications with the efficiency of unchecked code. You can achieve a similar capability in C++ by using conditional code generation (*#if*).

Although C++ doesn't have Eiffel's built-in support for invariants, I think it is important when using C++ to adopt the careful attitude that Eiffel encourages. We should look to class hierarchies, and especially to base classes, for opportunities to express invariants, so that our code can be more reliable and our failures more revealing.

Polymorphism

"Polymorphism" is a 50-cent word that means "the quality of having many forms," and it's a common, ordinary occurrence. For example, I have several outdoor power tools—lawn mower, tiller, chain saw—that all have small gasoline engines. Each engine needs gasoline, but the mixes vary. The mower likes its gasoline straight, the tiller wants a 40:1 gas:oil mixture, and the chain saw prefers a 32:1 gas:oil mixture. Filling their tanks is the same basic operation for each, but the details are different.

Polymorphism is fundamental to most programming languages. If you write $x + y$ where x and y are *doubles*, the compiler will generate a sequence of floating point arithmetic instructions, but when x and y are *ints*, the compiler will generate a completely different set of integer arithmetic instructions.

In C++, polymorphism allows you to create a family of classes that have common behaviors that vary according to what's appropriate for each class. The common behaviors are provided by polymorphic member functions, often called "virtual member functions" because the keyword *virtual* is used to declare a polymorphic member function. A derived class is free to either define its own version of the behavior or accept the version of the behavior that it inherits from its base class.

For example, imagine a *SmallGasEngine* class that has a *FillTank()* polymorphic member function that simply puts unmixed gasoline into the tank. From the *SmallGasEngine* base class we might derive the *LawnMowerEngine* class, the *TillerEngine* class, and the *ChainSawEngine* class. In the *LawnMowerEngine* class we would probably not redefine *FillTank()* because the base class behavior is appropriate. But in the *TillerEngine* class we would need to create a *FillTank()* procedure that filled the tank with the 40:1 gas:oil mixture the tiller needs, and in the *ChainSawEngine* class we'd need a 32:1 version of *FillTank()*. Figure 4-4 diagrams the polymorphic relationships.

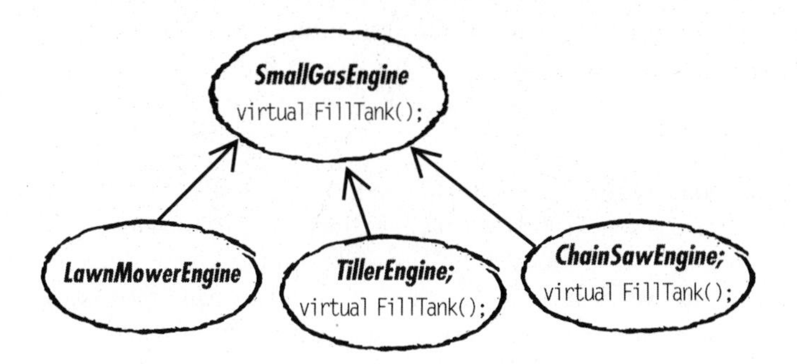

Figure 4-4.
The SmallGasEngine *class hierarchy with the polymorphic* virtual FillTank() *function.*

If we simply have any one of the four object types, it's easy for the compiler to invoke the correct version of *FillTank()*. That's similar to what the compiler does when it generates arithmetic code that depends on data type.

```
SmallGasEngine guzzler;
ChainSawEngine buz;
TillerEngine roto;
LawnMowerEngine briggs;

guzzler.FillTank();        // invoke SmallGasEngine class's FillTank()
buz.FillTank();            // invoke ChainSawEngine class's FillTank()
roto.FillTank();           // invoke TillerEngine class's FillTank()
briggs.FillTank();         // invoke SmallGasEngine class's FillTank()
```

But a C++ compiler is also able to invoke the correct *FillTank()* routine even when it can't tell, during compilation, which type of engine object will be used at runtime.

```
SmallGasEngine *engine;
switch(rand() % 4) {
    case 0: engine = &guzzler; break;
    case 1: engine = &buz; break;
    case 2: engine = &roto; break;
    case 3: engine = &briggs; break;
}
engine->FillTank();        // invoke the appropriate FillTank()
```

Following the switch statement, the *engine* pointer will be pointing at one of the four objects, but we can't know in advance which one. The C++ compiler is therefore forced to use a runtime mechanism that determines, based on what the *engine* pointer is actually pointing to at runtime, which *FillTank()* to invoke.

The mechanism that enables runtime polymorphism is quite simple. Every object of a class that has polymorphic member functions has a hidden table of pointers to those functions. If a derived class hasn't redefined a polymorphic member function, the entry in that table points to the base class's member function, but if there has been a class-specific member function redefinition, the table entry points to the function as redefined. This runtime mechanism makes it impossible to invoke the inappropriate member function by mistake. (Of course, you can gain control when necessary by using overrides.)

The term "late binding" is sometimes used to refer to the invoking of this or that routine based on runtime type checking. The "late" refers to the fact that the call occurs after a program starts to run, and "binding" refers to making a relationship between a function name and a particular version of the function. Binding is ordinary linking, or linkage editing. And because one term for something is never enough, late binding is also called "dynamic binding" because the binding is done dynamically, as the program runs. Of course, if we have late binding, we also have "early binding," also called "static binding," which is just ordinary compile time binding during the linking process.

Example: The *CShape* Classes

I've long been interested in recursive drawing algorithms because simple recursive operations often produce interesting and attractive designs. As an exercise in Windows programming, I created a Quilt program that is able to draw several recursively defined shapes, some of which are shown in Figure 4-5.

The Quilt program is organized into two parts, one that deals mostly with windows, dialog boxes, menus, and the like, and another that focuses on the graphical algorithms. In this chapter, we'll look at the set of classes for Quilt's graphics because they are a good example of inheritance and polymorphism. We'll take up the Quilt program as a whole in Chapter 15.

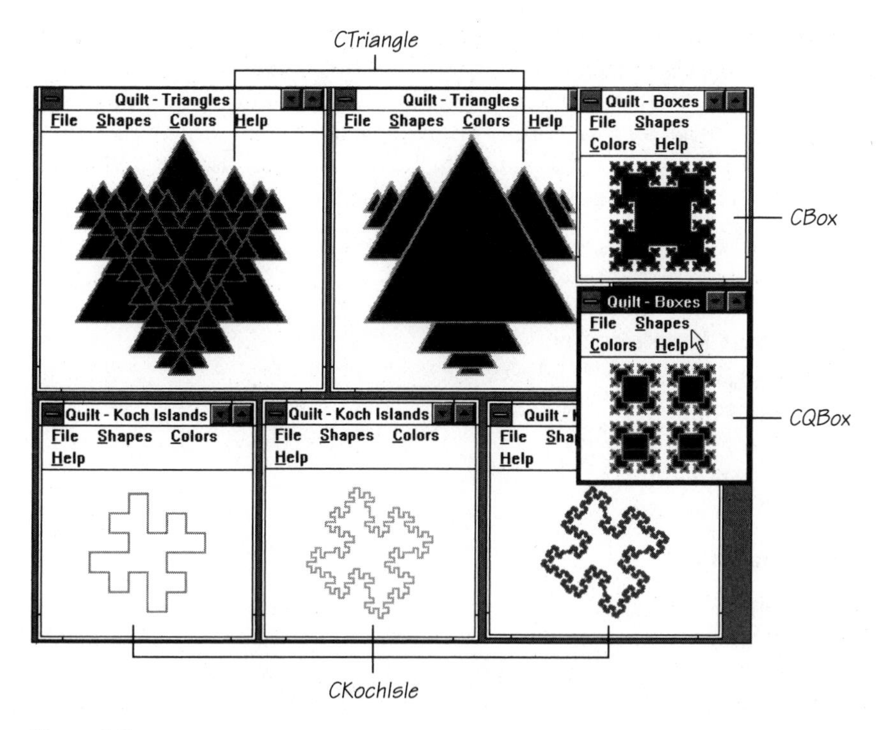

Figure 4-5.
Some of the recursively drawn shapes produced by the Quilt program, and the classes that drew them.

In Quilt, the classes for drawing several recursively defined shapes are organized into the hierarchical family shown in Figure 4-6.

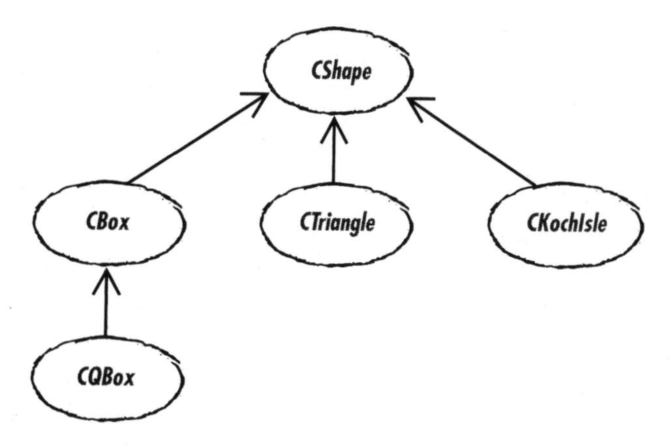

Figure 4-6.
The CShape *class hierarchy.*

The *CShape* base class is responsible for storing status information about the drawing environment, and it also contains a polymorphic virtual member function named *Draw()*. *Draw()* is the interface to the family of classes. The four derived classes—*CBox*, *CQBox*, *CTriangle*, and *CKochIsle*—draw specific graphical patterns. Each derived class redefines *Draw()* to meet its own needs, and each also has additional member functions that do most of the work of drawing a specific shape.

Here is the structure of the *CShape* class hierarchy in more detail, showing the members of each class in the hierarchy.

CShape Base Class Members

Member Variables	Member Functions
m_pDC	*CShape(CDC,CRect,int)*
m_pRect	*~CShape()*
m_pDepth	*Draw()*

CBox Class Members

Member Variables	Member Functions	
m_pDC	*CShape(CDC,CRect,int)*	From the *CShape* base class
m_pRect	*~CShape()*	From the *CShape* base class
m_pDepth	*Draw()*	From the *CShape* base class
	CBox(CDC,CRect,int)	
	Draw()	
	Draw(int,CPoint,int)	

CQBox Class Members

Member Variables	Member Functions		
m_pDC	*CShape(CDC,CRect,int)*	From the *CShape* base class	From the *CBox* base class
m_pRect	*~CShape()*	From the *CShape* base class	From the *CBox* base class
m_pDepth	*Draw()*	From the *CShape* base class	From the *CBox* base class
	CBox(CDC,CRect,int)		From the *CBox* base class
	Draw()		From the *CBox* base class
	Draw(int,CPoint,int)		From the *CBox* base class
	CQBox(CDC,CRect,int)		
	Draw()		

CTriangle Class Members

Member Variables	Member Functions	
m_pDC	*CShape(CDC,CRect,int)*	From the *CShape* base class
m_pRect	*~CShape()*	From the *CShape* base class
m_pDepth	*Draw()*	From the *CShape* base class
m_bFront	*CTriangle(CDC,CRect,int,BOOL)*	
	Draw()	
	Draw(int,CPoint,int)	
	Drawone(CPoint,int)	

CKochIsle Class Members

Member Variables	Member Functions	
m_pDC	*CShape(CDC,CPoint,int)*	From the *CShape* base class
m_pRect	*~CShape()*	
m_pDepth	*Draw()*	
	CKochIsle(CDC,CRect,int)	
	Draw()	
	Line(CPoint,CPoint,int)	

In the derived classes, the virtual *Draw()* member function of the base class is dimmed because it has been overriden by the derived class's *Draw()*. Each class in the hierarchy has implemented its own *Draw()* member function and its own constructor. Only the *CTriangle* class has added a member variable to the member variables defined by *CShape*, and only *CQBox*, which is derived from *CBox*, has failed to add member functions other than its own constructor and its own *Draw()*.

Here is the declaration of *CShape*:

```
class CShape {
public:
    virtual void Draw() = 0;        // Draw()--the interface
    virtual ~CShape() {}            // virtual destructor
protected:
    CDC *m_pDC;                     // pointer to a device context
    CRect *m_pRect;                 // pointer to a drawing rectangle
    int m_nDepth;                   // desired recursion depth
    CShape(CDC *dc, CRect *r, int depth);   // constructor
};
```

The *CDC* and *CRect* types are classes from the Microsoft Foundation Class library. They encapsulate a device context and a Windows *RECT*, respectively. All you need to know about these two items right now is that they are used for drawing: The *CDC* is the drawing environment, and the *CRect* specifies the drawing dimensions. (We'll look at the MFC library in Part 3 of this book.)

The *m_nDepth* integer member variable specifies the desired recursion depth. For these routines, I felt it best to terminate the graphical recursion at a specified depth because that approach provides more control over appearance. Another approach in drawing successively smaller recursive graphics is to terminate recursion when the dimensions grow smaller than some specified size, which is often 1 pixel. This approach automatically adapts to display resolution, but it usually produces fuzzy-looking drawings because the last drawn items are usually single pixels.

The public interface of the *CShape* family of classes contains three elements: each class's constructor, the *CShape* class's virtual destructor, and the virtual *Draw()* member function. The *CShape* destructor is virtual so that objects in the *CShape* family will always be destroyed correctly. We'll look further at this subtle but important aspect of C++ classes in Chapter 10. The *CShape* destructor is public so that

CShape objects can be deleted anywhere—that is, from within objects of other classes. The *Draw()* member function is virtual because *Draw()* is the main interface to the *CShape* family of classes.

Each derived class defines a constructor that initializes an object of that class, each defines its own public virtual *Draw()*, and each (except *CQBox*) has some drawing helper member functions in addition. Remember that the role of *Draw()* is simply to start the drawing process; some other routine in the class implements the recursive drawing algorithm. Here is the declaration of the derived *CBox* class, which draws the box shape in the upper right corner of Figure 4-5.

```
class CBox : public CShape {
public:
    CBox(CDC *dc, CRect *rect, int nDepth);      // constructor
    virtual void Draw();                          // drawing process
                                                  //  initiation
protected:
    void Draw(int nRadius, CPoint pt, int nDepth);     // recursive
                                                       //  Draw()
};
```

The *CBox* class has three member functions of its own: a virtual *Draw()* that replaces *CShape*'s *Draw()*, a constructor whose chief job is to invoke the *CShape* constructor, and a *Draw(int,CPoint,int)* routine that does the drawing. The two *Draw()* functions appear to have the same name, but to a C++ compiler they are completely different because they take different arguments.

The virtual *Draw()* is the interface; it is the function invoked, after a *CBox* object has been created, to initiate the drawing process. It calculates the center of the drawing region and determines a good size (radius) for the drawing. Then the virtual *Draw()* invokes the other *Draw()*, the one with three parameters, to do the actual drawing. This second *Draw()* is the recursive implementation of the box algorithm, in which a half-size box is recursively placed behind a quadrant of the central box.

You'll find the declarations for the other classes derived from *CShape* in Figure 4-7, and you'll find the full source code listings for all the classes in the *CShape* hierarchy in Chapter 15.

```
//
// A quad box shape--four CBox patterns
//
class CQBox : public CBox {
public:
    CQBox(CDC *dc, CRect *rect, int nDepth);
    virtual void Draw();
};
```

Figure 4-7. *(continued)*
Declarations for the other CShape *classes:* CQBox, CTriangle, *and* CKochIsle.

Figure 4-7. *continued*

```
//
// A triangle shape, on top of other triangles
//
class CTriangle : public CShape {
public:
    CTriangle(CDC *dc, CRect *rect, int nDepth, BOOL front);
    virtual void Draw();
protected:
    void Draw(int nRadius, CPoint pt, int nDepth);
    void Drawone(CPoint pt, int nRadius);
    BOOL m_bFront;
    static const double dSin30;         // sines and cosines
    static const double dCos30;         //  of some common angles
    static const double dSin30Cos30;
    static const double dSin30Sin30;
};
//
// A quadratic Koch Island
//
class CKochIsle : public CShape {
public:
    CKochIsle(CDC *dc, CRect *rect, int nDepth);
    virtual void Draw();
protected:
    void Line(CPoint from, CPoint to, int nDepth);
};
```

The other classes derived from *CShape* differ only in detail from *CBox*. More interesting than the particulars of their differences is the way these classes are used in the Windows context of the Quilt program.

In a Microsoft Foundation Class library application for Windows, the client window is painted by a function named *OnPaint()* that is executed each time the *WM_PAINT* message arrives. *OnPaint()* is a member of the *CMainWindow* class, which manages the Quilt application's main window. We'll look further at *CMainWindow* in Chapter 15.

These details merely set the stage; you needn't be familiar with programming for Windows or with the MFC library to get the idea: *OnPaint()* is the start of the drawing process, even before the virtual *Draw()* member function is invoked. Figure 4-8 on the next page shows the Quilt application's *OnPaint()* member function.

The beginning of *OnPaint()* attends to the user's menu choices for color, creates corresponding pens and brushes, and starts the painting process by creating a *CPaintDC* object. Following this initialization, a switch statement creates an object of the *CShape* family based on the currently selected shape choice, which is stored in the *m_wShape* variable. The presence of the switch statement illustrates the fact that

```
void CMainWindow::OnPaint()
{
    CPaintDC paintDC(this);
    CRect rect;
    GetClientRect(&rect);
    int clr = m_wColor - IDM_BLACK;
    int r = clrArray[clr].rgbtRed;
    int g = clrArray[clr].rgbtGreen;
    int b = clrArray[clr].rgbtBlue;

    DWORD rgbPen = RGB(r, g, b);
    if rgbPen == paintDC.GetBkColor())
         rgbPen = RGB(3*r/4, 3*g/4, 3*b/4);
    CPen Pen(PS_SOLID, 2, rgbPen);
    CPen *oldPen = paintDC.SelectObject(&Pen);

    DWORD rgbBrush = RGB(r/2, g/2, b/2);
    if rgbBrush == paintDC.GetBkColor())
         rgbBrush = RGB(3*r/4, 3*g/4, 3*b/4);
    CBrush Brush(rgbBrush);
    CBrush *oldBrush = paintDC.SelectObject(&Brush);

    switch(m_wShape) {
        case IDM_TRIA:
            shape = new CTriangle(&paintDC, &rect, 4, TRUE);
            break;
        case IDM_TRIB:
            shape = new CTriangle(&paintDC, &rect, 4, FALSE);
            break;
        case IDM_BOXESA:
            shape = new CBox(&paintDC, &rect, 6);
            break;
        case IDM_BOXESB:
            shape = new CQBox(&paintDC, &rect, 5);
            break;
        case IDM_KOCH1:
            shape = new CKochIsle(&paintDC, &rect, 1);
            break;
        case IDM_KOCH2:
            shape = new CKochIsle(&paintDC, &rect, 2);
            break;
        case IDM_KOCH3:
            shape = new CKochIsle(&paintDC, &rect, 3);
            break;
    }
```

Figure 4-8. *(continued)*
The OnPaint() *function draws the client window by creating an object belonging to one of the classes of the* CShape *family and then invoking that object's* Draw() *member function.*

Figure 4-8. *continued*

```
        if (shape) {
                shape->Draw();
                delete shape;
        }
        paintDC.SelectObject(oldPen);
        paintDC.SelectObject(oldBrush);
}
```

polymorphism doesn't apply to object creation. In the beginning, you must specify exactly what kind of object you want to create. However, once a *CShape*-family object is created, polymorphism can bloom. Following the *OnPaint()* function's switch statement is this simple statement that starts the drawing process and then deletes the object:

```
if (shape) {
    shape->Draw();
    delete shape;
}
```

The invocation of *Draw()* (by means of a generic *CShape* pointer named *shape*) is a perfect example of polymorphism. It doesn't matter what kind of object has been created—the proper *Draw()* will be invoked. Similarly, the delete statement works polymorphically: Because the base class's destructor is virtual, the appropriate derived class destructor will always be invoked. (In the *CShape* family, no derived class defines its own destructor, so this capability is, for the moment, dormant.)

Although this example clearly demonstrates the idea of polymorphism, it isn't a very strong argument for polymorphism. In this simple context, each *CShape*-family object exists for only a short time, and it would be easy to move the invocation of *Draw()* up into the cases of the switch statement, obviating the need for polymorphism. In more realistic circumstances, great collections of objects often survive for long periods, and manually keeping track of each object's type and capabilities would be onerous. Polymorphism frees you from that chore. It lets you define a class hierarchy, specify a generic interface that will be common to all the classes in the hierarchy, and then use that interface without worrying about the type of the current object.

5

Object-Oriented Design

Object-oriented design is a matter of specifying a set of classes and their relationships in order to solve a given problem. In this chapter, we'll look at some of the fundamental principles of object-oriented design. We'll take the concepts we've looked at in earlier chapters—objects, classes, encapsulation, abstraction, inheritance, and polymorphism—and see how they interact in the object-oriented design process.

Object-oriented design is a subject for a full-length book. In this chapter, we'll just treat the basics, enough so that you can move to C++ and simultaneously move to an object-oriented methodology.

Keep in mind that much of what the best object-oriented designers know, they know from experience. You shouldn't skip textbook or classroom learning, but you also need to get some real-world experience. Just as a well-equipped pantry doesn't make you a chef, a well-stocked larder of object-oriented principles doesn't necessarily make you a master designer. To become adept at design, you need to design.

Identifying Classes

Don't expect facility with object-oriented design to come to you instantly, especially if you have years of experience in more procedure-oriented methodologies. Identifying a concept that can be a good basis for the formation of a class is not a black art, but neither is it a trivial undertaking.

A major aspect of class design is coming up with classes that relate productively to other classes. I've discovered a few guidelines that should help you identify useful classes. Don't follow these suggestions slavishly. Just be aware of them as you struggle to partition a complex problem domain into groups of related classes.

- Make a class represent a concept or entity that you could explain to someone who isn't a programmer. Real-world objects rarely have functions so obscure or so subtle that you can't summarize them in a sentence or two. Software objects should also be easy to discuss. If your rationale for the creation of a class is long and involved, mentally step back from your concept and try to come up with a simpler one.

- Make the class small and simple enough for an ordinary programmer to understand it readily. A class can be easy to describe but still too complex to be useful. Remember that most classes grow over time, so today's 10-page class might be next year's 50-page headache. The obverse is true too: You need to make each class big enough to do something useful.
- Make the class embody an active concept. An ordinary data type or structure "is" something. A class is a data type or structure plus operations—it should "do" something.
- Use encapsulation to make the class self-reliant and reliable. Code reuse works only if the class can be taken from one environment and used in another.
- Use inheritance to create families of classes that can exploit the advantages offered by polymorphism. Traditional data structures permit only "member of" relationships, which can't be used to create a family of data structures. Class derivation permits *is a* relationships, which make families of classes possible.
- Regard your first design as a prototype. You need to get some experience with a design before you commit yourself to that design.

Experience is one of the best guides for identifying potential classes. If you work in a given problem domain over time, you start to see common problems and common solutions. The issues that you need to address every time you start a software project can suggest useful classes. Code that you have copied from one application to use in others is a good candidate for a class. Data structures that you've used in multiple projects are good candidates for expansion into classes. Once you have identified a potential class, analyze it in light of the guidelines we've just looked at to see how it holds up.

Usually, you can look at a problem domain from several perspectives. There are usually several candidates for the base class from which most of the other classes will be derived. Is a machine screw a type of metal object, or is the kind of metal a characteristic of a machine screw? In a factory that molds metal parts from raw stock, clearly a machine screw is just one of the kinds of objects that can be produced. But in a factory that uses machine screws to build more complex assemblies, a machine screw is a type of basic part, and its material (steel, brass, nylon) is just one of its characteristics.

Top-Down Design vs. Bottom-Up Design

In top-down design, you try to see and understand the big picture and to create a broad-stroke solution whose structure will address the major difficulties revealed by looking at the big picture. Once you've accomplished this step, you address the remaining, smaller, problems, whose details have been of secondary importance, in a similar way. Eventually, you arrive at a complete, fleshed-out solution.

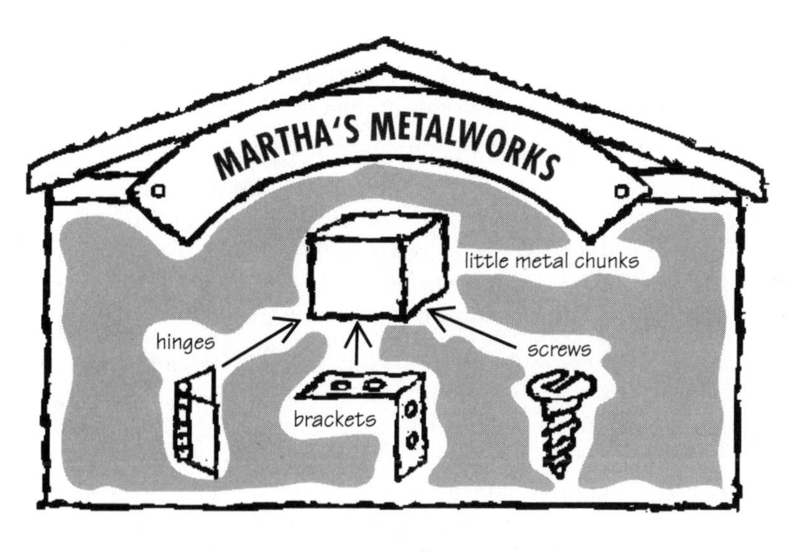

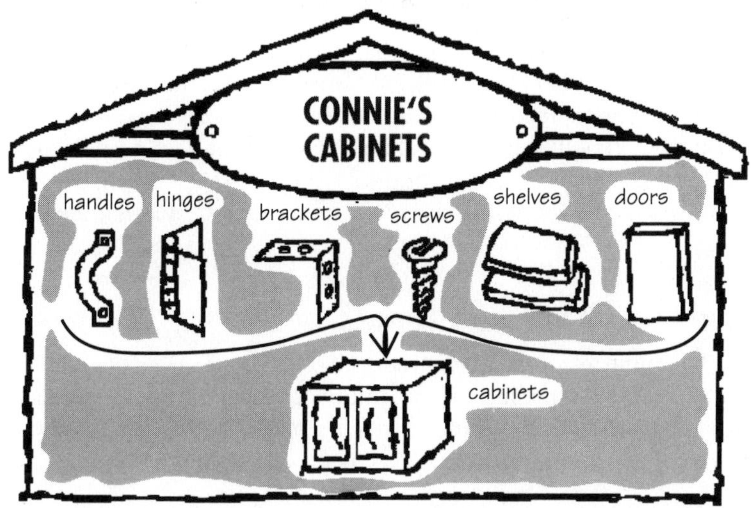

An object, such as a machine screw, can be viewed from different perspectives. To Martha, a machine screw is one of the many kinds of things she manufactures from raw stock. To Connie, a machine screw is one of the many components used to build a cabinet.

In top-down design, the trick to managing each level of the structure is to cultivate a form of selective blindness. You don't want to be overwhelmed by the details of the lower levels, but you also can't be completely ignorant of likely difficulties. Good designers can put on selective blinders, focusing on the current design region without being completely oblivious to the requirements of other parts of the problem.

The opposite of a top-down design is a bottom-up design, in which you start by solving basic, simple problems. Then you build additional capabilities on top of the basic facilities until, ideally, you've solved the entire problem. While you build each layer of capability, it helps to have some awareness of the complex higher-level goals, even though your main focus is on the problems in the current layer.

In a perfect top-down program design, an intellectually challenging problem is reduced to a series of technical problems, each amenable to the skills of one or more good programmers. But perfect designs are not the rule because it's hard to state problems clearly, because designers aren't always gifted, because requirements change, and so forth. Given a flawed top-down design spec, the implementors must do their best to fit together a puzzle whose pieces can never match perfectly.

Object-oriented design is neither top down nor bottom up, although it involves elements of both approaches. Among other things, object-oriented design encourages you to think about the simple, fundamental aspects of the problem domain and to think about representing many of the fundamental aspects as objects. This is the essence of bottom-up design. But object-oriented design also suggests that you look toward your goals, thinking about how fundamental objects can be composed to reach your goals. This is the essence of top-down design.

A major advantage of object-oriented design is that it emphasizes code sharing and reuse. In any problem domain, there are likely to be many applications that need to be developed, all of which manipulate the basic elements of the problem domain. In an object-oriented design, reusable software objects capture the key properties of the problem domain's basic elements. This is in stark contrast to the lower-level routines created in a top-down design, which are incidental creations and not likely to be reusable.

Forests of Classes vs. Trees of Classes

In the C language, the only way to combine structs is to have one struct contain another. This capability, or rather this lack of capability, leads us to think of structs as independent entities, in isolation. When we need a struct, we create one from scratch, even though it might have other structs as members.

We can see a C++ class as an independent entity too. Within a given area, a group of classes might be related by inheritance, but classes and class families for different areas might not be related to one another. For example, within a group of classes that represent graphical objects, we might have a rich set of relationships, but the graphical object classes might be unrelated to the set of classes that represent, say, complex numbers. This type of organization is often called a "forest of classes" because it is composed of many independent classes and class hierarchies (trees). This type of organization is shown in Figure 5-1.

It is also possible to organize classes into a single tree, so that all classes, no matter how distinct their functions, are related to a common ancestor class. This, quite naturally, is called a "tree of classes," and it is the approach taken in many traditional object-oriented programming language designs, such as those done in Smalltalk. A tree of classes type of organization is shown in Figure 5-2.

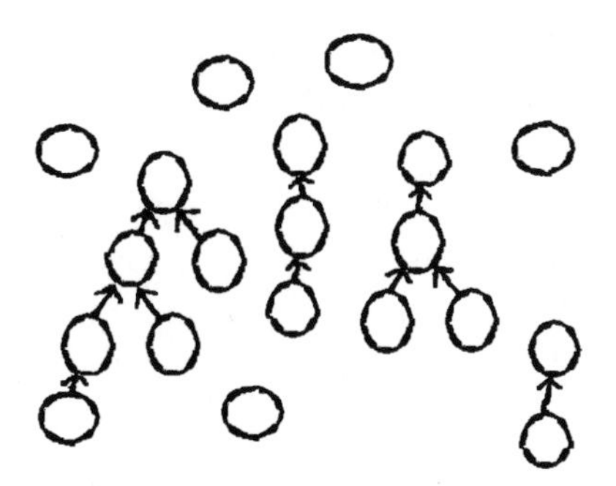

Figure 5-1.
A forest of classes.

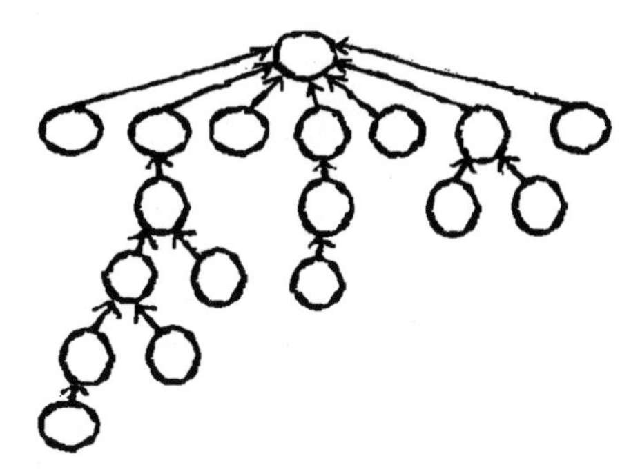

Figure 5-2.
A tree of classes.

The advantage of a tree of classes is that all classes will have characteristics in common. For example, many software classes need a mechanism for being saved on disk or transmitted across a network (serialization), many need to be converted to and from text, and many need runtime typing information. A tree of classes is a framework for efficiently providing a number of classes with the features they all need.

Practical considerations often lead to a design that is neither a pure tree nor a forest. The Microsoft Foundation Class (MFC) library is, mostly, a tree design based on the *CObject* class. *CObject* addresses basic issues, such as runtime typing and persistence, that are common to the library. *CObject*, like the entire library, is lean and trim, but it has one member variable and one virtual member function, which means that classes derived from *CObject* will have at least two inherited members. For most classes in the MFC library, the benefit from *CObject*'s facilities far outweighs the cost. But some of the classes in the MFC library are "value" classes, which means that they will often be returned from functions, involved in expressions, and the like. Efficiency is critical for value classes; if they aren't efficient, they won't be used. MFC's handful of value classes such as *CString* and *CPoint* are not derived from *CObject*—to avoid the slight space overhead imposed by *CObject*. Part of the MFC library is diagrammed in Figure 5-3 on the next page.

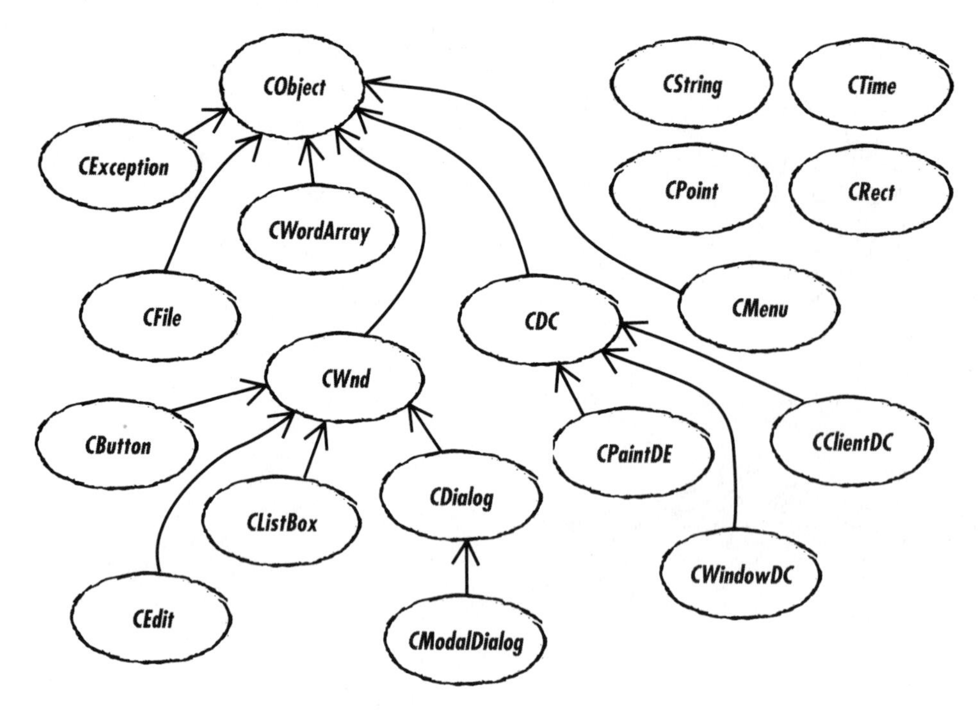

Figure 5-3.
Part of the Microsoft Foundation Class (MFC) library.

If you're a programmer trained in C, the idea of having a tree of classes probably seems foreign to you. It might seem less strange if you think about the C language's built-in types. The built-in types don't form a hierarchy, but they do have a standard set of operations: They all can be copied to and from disk storage by means of the read and write routines, they all can be converted to text by means of the *printf()* routine, their sizes are known, their types are known, and so forth. If you were to create independent classes, you would have to produce most of these capabilities from scratch for each class. That's why several research groups have created generic "superclasses," each of which can be used as the basis for all the classes in a particular system.

Part of the challenge of the 1990s is the wide variety of popular computing environments and the consequent need for vendors to produce software for multiple environments. A class library based on a single tree of classes helps to address this problem by pushing many environment problems into single superclasses that can be specially tailored for each environment. For example, routines need to produce error messages in various environments. In a graphics or character windowing environment, the message might pop up in a box and remain on screen until the user actively removes it. In a more traditional environment, the message might simply be output to a character stream or a file. These differences can be handled in each environment's superclass.

Although there are many benefits to the tree of classes approach, it does have some drawbacks. One is that you have to learn about the superclass and probably study some of the supplied derived classes before you can create your own derived classes. In the long run, this extra effort might seem trivial, but it is a significant initial hurdle. Another liability is that you have to standardize your classes on a single superclass, and that can be difficult in this changing, multivendor, multienvironment world. Once you've standardized your classes on a superclass, you've made a decision that rules out certain options in the future. De facto (or even more formal) superclass standards will probably develop eventually, but until that happens, you're working in rough, unknown terrain.

Example: A NetBIOS Interface Tree of Classes

NetBIOS is a software network interface specification that was first introduced in the early 1980s by IBM. It was originally designed as an interface specification for the Sytek networking hardware IBM was selling, but it soon became a de facto standard in the PC marketplace, and today virtually every network adapter card for the PC has driver software that implements a NetBIOS compatibility layer. Software written to the original NetBIOS specification will work on most PC networks today.

In many areas—manufacturing, process control, laboratory automation—multiple PCs are used to manage a complex, distributed process. Such a distributed control system is much more flexible and powerful if its individual PCs can communicate. I'm most familiar with this requirement from my work in laboratory automation at the Rockefeller University. In many experiments there, several PCs are used simultaneously to manage the experiment. One PC might exercise overall control of the experiment, another be busy managing specialized equipment such as the Gilbert prism system, and a third be constantly collecting data. This kind of management is diagrammed in Figure 5-4 on the next page.

The NetBIOS protocol provides a foundation for enabling communication among PCs, but it is a very low-level, detail-oriented protocol. What's needed is a much more convenient interface, so that a developer can establish a communication session between two machines without first attending NetBIOS University.

The NetBIOS protocol specifies 20 commands that an application program can issue to the NetBIOS communication layer (the driver). Some of these commands specify names and communications channels, and others are used to send or receive messages. But all the commands revolve around a 64-byte network control block (NCB) that has 14 clearly specified fields. A program interacts with a NetBIOS driver by filling in the fields of the NCB and then issuing software INT 0x5c with the ES:BX registers pointing at the NCB. The NetBIOS driver performs the command, which might include filling in certain response fields in the NCB. Most NetBIOS commands can be issued either synchronously, which means that control doesn't return to the application until the command is complete, or asynchronously, which means that the application regains control as soon as possible. When asynchronous commands are issued, the easiest way to determine command completion is to examine the command complete field of the NCB.

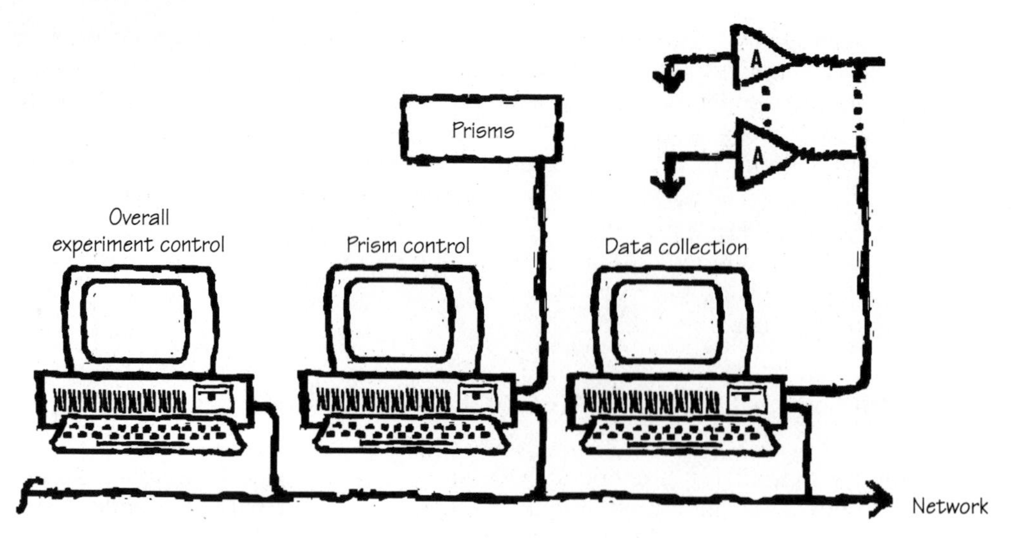

Figure 5-4.
Several PCs managing an experiment and communicating over a network.

A C-Style Single Class Approach

As I thought about how to use C++ to create a convenient interface to NetBIOS communications, I considered two approaches. In the first, I envisioned a NetBIOS object that would have member functions for handling the details of the different types of messages, plus member functions for more mundane chores, such as specifying communications names. This approach is conceptually similar to what most programmers would do in C—create a NetBIOS struct and then create a series of subroutines to send the messages. In this essentially C-style approach, the C++ class declaration would resemble this one:

```
class Net {
protected:
    NCB ncb;          // network control block
                      // other data
    int DoMsg();      // send the message
    int MsgStat();    // get status
public:
    Net();            // constructor, initialize data items
    void Call();      // send the Call message
    void Listen();    // send the Listen message
    void HangUp();    // send the Hangup message
    // 16 additional message-sending member functions
};
```

Although this isn't the approach I finally chose, I don't think it's a bad approach. It lets you use the object-oriented features of C++ to guarantee that network control blocks are filled in correctly, and it provides a basis for building a convenient high-level interface. The major failing of this approach is that the single class will have to contain all the member variables and all the member functions needed by any and all of the message types, which means that there will always be extra baggage—and it might be difficult to understand.

A Multiple Class Approach

In the second approach, the approach I eventually chose, I created a relatively simple NetBIOS class that performs a small number of simple but important chores. This low-level class knows how to send a command to the NetBIOS driver (using software INTs), contains a few simple status functions, and contains a network control block. From this basic class, I derived classes to handle all the specific NetBIOS messages. These slightly higher-level classes each "know" the ins and outs of a specific NetBIOS message. A few intermediate classes know how to handle features common to a set of similar messages. Figure 5-5 shows the class hierarchy that grew out of this approach.

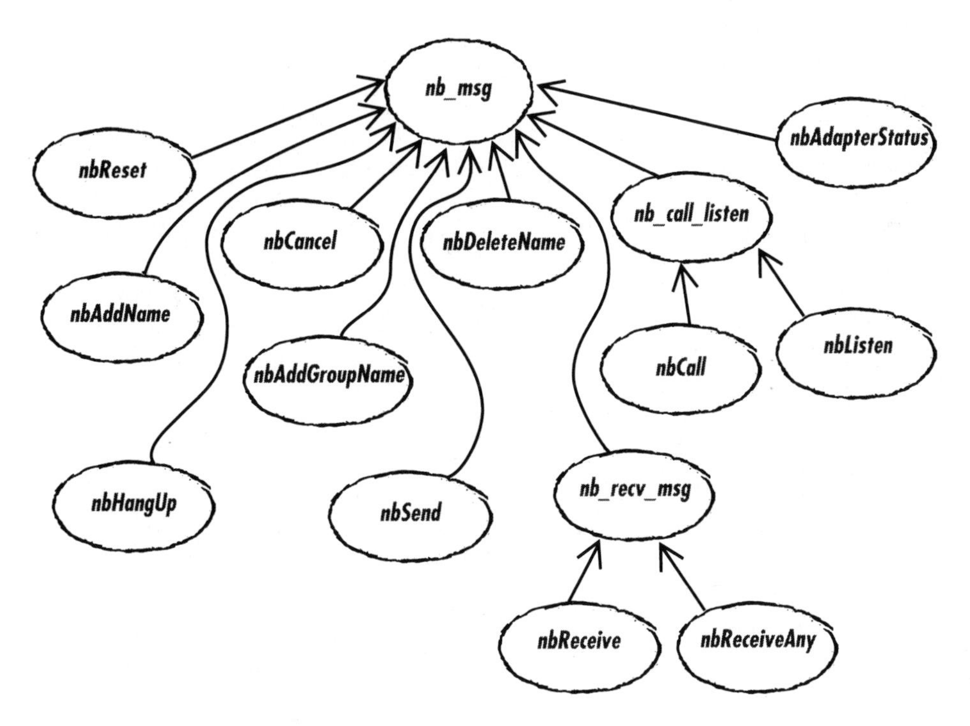

Figure 5-5.
The NetBIOS class hierarchy.

Three of the classes that are shown in Figure 5-5, *nb_msg, nb_call_listen,* and *nb_recv_msg,* have protected constructors, which means that objects can be created only in their offspring classes. Objects of the other classes can be created as necessary, whenever a message of that type is needed. As an organizing aid, I used fully lowercase names for the underlying helper classes and mixed-case names for the classes whose objects can be created publicly.

One advantage of this approach is that it lets C++ do more of the usage checking of these objects. For example, before sending data the user must open a session. I thus created an *nbSend* class that requires a reference to an *nbCall* object or an *nbListen* object. This lets the *nbSend* object pick up the session number and status informa-

The *nb_msg* Class Family

Class *nb_msg* is the base class for all the NetBIOS classes. It sends commands to the NetBIOS driver using software INTs and manages status information.

Class *nbReset* sends the Reset message. It is derived from *nb_msg.*

Class *nbCancel* sends the Cancel message. It is derived from *nb_msg.*

Class *nbAdapterStatus* sends the Adapter Status message. It is derived from *nb_msg.*

Class *nbAddName* sends the Add Name message. It is derived from *nb_msg.*

Class *nbAddGroupName* sends the Add Group Name message. It is derived from *nb_msg.*

Class *nbDeleteName* sends the Delete Name message. It is derived from *nb_msg.*

Class *nb_call_listen* is the base class for class *nbCall* and class *nbListen.* It manages the tasks common to sending the (similar) Call and Listen messages. It is derived from *nb_msg.*

Class *nbCall* sends the Call message. It is derived from *nb_call_listen.*

Class *nbListen* sends the Listen message. It is derived from *nb_call_listen.*

Class *nbHangUp* sends the Hangup message. It is derived from *nb_msg.*

Class *nbSend* sends the Send message. It is derived from *nb_msg.*

Class *nb_recv_msg* is the base class for *nbReceive* and *nbReceiveAny.* It manages the tasks common to both receiving a message and receiving any message. It is derived from *nb_msg.*

Class *nbReceive* sends the Receive message. It is derived from *nb_recv_msg.*

Class *nbReceiveAny* sends the Receive Any message. It is derived from *nb_recv_msg.*

tion directly from the message object that opened the session, and it ensures that the user has a session before he or she tries to send a message. These relationships, which were enforced by the compiler, mirrored the basic relationships specified in the NetBIOS manual. Similar guarantees could have been written into non-object-oriented code as a series of *if* statements, but not as naturally or transparently. And *if* statements are runtime checks, whereas the object-oriented approach introduces a great deal of checking during compilation.

Creating a separate class for each message type also enabled me to control which parts of the message would be public on a message-by-message basis. For example, when the user issues a Call or Listen NetBIOS request, the NetBIOS handler fills in the Logical Session Number (LSN) field of the network control block. The *nbCall* and *nbListen* classes therefore contain a member function that returns the number for the LSN field. (Actually, the member function is in the *nb_call_listen* base class and is one reason for creating the *nb_call_listen* intermediary class.) For the other messages, the LSN doesn't need to be read, so those classes don't implement an LSN access member function.

Another design decision was whether to use C++'s constructors solely for initializing message data elements. Initially, it seemed like an interesting approach to have the constructor actually send the message, so that simply creating a message would cause it to be sent automatically. After some thought, this seemed like a bad idea, one affording too little control. And although some messages, like those for registering names and starting sessions, need to be issued only once, other messages, like the send and receive data messages, are typically sent many times. Messages that are sent many times obviously don't lend themselves to the model of having the constructor automatically send a message at initialization. Although there are a few examples of having constructors cleverly perform multiple tasks, in general it's a good idea to restrict constructors to simple tasks that have little chance of failure. Initializing a message block is a clear, simple task that offers little chance of failure; sending that message on a network is not.

Somewhat surprisingly, in this design the network control block itself is not a class; instead, it is a C struct. This gives us precise control over the layout of the structure, so that it will conform to the NetBIOS specification. Even in C++, structs must follow the predictable layout rules first established in C, whereas C++ classes can be rearranged by the compiler. Use structs when you must conform to external structure layout requirements. The second reason to make the network control block a struct, not a class, had to do with my plan to derive the specific message classes from a generic base message class. Derivation expresses an *is a* relationship. The network control block is an appropriate member of the generic base message class, but the network control block is not an *nb_msg*.

You'll find the complete code for the NetBIOS class library at the end of this chapter. Right now, we'll focus on several aspects of the library, and we'll look at some fragments of the library as illustrations of design decisions.

The ultimate base message class

Let's start by looking at the *nb_msg* class declaration. Remember that *nb_msg* is the ultimate base class, the base class from which all the other NetBIOS classes are directly or indirectly derived.

```
class nb_msg {
friend class nbCancel;
private:
    static int handlerok;
protected:
    NCB *ncb;
    int protocmd;
    nb_msg(netbios_cmd cmd); // constructor
public:
    virtual int DoitNoWait(void);
    virtual int DoitWait(void);
    virtual int Complete(void) { return ncb->cmd_cplt == 0xff ? 0 : 1; }
    int ReturnCode(void) { return ncb->retcode; }
    int NameID() { return ncb->num; }
    int HandlerOK() { return handlerok; }
    void assign_name(NetName &n) { ncb->name = n; }
    void assign_callname(NetName &n)
        { ncb->callname = n; }
};
```

Notice that the *nb_msg* class references several items we haven't seen before. One is the NCB struct we've talked about, the 64-byte network control block. Another is the enumeration *netbios_cmd*, a symbolic, type-safe way to refer to the actual numeric values that specify NetBIOS commands. A third is the *NetName* class, which is essentially a 16-byte character array with a couple of special facilities that speak to unique NetBIOS naming conventions. These elements are shown in detail in the full source code at the end of the chapter.

A significant aspect of the *nb_msg* class is that its constructor is protected, which means that instances of *nb_msg* can be created only by *nb_msg* and classes derived from *nb_msg*. Another aspect of *nb_msg* to notice, and this is something you should always look for as you examine a class declaration, is that there are three polymorphic member functions: *DoitNoWait(), DoitWait(),* and *Complete()*. The *Doit()* (pronounced "do it") twins are the member functions that actually cause a message to be sent to the NetBIOS interface: The *DoitNoWait()* version returns control to the application as early as possible, and the *DoitWait()* version waits for the task to be completed before returning control to the application. Originally, the *DoitNoWait()* function was virtual because some messages don't have a *DoitNoWait()* version. Those classes implemented *DoitNoWait()* by invoking *DoitWait()*. (A more rigorous, less forgiving choice would be to have *DoitNoWait()* generate an error for those classes that don't have a *DoitNoWait()* version.)

Later I realized that some classes need to do certain tasks each time a message is sent; those classes implement their own *Doit()* functions, which do the per-call tasks and then call the base class *Doit()* functions. As realizations like these occurred to me, I made adjustments, but none of the adjustments compromised the original design. On the contrary, the ease with which unforeseen requirements were accommodated speaks well of the original design—if I do say so myself.

The *ReturnCode()*, *NameID()*, and *HandlerOK()* member functions are simply read-only ways to access elements of the NCB. I could have chosen to make the entire NCB public, but I felt that there should be as few publicly visible elements as possible. The minimal burden of writing these few access member functions was a small price to pay in exchange for completely hiding the NCB data structure. I wrote the *assign_name()* and *assign_callname()* member functions for similar reasons. The two *NetName* elements of the NCB needed to be assigned names, but I didn't want the NCB to be public. I was thus forced to write the two trivial assignment member functions.

A leaf message class

To get an idea of what one of the leaf classes, a class with no descendants, is like, let's look at *nbCancel*. The Cancel message is relatively simple: It tells the NetBIOS driver to cancel a pending message, which is usually a Receive message, although some of the other message types can be canceled too.

```
class nbCancel : public nb_msg {
public:
    // constructor
    nbCancel(nb_msg *tocancel) : nb_msg(ncCancel)
    {
        // note no check for commands that can't be canceled
        ncb->buffer = tocancel->ncb;
    }
    int DoitNoWait() { return DoitWait(); }
};
```

The *nbCancel* header says that the class is publicly derived from *nb_msg*. Public derivation means that the public and protected members of the base class have their accessibility levels preserved in the derived class. In this case, that means that each *nbCancel* object has a public *Complete()* function, a public *HandlerOK()*, and so on, just as if it were an *nb_msg* object.

The *nbCancel* class contains only two members, both public: the *nbCancel()* constructor and the *DoitNoWait()* polymorphic function. It needs the *DoitNoWait()* member function because NetBIOS's Cancel message doesn't have a *NoWait()* form; *nbCancel*'s *DoitNoWait()* function simply reissues the request as a *DoitWait()* invocation.

The *nbCancel* constructor must be supplied with a pointer to some other message object, which is the message that will be canceled. It invokes the parent constructor with the value *ncCancel*, which is a *netbios_cmd* enumeration constant. The body of the constructor fills in the buffer slot of the network control block with the address of the message to be canceled. This is the only instance in the NetBIOS class library in which one class needs to know the location of another class's NCB. This oddity mirrors the structure of NetBIOS itself: In canceling a message, you need one message that refers to another. To handle this exception, I made the *nbCancel* class a friend of the *nb_msg* class. Friendship allows *nbCancel*'s constructor to include the statement

```
ncb->buffer = tocancel->ncb;
```

Without friendship, the expression *tocancel->ncb* would have been a violation of the access rules because *ncb* was declared protected in the *nb_msg* class declaration. An *nbCancel* object would have been able to access its own *ncb*, but it would not have been able to access the *ncb* of an object supplied as a parameter. Information hiding and access rules are important safeguards, but it's also important to open the gates every once in a while.

The *nbCancel* class illustrates another aspect of object-oriented design. Notice that the parameter for the constructor is declared to be an *nb_msg* * (a pointer to an *nb_msg* object). Actually, a pointer to any object derived from *nb_msg* can also be used. This will always be the case in this set of classes because we don't have any pure *nb_msg* objects; we have only objects of classes derived from *nb_msg*. Without the hierarchy of classes, we would need a separate way to cancel each separate type of message; with the hierarchy, we can write a generic *nbCancel()*, and it can take a pointer to any NetBIOS object.

Session Classes

The NetBIOS message objects are a useful abstraction that makes it much easier and safer to interact with a NetBIOS driver. But they don't implement what many programmers want, a simple way of sending a message to a program on another machine. The NetBIOS message objects are a big step in that direction, but we can take at least one more step. The key idea is that of a "session"—NetBIOS-speak for a conversation between two machines.

A session isn't any particular type of message; rather, a session is a series of messages. Therefore, I didn't derive session-level classes from the message classes we've just looked at. Instead, I created two new classes: *nbCallSend_Session* for a session that sends messages and *nbListenReceive_Session* for a session that receives messages. The two are similar, so we'll look at the class declaration for only one class, *nbCallSend_Session*. Both classes are shown in full in the source code at the end of the chapter.

```
// session-level NetBIOS send interface
class nbCallSend_Session {
private:
    // a local buffer
    void *buf;
    int buflen;
protected:
    // NetBIOS message objects, about 64 bytes each
    NetName myname;
```

```
    NetName yourname;
    nbAddName addmsg;
    nbDeleteName delmsg;
    nbCall callmsg;
    nbSend sendmsg;
    nbHangUp hangupmsg;
public:
    nbCallSend_Session(char *name); // constructor
    ~nbCallSend_Session(void);      // destructor
    enum WaitType { NoWait, Wait };
    int Send(void *buf, int len, WaitType t = Wait);
    int SendCopy(void *buf, int len, WaitType t = Wait);
    int IsSessionOpen();
    int IsSendComplete();
    int IsNetOK() { return addmsg.HandlerOK(); }
};
```

The private part of *nbCallSend_Session* contains a buffer pointer; the buffer is allocated when an *nbCallSend_Session* object is created, and it is used when copies of user data are sent.

The protected part of a session contains a set of NetBIOS message objects that are used to implement the session. You'll find details of using these objects in the actual code at the end of the chapter. I made these message objects protected so that they would be accessible to specialized session classes derived from *nbCallSend_Session.*

The public interface of *nbCallSend_Session* is a simple set of functions for sending messages. The constructor requires only a single parameter, a character pointer to a name that will be used to identify the session. The other member functions actually cause some data to be sent, or they return status information about the session.

In the *nbCallSend_Session* class, I decided to have the class constructor actually start the process of opening a session. This seemed sensible for several reasons but mainly because I wanted the *nbCallSend_Session* facility to be as simple to use as possible. It therefore seemed reasonable to make it as automatic as possible. And opening a session takes a few seconds because the NetBIOS driver polls the stations on the network to see whether the proposed session name is acceptable (that is, not already in use). If the *nbCallSend_Session* object is created when the program starts to execute, the network station polling can proceed in the background and will probably be complete by the time the *nbCallSend_Session* object needs to be used.

Note that the decision here, to make the constructor do a great deal, is very different from the decision made for the underlying classes, in which I decided that constructors would do minimal initialization only. The *nb_msg* classes are intended to be flexible building blocks for creating a NetBIOS access system. Making them too automatic makes them a poor foundation. For the *nbCallSend_Session* class, the opposite is true. Ease of use, not flexibility, is the paramount consideration.

The NetSend program and the NetRecv program at the end of the chapter show how the session-level classes are used in practice.

The NetSend program allows the user to type in messages to be sent to another PC. When the user enters a blank line, the program terminates.

The NetRecv program opens a receive session and displays whatever text it receives on the screen.

In scientific laboratory automation programs, I've used the *nbCallSend_Session* class and its complement, the *nbListenReceive_Session* class, so that one PC could communicate with another. Because the session classes are complete objects, it's as easy to have several conversations as to have one, and in fact some of the programs do actually use several session communication objects to communicate with a number of other machines. In all of these laboratory automation programs, the session-level interface is ideal because the programs are concerned with lab automation; reveling in the details of NetBIOS is not their object.

The NetBIOS Class Hierarchy

Here is the complete source code for the NetBIOS family of classes and the NetSend and NetRecv programs.

netbios.h

```
//
// NetBIOS classes
//
#include <stdlib.h>
#include <string.h>
#include <stddef.h>

#define SendBufSize 1500

// local fixed size types
typedef unsigned char uchar;
typedef short int16;
typedef unsigned short uns16;
typedef long int32;
typedef void _far *ptr32;

//
//  A NetBIOS name should be exactly 16 bytes long;
//    not a null-terminated C string--
//    rather, a 16-byte char array

class NetName {
    private:
        char name[16];
```

(continued)

continued

```
    public:
        NetName() { memset(name, 0, 16); }
        NetName(char *nm, char ext = 0) {
            strncpy(name, nm, 16);
            int n = strlen(name);
            if (ext && n < 16)
                name[n++] = ext;
            while(n < 16)
                name[n++] = ' ';    // not an asciiz string
        }
        operator char *() { return name; }
};

//
//  A NetBIOS control block should be 64 bytes long;
//   used in all NetBIOS transactions
//
struct NCB {
    public:
        uchar command;
        volatile uchar retcode;
        uchar lsn;
        uchar num;
        ptr32 buffer;
        uns16 length;
        NetName callname;
        NetName name;
        uchar rto;
        uchar sto;
        ptr32 post;
        uchar lana_num;
        volatile uchar cmd_cplt;
        char reserve[14];
};

// A NetBIOS status_buf should be 348 bytes long
struct _status_buf {
        uchar unitid[6];
        uchar jumpers;
        uchar last_post;
        uchar rev_major;
        uchar rev_minor;
        uchar traffic[22];
        uchar _reserved1[8];
        int16 free_cmd_blocks;
        int16 max_cmd_blocks;
        int16 max_cmd_free_cmd;
        uchar _reserved2[4];
        int16 pending;
```

(continued)

continued

```
        int16 max_pending;
        int16 max_sessions;
        int16 max_packet;
        int16 num_names;
        struct {
            NetName name;
            uchar nameid;
            uchar flags;
        } names[16];
};
class status_buf {
    public:
        _status_buf *buf;
        status_buf() {
            buf = (_status_buf *)malloc(sizeof(_status_buf));
            memset(buf, 0, sizeof(_status_buf));
        }
        void dump(void);
};

//
// NetBIOS command constants
//
enum netbios_cmd {
    ncReset = 0x32,
    ncCancel = 0x35,
    ncAdapterStatus = 0x33,
    ncUnlink = 0x70,
    ncAddName = 0x30,
    ncAddGroupName = 0x36,
    ncDeleteName = 0x31,
    ncCall = 0x10,
    ncListen = 0x11,
    ncHangUp = 0x12,
    ncSend = 0x14,
    ncChainSend = 0x17,
    ncReceive = 0x15,
    ncReceiveAny = 0x16,
    ncSessionStatus = 0x34,
    ncSendDatagram = 0x20,
    ncSendBroadcastDatagram = 0x22,
    ncReceiveDatagram = 0x21,
    ncReceiveBroadcastDatagram = 0x23,
    ncCmdNoWait = 0x80
};

//
//  A NetBIOS message
//  base class for the individual message classes
//
```

(continued)

continued

```
class nb_msg {
    friend class nbCancel;
    private:
        static int handlerok;
    protected:
        NCB *ncb;
        int protocmd;              // store ncb.command here until needed
        nb_msg(netbios_cmd cmd);   // constructor
    public:
        virtual int DoitNoWait(void);
        virtual int DoitWait(void);
        virtual int Complete(void) { return ncb->cmd_cplt == 0xff ? 0 : 1; }
        int ReturnCode(void) { return ncb->retcode; }
        int NameID() { return ncb->num; }
        int HandlerOK() { return handlerok; }
        void assign_name(NetName &n) { ncb->name = n; }
        void assign_callname(NetName &n) { ncb->callname = n; }
};

//
//  The NetBIOS Reset message
//
class nbReset : public nb_msg {
    public:
        nbReset(int sessions = 0, int cmdblocks = 0) :
            nb_msg(ncReset)
        {
            ncb->lsn = sessions;
            ncb->num = cmdblocks;
        }
        int DoitNoWait() { return DoitWait(); }
};

//
//  The NetBIOS Cancel message
//
class nbCancel : public nb_msg {
    public:
        nbCancel(nb_msg *tocancel) : nb_msg(ncCancel)
        {
            // note no check for commands that can't be canceled
            ncb->buffer = tocancel->ncb;
        }
        int DoitNoWait() { return DoitWait(); }
};

//
//  The NetBIOS Adapter Status message
//
```

(continued)

continued

```
class nbAdapterStatus : public nb_msg {
    private:
        status_buf status;
    public:
        nbAdapterStatus() : nb_msg(ncAdapterStatus)
        {
            ncb->buffer = status.buf;
            assign_callname(NetName("*"));
            ncb->length = sizeof(status_buf);
        }
        void dump() { status.dump(); }
        int DoitNoWait() {
            ncb->length = sizeof(status_buf); return nb_msg::DoitNoWait(); }
        int DoitWait() {
            ncb->length = sizeof(status_buf); return nb_msg::DoitWait(); }
};

//
//  The NetBIOS Add Name message
//
class nbAddName : public nb_msg {
    public:
        nbAddName(NetName &nm) : nb_msg(ncAddName)
        {
            assign_name(nm);
        }
};

//
//  The NetBIOS Add Group Name message
//
class nbAddGroupName : public nb_msg {
    public:
        nbAddGroupName(NetName &nm) : nb_msg(ncAddGroupName)
        {
            assign_name(nm);
        }
};

//
//  The NetBIOS Delete Name message
//
class nbDeleteName : public nb_msg {
    public:
        nbDeleteName(NetName &nm) : nb_msg(ncDeleteName)
        {
            assign_name(nm);
        }
};
```

(continued)

continued

```
//
// The base class for Call and Listen messages
//
class nb_call_listen : public nb_msg {
    protected:
        // note--can be constructed only in derived classes
        nb_call_listen(netbios_cmd cmd, NetName& local, NetName& remote,
            int rectmout, int sendtmout) :
            nb_msg(cmd)
        {
            assign_name(local);
            assign_callname(remote);
            ncb->rto = rectmout;
            ncb->sto = sendtmout;
        }
    public:
        int sessionnumber() { return ncb->lsn; }
};

//
//  The NetBIOS Call message
//
class nbCall : public nb_call_listen {
    public:
        nbCall(NetName& local, NetName& remote,
            int rectmout = 0, int sendtmout = 0) :
            nb_call_listen(ncCall, local, remote, rectmout, sendtmout)
        {
        }
};

//
//  The NetBIOS Listen message
//
class nbListen : public nb_call_listen {
    public:
        // listen for a request from remote
        nbListen(NetName& local, NetName& remote,
            int rectmout = 0, int sendtmout = 0) :
            nb_call_listen(ncListen, local, remote, rectmout, sendtmout)
        {
        }
        // listen for any request
        nbListen(NetName& local, int rectmout = 0, int sendtmout = 0) :
            nb_call_listen(ncListen, local, NetName("*"), rectmout,
            sendtmout)
        {
        }
        NetName caller() { return ncb->callname; }
};
```

(continued)

continued

```
//
//  The NetBIOS Hangup message
//
class nbHangUp : public nb_msg {
    private:
        nb_call_listen* which_session;
    public:
        nbHangUp(int session) : nb_msg(ncHangUp), which_session(0)
        {
            ncb->lsn = session;
        }
        nbHangUp(nbListen& x) : nb_msg(ncHangUp), which_session(&x)
        {   // defer assignment to lsn
        }   // x might not be an established session
        nbHangUp(nbCall& x) : nb_msg(ncHangUp), which_session(&x)
        {
        }
        int DoitNoWait() {
            if (which_session)
                ncb->lsn = which_session->sessionnumber();
            return nb_msg::DoitNoWait();
        }
        int DoitWait() {
            if (which_session)
                ncb->lsn = which_session->sessionnumber();
            return nb_msg::DoitWait();
        }
};

//
//  The NetBIOS Send message
//
class nbSend : public nb_msg {
    private:
        nb_call_listen* which_session;
    public:
        nbSend(int session) : nb_msg(ncSend) {
            ncb->lsn = session;
        }
        nbSend(nbListen& x) : nb_msg(ncSend), which_session(&x) {
        }
        nbSend(nbCall& x) : nb_msg(ncSend), which_session(&x) {
        }
        int SendWait(void *buf, int n) {
            ncb->buffer = buf;
            ncb->length = n;
            if (which_session)
                ncb->lsn = which_session->sessionnumber();
            nb_msg::DoitWait();
```

(continued)

continued

```
            return ncb->retcode;
        }
        int SendNoWait(void *buf, int n) {
            ncb->buffer = buf;
            ncb->length = n;
            if (which_session)
                ncb->lsn = which_session->sessionnumber();
            return nb_msg::DoitNoWait();
        }
};

//
// The base class for Receive and Receive Any messages
//
class nb_recv_msg : public nb_msg {
    private:
        nb_call_listen *which_session;
    protected:
        // note -- can be constructed only in its derived classes
        nb_recv_msg(netbios_cmd cmd, nb_call_listen *which = 0) :
            nb_msg(cmd),
            which_session(which)
            { }
    public:
        virtual int ReceiveWait(void *buf, int max) {
            ncb->buffer = buf;
            ncb->length = max;
            if (which_session)
                ncb->lsn = which_session->sessionnumber();
            DoitWait();
            return ncb->retcode;
        }
        virtual int ReceiveNoWait(void *buf, int max) {
            ncb->buffer = buf;
            ncb->length = max;
            if (which_session)
                ncb->lsn = which_session->sessionnumber();
            return DoitNoWait();
        }
        int RecLength() { return ncb->length; }
        int RecError() { return ncb->retcode; }
};

//
//  The NetBIOS Receive message
//
class nbReceive : public nb_recv_msg {
    public:
        nbReceive(int session) : nb_recv_msg(ncReceive) {
```

(continued)

continued

```
            ncb->lsn = session;
        }
        nbReceive(nbListen& x) : nb_recv_msg(ncReceive, &x) {
        }
        nbReceive(nbCall& x) : nb_recv_msg(ncReceive, &x) {
        }
};

//
//  The NetBIOS Receive Any message
//
class nbReceiveAny : public nb_recv_msg {
    private:
        int req_num;
        nb_msg *nameptr;
    public:
        nbReceiveAny() :
            nb_recv_msg(ncReceiveAny),
            req_num(0xff),    // any
            nameptr(0)
        { }
        nbReceiveAny(nbAddName& x) :
            nb_recv_msg(ncReceive),
            nameptr(&x)
        { }
        nbReceiveAny(nbAddGroupName& x) :
            nb_recv_msg(ncReceive),
            nameptr(&x)
        { }
        virtual int ReceiveWait(void *buf, int max) {
            if (nameptr)
                ncb->num = nameptr->NameID();
            else
                ncb->num = req_num;
            return nb_recv_msg::ReceiveWait(buf, max);
        }
        virtual int ReceiveNoWait(void *buf, int max) {
            if (nameptr)
                ncb->num = nameptr->NameID();
            else
                ncb->num = req_num;
            return nb_recv_msg::ReceiveWait(buf, max);
        }
};

//
// Session-level NetBIOS send interface
//
class nbCallSend_Session {
```

(continued)

continued

```
    private:
        // a local buffer
        void *buf;
        int buflen;
    protected:
        // NetBIOS message objects, about 64 bytes each
        NetName myname;
        NetName yourname;
        nbAddName addmsg;
        nbDeleteName delmsg;
        nbCall callmsg;
        nbSend sendmsg;
        nbHangUp hangupmsg;
    public:
        nbCallSend_Session(char *name);
        ~nbCallSend_Session(void);
        enum WaitType { NoWait, Wait };
        int Send(void *buf, int len, WaitType t = Wait);
        int SendCopy(void *buf, int len, WaitType t = Wait);
        int IsSessionOpen();
        int IsSendComplete();
        int IsNetOK() { return addmsg.HandlerOK(); }
};

//
// Session-level NetBIOS receive interface
//
class nbListenReceive_Session {
    private:
        // a local buffer
        void *buf;
        int buflen;
    protected:
        // NetBIOS message objects
        NetName myname;
        NetName yourname;
        nbAddName addmsg;
        nbDeleteName delmsg;
        nbListen listenmsg;
        nbReceive recvmsg;
        nbHangUp hangupmsg;
        // some simple status stuff
        enum Status { Listening, Receiving, Abort, Unknown };
        Status stat;
    public:
        nbListenReceive_Session(char *name);
        ~nbListenReceive_Session();
        int Receive(void *buf, int len);
        int IsSessionOpen();
```

(continued)

continued

```
        int IsReceiveComplete();
        int IsNetOK() { return addmsg.HandlerOK(); }
};
```

netbios.cpp

```
#include <dos.h>
#include "netbios.h"

int nb_msg::handlerok = 0;

nb_msg::nb_msg(netbios_cmd cmd)
{
    ncb = (NCB *)malloc(sizeof(NCB));
    memset(ncb, 0, sizeof(NCB));
    protocmd = cmd;
    if (handlerok == 0) {
        void far *fp;
        fp = _dos_getvect(0x5c);
        if (_FP_SEG(fp) !=0 || _FP_OFF(fp) !=0) {
            // try an illegal command; should get al == 3 response
            int c = protocmd;
            protocmd = 0;
            handlerok = 1;    // so DoitWait can at least try
            int ret = DoitWait();
            protocmd = c;
            if (ret == 3)
                handlerok = 1;
            else
                handlerok = 0;
        }
    }
}

int nb_msg::DoitNoWait(void)
{
    if (!handlerok) {
        ncb->cmd_cplt = 0;
        ncb->retcode = -1;
        return -1;
    }
    protocmd |= ncCmdNoWait;
    int ret = nb_msg::DoitWait();
    protocmd &= ~ncCmdNoWait;
    return ret;
}

int nb_msg::DoitWait(void)
{
    if (!handlerok) {
        ncb->cmd_cplt = 0;
```

(continued)

continued

```
        ncb->retcode = -1;
        return -1;
    }
    ncb->command = protocmd;
    union REGS r;
    struct SREGS s;
    void far *ptr = ncb;
    s.es = FP_SEG(ptr);
    r.x.bx = FP_OFF(ptr);
    r.x.ax = 0xffff;
    int86x(0x5c, &r, &r, &s);

    return(r.h.al);
}

void status_buf::dump()
{
#ifdef __STDIO_H
    int i;
    printf("Unit ID %02x%02x%02x%02x%02x%02x, jumpers %x, last post %x, "
        "rev %x.%x\n",
        buf->unitid[5],
        buf->unitid[4],
        buf->unitid[3],
        buf->unitid[2],
        buf->unitid[1],
        buf->unitid[0],
        buf->jumpers,
        buf->last_post,
        buf->rev_major,
        buf->rev_minor);
    printf("free cmd blocks %d, max %d; pending %d, max %d;"
        "max sessions %d\n",
        buf->free_cmd_blocks,
        buf->max_cmd_blocks,
        buf->pending,
        buf->max_pending,
        buf->max_sessions);
    printf("max packet size %d\n%d names:\n", buf->max_packet,
        buf->num_names);
    for(i=0; i < buf->num_names && i < 16; i++) {
        printf("%-16.16s %2d %02x  ",
            (char *)buf->names[i].name,
            buf->names[i].nameid,
            buf->names[i].flags);
        printf("\n");
    }
#endif
};
```

(continued)

continued

```
//
// A call-to-someone session
//
nbCallSend_Session::nbCallSend_Session(char *name) :
    myname(name, 'X'),
    yourname(name, 'R'),
    addmsg(myname),
    delmsg(myname),
    callmsg(myname, yourname),
    sendmsg(callmsg),
    hangupmsg(callmsg),
    buf(0),
    buflen(0)
{
    addmsg.DoitWait();
    callmsg.DoitNoWait();
}

nbCallSend_Session::~nbCallSend_Session(void)
{
    hangupmsg.DoitWait();
    delmsg.DoitWait();
    if (buf) delete buf;
}

// all sends should pass through here
int nbCallSend_Session::Send(void *srcbuf, int len, WaitType t)
{
    while (!callmsg.Complete())  // wait for any previous call to complete
        ;    // this will never hang forever; there is a default
             // call time-out
    if (callmsg.ReturnCode())    // try again
        callmsg.DoitWait();        // this time be patient

    if (!IsSessionOpen())
        return -2;
    if (t == Wait)
        return sendmsg.SendWait(srcbuf, len);
    else
        return sendmsg.SendWait(srcbuf, len);
}

// copy message and then pass on to buddy
int nbCallSend_Session::SendCopy(void *srcbuf, int len, WaitType t)
{
    // SendBufSize is maximum packet size allowed
    if (!buf && buflen == 0) {
        buf = new char[SendBufSize];
        if (buf) buflen = SendBufSize;
    }
```

(continued)

continued

```
    if (len > buflen)
        return -1;
    memcpy(buf, srcbuf, len);
    return Send(buf, len, t);
}
int nbCallSend_Session::IsSessionOpen()
{
    return (callmsg.Complete() && !callmsg.ReturnCode());
}
int nbCallSend_Session::IsSendComplete()
{
    return (sendmsg.Complete() && !sendmsg.ReturnCode());
}

//
// A listen-receive session
//
nbListenReceive_Session::
    nbListenReceive_Session(char *name) :
        myname(name, 'R'),
        yourname(name, 'X'),
        addmsg(myname),
        delmsg(myname),
        listenmsg(myname, yourname),
        recvmsg(listenmsg),
        hangupmsg(listenmsg),
        stat(Listening),
        buf(0),
        buflen(0)
{
    addmsg.DoitWait();
    listenmsg.DoitNoWait();
    buf = new char[SendBufSize];
    buflen = SendBufSize;
}
nbListenReceive_Session::~nbListenReceive_Session()
{
    if (buf) delete buf;
    hangupmsg.DoitWait();
    delmsg.DoitWait();
}
//
// test for a message
// return:
//       -1 = bad error
//        0 = nothing ready
//       >0 = message length
int nbListenReceive_Session::Receive(void *userbuf, int userlen)
{
```

(continued)

continued

```
    if (stat == Abort)
        return -1;
    if (stat == Listening) {
        if (listenmsg.Complete()) {
            int rc = listenmsg.ReturnCode();
            if (!rc) {
//              Connect
                recvmsg.ReceiveNoWait(buf, buflen);
                stat = Receiving;
                return 0;
            }
            else {
//              Listen failed
                stat = Abort;
                return -1;
            }
        }
    }
    if (stat == Receiving) {
        if (recvmsg.Complete()) {
            int rc = recvmsg.ReturnCode();
            if (!rc) {    // OK
                int recvlen = recvmsg.RecLength();
                if (userlen < recvlen)
                    recvlen = userlen;    // truncate
                memcpy(userbuf, buf, recvlen);
                recvmsg.ReceiveNoWait(buf, buflen);
                return recvlen;
            }
            else if (rc == 0xA) {
//              Disconnected
                stat = Listening;
                listenmsg.DoitNoWait();
                return 0;
            }
            else {
//              Receive died
                stat = Abort;
                return -1;
            }
        }
    }
    return 0;
}

int nbListenReceive_Session::IsSessionOpen()
{
    return (stat == Receiving);
}
```

(continued)

continued

```
int nbListenReceive_Session::IsReceiveComplete()
{

    if (stat == Receiving)
        return (recvmsg.Complete() && !recvmsg.ReturnCode());
    return 0;
}
```

The NetSend Program

Here is the complete source code for the NetSend program.

netsend.cpp

```
#include <stdlib.h>
#include <iostream.h>
#include "netbios.h"

void main(int c, char **v)
{
    char str[100];

    if (c != 2) {
        cerr << "Usage: netsend name" << endl;
        exit(-1);
    }
    cout << "Local " << v[1] << 'X' << " Remote " << v[1] << 'R' << endl;

    // NetBIOS message objects
    nbCallSend_Session net(v[1]);

    if (!net.IsNetOK()) {
        cerr << "Net not loaded" << endl;
        return;
    }

    cout << "Enter text to send. Enter a blank line to hang up." << endl;
    while(1) {
        cin.get(str, sizeof(str));
        if (*str == 0) {
            cout << "Done" << endl;
            break;
        }
        if (net.Send(str, strlen(str) + 1)) {     // +1 to send null
            cout << "Bad send, aborting" << endl;
            break;
        }
```

(continued)

continued

```
        if (!net.IsSessionOpen()) {
            cout << "Session is closed" << endl;
            break;
        }
        cin.getline(str, sizeof(str));    // read endofline
    }
}
```

The NetRecv Program

Here is the complete source code for the NetRecv program.

netrecv.cpp

```
#include <stdlib.h>
#include <conio.h>
#include <iostream.h>
#include "netbios.h"

void main(int c, char **v)
{
    char str[100];

    // cout << endl  causes an end of line to be output and
    //  cout to be flushed
    if (c != 2) {
    cout << "Usage: netrecv name" << endl;
        exit(-1);
    }
    cout << "Receive: ";
    cout << "Local " << v[1] << 'R' << ", Remote " << v[1] << 'X' << endl;

    nbListenReceive_Session nbmsg(v[1]);

    if (!nbmsg.IsNetOK()) {
        cout << "Net not loaded" << endl;
        return;
    }

    cout << "Starting" << endl;
    while(1) {
        int n = nbmsg.Receive(str, sizeof(str));
        if (n < 0) {
            cout << "Closing" << endl;
            break;
        }
```

(continued)

continued

```
        if (n > 0)
            cout << "Rec " << n << " chars: " << str << endl;
        if (kbhit()) {
            cout << "Done" << endl;
            cin.getline(str, sizeof(str));
            break;
        }
    }
}
```

PART
2

THE C++ PROGRAMMING LANGUAGE

Part 2 of this book is a comprehensive guide to the C++ language for those who are already proficient in C and for those who have been exposed in Part 1 to the basic ideas of object-oriented programming. We won't go into standard C features and topics but will focus instead on C++'s new ideas and capabilities. In large part, this section of the book explicates and expands upon Bjarne Stroustrup's pioneering work at AT&T to extend the C language into C with Classes and then C++. You can consult the second edition of Stroustrup's *The C++ Programming Language* (Addison-Wesley, 1991) and Stroustrup and Margaret Ellis's *The Annotated C++ Reference Manual* (Addison-Wesley, 1990), known fondly among C++ programmers as *ARM*.

Chapter 6 is a guide to moving from C to C++. Some of the chapter offers general advice, and other parts of the chapter take up issues that must be decided individually. Its compatibility with C is one inducement for migrating to C++, and Chapter 6 will help you take advantage of that compatibility.

In Chapter 7, we'll look at features of C++ that can be thought of as mere improvements to C. None of these C++ features is central to object-oriented programming, although as a group they certainly support the cause. References and inline functions, for example, are important efficiency boosters that buck the general trend in the more abstract programming languages toward less efficiency.

Chapter 8 is the heart of this book because it covers classes, the heart of C++. In Chapter 8, we'll look at most features of classes: access rules; *static*, *const*, and *volatile* members; constructors and destructors; and friends. Class constructors and destructors are so important and so rich a topic that they warrant their own fuller treatment, in all their variety, in a brief Chapter 10.

Chapter 9 focuses on derivation, C++'s most powerful tool for code reuse and polymorphic runtime binding. Think "derivation" every time you think about objects that share many traits.

In Chapter 11, we'll look at the class operator functions that allow us to manipulate objects using algebraic notation. Class operator functions also allow us to implement class-specific memory allocation and type conversions.

Chapter 12 provides some perspective on the various input/output schemes available to C and C++ programmers and makes contextual recommendations. Then the chapter describes the type-safe C++ iostream class library hierarchy.

The examples in this part of the book will illustrate object-oriented techniques. Many short examples will illustrate specific points, and longer examples excerpted from software developed in my work at the Rockefeller University will reinforce your education in the C++ paradigm.

6

Moving to C++

Compatibility with C is one of C++'s biggest advantages. C++ lets you move to object-oriented programming without abandoning your C code. This is extremely important if your company depends on its successful products written in C. Companies rewrite working software only under duress. The compatibility of C++ code with C code lets you choose a dual track: You retain your current C software while you develop new software in C++. You can use both languages in a single program because C++ has explicit features for linking C++ modules to modules in other languages, most obviously including modules in C.

But C++'s compatibility with C is double edged. You can get hurt by retaining C habits and mind-sets while working with C++. As a superset of C, C++ is technically compatible with C, but it is a very different language conceptually, one you should learn how to use in its own way. Merely using a C++ compiler is not enough; you need C++ thinking, C++ designs, C++ habits.

C++ != C + Goodies()

Many C++ programmers, including some authors of books on C++, have adopted the attitude that C++ is just C plus a bunch of new goodies that need to be admired, learned, and perhaps used. The "goodies" doctrine suggests that you need to learn about references, which are a snap if you are already pretty good with pointers, plus *const* and *void*. And of course, you should learn a bit about classes, which you can think of as structures with a few new features (goodies). The allure of the goodies approach is that it shouldn't take more than a few days to learn how to use the new goodies. In this approach, none of the new C++ features requires more brainpower or thought to exercise than, say, declaring a pointer to an array of character pointers, and none of the features requires you to adopt a new way of thinking about how you do your job.

The problem with the "C++ is just C plus goodies" attitude is that it won't unleash the power of C++. Even worse, the abuse of C++ can result in programs whose coding style is inferior to that of typical C programs—and we all know that much C code is not exemplary. The rich C++ feature set can be misused, especially by gadget-minded programmers who manage to find some way to use every tool in the kit, no matter how inappropriately.

C++'s features are meant to facilitate object-oriented software development. Assimilating the object-oriented paradigm requires flexibility because you have to learn to think differently—and to look at the world differently. The assimilation requires some time because the approaches and methods that worked well for you in C will be less important in C++. You'll need to unlearn some old C habits. Absorbing the key ideas of object-oriented programming is easy, almost too easy, but applying those ideas productively is difficult. It takes time and commitment.

Recompile vs. Redesign

The simplest way to move from C to C++ is to recompile your existing C code using a C++ compiler. Because C++ compilers are much stricter than most C compilers, the recompilation will probably reveal numerous inconsistencies and minor problems. You can fix most of them by inserting casts, by coming up with accurate function prototypes to describe your own functions, and by adding *#include* directives to pull in relevant header files so that system functions are properly prototyped. You should be able to convert 500 to 1000 lines of C code per day, assuming that the existing C code is already in pretty good shape.

You can expect several tangible gains from this simple exercise. One windfall is a cheap lesson in some of the pitfalls of C. The C++ compiler's flagging myriad difficulties encourages most programmers to code a bit more carefully.

You also might learn that you can commit one minor error after another while producing something that, for the moment, is a working program. That lesson is a serious one. Testing can't find all the problems in a program, and formal proofs of correctness are still useful primarily in only restricted circumstances.

Simple recompilation is an eye-opening exercise, but it won't give you any new skills for writing better software. And although C++ is a language with new capabilities, its point isn't the new set of language features, but rather the new thinking that allows you to take advantage of those language facilities.

The way to move from C to C++ at the other extreme is to completely redesign your existing software in C++, using true object-oriented methodology. The pros and cons should be obvious. Using consistent object-oriented methodology will create consistent and maintainable software, but reimplementing working software involves a huge and costly duplication of work.

C++ also lends itself to a middle tack, in which you keep your current software coded in C but add new features in C++. This is less awkward than it sounds because of the close relationship between the two languages. This approach also allows you to select key parts of your software for conversion to C++ while leaving other parts unaltered.

New C Habits

For the most part, the object-oriented paradigm is a new skill that overarches your existing programming skills. Even though it's a new paradigm, you still need to declare data, create procedures, work with control statements, comment your code, and so forth. These programmer's chores don't change.

But you should reduce or eliminate some C habits as you start to use C++. I don't believe in being too fanatical on this subject; many of the practices I'm about to suggest you disown will start to seem a bit quaint anyway as you become more familiar with C++. And none of the practices are completely incompatible with object-oriented programming in C++. They simply stand in the way of your getting the most from C++.

Move all extern declarations to header files. Extern declarations are critical to large software projects because the compiler relies on them. An extern declaration is a pledge, a contract between you and the compiler. The statement

```
extern double sin(double);
```

promises the compiler that it will encounter a function named *sin()*, that the function takes a *double* parameter, and that the function returns a *double* value. Most violations of the pledge, such as omitting *sin()* from the standard object library file, will be detected at some point in the compilation and linking process. But as we'll see in Chapter 7's discussion of type-safe linkage, you can violate your pledge in a few ways that will lead silently and inexorably to serious errors.

The easiest way to avoid these errors is to see that all extern declarations are correct and that they are in header files. It is common to see extern declarations placed in individual functions in C code in order to avoid the compilation-time overhead of pulling in an entire include file, say math.h, just to declare one function. But individual extern declarations are too often incorrect or out of date. Scan your .c and .cpp files for extern declarations, remove them, and include additional .h files as necessary to take their places.

Reduce your use of the preprocessor. Use of the preprocessor in traditional C programs is often criticized as excessive and rightly defended as necessary. Of course, it is a bit of both. *#if, #ifdef,* and *#include* are uncontroversial—in both C and C++. What changes in C++ is the use of *#define.* In C++, *#define* is used mainly to create compile-time constants for *#if* and *#ifdef* controls; its other traditional uses in C are delegated to language features that are new in C++.

For example, one major use of *#define* in C has been for the creation of short inline subroutines. The *getc()* routine and related macros from the C standard I/O library are the most familiar examples. C++ recognizes this need as well and provides inline subroutines. The advantage of C++ inline subroutines is that they provide the same scoping and semantics as ordinary subroutines; they are part of the language, not part of a text substitution preprocessor. All of your *#defined* functions should be recast as C++ inline functions.

C

```
#define max(a,b) \
  ((a) > (b) ? (a) : (b))
```

C++

```
inline int max(int a, int b)
{
    return a > b ? a : b;
}
```

Another major use of *#define* in C has been to create named constants. In C++, two facilities take over this role. The first is the *const* data type, which allows you not only to declare data but also to state that it is constant, that its value cannot be changed. *const* data has various advantages over *#defined* constants. One is that independently compiled modules can share a single copy of a *const* datum. This avoids the notorious problems that occur when *#defined* values are changed but all the dependent modules aren't recompiled. Another advantage of *const* is that it produces a true datum, which sometimes makes debugging easier. And finally, *const* can be applied to structures, classes, unions, and arrays, which are beyond the reach of *#define*.

C

```
#define MAX_X 639
```

C++

```
const int MAX_X = 639;
```

The second C++ method for reducing use of *#defined* named constants is to use enumerations. Although this feature has always been part of C, its use is much more common in C++ code. Partly this is because each *enum* in C++ is its own type, and partly it's because C++'s tighter type checking makes it more worthwhile to segregate *enums* from *ints*. In C++, a group of related numeric constants, such as a set of NetBIOS command codes, should be declared as an enumeration constant.

C

```
#define NetRESET  0x32
#define NetCANCEL 0x35
#define NetSTATUS 0x33
/* . . . */
```

C++

```
enum netbios_cmd {
    NetRESET = 0x32,
    NetCANCEL = 0x35,
    NetSTATUS = 0x33
    /* . . . */
};
```

Reduce your reliance on free global variables. A "free global" is a variable that isn't a member of a class. Everybody seems to acknowledge that free global variables present problems, but in C there isn't much you can do about that. Parts of a program have legitimate needs to know certain things about other parts of a program, and in C, global variables are the easiest and most (machine) efficient way to accomplish this awareness. The trouble is that unconstrained use of globals leads slowly but inexorably to code anarchy.

C++ introduces several facilities that help you reduce and possibly even eliminate (in new code) the use of free global variables. The first is the ability to assign the ownership of each global variable to a specific class of objects. Make each global a static class member variable. This clarifies the use of the global, focusing responsibility for the global in one place. Most globals are clearly "owned" by some specific part of a program; binding each to a class formalizes that ownership.

A second advantage of putting globals into classes is that the global's name goes into the class's namespace. The global will still be accessible, if that's what you want, but its name will be composed of two parts, its class name and its individual name. This reduces the likelihood of namespace collisions.

A third advantage is that it is possible to use some of the features of C++ objects to create globally accessible variables that have special characteristics, such as being modifiable by certain privileged routines but read-only to all other routines.

Reduce your use of free procedures. A free procedure is a procedure that is not part of a class. Some examples of free procedures are *main()*, all the procedures in the standard C library, and all the procedures you have written in C. Until the advent of classes in C++, it was inconceivable that you could reduce or eliminate your use of free procedures. But the rules are changing. You should strive to create procedures that are members of classes instead of creating free procedures.

Class member functions offer several advantages. One is organizational. In C++, the class is the center of attention, and procedures naturally belong to classes. Another advantage has to do with namespace pollution. Free procedures are in the precious global namespace, where name collisions often occur. Moving a procedure into a class removes the procedure's name from the global namespace, which reduces the likelihood of a collision.

In several areas, the goal of reducing the use of free procedures is at odds with other goals and requirements. For example, in most environments, you can't expect to eliminate *main()*, and I'm not suggesting that you completely eschew the standard C library or other useful C libraries. Also, the programming environment sometimes requires the use of free procedures. Some graphical environments, for instance, use callback functions, which often must be free functions, and hardware and software interrupt handlers usually must be free functions. A final exception to the general rule is in the use of operator functions, some of which are most flexibly written as free functions.

Reduce your type laxity. Become type correct. In object-oriented systems, much of a program's runtime behavior depends on the types of its objects. Consider a generic graphical shape object class from which you derive various specialized graphics classes. In this family of classes, each class implements a *Draw()* procedure that draws the shape represented by that class. Each time the program calls the *Draw()* function, what gets drawn depends on the type of object the program is manipulating at runtime. If you "lie" about the type by writing a cast, the wrong shape will be drawn. In a drawing system, such a bug will probably surface early and visibly, but in many other kinds of systems, the problem might be well disguised. That's why some OOP practitioners say that casting is to object-oriented programming as the harmful *goto* statement is to structured programming.

The first line of defense is the programmer's increased emphasis on type correct programming. With some effort, most programs can be made to use far fewer casts. In the past, the programmer attitude has been something like "Well, if the compiler is complaining, I guess I'll stick in a cast to shut it up." The new attitude strives to see what aspect of the program's design has led one down the thorny path to a cast, so that the underlying problem can be addressed.

One remedy is to completely prototype all the functions you use. C++'s strict type checking requires a full prototype for every external function. The prototype must specify both the return value type and the parameter types. Functions that don't return a value should be declared *void*; it is no longer acceptable to let the return type default to *int* when nothing is actually returned.

Similarly, you should declare the parameters for a function completely. If a function such as *sin()* returns a *double* value and takes a *double* parameter, it should appear in a header file as

```
double sin(double);
```

not as

```
double sin();
```

This goes for both the standard C library functions, for which prototypes will be supplied by the compiler vendor, and your own functions, which you must prototype yourself.

Many C programmers are cavalier about pointer types, and this attitude has been abetted over the years by many of the C compilers. In C++, you should take care to declare your pointers correctly and to learn the difference between, say, a pointer to a pointer to *int* and a pointer to an array of ten *int*s. On a given machine, a number of type errors might not lead to failures; the problems show up when the environment changes—for example, when 16-bit MS-DOS code is upgraded to run in the 32-bit extended DOS environment.

Fortunately, C++ furnishes the means to a number of remedies that can help you reduce your reliance on casting. One improvement is a new system for allocating memory, which can be used without resorting to casts. Another is the object-oriented paradigm itself, in which the proper design of class hierarchies can create a family of compatible types, eliminating many situations in which casts were once necessary.

7

A Better C

This chapter's goal is simple—to show you the elements of C++ that are incidental to object-oriented programming. You can think of these features, some of which have been incorporated into the ANSI C standard, as improvements to C. They tighten up C's notoriously lax type system and provide other useful facilities that have never been a part of the C language before.

Another useful way to think about many of these features is as improvements that turn C into a more suitable base language for C++. Without strong type checking, inline functions, overloaded functions, smart linkage, and the like, it would be inconceivable to add an object-oriented facility atop C. C's low-level view of the world creates a framework for adding higher-level facilities. The enhancements described in this chapter further develop that framework so that C++'s object-oriented extensions are fully enabled.

Mastering these new C features is a mundane but necessary step in the process of mastering C++—"mundane" because they can seem to have little directly to do with objects. Be patient. Objects are on their way.

Comments

C++ allows two forms of comments: the traditional /* *comment* */ variety you're used to seeing in C code, and a new form in which the comment is started with // and is terminated by the line's ending. The new form of comment, which is sometimes called a single-line comment, is convenient for short comments and an easy way to comment out a few lines of code.

You can use a \ at the end of a single-line comment to escape the new line, but that complicates matters and thus isn't very good practice. If you want to entertain the idea, here's the rule: The compiler glues the lines together in response to the \ before it removes the comment in response to //. Thus, in this example, the text *and continues here* is part of the comment:

```
// comment starts here \
and continues here.
```

But don't complicate matters with this style. Use single-line comments the way they were meant to be used.

As in C, you can't nest traditional /* *comment* */ style comments, although some compilers will let you do it. However, once the compiler sees //, it ignores everything to the end of the line, so you can use // to comment out a traditional comment:

```
// i = 1; /* traditional comment */
```

Similarly, within the bounds of a /* *comment* */, the only thing the compiler is looking for is */, so you can use a traditional comment to comment out code that already contains // comments:

```
/* traditional comment
i = 1; // something examined
*/
```

The Preprocessor

The C++ preprocessor is better defined than the traditional C preprocessor, which came in two similar but subtly different versions. The C++ preprocessor also contains a few new features that make program entry more convenient and the macro language more powerful.

Much of the C++ preprocessor is the C preprocessor unchanged. The *#ifdef*, *#ifndef*, *#if*, *#elif*, *#else*, and *#endif* controls for conditional compilation are unchanged. You'll recall that *#ifdef* and *#ifndef* test to see whether a preprocessor identifier has been defined and that *#if* and *#elif* test the value of a constant expression. In *#if* and

#elif expressions, it is often useful to use the *defined* operator to determine whether a preprocessor identifier has been defined. Also unchanged in C++ is *#include* for file inclusion and *#undef* for undefining a preprocessor identifier.

String Literal Concatenation

In C++, the preprocessor concatenates adjacent string constants. This convenient facility makes it much easier to enter long strings by writing them in several pieces, and it also works well with token stringization, which we'll take up a little later in this chapter. Here's an example of C++'s concatenation of adjacent strings:

```
#include <stdio.h>

void main()
{
    printf("Line 1\n" "Line 2\n"
        "Line 3\n" );
}
```

The three adjacent strings are concatenated to form a single string, which becomes the single argument for *printf()*. Here's the output:

```
Line 1
Line 2
Line 3
```

Trigraph Replacement

Trigraphs are an attempt to make it easier to write C and C++ software using character sets that don't have some of the heavily used C symbols. Most European character sets are missing the curly and square brackets, the pound sign, the vertical bar, the backslash, the caret, and the tilde. The trigraph replacement sequences, which all start with a pair of question marks, are shown in the following table, adapted from Stroustrup and Ellis's *Annotated C++ Reference Manual*:

{	??<	}	??>
[	??(	]	??)
#	??=	|	??!
\	??/	^	??'
~	??-		

Here is the string concatenation example rewritten using trigraphs:

```
??=include <stdio.h>

void main()
??<
    printf("Line 1??/n" "Line 2??/n"
        "Line 3??/n" );
??>
```

Trigraph support is sometimes omitted from compilers marketed only in the United States. Trigraphs are supported in Microsoft C++.

Token Stringization—the # Preprocessor Operator

The # preprocessor operator can convert a *#define* parameter into a string literal that contains the text of the replacement. This is sometimes called "stringizing" because the parameter is converted to a character string. Here is a simple example:

```
#include <stdio.h>

#define print(a) printf(#a ": %d\n", (a))

void main()
{
    int alpha = 100;
    print(alpha);
}
```

In the *print()* macro, the expression *#a* is replaced by a string containing the original parameter, which is *"alpha"* in the example. After token stringization, the main routine would be transformed:

```
void main()
{
    int alpha = 100;
    printf("alpha" ": %d\n", (alpha));
}
```

The preprocessor's string concatenation facility will combine the two adjacent strings, producing this result:

```
void main()
{
    int alpha = 100;
    printf("alpha: %d\n", (alpha));
}
```

Stringization is often used this way to build a string that contains the name of a parameter, not its value.

Token Concatenation—the ## Preprocessor Operator

The ## preprocessor operator is used to glue a pair of tokens together, to create one token from two. This is useful when you are creating lists of identifiers with similar names. Here is a simple example of token concatenation, also called "token pasting":

```
#include <stdio.h>

#define ErrMsg(n,txt) char Err##n[] = "Error " #n ": " txt "\n";
```

```
// Declare the error messages
ErrMsg(0, "Too many chips")
ErrMsg(1, "Too much soda")
ErrMsg(2, "Too little sunlight")

void main()
{
    printf(Err0);
    printf(Err1);
    printf(Err2);
}
```

The *ErrMsg()* macro uses token concatenation to create identifiers containing *Err* followed by one of the parameters. The *ErrMsg()* macro also uses token stringization to help build the individual error strings. The three invocations of *ErrMsg()* in the example create three character strings. After macro replacement, token stringization, and token concatenation, the trio of declarations looks like this:

```
char Err0[] = "Error " "0" ": " "Too many chips" "\n";
char Err1[] = "Error " "1" ": " "Too much soda" "\n";
char Err2[] = "Error " "2" ": " "Too little sunlight" "\n";
```

And then, after the adjacent strings are concatenated, the declarations look like this:

```
char Err0[] = "Error 0: Too many chips\n";
char Err1[] = "Error 1: Too much soda\n";
char Err2[] = "Error 2: Too little sunlight\n";
```

When the program is executed, the three messages are output.

Predefined Identifiers

These four preprocessor identifiers are always defined in ANSI C compilers and in C++ compilers:

__LINE__	The current line number, a numeric value
__FILE__	The current file name, a string literal
__TIME__	The current time in HH:MM:SS format, a string literal
__DATE__	The current date in MMM DD YYYY format, a string literal

These identifiers aren't present in all classic C compilers, although they are certainly present in most.

In addition, C++ compilers always define the identifier *__cplusplus*. The *__cplusplus* identifier is often used to create header files that can be processed by either C++ or C compilers.

Declaration Placement

C practice has always been very restrictive when it comes to data declarations, insisting that they appear only at the beginning of a block, which is the group of statements enclosed by curly braces. Inside a block, once the C compiler has seen a statement, it will be shocked if it encounters a data declaration and will print a (probably confusing) error message. In C++, this rule has been relaxed to allow data declarations to appear anywhere in a block that a statement can appear.

The following, for example, is legal in C++ though not in C:

```
{
    double ds = sin(1.0);
    ds *= ds;
    double dc = cos(1.0);
    dc *= dc;
}
```

You can get the same effect in C by introducing extra nested blocks:

```
{
    double ds = sin(1.0);
    ds *= ds;
    {
        double dc = cos(1.0);
        dc *= dc;
    }
}
```

The scope of a variable extends from its point of declaration to the end of the block, so you do have to put a data declaration above the part of the block in which the variable will be used.

You need to be careful to avoid putting a data declaration in a spot in which it might be bypassed by a *goto* or other kind of control statement. The following, for example, is not legal in C++:

```
{
    extern int x;
    if (x < 100)
        double g = x;
    g *= 2;
}
```

Novices sometimes hope that this will work:

```
if (x < 100)
    double g = sin(x);
else
    double g = cos(x);
```

That looks reasonable because there is no way to avoid the initialization of *g*. Even so, it isn't allowed. The safety of such code would, in general, be too hard to verify. But in both C and C++, this is allowed:

```
double g = x < 100 ? sin(x) : cos(x);
```

You aren't allowed to put a declaration where only an expression is legal. You can't put a declaration where the test expression in an *if* or *while* statement would fall, for instance. However, you can put a declaration in the first part of a *for* statement, which in C++ is truly a statement, not an expression:[1]

```
for(int y = 0; y < 100; y++) {
    // stuff
}
```

Although that's legal, you should be aware that the scope of the newly minted variable *y* is not confined to the body of the *for* loop. To understand why, note that the *for* loop is equivalent to this *while* loop:[2]

```
int y = 0;
while(y < 100) {
    // stuff
    y++;
}
```

The *while* loop example makes it obvious that the scope of *y* extends through the body of the loop plus the remaining body of the block in which the loop resides.

You can use the new freedom constructively to scatter declarations throughout a block to produce better code. Putting declarations close to where they are used can improve readability, and reducing the scope of variables is, in general, a good rule of thumb practice. But it is also possible to use this facility to create a real mess. Don't introduce a new variable every line or two; try to group them sensibly, in clusters. You can use the new freedom in the placement of declarations to make your code reflect the problems you are solving, but when in doubt, declare at the top.

The *const* Type Specifier

Some things never change; they should be declared *const* so that the compiler will know that they are constant and check your usage to be sure that you don't change a *const* datum. This also gives the compiler flexibility in implementation, allowing different (possibly better) code generation for a *const* datum. And a *const* datum is a

---

1. The C++ *for* statement has the syntax *for(stmt expr;expr;expr) stmt*, in contrast to the C *for* statement, which has the syntax *for(expr;expr;expr) stmt*.

2. The loops aren't equivalent from the point of view of the *continue* statement, but that's beside the point as far as this discussion is concerned.

true datum—in the symbol table, with a name, a type, and a value. This can sometimes greatly facilitate debugging because it allows the debugger to treat the *const* datum as a full-fledged item.

Const data takes on a variety of roles in typical programs. One role is for a *const* datum to replace a traditional *#define* macro constant. For example, instead of writing

```
#define MAX_ELEMENTS 5000;
```

you could write

```
const int MAX_ELEMENTS = 5000;
```

Because the default linkage for *const* data is internal, the statement above is really equivalent to writing

```
static const int MAX_ELEMENTS = 5000;
```

This means that, unless you specify otherwise by using the *extern* keyword, *const* data is accessible only inside the current file.

To create a global *const* value (which is something you should think about at least twice because free globals should be reduced or eliminated), simply declare a *private const* (*static*, not *extern*) in a header file and include that header file as necessary. Each module will have a private copy of the datum.

Things get a bit more complex when you can't afford to have a private (static) copy of a *const* in multiple object files. For example, if the *const* is a large read-only table, it should reside in a single place. To have a single shared copy of a *const* datum, you need to declare the *const* as *extern* and omit the initialization in the appropriate header file:

```
extern const int MY_TABLE[];
```

You can include this header file in all the modules that need to use *MY_TABLE*; it is all they need to see. Then, in one place in your program, you initialize *MY_TABLE* this way:

```
extern const int MY_TABLE[] = {
    1, 2, 3, 4, 5
};
```

If the line appears more than once in your program, you will have problems. If it is visible to the compiler twice, you will get a compilation error; otherwise, you will get an error when you try to link.

You are allowed to put the line

```
const int MAX = 50;
```

into a header file that is included into multiple other files. The result will be a separate copy of *MAX* in each of your separately compiled modules. You are not allowed to put the following into multiple header files:

```
extern const int MAX = 50;
```

because you can initialize a *const* only once; otherwise, you'll get linkage errors. A *const* datum is, like any other true datum or procedure, something that can be defined only once.

A *const* datum is compatible with its non-*const* counterparts, but the reverse is not true. For example, if *i* is an *int* and *ci* is a *const int*, *i* can be assigned the value of *ci* but *ci* cannot be assigned the value of *i*. (Using casts to remove "*const*ness" from a variable is an implementation dependent issue, but the only safe policy is to avoid casting away *const*ness.)

The keyword *const* gets to be a lot of fun when it is used with pointers. Naturally, there are several possibilities. In

```
const int *pci;*
```

pci is a pointer to a *const int*. *pci* is free to point at something else, but whatever it points at can't be changed. In

```
int i;
int *const cpi = &i;
```

cpi is a *const* pointer to an ordinary *int*. *cpi* can't point at anything else, but what it points at can have its value altered. In

```
const int ci;
const int *const cpci = &ci;
```

cpci is a *const* pointer to a *const int*. *cpci* can't point at anything else; and what it points at can't be altered.

Declaring *const* pointers and pointers to *const* is easy if you keep in mind that C (and C++) declarations should be read from the inside out. Let's start with a pointer to a *const*:

```
const double *pcd;  // pointer to const double
```

Reading from the inside out, we'd say, "*pcd* is a pointer to a *double* that is constant." This code fragment shows what is legal and what is not legal for a pointer to a *const*:

```
double d;
const double cd;
const double *pcd;
pcd = &d;       // OK--can point at a double
pcd = &cd;      // OK--can point at a const double
*pcd = 1.23;    // no good--can't assign by means of a pointer to const
```

Be careful when declaring a "*const* pointer to a *double*":

```
double *const cpd;
```

Unfortunately, that doesn't quite work because a *const* pointer must be initialized—if it doesn't point to something initially, how can it ever point to something? This *const* pointer definition is OK:

```
double d;
double *const cpd = &d;
```

The definition creates a *const* pointer to a *double* and points it at a willing *double*. Reading from the inside out, we'd say, "*cpd* is a *const* pointer to a *double* that is initialized with the address of *d*." Given the above, this is an OK assignment:

```
*cpd = 1.23;
```

Note that you can't point a "*const* pointer to a *double*" at a *const double*:

```
const double cd;
double *const cpd = &cd; // no good--can't point at a const
```

Having digested the above, you'll find the third variety, "a *const* pointer to a *const*," easy to declare:

```
const double *const cpcd = &d;
```

The only thing you can do with a "*const* pointer to a *const*" is test its value—that is, use it in a test as the right side of an assignment in an expression. You can't assign to the pointer, and you can't assign to the item pointed at.

A *const* declaration often appears in a function declaration. This lets the user of a function know that certain arguments won't be changed inside the function, and it lets the function's author use compiler checking to ensure that the contract is honored.

In new code, you should strive to be "*const* correct." Everything that is truly *const* should be declared *const*, and this goes double for function parameters. The C++ language does not force you to write "*const* correct" programs—at least, it doesn't force you in the same way that it forces you to write "type correct" programs. You can write huge C++ programs without using the *const* keyword, and you will never see a complaint from the compiler. The mere fact that this is allowed doesn't mean it is a good idea; on the contrary, in new code you should use *const*, so that you have yet another layer of compilation safeguards.

It is much harder to come up with a recommendation for making your existing code "*const* correct." The *const* keyword is a somewhat insidious construct. Once *const* gets into your code, you'll find that it has a way of multiplying. One *const* datum requires another, and so forth. Eventually, the growth reaches a natural limit, your code is partitioned into *const* and non-*const* data, and rarely do the twain meet. For existing code, this can be an enormous amount of work that might not be worth the trouble. Before making any large projects "*const* correct," you should first tackle a few-hundred-lines program and then decide for yourself.

The *volatile* Type Specifier

The *volatile* type specifier informs the compiler that the given datum is special in some way and that it might be modified behind the compiler's back. This is important in a world in which compilers have ever-increasing levels of optimization, because modern compilers keep more variables in registers, and for longer times, than previous generations of compilers did.

Variables are modified, unbeknownst to a compiler, by concurrent threads (processes), interrupt handlers, graphics callback routines, and the like. In a "load-store" type of compiler, which usually loads a variable from memory when it is needed, behind-the-back modification of a variable doesn't usually matter. When the variable is next used, the new value will probably be loaded from memory. But in a modern, "register intensive" compiler, the compiler might have a copy of the variable in a register and not load the variable from memory each time it is used. Even more unsettling, optimizations can transform or eliminate a variable in ways that are incompatible with the changes made in the background.

For example, the following code loops on the value of a variable, waiting for it to be changed by an interrupt handler:

```
int int_done;         // set to 1 by interrupt handler
. . .
void iwait(void)
{
    while(!int_done) // wait
        ;
}
```

This code is likely to fail, or even worse, to fail depending on what level of optimization you have selected, because *int_done* is not declared to be volatile. When the compiler generates optimized code for the *while* loop, it is likely that *int_done*'s initial value will be loaded into a register and then tested repeatedly.

To prevent such problems, use *volatile* to identify asynchronously modified datums. The *int_done* variable from our earlier example should be declared this way:

```
volatile int int_done;     // set to 1 by interrupt handler
. . .
void iwait(void)
{
    while(!int_done)       // wait
        ;
}
```

The *void* Type

The *void* data type has several similar but distinct uses in both ANSI C and C++. Note that *void* is a C++ innovation that was carried back into ANSI C, so that most of what is true of *void* in C++ is true of *void* in ANSI C but not in classic C.

The first meaning of *void* is that it is a data type that has no values. A function that doesn't return a value should be declared *void*:

```
void fn(int *);
```

This declaration says that *fn()* is a function that takes a pointer to an *int* argument and doesn't return a value. In the body of *fn()*, you can have a return statement but you can't have a return expression. In C++, the compiler is careful to check the obverse; in a non-*void* function, your return statements must be return expressions, not simply returns. One common task in converting C code to be compatible with a C++ compiler is to find all the functions that don't return values and declare them to have the *void* return type.

You can also use the *void* keyword in a function declaration to mean that the function doesn't take any arguments:

```
int g(void);
```

This says that *g()* is a function that doesn't take an argument and returns an *int*. In C++, you could equivalently state

```
int g();
```

because an empty parameter list in C++ means no parameters. The two are not equivalent in classic C because an empty parameter list in C simply means that the lazy prototype writer hasn't bothered to fill in the argument types—the parameters might be of any type.

You can't declare an ordinary datum to be a *void*—it wouldn't mean anything for a variable not to have a value:

```
void v;    // no way
```

However, you can use *void* in declaring data when you're talking about *void* pointers. A *void* pointer is C++'s generic pointer type, taking on the role that is performed by *char* pointers in classic C. This declaration creates a generic pointer:

```
void *ptr;
```

The generic pointer *ptr* can be assigned the value of any pointer. For example, if *fptr* is a pointer to a *float*, this is an acceptable assignment:

```
ptr = fptr;
```

The C++ language also guarantees that a pointer value assigned to a *void* pointer can be converted back to its original type without loss of information. But that's it—there are no arithmetic operations, no guarantees on conversions to other types, and no facilities to dereference a *void*. All you can do with the value in a *void* pointer is convert it back to its original type:

```
fptr = (float *)ptr;
```

When a *void* pointer is converted back to a pointer of the original type, you must use a cast. This is partly because converting from a *void* pointer is considered to be a dangerous operation, one that should be flagged in the code, and partly because of some subtle properties of pointers to classes that we needn't go into here.

Although I don't heartily recommend the following, the circumventions shown in the next two examples are common, and occasionally necessary. To add a value to a *void* pointer, you can use the "cast to *char* *" subterfuge:

```
v = (char *)v + 1;
```

To dereference through a void, you can use this subterfuge:

```
*(float *)v = 1.23;
```

The *char* Family

C++ has improved and clarified the handling of character data. In classic C, character data is not quite a full-fledged data type. One shortcoming is the lack of true character constants. In classic C, the constant *'a'* only looks like a character constant; in reality, it is an integer constant. That's why in classic C the expression *sizeof('a')* always produces the same result as *sizeof(1)*, which is *2* in 16-bit C implementations. Another shortcoming in classic C is the automatic promotion of all *char*s to *int*s when they are passed to functions or used in expressions.

C++ has removed these limitations. C++ character constants are true character constants; in C++, *sizeof('a')* is *1*. And C++ allows *char* expressions and *char* arguments without the automatic promotion to *int*. Another change in C++ is that there are three distinct character types: *unsigned char*, *signed char*, and *char*. The expectation is that *char* will be implemented optimally for a given machine. But however *char* is implemented, it is a distinct type; *char* isn't a synonym for either *unsigned char* or *signed char*. When you don't really care about the arithmetic properties of true character data, you should simply use the *char* type. But when you do care about arithmetic properties, be careful to specify either *signed char* or *unsigned char* so that you will produce portable and predictable programs.

C++ also contains a wide character type called *wchar_t* that is used for character sets, such as many Asian character sets, that don't fit into a traditional character variable's single byte. The *wchar_t* type isn't a fundamental, built-in type in the same way that *char* is a built-in type because it is defined as a *typedef* in stddef.h. Thus, *wchar_t* isn't a keyword, although you should avoid making up your own meaning for *wchar_t*. Even though *wchar_t* isn't a first-class type, it does sit at the front of the second-class seats. The C++ compiler is aware of *wchar_t*, and it will build a wide character constant or array whenever a traditional character constant or character array literal is immediately preceded by the letter *L*. This is somewhat analogous to using an *L* after an integral constant to indicate a long constant.

Here are declarations of a single wide character, an array of wide characters, and a pointer to wide characters that is pointing at a wide character literal:

```
#include <stddef.h>

wchar_t wc = L'a';
wchar_t awc[80];
wchar_t *pwc = L"hello";
```

Many compilers marketed primarily for the US or the European market will make *wchar_t* a synonym for *char*.

The Reference Type

Although C has made extensive (many would say excessive) use of pointers, at heart it is really a call-by-value language. Each time a function is called, the calling argument is copied and the function receives that copy. The underlying mechanism is a call by value, but C programmers routinely use a call by value to get the effect of a call by reference, by explicitly passing pointer parameters.

The major problem with pointer parameters is that they are explicit. If a function requires a pointer to point to a *double*, when you invoke the function you must explicitly use the address-of operator to supply the address. Inside the function, additional complications arise because you must use the dereference operator to get at the value. Similarly, a C function can return a pointer, but it can't return a true *lvalue*.[3]

C++ has added a reference data type to address these problems. A reference declaration looks like a pointer declaration, but once created, a reference is a true alias; operations on the reference always refer to the target datum, never to the reference itself. In a declaration, and only in a declaration, the ampersand (&) is used to specify the reference data type, in somewhat the way that the asterisk (*) is used to declare a pointer:

```
double d = 0;
double& dr = d;       // dr is a reference to d
double *dp;           // dp is a pointer to a double
dr += 1.0;            // add 1.0 to d
dp = &dr;             // point dp at d
```

3. An *lvalue* is any expression that can be assigned a value. It is so named because it can appear to the left of an assignment operator.

Everything you do to a reference is actually done to whatever the reference refers to. In the example we just looked at, the expression *d==dr* is always true, the expression *&d==&dr* is always true, the expression *dr+=1.0* adds *1.0* to *d*, and so on.

References are often used as function parameters to achieve transparent call by reference. Reference parameters are sometimes used to make it easy for the function to change its arguments, and they are sometimes used so that very large arguments can be passed efficiently. The following short program contains a trivial procedure named *max()* that both takes reference parameters and returns a reference to one of them. Because *max()* returns a reference to an *int*, it can be used in any situation in which an ordinary *int* variable can be used; *max()* is an *lvalue*.

```
#include <stdio.h>

int& max(int& a, int& b)
{
    if (a > b)
        return a;
    return b;
}

void main()
{
    int x = 20, y = 30;
    max(x,y)--;
    printf("%d %d\n", x, y);
}
```

The output of the program is

```
20 29
```

Yes, the same effect could have been achieved with pointers, but not as cleanly. Also notice that the references in the example aren't initialized. In general, references must be initialized unless they are procedure parameters, procedure return values, class members, or *extern* references.

An ordinary reference must be initialized with some variable of the appropriate type. For example, a reference to a *double* must be initialized with a *double* variable:

```
double    d1;
double&   rd1 = d1;    // OK
```

not with a *const double*:

```
const   double  d2 = 2.0;
        double& rd2 = d2;    // error
```

or a *double* constant:

```
double&   rd3 = 3.0    // error
```

If you want a reference to be able to refer to a *const*, either to a true constant or to a *const* variable, you should declare a *const* reference, as in this declaration:

```
const double& rd4 = 4.0;  // OK
```

This restriction, which is reinforced by Microsoft C++, is relatively recent, and many compilers remain compatible with the old rule, in which a non-*const* reference to a constant is allowed. Under the old rule, the compiler creates an anonymous temporary, the constant is copied into that temporary, and then the reference is made to refer to that temporary. This feature was removed from the language because it produced surprising results.

One final note: You obviously cannot have a reference to a *void*, although a reference to a *void* pointer is fine.

Initialization

Initialization is the initial assignment of value to a datum. All data is initialized somehow, either by the programmer, by default, or randomly by the bit pattern that happens to reside wherever the datum is located. Randomly initialized data is technically called "uninitialized data," but even uninitialized data has some initial value—we just don't know what it is.

Initialization is the focus of much effort and thought in C++, by both the designer of the language and programmers using the language. C++ carefully distinguishes between initialization and assignment—yet another classic C shortcoming that has been corrected. The distinction between initialization and assignment is very important in many aspects of C++:

- A reference must be initialized. After initialization, a reference can't be made to refer to some other datum.
- A *const* datum must be initialized.
- A class has a constructor, so that objects of the class can be guaranteed to be initialized.
- A class has different mechanisms for initialization and assignment, so that a programmer can manage the two operations differently.

Another C++ enhancement is that external data can be initialized by full expressions, instead of by mere constant expressions, as in C. This gives external datums the same flexibility that has always been available to local data. Here is a simple program that initializes two external *const* variables by calling functions from the math library. If the following program were compiled by a C compiler, you would see an error message complaining about the non-constant initializer, but in C++, this is perfectly legal:

```
#include <math.h>
#include <stdio.h>

const double pi = acos(-1.0);
const double e = exp(1.0);

void main()
{
    printf("%14.12g\n", pi);
    printf("%14.12g\n", e);
}
```

This program produces the following output:

```
3.14159265359
2.71828182846
```

Another C++ addition is the parenthesized initialization syntax, which makes initialization look like a function call. In traditional C, data is initialized using a syntax that looks like assignment:

```
int i = 0;

double x = 1.0;

char p[] = "ROBIN";
```

This works well for numeric data. For character string data, initialization using assignment syntax is slightly odd because C and C++ don't have array assignment.

C++'s new form of initialization uses a notation taken from Simula that resembles a function call. Here is the same set of initializations rewritten using the Simula-style syntax:

```
int i(0);

double x(1.0);

char p[]("ROBIN");
```

The chief advantage of the Simula-style initialization is that it allows more than one initializer. This isn't too important for the built-in types, but it is very convenient for class types, which are commonly initialized by several values. For example, imagine a *Complex* class type that can be initialized using a pair of doubles:

```
Complex c(1.0, 2.0);
```

Even though the Simula-style initialization is convenient, the same effect can be achieved using the old assignment style:

```
Complex c = Complex(1.0, 2.0);
```

The difference between the old assignment-style initialization syntax and the new Simula-style syntax is largely a matter of taste. For numeric values and for other types for which assignment "looks right," you should use the old style; for most class object initialization, you should use the Simula style.

Casts

A cast is an operation that converts something of one type to another type. Casts are sometimes necessary, but excessive casting is a sign of problems. Even though C++ imposes a much stricter type checking system on code than C does, there is actually a reduced need to cast. This is partly because of C++'s replacement for *malloc*, which eliminates casts as a standard part of memory allocation, and partly because of type-safe class mechanisms that are used in places in which C techniques force you to cast.

The traditional C cast uses a parenthesized type specifier in front of the expression to be converted. For example, this C-style cast converts the integer *1* to a *double* to make it a suitable argument for the *sin* procedure:

```
double d = sin((double)1);
```

C++ has an additional syntax for specifying casts. This isn't a gratuitous addition; it originates with the notation used with classes to specify conversions. For example, a *Complex* number class would probably have a conversion from a pair of numbers to a *Complex* number. If *c* is a *Complex* object, it can be assigned the complex value *1+2i* by means of this statement, assuming that suitable facilities have been built into our hypothetical *Complex* class:

```
c = Complex(1,2);
```

The traditional C notation for expressing casts, in which a parenthesized type specifier is followed by an expression, is clearly inadequate for more complex conversions such as this one. Enter the new functional notation, in which a type name is followed by an expression or by a list of expressions for suitably defined class types:

```
typedef char *charptr;
typedef void (*fnptr)(void);
struct point { short x, y; };
typedef point *point_ptr;

double d;
charptr p;
fnptr q;
point *r;
d = double(10);
p = charptr(0);
q = fnptr(0);
r = point_ptr(0);
```

The main requirement for using the new form of cast is that you must have prepared the way with a simple type name for the type that you want to cast. You can't cast a value into a "pointer to *char*" using this form of casting unless you have a type name for "pointer to *char*." That's why you see the *typedef*s in the example.

A cast to any type other than a reference type produces a value, not an *lvalue*. Therefore, if you want a casted datum to be assigned a value, you must use a cast to reference. Let's say that you want to explicitly cast a *long* to an *unsigned long*. Here's the ordinary, right-hand-side method:

```
long l = -1L;
unsigned long ul;
ul = (unsigned long)l;
```

If you try to place the cast on the left, as in the example below, you will get a compilation error because ordinary casts don't produce *lvalues*:

```
(long)ul = l;
```

But you can place the cast on the left if you change it to "reference to *long*":

```
(long&)ul = l;
```

C++ requires an explicit cast when you convert a "pointer to *void*" to any other pointer type and when you convert any integral type to an enumeration type.

Function Prototypes

A function prototype is a declaration that states a function's argument types and return type. The compiler uses the function prototype to ensure that you at least supply the correct number and kinds of arguments each time you use the function. C++ requires a full function prototype, a prototype that includes parameter types, for every function in a scope that you use. It is no longer acceptable to simply use a function without first telling the compiler about the function.

The advent of function prototypes has introduced a number of interesting compile-time side effects. Because all functions are prototyped, the compiler can differentiate, for example, between a *char* argument and an *int* argument, or between a *float* argument and a *double* argument. Such distinctions could not be made in C because the compiler didn't know what types of arguments a function was expecting.

The C++ function prototype style is somewhat different from the typical C function header style. The traditional C style comes from the header libraries that have been used by the lint utility, the C source code checking program, on Unix systems. In classic C, a function definition for, let's say, the *strtol()* function from the C standard library looks like the code on the next page.

```
long strtol(p, pp, base)
char *p;
char **pp;
int base;
{
    /* body here */
}
```

In a lint header library, *strtol()* is described by this prototype:

```
long strtol(char*, char**, int);
```

In C++, most of the type checking that lint used to do has been incorporated into the compiler, so a C++ compiler not only allows but requires a prototype similar to lint's. As an added feature, the C++ prototype can optionally include parameter names, which is useful to us humans, who want hints to help us understand how the arguments are used. Here is a C++ prototype for *strtol()*, in which the first argument type is tightened to *const*:

```
long strtol(const char *p, char **pp, int base);
```

C++ also allows this style to be used in a function definition. In a function definition, which contains both the header and the body, the argument names must be present if you plan to use them.[4] Here is the skeleton of a C++ style *strtol()*:

```
long strtol(const char *p, char **pp, int base)
{
    /* body here */
}
```

C++ prototypes don't follow exactly the same rules as C prototypes. In C++, this prototype indicates that *rand()* is a function that doesn't take any arguments and that returns an *int*:

```
int rand();
```

This is different from the C interpretation. In C, the same prototype indicates that *rand()* is a function that takes an unknown set of arguments and returns an *int.* Of course, a better function prototype for *rand()* in C++ is this one, because it doesn't leave anything unstated:

```
int rand(void);
```

In C++, we haven't lost the ability to have functions such as *printf()* and *scanf()* that take varying numbers and types of arguments. In C++, we use ellipses to indicate

---

4. In a C++ function definition, if you omit an argument name, an argument of the proper type must be supplied, but it will not be accessible in the body of the function. This rarely used feature allows you to have placeholder arguments and to avoid "argument not used" gripes from the compiler.

that varying numbers and types of arguments are acceptable. Here's the C++ *printf()* prototype:

```
int printf(const char *, ...);
```

In C, we have a number of tricks at our disposal to manage functions that, like *printf()*, have varying argument lists. The only acceptable way to have varying argument lists in C++ is to use the variable argument list macros in stdarg.h.

In general, if you are going to use a C++ compiler with code originally written in C, you should convert all your function headers to the new C++ style. C++ compilers are required to accept both styles, but they don't treat the styles identically, and this can cause problems. Consider this sketch of a function that uses the traditional C header style:

```
int cfn(c)
char c;
{    /* body */    }
```

When a C++ compiler sees this definition, it believes that *cfn()* takes an *int* argument because it follows the C rules when it sees a traditional C function header. If instead, the compiler sees this style, it will follow C++ rules:

```
int dfn(char c)
{    /* body */    }
```

The part of all this that trips people up is that the function prototypes for the two functions shown above should be

```
int cfn(int);
int dfn(char);
```

Don't get tripped up. Be consistent: Rewrite your C function headers in C++ style.

Overloaded Functions

A common problem is having groups of functions that perform similar tasks but that work with different data types. Graphical coordinates, for example, might be expressed as pairs of integers, as pairs of floating point numbers, or as a structure that contains the two coordinates. In C, you might write these functions to plot points whose coordinates are expressed by the three types:

```
void drawpoint_i(int, int);
void drawpoint_f(double, double);
void drawpoint_s(struct point);
```

Because this can get very tedious, and because such a diversity of operations takes on even more importance in much object-oriented code, C++ allows you to have "overloaded" functions. Overloaded functions have the same name but differ in the types of arguments that they accept. Here are the same point plotting functions redone in C++ overloaded style:

```
void drawpoint(int, int);
void drawpoint(double, double);
void drawpoint(struct point);
```

This is a mundane idea; we commonly accept the notion that *i+j* for *int* types will produce one result, and *x+y* for *double* types quite another, even though both expressions use the plus operator. Overloading functions is the same idea applied to functions. If the compiler can tell from the argument types which function to call, all you need to do is supply the various functions.

It is tempting to expect that the function return type will be considered when the compiler is deciding which of a set of functions to call, but the return type doesn't enter into the process at all. Once the compiler has selected a function, the function's return type is converted as necessary, but the return type has no impact on the compiler's selection of the function.

Function overloading starts out as a simple idea, but then the complexity of the C++ environment intrudes, calling for a fairly big set of ensuing rules. I'll try to lay out the rules that Stroustrup describes succinctly, but first some advice: Don't get into situations in which the nuances of these rules become significant. Instead, try to keep it simple, so that it doesn't take someone else a lot of effort to understand your overloaded functions.

First, here are the rules for how a C++ compiler decides which overloaded function to call, based on the parameters that are being supplied in the function call:

1. The compiler looks first for an exact match of parameter type with function.
2. Barring an exact match, the compiler tries to match promoted parameter types, such as a parameter promoted from *char* to *int* or from *float* to *double*, with a function.
3. Then the compiler tries to match standard converted parameter types, such as a parameter converted from *int* to *double*, with a function.
4. Then the compiler tries to match parameter types resulting from using user-defined conversions with a function.
5. Finally, the compiler resorts to trying to match parameter types indicated by an ellipsis with a function—a catchall match.

We also have to consider the fact that many overloaded functions have more than one argument, and that what might be a good function to match with one argument might not be a good match for another. The reigning principle for multiple arguments is that the best matching function overall must also be the best match for each argument. If it isn't, the situation is ambiguous and the compiler will complain.

When you create a set of overloaded functions, keep several things in mind. One is that *typedef* doesn't really manufacture types, so parameters that are really the same type but that have different *typedef* names can't be distinguished. Another consideration is that if you have a type *T*, to use Stroustrup's example, you can't create a family of functions that differentiate among *T*, *T&*, *const T*, and *volatile T*, although you can distinguish among *T*, *const T&*, and *volatile T&*. *T&*, *const T*, and *volatile T* specify only how arguments are treated inside a function—any *T* can be trivially converted to one of these variants. However, there are real differences among *T*, a reference to a *constT*, and a reference to a *volatile T*. You can't hand a *T* to a procedure that expects a reference to a *const T*. You need to hand the procedure a true *const T*. The same is true for a reference to a *volatile T*.

But as I mentioned above, the best way to cope with these arcane rules is to stay away from them, to design your code so that you don't rely on these details.

Type-Safe Linkage

The phrase "type-safe linkage" refers to a function naming system that guarantees that you will supply the correct numbers and kinds of arguments to your functions. We've looked at prototypes and how they are used by the compiler to check your function usage. But what if the actual function in the library doesn't match the prototype? And how does the compiler manage overloaded functions, which appear to have the same name? The answer to these questions is "type-safe linkage."

Type-safe linkage is a naming system that guarantees that functions will be tagged with information regarding their argument types so that, during linkage, functions will be called with the correct parameters. Type-safe linkage doesn't guarantee that function return types will be correct, or that externally referenced variables will be of the correct types. We'll look at an example of these holes in the type-safe linkage naming system shortly.

Although a variety of mechanisms can be envisioned, the standard method for implementing type-safe linkage is a technique variously called "name mangling" or "name decoration." Name mangling is one of the more illuminating technical terms to emerge in the last few years. It involves adding a signature to the end of every function name that encodes the argument types that the function expects.

C++'s type-safe linkage system guarantees that you will supply the correct argument types for all functions that you call, even across module boundaries. But as we noted earlier, for a variety of technical reasons, the system doesn't make any guarantees about function return types or about the types of variables referenced by *extern* statements. We should look at an example of each deficiency, just so that you can see the potential difficulties.

The return type deficiency

Consider this function, which implements a Euclidean distance calculation:

```
#include <math.h>
double distance(double x1, double y1, double x2, double y2)
{
    double d1 = x2-x1;
    double d2 = y2-y1;
    return sqrt(d1 * d1 + d2 * d2);
}
```

If in another file, we write the following code, neither the compiler nor the linker will notice that we have lied about the return type of the *distance()* function:

```
#include <stdio.h>
void main()
{
    extern int distance(double, double, double, double);
    printf("%d\n", distance(1,1,2,2));
}
```

If we had lied about the argument types for the *distance()* procedure, we would have produced a link error. But because the lie concerns one of the blind spots in the type-safe linkage system, no errors are noticed by the compiler or the linker. When executed, the program prints *16374*, a nonsense return reminiscent of C programs that used floating point but neglected to *#include <math.h>*. If the prototype is changed to reflect the *double* return value and the *printf()* format string is changed to *%g*, the correct result, *1.41421*, is printed.

Also notice in the example that when *distance()* is invoked, it is supplied with four integer arguments. Because of the function prototype, the compiler knows that *distance()* requires *doubles*, not *ints*, and the compiler automatically converts the *ints* to *doubles*. This is exactly the same thing that happens in an expression such as *d+i*, in which *d* is a *double* and *i* is an *int*; the compiler automatically converts *i* to *double* before performing the addition. Ordinary C compilers can't perform this feat for function arguments because they, in general, don't know what arguments are expected, but C++ compilers can do the conversion because they always know what arguments a function is expecting.

The externally referenced variable type deficiency

Here is an example of the other hole in the type-safe linkage system. Consider one file, which contains this declaration of a *const double* to store the value of *pi*:

```
extern const double pi = 3.14159265;
```

In another file, we reference this constant incorrectly, by suggesting that *pi* is an *int*. (Note that the type *int* isn't mentioned explicitly; it is the default type.)

```
#include <stdio.h>
void main()
{
    extern const pi;    // int by default
    printf("%d\n", pi);
}
```

Again, because the *extern* declaration is a lie, the output of the program is nonsense. If the declaration is changed to a *const double* and the *printf()* format string is changed to *%g*, the output is correct.

Note that both of these demonstrations of holes in the C++ type-safe linkage system rely upon placing an *extern* declaration inside a function. Yes, this is a bad idea. Don't put *extern* declarations inside functions, and don't place them in your .cpp source files. Your *extern* declarations belong in .h files. This helps guarantee consistency in large projects.

The Linkage Directive

One major design goal of C++ is to be compatible with the existing body of C software, even while moving forward to object-oriented technology. This is not a trivial undertaking. One major barrier between the two languages is the type-safe linkage system. Type-safe linkage is vital to C++ in increasing the type safety of the language, but it is not a part of any C compiler.

When you have a choice, you should modify your existing C software so that it can pass through a C++ compiler. This will create a type-safe version of your existing C software, which is a big improvement.

But recompilation of existing C software is not always an option. Sometimes routines must remain callable by C programs, which means that they can't reside in type-safe object files. That's why the standard C library doesn't exist in a type-safe form; it must be callable from both C and C++. And some software is provided without source, so that you must continue to use a C-callable library until the vendor provides a type-safe C++ version of the library.

The problem of linking to foreign languages, languages that are not C++, actually runs deeper than merely what names to call the functions. Different languages have different conventions for the way arguments are passed to functions, for what registers are saved, for the way the stack is managed, and so on.

To address these problems, C++ has a "linkage directive," which tells the compiler that a given function is written in a foreign language. Different C++ compilers understand different foreign languages, although all C++ compilers know about the C foreign language. Most MS-DOS C++ compilers also know about Pascal linkage because Pascal linkage is the standard linkage for Microsoft Windows functions.

The linkage directive consists of the word *extern* followed by a string constant naming a language. Following that is either a simple declaration or a block of declarations. For example, the directive on the next page indicates that *sin()* is a C linkage function.

```
extern "C" double sin(double);
```

Note that the linkage directive must occur in global scope.

You can also make a linkage directive apply to a whole group of declarations:

```
extern "C" {
    double sin(double);
    double cos(double);
    double sqrt(double);
}
```

Linkage directives can even be nested, although you should try to keep things simpler than that.

Because the C language doesn't understand C++'s linkage directive, you must be careful when you add linkage directives to a C header file. The best method is to use the *__cplusplus* predefined macro, which is defined in every C++ compiler, to delimit C++ constructs inside C header files. This will allow the C++ compiler to see the C linkage directive and the C function prototypes, while the C compiler will see the prototypes only. Using the *__cplusplus* macro, the example is written this way:

```
#ifdef __cplusplus
extern "C" {
#endif
    double sin(double);
    double cos(double);
    double sqrt(double);
#ifdef __cplusplus
}
#endif
```

C++ has taken the middle ground with respect to linking to foreign languages. By incorporating a linkage directive, it has done more than most languages have, but the linkage directive doesn't offer a complete solution. The linkage directive helps address low-level compatibility issues, such as pushing arguments onto the stack in the correct order, unwinding the stack properly, and the like. It does not address issues such as the difference between Pascal strings and C strings, or FORTRAN's ubiquitous call by reference. C++ assumes that those issues will be addressed in library routines and data structures and that type-safe linkage will help to create a secure interface.

The linkage directive has an impact on the effectiveness of C++'s type-safe linkage system. When all code is written in C++, type-safe linkage guarantees that functions will get proper arguments. This guarantee holds even if a function prototype is wrong, because the function names are mangled to include an argument type signature. But foreign languages don't use C++ name mangling schemes. This means that incorrect prototypes of foreign language functions will cause erroneous linkage, although you're not likely to see any linkage error messages.

Inline Functions

In C, most of us have used preprocessor macro definitions to create short code sequences. The most famous example is probably the standard C I/O library, which usually uses preprocessor macros to implement several functions, including *getc()* to read in characters and *putc()* to output characters. Building functions from macros is a problem for several reasons. One difficulty is that the preprocessor doesn't know C, which means that the macro rules are slightly different. For example, arguments to a macro can be evaluated multiple times, but arguments to a true C function are evaluated only once.

Even with these and other problems, macros have been heavily used in C in situations in which it is vital to avoid the overhead of a function call, even when a complex functionlike operation is required. To address this need, C++ has inline functions. An inline function is like a true function in all regards—with respect to scope, local variables, and argument evaluation—except one. An inline function is expanded inline. The trade-off is between the increased space occupied by multiple inline copies of the routine and the decreased time of execution (because there is no function call overhead).

Like the register declaration, the inline specifier is what Stroustrup calls "a hint to the compiler" that the compiler can choose to ignore. The compiler can instead supply an ordinary callable function. Compilers differ on what they are able to inline. Some can handle inline functions containing loops; others will automatically outline if a loop is detected. Some compilers have size limitations and will automatically outline once a threshold is crossed. All compilers will outline recursive inline procedures, or inline procedures whose address is taken. Consider this example:

```
extern "C" double sqrt(double);

inline double distance(double x1, double y1,
    double x2, double y2)
{
    double d1 = x2-x1;
    double d2 = y2-y1;
    return sqrt(d1 * d1 + d2 * d2);
}

void main()
{
    double (*fn)(double, double, double, double);
    double x = distance(1, 2, 3, 4);
    fn = distance;
    double y = fn(5, 6, 7, 8);
}
```

In this example, the *distance()* procedure is inlined when it is invoked explicitly inside *main()* to provide a value for *x*. But the compiler also creates an outline version, whose address is assigned to the function pointer named *fn*, and this outlined version is used when *y* is assigned a value by a call to the function pointed at by *fn*.

Notice also the declaration of the function pointer *fn*. Its declaration states that it is a pointer to a function that takes four *double* arguments and that returns a *double*. C++ is picky about function pointers, requiring that the type of a function pointer match the type of the function that it points toward. This is different from many C compilers, which were often lax about the types of functions and function pointers.

Default Function Arguments

Sometimes you want to have default values for certain function arguments, as in the *distance()* function defined above, which computes the distance between two points—but what about the distance between a point and the origin? Of course, we could write a version of *distance()* that accepted a pair of coordinate arguments and returned the distance from that point to the origin, but a simpler method is to make *0* the default value for the last two arguments:

```
extern "C" double sqrt(double);

double distance(double x1, double y1,
    double x2 = 0, double y2 = 0)
{
    double d1 = x2-x1;
    double d2 = y2-y1;
    return sqrt(d1 * d1 + d2 * d2);
}

void main()
{
    double x = distance(1, 2);
    double y = distance(-1, -1, -1, 1);
}
```

The default arguments are specified by writing what looks like an initialized declaration in the function header. When the argument is supplied, the actual argument's value is used; when the argument is omitted, the default value is used.

The version of *distance()* shown above accepts either two, three, or four arguments. Note that default arguments must always be at the end of the argument list, not at the beginning or in the middle. Also note in the example above that it is the actual function definition that contains the default argument values. It is important that the compiler see the default arguments only once, so if you use function prototypes in a header file, the function prototype should contain the default argument specification and the actual function definition should omit all mention of the default arguments. Here's this more usual arrangement:

```
// prototype, usually in a header file
double distance(double x1, double y1,
    double x2 = 0, double y2 = 0);
// definition
```

```
double distance(double x1, double y1,
    double x2, double y2)
{    /* body */     }
```

Keep in mind that default arguments are simply filled in by the compiler when it generates code for the procedure call. The presence of default arguments has no effect on the signature of a function or on type-safe linkage. Also note that there isn't any efficiency to be gained from using default arguments. If we wanted a version of *distance()* that had only two arguments so that we'd have a lower function call overhead, we would need to write a separate version that actually contained only two arguments.

Structure Tags and Declarations

In classic C, you can provide a tag name[5] for a structure, so that you can declare structures conveniently. In C, the tag name isn't a true type name in the sense that *int* is a type name. The tag name is merely a shortcut for declaring additional copies of the struct. In C++, structure tag names have been elevated to the status of true type names:

```
struct point { short x; short y; };
```

In C++, this declaration creates a new type called *point.* We can then declare *point*s:

```
point origin = { 0, 0};
point box[4];
point *pnt_ptr;
struct rect { point origin; point extent; };
```

In C, it is common to use *typedef* to make declaring structures more convenient. This technique also works in C++, although it is needed only for compatibility with existing C source code. There are a few cases to consider.

When the tag name is omitted in a *struct typedef* declaration:

```
typedef struct { int a, b, d; } trio;
```

the *typedef* name, *trio* in the example above, is used as the tag name. Remember that tag names are, above all, class type names. This is compatible with the intent of the C-language style construct above but slightly different in detail.

When the tag name is included in a *typedef struct* declaration:

```
typedef struct TRIO { int a, b, d; } trio;
```

5. Recall that a tag name is one that comes between the word *struct* and the opening brace of the struct.

the *typedef* name (*trio*) is a *typedef* for the true type name (*TRIO*). This is a lot of effort to get very little result. It can also lead to confusing errors because wherever you write *trio*, the compiler is thinking *TRIO*.

For C code that is being compiled by a C++ compiler, it is probably best to rewrite all the *typedef*'d *struct* declarations as tagged structs, like the *point* struct at the beginning of this section. Unfortunately, this is not an option for code that must still be compatible with C, and it can be a lot of work.

Anonymous Unions

Anonymity is certainly the exception in software, where innumerable program elements need names. In traditional C unions, the penchant for naming was carried one step too far. Consider a *union* named *u* of an *int* named *i* and a *double* named *d*. That's three separate names for a single spot in memory. Recognizing that only two of those names are needed, C++ allows "anonymous unions," as in this statement:

```
union { int i; double d; };
```

The anonymous union above can be used anywhere that an ordinary named union can be used, although the predominant use of anonymous unions is inside structs and classes. The main restriction on anonymous unions is that global anonymous unions must be declared *static* explicitly; they must be confined to file scope. We'll see a useful example of anonymous unions when we look at fixed point numbers in Chapter 11.

Enumerations

Enumerations have been part of C for a long time, but they have been little used. Partly this is a result of several notorious bugs in some of the early C compilers, and partly this is because there is little advantage in using enumerations in a weakly typed language such as C. But in C++, enumerations have been spruced up, and you should strongly consider increased use of enumerations to provide type-safe symbolic numeric constants in your software.

In C++, the tag name of an enumeration is a type name. This lets you use an *enum* tag name to declare an enumeration variable just as a *struct* tag name can be used to declare a structure. And in C++, each enumeration is its own type, which gives you a real benefit—type safety—in exchange for the effort of using *enums*.

C++ *enums* have only one operation, assignment. You cannot use any of the arithmetic operators on *enums*, and you cannot, without casting, assign an integer value to an *enum*. These C++ rules are much stricter than those you might be used to in C. This program shows typical C use of *enums*:

```
enum window {
    casement, doublehung, sliding };

void goo()
{
    enum window w = casement;
    w--;
    w = 3;
}
```

Note that in C the arithmetic operations are allowed, even though each of them will make *w* into an illegal value for the *window* enumeration.

This program is not a legal C++ program because of the operations on *w*. If you must perform arithmetic on enumeration values in C++, you need to use type casts to signal your intentions. Here is the C++ equivalent of the *goo()* procedure:

```
void goo()
{
    window w = casement;      // enum keyword not needed;
                              //  window a type name
    ((int&)w)--;
    w = (window)3;
}
```

In this version of the *goo()* procedure, I declared an enumeration variable without using the *enum* keyword. That's because the name of a C++ enumeration is a type name, just like the tag name of a struct or a class.

C++, like C, allows you to explicitly specify the numeric values that are assigned to the enumeration constants. In our example, the default values *0*, *1*, and *2* would be applied to the *enum* constants *casement*, *doublehung*, and *sliding*, respectively. This declaration shows how the values could be specified explicitly:

```
enum window {
    casement = 0x10, doublehung = 0x20, sliding = 0x40 };
```

Also note that *enum* constants don't need to have distinct values; *sliding*, as well as *doublehung*, could have been assigned the value *0x20* in the example above.

new and *delete*

Dynamic memory allocation allows an executing program to get use of memory from a large pool of storage called "the heap." Dynamic memory allocation gives a program great flexibility because the program can decide during execution how much memory is used and for what purposes. In C, memory is allocated by means of the library routines *malloc()* and *free()*. In C++, there is an additional, language-sponsored, interface to memory allocation, *new* and *delete*. Here we'll look at the mundane uses of C++'s *new* and *delete* for ordinary data. In Chapter 11, we'll look at the class-specific memory allocators *operator new()* and *operator delete()*.

new

Memory allocation in C++ is less troublesome and more reliable than in C because the memory allocation operator, operator *new*, is handled in a special way by the compiler. This lets the compiler perform type checking each time memory is allocated, reducing the likelihood of problems such as allocating space for an *int* having placed the pointer to that *int* in a pointer to a *double*. However, C++'s additional type checking of memory allocation doesn't extend into the realm of usage checking. You can still overrun the bounds of memory that you have allocated, you can still free memory that was never allocated, and so forth.

Here are some examples of allocating memory using *new*:

```
double *d = new double;

float *f = new float[1000];

char *p = new char[100];
```

In each of the statements, the compiler would have complained if the pointer type on the left hadn't been the correct type for what was being allocated on the right. This isn't all that important in this simple example, but it becomes a very important aid to getting things right in more complex settings. Remember that *malloc()* returns a pointer to *void* which the programmer must cast to the correct type. When the cast is incorrect for what has been allocated, things go silently awry. This cannot happen in C++ when you use *new*.

Following the indication of what type is to be allocated, *new* allows an initialization expression or expression list. This capability, which is not available for arrays, is used primarily to pass information to class constructors and will be discussed more in the "Dynamically Allocated Objects" section of Appendix B. Here is an example of using an initialization expression with an ordinary variable:

```
int *iptr = new int (0);
```

This statement allocates storage for an *int*, initializes the storage to *0*, and then saves a pointer to the storage in the *iptr* variable.

This much more useful construct is unfortunately not available:

```
int *iptr = new int[100] (0);
```

There is no automatic way to use *new* and initialize an array—a rather odd omission for a language that has so many other features related to initialization and safety.

The *new* operator also allows an expression, called a "placement expression," to appear in front of the type information. Placement expressions are used when you need to pass information to an allocator of your own design.

delete

Memory that has been allocated using *new* can be deallocated using *delete.* You should be very careful that whatever you pass to *delete* was given to you by *new*; mistakes here are usually disastrous, never caught at compile time, and not usually apparent during execution until sometime after the mistaken call to delete. You should also refrain from accessing memory after it has been freed.

When you have allocated a single object, you can simply delete that object:

```
double *p = new double;
// . . .
delete p;
```

However, when you allocate an array, you are supposed to inform the compiler that you are deleting an array by using the *delete[]* syntax. In older versions of C++, the expression inside the square brackets specified the number of elements in the array, but that information no longer needs to be supplied by the programmer.

```
delete [] q;    // delete an array pointed at by q
```

Informing the compiler that you are actually deleting an array is critically important when you have an array of class objects, because those objects might have destructors that must be called individually.

In a special dispensation, it's always OK to delete a null pointer. This allows you to write a routine that cleans up allocated memory simply by deleting each pointer in a set of pointers, provided you are absolutely sure that all the pointers are either valid or null. This feature is useful for cleaning up class objects.

C++ provides several hooks that you can use to fine-tune the memory allocation system. One is a function called *set_new_handler()* that you can call to install a function that will take control when the allocator fails because it is out of memory. By default there is no such handler; if you write such a handler, it should not take arguments or return a value.

Another feature of C++ is that you can write your own allocator. This feature has always been available to C programmers; just think of the number of C mavens who, for various reasons, wrote their own *malloc().* In C++, the operator *new* is known to the compiler and treated in a special way, but the actual allocation of memory isn't done by the compiler; rather, it is done by a library function called *operator new().* We'll look at C++ operator functions in detail in Chapter 11, but you don't really need to know about operator functions to understand the following, which is an example of a user-written *operator new().*

```
#include <stdlib.h>          // pull in def of size_t

void *operator new(size_t t)
{
    const int poolsize = 20000;
    static char pool[poolsize];
    static char *base = pool;
    char *obase = base;
    base += t;
    if (base > pool + poolsize)
        return 0;
    return obase;
}
```

The simpleminded allocator shown above has a private fixed size pool of memory that it doles out each time it is called. When the pool is exhausted, it returns *0*. Because the *operator new()* above uses a private memory pool and because it doesn't keep track of allocation locations and sizes, you cannot write a matching *operator delete()*. Thus the example above is not so much a good example as it is a simple example. This small routine exercises the *operator new()*:

```
#include <stdio.h>
void main()
{
    double *d = new double;
    float *f = new float[1000];
    char *p = new char[100];
    printf("%d %d %d\n", d, f, p);
}
```

When you write your own *operator new()*, you usually also need to write your own *operator delete()*.

8

Classes

Finally we arrive at the heart of the matter, classes. A class is a user-defined data type that contains both data elements and procedural elements. In C programming terms, a class is a structure combined with functions that operate on that structure. The default status of its members is private.

But the simple explanation is inadequate because classes also support information hiding, allow you to gain control automatically when they are created and destroyed, and can be manipulated using the standard operators. Most important, classes are the basis of inheritance, which enables you to create new classes by specifying the ways in which they will differ from existing classes. And inheritance is the basis of polymorphic runtime behavior.

In this chapter, we'll look at all the fundamental aspects of classes—access controls, constructors and destructors, scope issues, and pointers to class members. In Chapter 9, we'll look at derivation; in Chapter 10, we'll revisit the important topic of constructors and destructors; and in Chapter 11, we'll look at operator functions.

Member Variables, Member Functions

Classes are declared much as structures are, except that the *class* keyword is used instead of *struct.* Because classes are targeted for extensive use, we usually create a class using a tag name, and then use the tag name, which has become a bona fide C++ type name, to declare objects of the class and pointers to the class. In this example, *cat* is a bona fide C++ type:

```
class cat {
    public:
        int age;
        int weight;
        void play(void);
        void hunt(void);
};
```

The class *cat* we've just declared has four members: the two member variables *age* and *weight* and the two member functions *play()* and *hunt()*. The *public:* part of the class declaration is an "access specifier." It makes everything that follows in the class—data and functions—fully accessible to other parts of a program.

The declaration doesn't provide a definition for either of the member functions, and it doesn't actually create any *cat* objects. Here's how we can use the *cat* type:

```
cat cozette;             // creates a cat object
cat family[6];           // creates an array of cat objects
cat *catptr;             // creates a pointer to a cat object
cat procreate(char *);   // creates a function prototype
```

These declarations create a *cat* object named *cozette*, an array of six *cat* objects named *family*, a pointer to a *cat* object named *catptr*, and a prototype of a function named *procreate()* that returns a *cat* object and has a pointer to a *char* as a parameter. We have not yet explicitly initialized either of the *cat* objects, *cozette* and *family*. We need to create a constructor for that. We'll get to constructors in this chapter, but first we'll take care of some business with our data and procedures.

Member Variables of the Object *cozette*

Let's start by accessing the members of the *cat* object *cozette*:

```
cozette.age = 2;
catptr = &cozette;
catptr->weight = 6;
```

So far, so good. The results of these operations are the same as they would be if the class *cat* were a structure: The *age* member variable of the object *cozette* is assigned the value *2*, the *catptr* pointer is assigned the address of *cozette*, and then the *weight* member variable of the object pointed at by *catptr* is assigned the value *6*.

Member Functions of the Object *cozette*

Now let's turn to the member functions. They are accessed just as the member variables are:

```
cozette.play();
catptr->hunt();
```

With their odd prefixes, these function call statements might look a bit drastic, but they are simple function calls and can be used in any way that an ordinary function call can be used. In each case, the function, *play()* or *hunt()*, is called to operate on a given object, the *cat* object *cozette* in the first case and the *cat* object pointed to by *catptr* in the second. This interplay of member functions and objects is the essence of objects, the central idea in object-oriented programming.

The point of accessing a member function with a specification for a particular object, *cozette* in the case of our example's *play()* function, is that we thus tell the member function which instance of the class—which object—should be used. The

C++ compiler actually passes a pointer to the specific object (*cozette*) as an implicit argument to the function. Inside the function, the implicit pointer named *this* is used to access members of the class. We'll look at the implicit pointer in more detail later in this chapter.

Member function definition

Now let's look at how a member function is defined. The point of our examination of the *play()* function here is not the trivial content of the function but the mechanics of writing a member function:

```
void cat::play(void)
{
    if (age < 2)
        // rough and tumble
    else
        // sleep on windowsill
}
```

The header of the function looks perfectly ordinary except for the *cat::* notation in front of the function name. The pair of colons is a new C++ operator with the formidable name "scope resolution operator." The scope resolution operator lets you explicitly specify a scope, which in this case is the scope of the class *cat.* Writing *cat::* indicates that what follows, a function definition in this case, is a member of the *cat* class.

Inside the *play()* member function the *if* statement tests the value of the *age* member variable. Note that we didn't have to use C++'s -> or . operator, even though *age* is a member of a class. If we call the *play()* function using the statement *cozette.play()*, the *if* statement inside *play()* will access *age* from the *cozette* object, but if we say *sammy.play()*, the same *if* statement inside *play()* will access *age* from the *sammy* cat object. This simple but profound treatment applies to both data and procedure members.

Member functions can be defined either inside the class declaration:

```
class X {
    // other class details
    void Y(void) {
    // function details
    }
};
```

or outside it, as the *play()* function was and this one is:

```
class X {
    // other class details
    void Y (void);
}
void X::Y(void) {
    // function details
}
```

When a member function is defined outside the class declaration, you must write the class name followed by the scope resolution operator to tell the compiler that you are defining something that belongs to a class it has already encountered.[1] By default, member functions defined inside the class declaration are inline functions; those defined outside the class declaration are ordinary functions.

Here's one way that the *cat* class could be declared with an inline *hunt()*:

```
class cat {
    public:
        int age;
        int weight;
        void play(void);
        void hunt(void) {
            weight++; // hunting makes the cat fatter
        }
};
```

Inline definitions of class member functions should be reserved for trivial functions, of which *hunt()* is an excellent example. Excessive function definition inside a class declaration makes the declaration hard to read, and human readability is a paramount objective in a class declaration. When you want to have a low-overhead, inline member function but you don't want to clutter the class declaration with implementation details, specify *inline* in the class declaration, and then supply the member function definition later in the header file.

The *hunt()* member function defined above will access the *weight* member of whatever object is used to access it. Using *cozette* as an example once again, note the call to the *hunt()* member function, whose action is to increment the *weight* of *cozette*:

```
cozette.hunt();
```

Because *hunt()* is inline, the overhead of the expression will be exactly the same as the overhead of this expression:

```
cozette.weight++;
```

In this trivial example, the efficiency certainly seems to be much ado about nothing. But as classes and situations get more complex, with more emphasis on access levels and abstractions, using inline procedures such as *hunt()* lets us have it all: the protection and control of member functions plus the efficiency of unfettered access to class member variables.

If a class is important and needs to be used by various clients, put the class declaration into a header file and use *#include* to include that file wherever the class is used. The class definition is complete in the sense that it contains everything a

---

1. If you omit the *classname::* scope resolution qualifier, you will define an ordinary function, not a member function.

client needs in order to use the class. The class declaration usually isn't a complete definition of the class; in a separate file you need to provide the definitions of outline member functions you haven't completely defined in the declaration.

For example, my *cat* class definition might be stored in a file called cat.h, and its member function definitions might be stored in cat.cpp. Program modules that needed to use *cat* objects would include cat.h; the linkage script for such modules would need to include cat.obj, which would be the result of compiling cat.cpp. And of course cat.cpp would include cat.h; the compiler must see the class definition before it can compile the member function definitions. These relationships among program modules are shown in Figure 8-1. Note that a class header file shouldn't contain definitions of outline functions because if the header were included multiple times, you would get "multiple definition" errors during linkage.

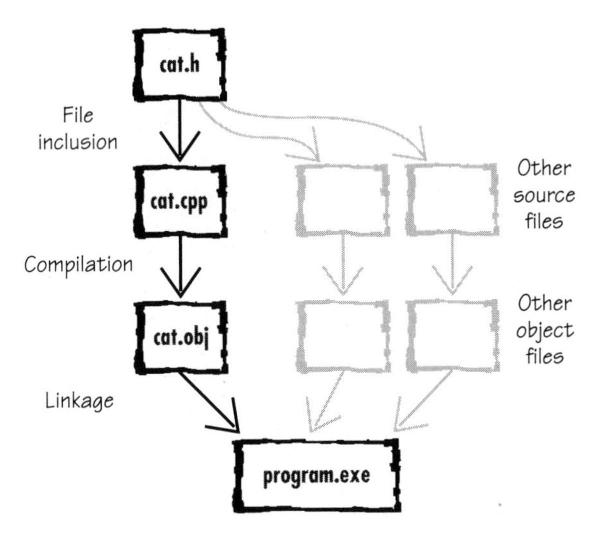

Figure 8-1.
The organization of a program among file modules.

Although the goal of object-oriented programming is to create important, reusable, sharable, apple pie–style classes, it's also common practice to whip up a class or two now and then for the needs of the moment. Often such a class is fully contained in a single file—the class declaration at the top followed by the class member function definitions. I often find it convenient to develop a class while it is contained in a single file. Then, when the code starts to stabilize, I separate it into the declaration file (.h) and the definition file (.cpp).

Public, Private, and Protected

Access controls facilitate a major goal of object-oriented programming: encapsulation and abstraction. Access controls are a central feature of C++, and you need to consider access needs as you plan your classes. There is a constant tension between the class user's right to know and the class designer's tendency to protect. As we've already noted, C++ provides three access controls that help you balance this tension:

- A *private* member can be accessed only by class member functions and by friends of the class. This is a severe but sometimes necessary restriction.
- A *protected* member can be accessed only by class member functions, by friends of the class, and by member functions of publicly derived classes. This restriction prevents mere clients from accessing a member but still makes the member available to derived classes.
- A *public* member is available to all. A class's *public* members constitute the public interface to the class.

C++ is consistent in its treatment of access controls across all members—both data and function—and the jurisdiction of the access controls extends to all the operator member functions, even to constructors and destructors.

In the example we've been working with, we've already made the expedient decision to make all the members of the *cat* class *public*. Although some fully public classes are useful, they are the exception because one of the most important reasons to create a class is to hide details. When I use a user-interface window class, I don't want to see all the gory details that go into implementing a GUI window system; I want to be able to examine the public part of the class declaration to find the simplest possible interface that will give me the requisite power and facility.

Let's use the *cat* class example again to see how access controls are imposed on a class. At the outset of a class definition, the default access privilege is *private*. An access keyword (followed by a colon) changes the access privilege. You can put access keywords into a class as many times as you want, and in whatever order you want.

I often put the *private* elements first, followed by the *protected*, followed by the *public*. This makes sense to me because the *protected* elements usually build on the *private*, and the *public* elements tend to make use of both the *private* and the *protected* elements. The argument for the opposite order is that human readers are primarily interested in the *public* elements and they should therefore be first.

Here is the *cat* class redefined to make use of access controls:

```
class cat {
    private:
        int age;
    protected:
        int weight;
    public:
        void play(void);
        void hunt(void) {
            weight++; // hunting makes the cat rotund
        }
};
```

Now we've made *age* private, presumably because *age* would never be changed by either a client or a derived class. The *weight* member is now protected, making it accessible to any class derived from *cat*. The *cat* class's public interface consists of the *play()* and *hunt()* functions. Access controls give a bit more meaning to the inline *hunt()* function.

```
void persian(void)
{
    cat tabby;
    tabby.weight = 0; // no good--weight is protected
    tabby.hunt();     // OK--hunt is public
}
```

A *cat* client can call *hunt()* to increase the *weight* even though the *weight* member isn't directly accessible to clients.

Constructors and Destructors

Constructors and destructors give you control over what happens when an object is created and what happens when it is destroyed. This lets you guarantee that necessary initializations and cleanups will be performed. And you can use constructors to implement conversions from a foreign type to a given object type.

A constructor is a member function that is invoked automatically each time an object (of a class with a constructor) is created. You can define multiple constructors for a class, so long as each constructor has a different argument list. We've seen the rules for this in Chapter 7's discussion of overloaded functions. Once a class has any constructors, object creation falls under control of the constructors and it becomes impossible to create an object without calling a constructor. Most of your classes will have constructors, and many of your classes will have several constructors. Constructors are your access to object creation, and you should give them careful attention during class design.

A destructor is a member function that is invoked when an object is destroyed. C++ objects are destroyed

- When an automatic object (one defined within a block) goes out of scope
- When a dynamically allocated object is deleted
- For global objects, when the program exits

In each of these three cases a destructor, if it exists, will be invoked. But if an object is dynamically allocated but is never deleted, its destructor will never be invoked.

Constructors can be overloaded, but each class has only a single destructor. This doesn't mean that only one destructor will be invoked each time an object is destroyed. The list on the next page shows the three sets of destructors that are invoked automatically each time an object is destroyed.

- The object's destructor, the destructor defined in the object's own class
- The destructors for member objects
- The destructors for the object's base class

In some object-oriented languages, a reserved name, such as *Create* in Eiffel, is used to implement a constructor function. C++ uses a slightly different approach. The constructor functions have the same name as the class. Destructors in C++ are named in a similar scheme. The destructor functions have the class name with a ~ (tilde) prepended.

Let's look at a trivial example, a version of the *cat* class that contains a constructor and a destructor:

```
#include <iostream.h>
class cat {
    protected:
        int age;
        int weight;
    public:
        cat(void) {         // inline constructor
            age = 0;
            weight = 0;
            cout << "cat " << age << ' ' << weight << '\n';
        }
        ~cat(void) {        // inline destructor
            cout << "~cat " << age << ' ' << weight << '\n';
        }
        void play(void);
        void hunt(void) {
            weight++;       // hunting makes the cat fatter
        }
};
```

The *cat* constructor initializes the *age* and *weight* member variables and then prints out a brief message. The destructor has nothing to do except print out a brief message so that we will have a record of its execution.

The role of *main()* is simply to create a *cat* object, call *hunt()*, and then exit, which causes the *cat* object to be destroyed:

```
void main(void)
{
    cat cozette;
    cozette.hunt();
}
```

When executed, the program prints this:

```
cat 0 0
~cat 0 1
```

The first line of output comes from the constructor, invoked automatically when the *cat* object is created, and the second line comes from the destructor, invoked automatically as *main()* returns. Note that in the interim, *hunt()* has fattened the cat!

I/O Connections

The class *cat* example uses C++'s iostream library for text output. We'll look at iostream in detail in Chapter 12, but in the meantime you should know enough about streams to be able to read such code. Each I/O statement starts on the left with the name of an I/O connection—*cout* for output in our example. Other predefined I/O connections are *cerr* for error output and *cin* for input.[2] Following the name of the I/O connection is a series of expressions separated by << for output statements and >> for input statements. For output, each expression is converted to text by a conversion function. The streams header file iostream.h tells the compiler about the conversion functions for the built-in types; you can create your own conversion functions for your class types. The role of a conversion function is to convert its argument to text and deliver the text to the I/O connection.

Let's look more closely at the I/O statement from the *cat* constructor:

```
cout << "cat " << age << ' ' << weight << '\n';
```

This line outputs five items: a string, an integer, another string, another integer, and a character.

Both the constructor and the destructor for the *cat* class have *void* specified as their argument type. For the constructor this is but one of many choices, although *void* signals that this particular constructor is a "default constructor." We'll look at that idea shortly. For the destructor, the only choice is to specify no arguments; destructors don't take arguments. And notice that neither the constructor nor the destructor specifies a return type, not even the *void* type. Constructors and destructors don't return values, and so naturally don't specify return types.

Default constructors

A "default constructor" is a constructor that doesn't take any arguments and can be useful in several situations. A default constructor is needed, for instance, when an array of objects is allocated by means of *new*, when an array of objects is created statically but there are too few initializers, and when an object is created without the specification of an initializer. A default constructor is also needed in a few obscure cases, such as when an object with constructors (say, object *m*) is a member of another object (say, object *c*). If *c* doesn't have a constructor, or if even one of *c*'s constructors doesn't explicitly invoke a constructor of *m*, *m* must have a default constructor. If no constructor has been specified for a class, the compiler will create a default constructor.

---

2. *cout* roughly corresponds to the standard C library's *stdout*; *cin* to *stdin*; and *cerr* to *stderr*.

Class Initialization

The C++ language is careful to differentiate between "initialization," which happens when something is created, and "assignment," which happens during the usual lifetime of an entity. We've already noted this distinction in Chapter 7, in which we saw that a *const* or a reference variable must be initialized and that after initialization, a new value cannot be assigned to it.

Knowing that initialization obeys a different set of rules than assignment does, we can ask ourselves what happens with respect to initialization when a class contains a *const* or a reference variable. Our first instinct, to initialize it in the body of the class definition, is just plain illegal. The following small class, although it might look reasonable, is not legal in C++:

```
class KandR {
    const int K = 1000;     // no good--can't initialize
                            //  in class definition
    const int& R = K;       // no good--can't initialize
                            //  in class definition
};
```

The correct method for initializing members of a class is to use the constructor. Again, our intuition might lead us astray—initialization of class members is not allowed in the body of a constructor. Instead, the initializations must occur in a series of initialization expressions that are placed between the constructor header and the opening curly brace of the constructor body. Here is the *KandR* class rewritten using a constructor to achieve the result we tried to achieve in our earlier attempt. Here's the class definition:

```
class KandR {
    const int K;
    const int& R;
public:
    KandR(void);              // constructor
};

KandR::KandR(void) :          // constructor
    K(1000),                  // initialize K constant to 1000
    R(K)                      // initialize R reference to refer to K
{ /* body */ }
```

We could have included class *KandR*'s constructor definition in the class declaration:

```
class KandR {
    const int K;
    const int& R;
public:
    KandR (void) : K(1000), R(K) { /* body */ }
}
```

But the constructor is defined outside the class declaration, so the header of the constructor, introduced by the *KandR::* class scope specification, is followed by a colon, which means that initialization expressions will follow. Each initialization expression consists of the name of a member datum and a parenthesized expression denoting its initial value, and the expressions are separated by commas. The parenthesized expression should be of the proper type, or of a type that the compiler can convert to the proper type. The constructor we've just written could be read aloud as "The *KandR* default class constructor initializes the *K* member to *1000* and the *R* member to reference *K*, and its body is empty." An assignment to either *K* or *R* in the body of the *KandR* constructor would be illegal. *K* and *R* must be initialized, but neither can be assigned.

Initialization is required for some types, but for *int*, *double*, and most of the other built-in types, it is merely a convenience. If, for argument's sake, the *KandR* class also had an ordinary *double* named *D*, we could either initialize *D* in an initialization expression such as those shown above for *K* and *R* or assign *D* an initial value in an assignment statement in the body of the constructor. Although the effect is the same, I prefer to place initializations in the specific spot reserved for them, to save the body of the constructor for noninitialization tasks.

Here's the class definition for *Param*, the parent of a family of classes that keeps track of parameter values. *Param*'s role is to keep track of the assigned name of a parameter; classes derived from *Param* handle the specific values and their types. In the *Param* declaration, *nm* is a *const* pointer to increase safety:

```
class Param {
    private:
        char *const nm;
    public:
        Param(char *name);  // constructor
        virtual ~Param();   // destructor
        const char *name();
        virtual void assign(const char *s) = 0;
        virtual const char *string() = 0;
};
```

Here's the simplest way to write the *Param* constructor:

```
Param::Param(char *name) :      // constructor
    nm(name)                    // initialize nm
{ /*body*/ }
```

This simply points *nm* at the *name* that has been passed to the constructor. The problem with this approach is that each object doesn't have under its own control its own copy of the name. Instead, each object is trusting whoever sent in the name for assurance that the name won't be changed, deallocated, or otherwise mangled. On the next page is a much more robust, less trusting version of the *Param()* constructor, in which space is allocated for a local copy of the name. This makes the object more self contained and less reliant on the vagaries of how it is used.

```
Param::Param(char *name) :          // constructor
    nm(new char[strlen(name)+1])    // initialize nm; allocate strlen+1
{
    if (!nm) {                      // new failed
        // error handling
        return;
    }
    strcpy(nm, name);               // copy name to private buffer
}
```

In the initialization part of *Param*, the *nm* pointer is initialized to point at a chunk of newly allocated memory that is just large enough to hold the name (plus 1 for the trailing null). In the body of the constructor, the name is copied into the newly allocated space. The same initialization could be accomplished with the following constructor, which for my taste is unnecessarily hard to read. This compact version also prevents us from testing the pointer returned by *new* before handing it to *strcpy()*, which I see as a major failing:

```
Param::Param(char *name) :         // constructor
    nm(strcpy(new char[strlen(name)+1], name))
{
}
```

This obfuscation does have one small advantage: It allows us to declare *nm* more restrictively as a *const pointer to const char* instead of as a mere *const pointer to char* as was done in the earlier version.

The role of the *Param* destructor is to free the space that was allocated for *nm*:

```
Param::~Param(void)
{
    delete nm;
}
```

The final constructor and destructor example we'll look at comes from the NetBIOS class library whose general organization was described in Chapter 5. A *NetName* is a NetBIOS data type that consists of a 16-byte array. An ordinary null terminated C string ends at the null, but all 16 bytes in a *NetName* are significant.

I designed the *NetName* class to have two constructors: a default constructor, which is a constructor that doesn't take any arguments, and a constructor that initializes the *NetName* object from a C string. Because all bytes of the *NetName* are significant, this constructor has somewhat more to do than simply invoke *strcpy()*. And as a convenience, this constructor takes an optional second argument that allows a single character to be appended to a *NetName*. This secondary feature arose during my construction of the session-level network interface to facilitate creating pairs of similar names, and we won't go into it here.

```
#include <string.h>
class NetName {
    private:
        enum NetNameConsts { NameLen = 16 };
        char name[NameLen];
    public:
        NetName() { memset(name, ' ', NameLen); }
        NetName(char *nm, char ext = 0) {
            strncpy(name, nm, NameLen);
            int n = strlen(name);
            if (ext && n < NameLen)
                name[n++] = ext;
            while(n < NameLen)
                name[n++] = ' ';     // not an asciiz string
        }
        operator char *() { return name; }
};
```

The only data member of the *NetName* class is *name*, a 16-byte array to store the network name. Both constructors are careful to completely fill in the 16-byte array because all 16 bytes are significant. All of the following declarations create *NetName* objects:

```
NetName local;

NetName remotea("alpha3");

NetName remoteb("alpha", '3');
```

The last two declarations create two separate names that have the same value.

In the NetBIOS code in Chapter 5, we used the explicit constant *16* to specify the length of the array. In this chapter's version, we use the preferred way to define a constant, an enumeration that specifies the length.

The enumeration called *NetNameConsts* in the private part of the *NetName* class definition is a common subterfuge in C++ classes. As we've noted, there isn't a way to initialize a *const* inside a class definition; we can't simply write

```
const namelen = 16;
```

in the class definition. The first difficulty is that C++ won't allow us to initialize a *const* in a class definition. The second problem is that a *const* takes up space in a class, and it is critical for each *NetName* object to occupy exactly 16 bytes; one byte more or less will prove fatal to the whole set of NetBIOS classes.

Of course, we could use *#define* to create a constant and use it for the array length inside the class. Unfortunately, the *#define* wouldn't be local to the class; instead, it would follow the usual rules for preprocessor constants. The alternative is to declare an enumeration type and use its enumeration constants where we would normally use a *const int* or a preprocessor *#define*. In the *NetName* class, the enumeration constant *NameLen* is set to *16*, which is the length of a network name. This symbolic constant is then used throughout the class. This works because C++ allows automatic conversion from an enumeration constant to an integer. (Conversion in the opposite direction, integer to enumeration, can be done only with an explicit cast.)

The *NetName* class also contains an operator function. We'll take a more detailed look at operator functions in Chapter 11.

The *this* Pointer

Inside a class member function, you can use all the accessible members of the current object without explicitly using a pointer because, as we noted earlier in this chapter, the member function is secretly passed a pointer to the current object. Each time you access one of the members of the current object, the compiler is actually using the implicit pointer to access the member.

The *this* pointer is the mostly hidden pointer that is passed to each (non-*static*) member function so that inside the member function, elements of the current object can be accessed. (As we'll see shortly, static member functions don't have access to the *this* pointer.) I say "mostly hidden" because the compiler uses the *this* pointer automatically. Each time you access a member variable or call a (non-*static*) member function, the compiler is using *this* to do your bidding.

Sometimes you need to take control at a lower level. Inside a class member function you can use the *this* pointer as necessary simply by writing its name. No declaration is necessary. To make clear how *this* should be used, you can write its exact type. In a member function of a class named *T*, the *this* pointer has the following type:

```
T *const this;
```

Because *this* is a *const* pointer, you can't write *this++* or do anything else to alter the value of the pointer. But you can use *this* to access elements of the current class. For example, in a class with a member variable named *x*, the expression *this->x* will access the *x* member. This example illustrates:

```
class xyz {
        short x, y, z;
    public:
        void setxyz(short x, short y, short z) {
            this->x = x; this->y = y; this->z = z;
        }
        void mockxyz(void);
};
```

Inside *setxyz*, the *x*, *y*, and *z* arguments hide the member variables of the same names; the *this* pointer makes the members explicitly accessible.

The *this* pointer is commonly used when a true pointer to the current object is required inside a member function. For example, in a member function of class *xyz* you would use *this* to call a nonmember function that requires a *pointer to uxyz* argument. An example of this is shown in the following definition of *mockxyz*, which was declared above:

```
void xyzgrok(xyz *);      // declare xyzgrok function
                          // its argument is a pointer to an xyz

void xyz::mockxyz(void)
{
    xyzgrok(this);        // call xyz, and pass it a pointer
                          // to the current object
}
```

Another legitimate use of *this* is to refer to the entire current object. For example, you might have an *xyz* member function that returns an *xyz* or one that returns a reference to an *xyz*. The return statement of such a member function would be

```
return *this;
```

There is also a Machiavellian use of *this*, to circumvent *const* or *volatile* restrictions that have been placed on a class member function. (We'll look at *const* and *volatile* member functions later in this chapter.) The restrictions can be circumvented by casting *this* to a more hospitable type.

Static Members

All the class data members that we've encountered so far in Part 2 have been "member variables." That means that the variables have been parts of class objects. In some sense, a class object is simply a collection of the class member variables. Each time we create an object of the class, we simply create each of the member variables, line 'em up in a row, and call that an object.

Static Member Variables

The flip side of a member variable is a "static member variable," a class member that

- Is shared by all class objects
- Exists for the lifetime of a program
- Exists even if there aren't any class objects
- Is a part of individual class objects

A static member variable is something like a traditional global variable in that it exists for the lifetime of the program. But unlike a traditional global variable, a static member variable is a member of a class and subject to the usual class member access rules. A static member variable can be accessed directly in member functions. In nonmembers, you must use the scope resolution operator to access a static member variable.

A static member variable is also something like a traditional static variable that is declared within a function, except that a static member variable is accessible to all of a class's member functions, not just to a single function. Because of this similarity, you use the *static* keyword in a class definition to specify that a given member is a static member variable.

The *ObjCount* class we define below contains a static member variable that keeps track of the number of *ObjCount* objects that are in existence. The constructor of the class increments the count each time a class object is created, and the destructor decrements the count.

```
class ObjCount {
    protected:
        double d;               // instance variable
    public:
        static int count;       // static count of objects
        ObjCount() :            // constructor
            d(0)                // initialize member
            { count++; }        // increment object count
        ~ObjCount()             // destructor
            { count--; }        // decrement object count
};
```

The *ObjCount* declaration would normally go into a header file, and the initialization of *count* would go into the .cpp file:

```
int ObjCount::count = 0;
```

You must initialize all static member variables exactly once; otherwise, you will get errors during linkage.

The *ObjCount* constructor initializes the member variable *d* and then increments the static member variable *count*. The destructor does the opposite: It decrements *count*. Notice that *count* in this class is public, which in general is not a very good idea because it might be modified anywhere in the program. We'll remedy this mistake shortly. Most static member variables should have one or two simple member functions that read and initialize them to stand guard over them, to prevent their abuse by outsiders. More to the point, static member variables should be variables that are of interest only to member functions, not to outsiders. Notice also that the static member variable *count* is truly a member of *ObjCount*; there can be other static member variables named *count* in other classes, but they will not interfere with or have any relationship to *count* in the *ObjCount* class.

The *main()* function demonstrates *ObjCount*'s functionality.

```
#include <iostream.h>

void main()
{
    cout << "Init " << ObjCount::count << '\n';
    ObjCount *one = new ObjCount;
    cout << "One " << ObjCount::count << '\n';
    ObjCount *ten = new ObjCount[10];
    cout << "+Ten " << ObjCount::count << '\n';
    delete [] ten;
    delete one;
    cout << "None " << ObjCount::count << '\n';
}
```

Inside a member function, inside the constructor and destructor above, for instance, a static member variable can be accessed by writing its name. But outside member functions, you must use the scope resolution operator to specify the class; that's why *count* is called *ObjCount::count* inside *main()*. If you do have an object available, you can use it to get at a static member variable. For example, inside *main()*, once you have initialized *one* to point at an *ObjCount* object, you can write *one->count* to get at the *count* static member variable. I generally avoid using a class object (or an object pointer) to access a static member variable; to me, using the class name and the scope resolution operator seems more in keeping with the nature of a static member variable.

Here is the output of the example program:

```
Init 0
One 1
+Ten 11
None 0
```

Notice one other small aspect of the example. When an array of *ObjCount* objects is created, the count is correctly maintained because C++ sees that the default constructor is called once for each member of the array. Similarly, when the array is deleted, the destructor is called once for each member of the array.

Static Member Functions

The glaring deficiency of our example is that *ObjCount*'s static member variable *count* is fully public. Any module, anywhere in your 100,000-line application, can completely destroy the value in *count* with the following little typo that assigns *1000* to *count* instead of testing whether *count* equals *1000*:

```
if (ObjCount::count = 1000) {
    // do this when we have 1000 ObjCount objects
}
```

We haven't practiced defensive, encapsulated, object-oriented programming. What's needed is a member function that will let us read the value in *count* but that will protect us from accidental modification. If we were to use a standard member function for this chore, we would need to call it with the *obj.mem* or *objptr->mem* syntax; that is, we would need an object. That would make it pretty difficult to code the first and last lines of *main()* in our example because there aren't any *ObjCount* objects at those points in the program.

The solution is to use a "static member function," a member function that can access only the static members of a class, either static member variables or other static member functions. Just as a static member variable can be accessed without using an object, a static member function can be accessed without resort to an object. Here is the *ObjCount* class, slightly altered to provide better safety. The simple *main()* exerciser is omitted.

```
class ObjCount {
    protected:
        double member;       // instance variable
        static int count;    // count of objects (static member variable)
    public:
        ObjCount() :         // constructor
            member(0)        // initialize member
            { count++; }     // increment count
        ~ObjCount()          // destructor
            { count--; }     // decrement count
        static int Count()   // return value of count static
                             //  member variable
            { return count; }
};
```

Using this version of *ObjCount*, we can write *ObjCount::Count()* to read the number of extant *ObjCount* objects. Notice that there isn't any function call overhead because *ObjCount::Count()* is an inline member function.

const and *volatile* Member Functions

Any variable or class object can be declared *const* or *volatile*. Remember from Chapter 6 that a *const* datum doesn't change and that a *volatile* datum can be changed asynchronously. The compiler is careful to prevent you from altering a *const*, and it is careful to reload a *volatile* from memory each time it is accessed. We noted in Chapter 7's discussion of the *const* type specifier and the *volatile* type specifier that pointers to or references to such variables can be passed only to a function that is equipped to handle them. For example, the *const double* named *cd* can be passed to the *sin()* procedure:

```
const double cd;
double altsin(double *);

sin(cd);  // OK--a const double can be converted trivially to a double
```

That's because a *const double* value (such as *cd*) can be trivially converted to an ordinary *double* value. If *sin()* changes its argument, that won't have any effect on *cd* because a copy of *cd* is passed to *sin()*. But things change drastically when we pass pointers or references. For example, imagine an alternative math library that takes pointers to its arguments. We might have an *altsin()* procedure whose prototype is

```
const double cd;
double altsin(double *);

altsin(&cd);  // error--a const double can't be converted
              //  automatically to a double
```

The trouble arises because a pointer to a *const double* can't be converted automatically to a pointer to *double*. The conversion is not automatic because no copying is performed; *altsin()* can modify whatever its pointer is pointing toward. The solution, assuming that *altsin()* doesn't actually modify the *double* that its argument points toward, is to correct the prototype:

```
const double cd;
double altsin(const double *);

altsin(&cd);  // OK--parameters match
```

The same principle applies to *const* class objects and to free procedures because the free procedures can be declared to take *const* parameters if they don't actually modify the class whose address they have been passed. Similarly, there is a way to declare class member functions and *volatile* class member functions so that you can indicate that a member function is compatible with *const* or *volatile* objects.

Our understanding of the *this* pointer discussion earlier in this chapter should lead us to the obvious inference that C++ implements member functions by passing a "hidden" first argument to each member function whose type is *T** for any class type *T*. To make this clearer, I'm going to show a simple class and a few class operations in a two-column format. On the left will be what we write in C++. On the right will be equivalent C pseudocode that implements the operations..

C++ Code

```
class Psych101 {
    double Troubled;
    public:
        double Freud(void) {
            return(Troubled);
        }
};
Psych101 Hysteria;
Hysteria.Freud();
```

C Pseudocode Equivalent

```
struct Psych101 {
    double Troubled;
};
double Freud(Psych101 *const this)
{
    return(this->Troubled);
};
struct Psych101 Hysteria;
Freud(&Hysteria);
```

Traditional C syntax lets us control two important aspects of a class member function: the return type and the argument types. However, it doesn't give us a handle on the type of the *this* pointer. Consider a *const* class object such as the one shown at the top of the next page.

C++ Code	C Pseudocode Equivalent
`const Psych101 Envy;`	`const struct Psych101 Envy;`

Because *Envy* is a *const*, we can't use it to invoke the *Freud()* member function:

C++ Code	C Pseudocode Equivalent
`Envy.Freud();   // no good`	`Freud(&Envy);   // no good`

The reason for the failure should be obvious from the right-hand column; *Freud()* is expecting a *Psych101 *const* parameter, but it is getting a *const Psych101 ** pointer.

The most obvious (but wrong) solution is to put the keyword *const* in front of the member function declaration:

C++ Code

```
class Psych101 {
        double Troubled;
    public:
        const double Freud(void) {
            return(Troubled);
        }
};
```

C Pseudocode Equivalent

```
struct Psych101 {
    double Troubled;
};
const double Freud
    (Psych101 *const this)
{
    return(this->Troubled);
}
```

But, as the C pseudocode equivalent on the right points up, this doesn't work. All it does is adjust the return type of *Freud()*, not the type of *Freud()*'s *this* pointer. The correct way to declare that *Freud()* is a *const* member function is to write the keyword *const* after the function header:

C++ Code

```
class Psych101 {
        double Troubled;
    public:
        double Freud(void) const {
            return(Troubled);
        }
};
```

C Pseudocode Equivalent

```
struct Psych101 {
    double Troubled;
};
double Freud
    (const Psych101 *const this)
{
    return(this->Troubled);
}
```

(The *const* that makes *Freud()* a *const* member function is italicized in the left column, and the corresponding usage of *const* in the declaration of *this* is italicized in the right column.) In a *const* member function, you can't modify instance variables, although you can modify static member variables. The reason, again, should be clear from the right column. Instance variables are accessed (implicitly) using *this*, which is a *const* pointer to *const*, but static member variables are accessed directly. A *const* member function can be invoked by either an ordinary or a *const* object, but an ordinary member function can be invoked only by an ordinary object.

Similar facilities and restrictions apply to *volatile* member functions. You declare a member function to be volatile by writing *volatile* after the header. A *volatile* member function can be invoked by either a *volatile* or an ordinary object, but an ordinary member function can be invoked only by an ordinary object. Similarly, there are *const volatile* member functions, so that something can be done with a *const volatile* object.

Nested and Local Classes

A nested class is simply a class that is contained within another class. Members inside a nested class can access the types and enumerations that have been declared in the outer class, and nested class members can also access the static members of the outer class. But members of the nested class can't access member variables of the enclosing class (except by using an explicit pointer). In a nested class situation, all access rules apply. The nested class members can access only the public members of the outer class, and the outer class can access only the public members of the nested class.

A local class is a class that is defined inside a procedure. There are two main restrictions on a local class. The first is that it cannot access the automatic variables of its enclosing function. This is similar to the rule for a nested class that it cannot access the member variables of its enclosing class. The second restriction on a local class is that all of its functions must be defined within the class. There is no way to defer the definition of a local class function until a later scope. This encourages the application of local classes to only simple chores that can be managed with modest inline functions.

Nested and local classes try to fill a niche, but they are far from the C++ mainstream and aren't often used. A class with an important and general role should receive first-class treatment, a full declaration in the global scope, usually in a header file.

Friends

C++ is a system of checks and balances whose net effect is to facilitate and encourage object-oriented programming without imposing an object-oriented reign of terror on the programmer. On the checks side are C++'s strict type checking and its access controls for private and protected class data. On the balances side are casts to release the type checking constraints and friends to provide unfettered access to private and protected class data.

Casts and friends are both aids for relaxing normally secure systems, but they operate from different perspectives. Casts help out wherever the current assemblage of types doesn't quite match and other types are needed. A cast is rarely planned for and is usually done almost impromptu—added to a program as the need for it becomes apparent. This might not be ideal, but it certainly is common practice.

Friendship is usually the product of thought and reflection, of a more considered approach to design and strategy alternatives. Friendship is granted by the designer of a class to a select group of other classes and functions so that they can access the private and protected elements of the class. Friendship is under the control of the class designer, the individual who has a reason for protecting the elements of the class. And sometimes a request for friendship is refused because the class designer decides that the rationale for friendship is not compelling.

In the ongoing debate about the C++ friendship capability, some programmers argue that friendship can be abused, that unfettered use of friendship violates a class's encapsulation and makes the class less reliable. Others argue that friendship is a necessary expedient, noting that it has been used successfully for years.

I've found friendship to be useful in my own work, and I haven't seen it cause problems. The ability to give a class friends can help you keep small independent classes from coalescing into a single large class.

To specify a friend in a class definition, you simply write the word *friend* followed by the name of the friend. A friend can be an ordinary procedure, a member function of another class, or an entire class. When you specify procedure and member function friends, you must specify the full function prototype. When you've designated an entire class as a friend, all the member functions in the class are treated as friends. Here's an example containing two friend declarations:

```
class X {
    // friends
        friend void makeAnX(void);      // ordinary procedure
        friend class Y;                 // entire class
    private:
        double treasure;
        X() : treasure(10000) {}
};
```

The most noteworthy feature of the class *X* definition, besides its friend declarations, is its private constructor. A constructor, like all other member functions, obeys the usual access rules. It can't be invoked unless it is accessible. This means that *X* objects can be created only in the two friends: in the *makeAnX()* procedure or in some member function of the *Y* class. *X* objects can't be created in the global scope because in the global scope the *X* constructor is inaccessible (private). And *X* objects can't be created in derived class objects, because the private constructor isn't accessible in a derived class (unless the derived class is also a friend).

This doesn't meant that there can't be a global pointer to an *X* object, but the object that it points to must be constructed in one of the two friend environments. This technique is, to some, a bit surprising, but it is often used. For example, if you want a class that can be constructed only within *main()*, simply make the class constructors private and make *main()* a friend of the class.

Here is a declaration of two globals, a global pointer to an *X* and the *makeAnX()* procedure. In this example, the sole task of *makeAnX()* is to allocate an *X* object that can be accessed by the *TheGlobalX* pointer.

```
X *TheGlobalX;

void makeAnX(void)
{
    // needs friendship to access constructor
    TheGlobalX = new X;
}
```

In the *Y* class, which is an *X* class friend, the constructor is public, but it requires a pointer to *X* argument. The task of the constructor is to copy the *treasure* member from the *X* object into *Y*'s own *Ytreasure* member. This operation on the private data of *X* wouldn't be possible without friendship.

```
class Y {
    private:
        double Ytreasure;
    public:
        Y(X *x) :            // constructor
            Ytreasure(x->treasure)
        {}
};
```

The friend declarations are not subject to access controls. It makes no difference whether a friend declaration occurs in a private region or in a public region. There are no gradations to friendship. A friend has full access to anything a class member function can access, which is more than a derived class can access.

Pointers to Members

An object is a complete entity, a self-sufficient world in miniature. To help support this encapsulation, C++ contains pointers to members. An ordinary pointer can be used to access any object (of a given type) in memory, and a pointer to a member can be used to access any member (of a given type) in a particular class of object.

C++ contains both pointers to member variables and pointers to member functions. Let's look at pointers to member variables first.

Pointers to Member Variables

A pointer to a member variable accesses a given type of member variable of any object of a given class. Consider this simple class:

```
class A {
    public:
        int a, b, c;
        void fa(void) {}
        void fb(void) {}
        void fc(void) {}
};
```

The following declaration states that *pai* is a pointer to an integer member variable of class *A*:

```
int A::*pai;    // pointer to an A integer member variable
```

Working from inside out, the declaration can be read "*pai* is a pointer (the *) to a member variable of class *A* (the *A::*[3]) that is an integer." *pai* can point at one of only three member variables, *a*, *b*, or *c*, the only integer member variables of class *A*.

pai can be pointed at one of the three eligible member variables of *A* with this assignment:

```
pai = &A::a;
```

Notice that we haven't created any *A* objects yet. That's the essence of a pointer to a member. *pai* will access the *a* member of any *A* object. To actually use a pointer to a member, you need to use the .* and ->* operators, which are new operators in C++.

```
int A::*pai;        // pointer to an A integer member variable
pai = &A::b;        // point pai at the b member variable
A x;                // an A object
A *px = new A;      // a pointer to an A object
x.*pai = 1;         // set x.b to one
pai = &A::c;        // point pai at the c member variable
px->*pai = 2;       // set (*px).c to two
```

The .* operator connects its left operand, which must be a class object, with its right operand, which specifies a particular member of that class. In the example above, *x* is an *A* class object, and the member of *A* indicated by *pai* is set to *1*. The ->* operator works similarly. Its left operand must be a pointer to a class object, and its right operand indicates a specific member of that class. In the example above, *px* is a pointer to an *A* object, and the member of *A* indicated by *pai* is set to *2*.

Pointers to Member Functions

Pointers to member functions work similarly to pointers to member variables and serve a similar need. The chief difference is that the syntax quickly escalates in difficulty. The following declaration creates a variable named *pafn* that can point to any *A* member function that has no parameters and no return value.

```
void (A::*pafn)(void);
```

Again, it is useful to pronounce the declaration "*pafn* is a pointer to a member of class *A* that is a function that takes no arguments and returns no value." Here is a brief example of how *pafn* could be assigned a value and then used to invoke a function:

---

3. Although *::* is the scope resolution operator, in a declaration, *T::* is best pronounced "member of *T*."

```
pafn = A::fa;        // point pafn at fa() member function of A
A x;                 // an A object
A *px = new A;       // a pointer to an A object
(x.*pafn)();         // call fa for object x via pafn
(px->*pafn)();       // call fa for object *px via pafn
```

You might be surprised by the extra set of parentheses in the last two lines of the example. They ensure that the entire expression designating the pointer to a function, *x.*pafn* in the first case, will be parsed as a unit. Without the parentheses, the compiler would attempt to parse *pafn()* as a function call and fail because *pafn* is not a function or a pointer to a function.

Like ordinary pointers, pointers to members can be assigned the value *0* to indicate that they aren't pointing at anything. However, pointers to members are unlike ordinary pointers in that they are not compatible with pointers to *void*. A member pointer can't be converted to a pointer to a *void* even by explicit casting.

Structs, Unions, and Classes

In C, the two types of data structures are structs and unions. A struct is a container for a group of elements, each element accessible by name. A union is nearly the same except that the elements are stored on top of each other, which means that only one of the elements is really present at a given time.

In C++ terms, a struct is a kind of class, one in which members are public by default. A union is a struct with all data members overlapped in memory. Figure 8-2 sets out the characteristics of classes, structs, and unions.

class
- Members private by default
- Good for creating objects: associated data and functions

struct
- Members and base class public by default
- Good for creating data structures that don't have associated functions

union
- Members public by default
- Members have same address—holds only one member at a time
- Can't have static data members
- Can't have virtual functions
- Can't have or be a base class
- Members can't have constructors and destructors

Figure 8-2.
The class, the struct, and the union. The union is the least object oriented of the three types.

If you want to keep things as simple as possible, use structs, unions, and classes straightforwardly. Use a struct to combine related elements into a data structure. Use a union to save space by storing one of several (mutually exclusive) data types in a single space. And use a class to implement objects some of whose members might be private or protected.

Even though this straightforward approach in the interest of simplicity is desirable, you should be aware that the relationships among structs, unions, and classes in C++ are complex.

Structs and Classes

A C++ struct is simply a class whose default access level is public. I suggest that you use structs primarily to create traditional C data structures, that is, data structures that don't have associated functions—even though C++ does allow structs to have member functions. Use classes, as usual, for data structures that have associated behaviors.

The most important aspect of the congruence between structs and classes is that their layouts are the same. This allows you to use either C or C++ to manipulate data structures, which is an important consideration when your program is migrating from C to C++. Of course, this capability exists only if both the C and the C++ sources are translated with a compiler that follows the same rules for layout.

Unions and Classes

The primary rule for a union in C++ is that union members cannot have constructors or destructors. A class can be a member of a union, but that class must not have constructors or destructors. The union itself can have many of the accoutrements of a class, including constructors and destructors, member functions, and access restrictions. But a union is prohibited from having some class characteristics, such as static members, virtual member functions, and parents and children. A union can't be derived from another class, and it can't serve as a base class for derivation.

Yes, this is surprising, and as with most of the surprising elements of C++, you should be both skeptical and careful. If I needed a class whose data elements were all stored at the same place, I'd have the class contain an anonymous *union* data member:

```
class C {
    union {          // anonymous union
        int a;
        double d;
    };
public:
    C();             // class constructor
    void fn(void);   // class member function
};
```

One advantage of this approach is that it holds no surprises. A union is used for its traditional purpose, saving space, and a class is used to endow a data structure with behaviors.

The other approach is to create a union with class features:

```
union U {
private:
    int a;
    double d;
public:
    U();            // union constructor
    void fn(void);  // union member function
}
```

By default, a union is fully public, so I've used the *private* keyword to make the data elements of *U* private, as they were by default in the preceding class *C*. The principal difference between the union *U* and the class *C* is that *C* can be used as a base class but *U* cannot.

The only classlike elements that I feel comfortable about using with unions are constructors and destructors. Constructors can guarantee that unions are properly initialized, and destructors can guarantee that unions containing pointers to allocated memory are properly deallocated.

9

Derived Classes

Creating new data types by specializing existing types is an exciting new technique that gives object-oriented languages great power and expressiveness. Derivation creates an *is a* relationship on two levels. At the conceptual level, class derivation lets you create a software structure that mirrors the structure of the problem domain. Equally important, in the software domain, class derivation creates a family of types. An object of a derived class *is an* object of its base class and can be used wherever its base class objects can be used. We can use polymorphic member functions to fine-tune this relationship, so that a derived class behaves identically to its base class in some respects but exhibits its own behavior in others.

In this chapter, we'll focus on the C++ facilities for class derivation. In the first few sections, we'll tackle deriving one class from another and creating polymorphic member functions. In later sections, we'll take on the more difficult topics of abstract classes, multiple inheritance, virtual base classes, and access declarations.

Publicly and Privately Derived Classes

Class derivation is an act of genesis, creating a new type from an existing type by extending, modifying, and specializing. Class derivation enables code reuse by creating families of objects that share key traits, and it is a profound means of expression.

The basic procedure for deriving one class from another is trivial. Here's how we create a derived class named *D* from a base class named *B*:

```
class D : public B {
    // declarations of D members
};
```

The *class D : public B* notation in the class header should be read "class *D* is publicly derived from *B*." It is the syntactical expression in C++ of the *is a* relationship; it tells the compiler that a *D is a B* but to expect the changes and additions that will be listed between the braces.

The top part of a derived class consists of its base class members; the bottom part is the derived class's own contribution. When the compiler stores the elements in memory, the base class members always come first, followed by the new members that are unique to the derived class. Figure 9-1 illustrates this layout.

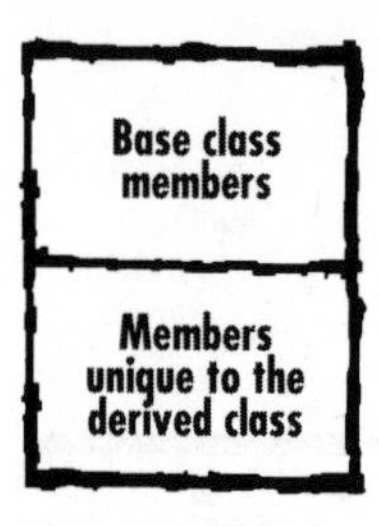

Figure 9-1.
Every derived class is the sum of base class elements and its own elements.

This memory layout means that a derived class can always be used where a base class is expected. The derived class has exactly the same layout in memory as its base class, up to the point at which the derived class's own members are stored.

When the compiler chances upon the definition of *D*, it must have already seen the definition of *B*. It is not enough for the compiler to have already seen the declaration of *B*. Recall that the definition of a class is a full list of the class's members. A declaration simply states that a given name refers to a class. You can declare a pointer to a class object with the compiler's having seen only a declaration, but to declare a class object or to define a derived class, you must arrange for the compiler to have already encountered the base class's definition.

```
class B;          // declaration of B; tells compiler that B
                  //  is a class name
B *pb;            // OK; compiler has encountered declaration of B
B b;              // no good; compiler has not encountered definition of B
class D : public B {  // no good; compiler has not encountered
                      //  definition of B
    // declarations of class D members here
};
```

One class can be derived from another either publicly or privately. There are two differences between public and private derivation. The first is that a publicly derived class can be automatically converted to its base class. This is the literal manifestation of the *is a* relationship. Automatic conversion to base is the technical description; *is a* is what's in your head during design. But a privately derived class isn't automatically converted to its base class. This implies an *is built from* relationship.

In a privately derived class, these access rules apply to the inherited base class members:

- Inaccessible and private members of the base class are inaccessible in the derived class.
- Protected and public members of the base class are private in the derived class.

In a publicly derived class, these rules apply to the inherited base class members:

- Inaccessible and private members of the base class are inaccessible in the derived class.
- Protected members of the base class remain protected in the derived class.
- Public members of the base class remain public in the derived class.

The access rules are summarized in Figure 9-2.

Base Class	***Privately Derived Class***	***Publicly Derived Class***
	`class Dpriv: private B`	`class Dpub : public B`
`class B { . . . };`	`{ . . . };`	`{ . . . };`
inaccessible members	inaccessible	inaccessible
private members	inaccessible	inaccessible
protected members	private	protected
public members	private	public

Figure 9-2.
The access status of base class members in privately and publicly derived classes.

Notice a few implications of these rules. Private base class members are inaccessible to members of both publicly derived classes and privately derived classes. That is exactly the point of privacy.

And notice that, for the first time, the term "inaccessible" is used. An inaccessible member is unavailable even to members of its own class. In a root class, a class that isn't derived from another class, no members are inaccessible. The only possible access levels for a root class are *private, protected,* and *public.* In derived classes, *inaccessible,* the fourth access level, is possible. Inaccessible members are always inherited from a base class; inaccessible members in a derived class were either inaccessible or private members of the base class.

The third thing to notice is the difference in member accessibility in private derivation and in public derivation. In *private* derivation, which is the default for classes,[1] the protected and public members of the base class become private members of the derived class. They are thus accessible to members of the derived class, but as private members of the derived class they become inaccessible in further derivations. In *public* derivation, which is by far the most common kind in practice, protected and public members of the base class retain their protected and public levels of accessibility in the derived class.

The important aspect of inheritance is that a publicly derived class can be used wherever the base class can be used. The next example shows a variety of situations

1. Structs and unions can also be derived; *public* derivation is the default for struct and union derivations.

in which *D* (derived) objects and pointers to *D* objects are used in places in which *B* (base) objects and pointers to *B* objects are expected. The compiler performs all the conversions shown in the example automatically.

```
class B {
    // B members
};
class D : public B {
    // D members
};
// functions that take B*, B&, and B arguments
void fa(B *p);
void fb(B& b);
void fc(B b);
void DeeBee(void)
{
    D d;
    fa(&d);          // fa is called with a pointer to a D object
    fb(d);           // fb is called with a reference to a D object
    fc(d);           // fc is called with a D object
    B b = d;         // b is initialized by a D object
    b = d;           // b is assigned a D object
    B *pb = &d;      // pb is initialized with a pointer to a D object
    pb = &d;         // pb is assigned a pointer to a D object
    B& rb = d;       // rb is initialized with a reference to a D object
}
```

When a *D* object is assigned to a *B* object, the base class *B* members are copied, and the additional *D*-specific members are ignored. This slicing can be surprising, but nothing else could be done, given the primacy of the rule that a publicly derived class *is a* base class and can be used wherever the base class can be used. When a pointer to a *D* object is assigned to a pointer to a *B* object, the *B* pointer can be used only to access the *B* members, even though additional members are likely to be present after the end of the *B* elements.

The opposite direction of conversion is not automatic and doesn't usually make sense. Remember that derived classes often have additional members. Not much could be done, say, inside a function that expected a *D* but was actually handed a smaller *B*:

```
void ga(D *p);      // ga expects a D object; it can use D members
void BeeDee(void)
{
    B *b = new D;
    ga(b);          // no good; no automatic conversion from B* to D*
    ga((D *)b);     // OK; manual conversion
}
```

Because this general problem has no solution, conversions from base class to derived class are not automatic, not often needed, and not generally recommended. In the rare situation in which such a conversion from base class to derived class is known to be safe, such as in the example above, the conversion can be accomplished by using a cast.

The ability to use a publicly derived class where a base class is expected is the profound advantage of derivation over membership. We've declared class *D* as publicly derived from *B*. We could have achieved the same memory layout of class members by making *B* a member instead of a base class:

```
class Dtwo {
    B bmember;
    // Dtwo members
};
```

The definition of class *Dtwo* is likely to have the same memory layout as the original *D*'s, but that's where the similarity ends. A *Dtwo* isn't a *B*. It can't be used where a *B* is used, and it can't be used in a manual conversion as *D* was earlier in function *DeeBee()*. And access rights are very different. In class *Dtwo* member functions, only the public members of *B* can be used, whereas in *D* member functions, access to both the protected and the public members of the base class was permitted.

Protected Derivation

Protected derivation is a compromise between public and private derivation. In protected derivation, accessibility of base class members is the same as for public derivation, except that public base class members are protected in the derived class. But protected derivation doesn't create an *is a* relationship; classes created using protected derivation can't be used in place of their base classes unless explicit casts are used.

In practice, public derivation is the rule. For example, in both the Microsoft Foundation Class library and the iostream class library, all derivation is public; neither private nor protected derivation is used. We've looked at private derivation in some detail because it is a significant feature of C++ even though lightly used. Protected derivation is a feature for language lawyers, not for programmers. Don't use protected derivation; its effects are too subtle.

Virtual Functions and Polymorphism

Virtual functions implement polymorphism in C++. When a virtual function is called, the version of the function appropriate for the current object will be executed, even when the current object's type isn't known until runtime. This is a marvelous and profound capability, but one that takes some acclimatization.

A polymorphic member function is declared with the keyword *virtual* in front of the function name in the base class definition. Once a function has been declared as *virtual*, it is virtual in all derived classes, even if it is not explicitly mentioned in their definitions. This feature of C++ inheritance can be helpful because it makes families of classes consistent, but it can also be surprising. And be careful—the reverse isn't true: A function declared as *virtual* in a derived class is not automatically virtual in the base class.

```
class B {
public:
    virtual int f(double);
            int g(double);    // not virtual, even though the derived
                              //  int g is declared as virtual
};

class D : public B {
public:
            int f(double);    // virtual because base class's f() is virtual
    virtual int g(double);
};
```

Virtual Function Signatures

Another important aspect of identifying virtual functions is their argument signatures.[2] The signatures must match if *virtual* is to be effective with a derived class's member function.

```
class B {
public:
        virtual int f(double);
};

class D : public B {
public:
    int f(double);        // virtual because base class's f() is virtual
    int f(int);           // not virtual; argument signature differs
};
```

Only the first *f()* in class *D* is virtual because only the first *f()* has an argument list that matches the base class *f()* argument list. The second *f()* in class *D* is an ordinary overloaded member function.

You must see to it that the return type of an overloaded function in a derived class matches the return type of the function in the base class:[3]

---

2. The keyword *virtual* doesn't contribute to a function's signature.

3. This gets tricky. Recall that when a C++ compiler is trying to determine which overloaded function to invoke, it examines only the argument types and ignores return types. But for virtual functions, the return types must match exactly—because the compiler can't generate different conversions based on the run-time object type.

```
class B {
    virtual B *f(double);
    virtual B *g(double);
};

class D : public B {
    virtual D *f(double);    // no good; return type differs
    virtual B *g(double);    // OK
};
```

The declaration of *f()* in derived class *D* is unacceptable because its return type differs from the original return type for *f()* declared in base class *B*. This type of polymorphism-cum-conversion is often desired, and programmers often naively assume it is a capability in C++. Unfortunately, it isn't. The polymorphic behavior of *g()* in the example above is assured because the parameter types and the return types match. Inside *g()*, you can return a pointer to a *D*:

```
virtual B *D::g
{
    return this;
}
```

even though *g()* is declared as returning a pointer to a *B*; the compiler will automatically convert the pointer return type.

Virtual Function Invocation

Polymorphism entails a small runtime overhead. When an ordinary member function is called, the compiler is able to invoke it directly because its address has been resolved during linking. But a polymorphic member function must be invoked indirectly. The compiler generates code so that at runtime the function's address is looked up in a virtual function table, and then that address is called. Every object that contains a virtual member function contains a hidden pointer to the table of addresses of polymorphic functions, so typical C++ implementations of polymorphism add a few instructions to each virtual function call. Use polymorphism with care in those rare but important functions whose performance determines an application's performance.

Virtual member functions can be written as inline functions. Whether such functions will actually be inline when they are invoked depends on how they are used. If the compiler detects a situation in which a virtual function is called with an object whose type is known during compilation, it might execute the inline expansion of the function. But in situations in which the object's type isn't known until runtime, the compiler is obliged to create an outline version of the function so that it can be called indirectly, by means of the virtual function dispatch table. An example of this slightly tricky distinction appears on the next page.

```
class A {
    public:
        int a;
        virtual void fn(void) { a = 0; }
};

void bee(A *pa)
{
    A a;
    a.fn();   // known type; use inline version
    pa->fn(); // pa could point at anything; use virtual function call
}
```

It's easy to confuse polymorphism with simple hiding. When a derived class redefines a virtual function from its base class, polymorphism applies. When a base class and a derived class each have a function with the same arguments but the function isn't declared as *virtual* in the base, ordinary scope rules apply. This example illustrates both cases:

```
#include <iostream.h>

class B {
    public:
        virtual void fa(void) { cout << "B::fa\n"; }
                void fb(void) { cout << "B::fb\n"; }
};

class D : public B {
    public:
        void fa(void) { cout << "D::fa\n"; }     // polymorphic fa()
        void fb(void) { cout << "D::fb\n"; }     // hides B::fb()
};

void main()
{       // two B* pointers
        B *pb = new B;
        B *pd = new D;

    /*1*/ cout << "B* pointer, B object\n";
    /*2*/ pb->fa();            // polymorphism; invoke B::fa()
    /*3*/ pb->fb();            // scope rules; invoke B::fb()
    /*4*/ cout << "B* pointer, D object\n";
    /*5*/ pd->fa();            // polymorphism; invoke D::fa()
    /*6*/ pd->B::fa();         // explicit; invoke B::fa()
    /*7*/ pd->fb();            // scope rules; invoke B::fb()
    /*8*/ ((D *)pd)->fb();     // explicit; invoke D::fb()
}
```

Note that both pointers are declared to be pointers to *B* objects, although only *pb* actually points at a *B* object; *pd* points at a *D* object. Because *fa()* is a virtual function, the actual type of object determines which *fa()* function is invoked unless an explicit override is used. Because *fb()* is an ordinary function, scope rules determine which *fb()* is called. This table explains in more detail what happens in the example above:

Line	*Output*	*Rationale*
/*1*/	B* pointer, B object	
/*2*/	B::fa()	Polymorphism. A pointer is pointing at a *B*, so *B*'s *fa()* is invoked.
/*3*/	B::fb()	Scope rules. A *B** pointer is being used, so *B*'s *fb()* is called.
/*4*/	B* pointer, D object	
/*5*/	D::fa()	Polymorphism. A pointer is pointing at a *D*, so *D*'s *fa()* is invoked. The type of the pointer is irrelevant.
/*6*/	B::fa()	Explicit override of polymorphism. The *B::* scope resolution operator specifies that *B*'s *fa()* should be called.
/*7*/	B::fb()	Scope rules. A *B** pointer is being used, so *B*'s *fb()* is called. The type of the object is irrelevant.
/*8*/	D::fb()	Explicit override of scope rules. The *B** pointer is cast to a *D** pointer, so *D*'s *fb()* is called.

It is a confusing practice to have functions of the same names and signatures in both a base class and a derived class unless they are polymorphic. Polymorphism is expected, useful, and powerful and should be used routinely. Hiding base class members in a derived class is usually unexpected and too subtle and should generally be avoided.

You need to understand what happens when object arguments from classes with polymorphic functions are passed to functions. There are just three cases to consider: functions that take objects as arguments, functions that take pointers to objects as arguments, and functions that take references to objects as arguments. This example shows all three situations:

```
void fobj(B b)    { b.fa();    }        // fobj--object as argument
void fptr(B *pb) { pb->fa(); }          // fptr--pointer to object
                                        //  as argument
void fref(B& rb) { rb.fa();  }          // fref--reference to object
                                        //  as argument

void f()
{
    D d;
    fobj(d);
    fptr(&d);
    fref(d);
}
```

When *d* is passed to *fobj()*, its *D* personality (that is, its *D* elements) is left behind and it becomes a *B* object, and inside *fobj()* the base class's *fa()* is invoked. When *&d* is passed to *fptr()*, it continues to point at a *D* object, and inside *fptr()* *D*'s *fa()* is invoked. The third case is surprising to some programmers. When a reference to *d* is passed to *fref()*, the *p* reference inside *fref()* refers to a *D*, even though it is declared to be a reference to *B*. Thus, inside *fref()*, the *D* class's *fa()* is invoked.

Here is another way to look at the example. The function *fobj()* has its own *B* object, with its own pointer to the *B* class virtual function dispatch table. When *d* is passed to *fobj()*, its *B* members are copied into *d*, and then from that point forward *fobj()* is using a pure *B* object. In the other two cases, *fptr()* and *fref()*, the function reaches out to the existing *D* object and uses the existing *D* object's virtual function dispatch table, which results in *D* behavior.

It is possible for a virtual function to have different accessibility in base and derived classes. The rule that resolves this dilemma is simple: Accessibility is checked at the point at which the virtual function is invoked.

```
class B {
    public:
        virtual void f() {}
};

class D : public B {
    private:
        virtual void f() {}
};

void g()
{
    B b;
    D d;
    b.f();     // OK; B's f() is public
    d.f();     // no good; D's f() is private
    B* pb = &d;
    pb->f();  // OK; B's f() is public, but D's f() will be invoked
    D* pd = &d;
    pd->f();  // no good; D's f() is private
}
```

In this example, virtual function *f()* can be invoked using a *B* object, or using a pointer to a *B* object, because it is a public *B* member function. This rule holds even when a pointer whose type is *B** is actually pointing at a *D* object. What matters is the type of the pointer, not the type of the object it is pointing at. Virtual function *f()* can't be invoked using a *D* object, or using a pointer to a *D* object, because it is a private *D* member function.

Abstract Base Classes

An abstract class is one designed solely to serve as a basis for other classes; creating an object from such a class makes no sense. The major role of an abstract class is to create an interface for a family of classes. C++ doesn't have a keyword to indicate that a class is an abstract class. Instead, you implicitly state that a class is abstract by creating a pure virtual function within the class:

```
class A {
    virtual void f() = 0;
};
```

The *f()* function is a pure virtual function because of the *=0* that follows its header. An ordinary class member function must be defined either in the class definition or elsewhere. A pure virtual function doesn't need to be defined in the class definition or elsewhere because it will be defined in a derived class. The notation *= 0* is reminiscent of assigning the value *0* to a pointer.

Because class *A* has a pure virtual function, it can't be instantiated. This is illegal:

```
A a;
```

And these somewhat more hopeful declarations are illegal too:

```
A get_a(void);
void put_a(A a);
```

The lack of true abstract class objects doesn't impede our ability to have pointers to or references to abstract class objects. So all of this is legal:

```
A *a
A& get_a(void);
void put_a(A& a);
```

In derived classes, all pure virtual functions in the base class must be fully defined. If they aren't, the derived classes are themselves abstract classes.

An obscure feature of pure virtual functions is worth mentioning, although I have serious doubts about the advisability of its use. The declaration of a pure virtual function specifies that there is no default definition for the pure virtual function, so it can't be accessed using the virtual function dispatch table. It is still possible to define a body for a pure virtual function, although the function can be used only by calling it explicitly. For example, given the declaration of *f()* as a pure virtual above, it is still possible to supply a definition for *f()* in class *A*:

```
void A::f(void) {
    // body of f()
}
```

To use this version of *f()*, you must call it explicitly. Inside an *A* member function, you could call it by writing

```
A::f();
```

Given a pointer to an *A*, you would have to write

```
objptr->A::f();
```

I can imagine wanting this sort of capability, but instead of using the confusing and obscure tactic of supplying a definition for a pure virtual function, it would be better to invent a new name for a new member function.

Multiple Base Classes

All of the uses of inheritance we've looked at so far—and the great majority of uses of inheritance in practical code—deal with single inheritance. In single inheritance, each derived class inherits the features of a single base class. In multiple inheritance, a derived class has multiple base classes from which it inherits features.

When a class is derived from multiple base classes, it has an *is a* relationship with each of its base classes. Inheriting from multiple base classes is sometimes called "mixing in" because the characteristics of the base classes are combined to create the derived class.

Let's first look at a few simple examples that demonstrate the mechanics of multiple inheritance and then conclude with a more detailed look at the organization of the iostream library we looked at briefly in Chapter 4. It is probably the best known C++ facility that relies on multiple inheritance.

The syntax for deriving a class from multiple base classes is a straightforward extension of single inheritance syntax:

```
class B1 {
    public:
        double d;
};
class B2 {
    public:
        double d;
};

class MI : public B1, public B2 {
    public:
        double d;
};
```

This is the simplest possible example of multiple inheritance. It states that class *MI* is derived from base classes *B1* and *B2*. Both base classes are public, which means that their protected elements are protected and their public elements are public in public *MI* objects. In multiple inheritance, as in single, the default access level for the base classes is private. And as in single inheritance, it is a good idea to explicitly specify either *public* or *private* for each base class, just to remove all doubt.

A class that is derived from multiple base classes still *is* each of the public base classes from which it is derived, and it can be used in any context that requires one of its public base class objects (or a pointer or a reference to an object of one of its base classes). This easy-to-describe trait is not so easy for a compiler to implement in a multiple inheritance situation. In single inheritance, a derived class pointer can be converted to a base class pointer without fuss because the base class always resides at the beginning of the object. Similarly, a pointer to, say, *MI* can easily be converted to a pointer to *B1* because *B1* is at the beginning of *MI*. But what about conversions to *B2*? The difficulty is that *B2* isn't at the beginning of *MI*. To make casting work, the compiler must adjust the pointer to *MI* by the offset of *B2* each time it converts a *MI** into a *B2**. The opposite conversion, from *B2** to *MI**, which can be done only by using an explicit cast, requires the opposite adjustment. These adjustments are shown in this example:

```
#include <iostream.h>

void needB1(B1 *b)        // requires a pointer to a B1
{
    cout << "&MI::B1  " << (unsigned)b << '\n';
}
void needB2(B2 *b)        // requires a pointer to a B2
{
    cout << "&MI::B2  " << (unsigned)b << '\n';
}

void main(void)
{
    MI m;
    cout << "&m       " << (unsigned)&m << '\n';
    needB1(&m);           // automatic conversion of MI object
                          //  to B1 object
    needB2(&m);           // automatic conversion of MI object
                          //  to B2 object
}
```

The output of the program looks like this:[4]

```
&m        9022
&MI::B1  9022
&MI::B2  9030
```

The interesting output is the second and third lines, which are printed by the functions *needB1()* and *needB2()*. They show that when a pointer to an *MI* object is converted to a pointer to a *B1*, its value is unchanged. But when a pointer to an *MI* object is converted to a pointer to a *B2*, its numeric value is increased by 8, which is the offset of *B2* inside *MI*.

Because even simple examples of multiple inheritance are a bit lengthy, I decided to make the example we've just looked at do double duty. Notice that all three of *MI*'s members are named *d*. This is a name collision of the first magnitude. Here is how it's straightened out. The name *m.d* refers to the native *d* member of *MI*, the member that isn't inherited from a base class. If you want to refer to the inherited

4. The size of a *double*, which is also the size of class *B1* and of class *B2*, is 8.

d members, you need to use the scope resolution operator, as shown in this example, to specify either the *B1* or the *B2 d* member:

```
#include <iostream.h>

void main(void)
{
    MI m;
    cout << "&m.B1::d " << (unsigned)&m.B1::d << '\n';
    cout << "&m.B2::d " << (unsigned)&m.B2::d << '\n';
    cout << "&m.d     " << (unsigned)&m.d << '\n';
}
```

Here is the output:

```
&m.B1::d 9022
&m.B2::d 9030
&m.d     9038
```

Multiple Inheritance and the iostream Library

The most widely known example of multiple inheritance is found in the iostream library, which was originally developed by Jerry Schwarz at AT&T. We'll take up the use and design of the iostream library in Chapter 12, but in this chapter we'll look specifically at the library's use of multiple inheritance.

Figure 9-3 shows a simplified diagram of the iostream library.

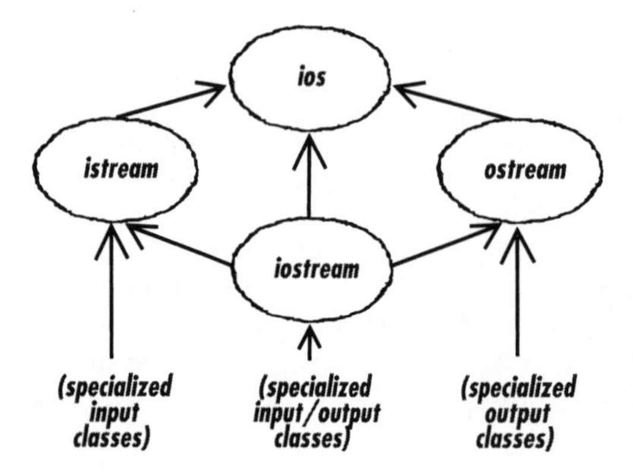

Figure 9-3.
A simplified diagram of the iostream *class hierarchy.*

The base class for the library is *ios*, which defines symbolic constants, stores status and format information, and contains a pointer to a *streambuf* class that is used for the unformatted input and output. Actual input and output operations are absent from *ios*; they are provided by the derived *istream* and *ostream* classes. The *istream* class contains a set of operations for input from a stream, and *ostream* contains stream output operations.

Using separate classes for input and output prevents opening a file for reading and then writing, but sometimes we need a true read and write, input and output connection. One possibility would be to derive a read/write class from *ios*, but that would duplicate much of the work in *istream* and *ostream*. Instead, the read/write class, called *iostream*, is multiply derived from *istream* and *ostream*. This provides an *iostream* with all the facilities of *istream*, *ostream*, and *ios*. An *iostream is an istream*, *is an ostream*, and *is an ios*.

Another important aspect of the *iostream* hierarchy is the fact that *istream* and *ostream* are both virtually derived from *ios*. This ensures that each *iostream* object will contain only one copy of *ios*—appropriate for the iostream library because *ios* contains status information and other elements that should be shared in an *iostream*.

Virtual Base Classes

The first rule of multiple inheritance has to be that a derived class can't inherit more than once from a single class, at least not directly. Thus the following, which might be the simplest illegal example of multiple inheritance, is not allowed:

```
class B {
    // B members
};
class D : public B, public B {
    // D members
};
```

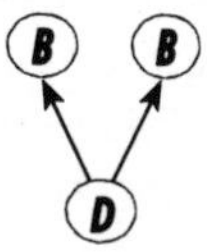

B B
D

This isn't allowed because there is no way in class *D* to distinguish between the two *B* classes that the new class *D* is based on.

You might think that simple subterfuge could achieve the same result. In the following, class *D* tries to disguise the double inheritance from *B* by making one of the derivations from *B* indirect. This isn't allowed because there is no way to disambiguate the direct base *B* of *B1* from the indirect base *B1*:

```
class B {
    // B members
};
class B1 : public B {
    // B1 members
};
class D: public B, public B1 {
    // D members
};
```

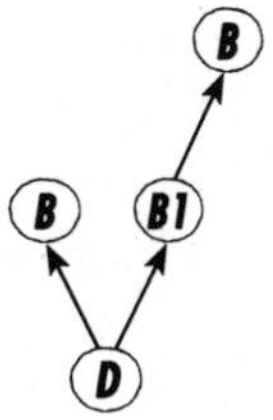

B
B B1
D

But a class can be derived twice or more from a single class, provided that none of the derivations are direct. Thus the derivation shown on the next page is allowed.

```
class B {
    // B members
};
class B1 : public B {
    // B1 members
};
class B2 : public B {
    // B2 members
};
class D: public B1, public B2 {
    // D members
};
```

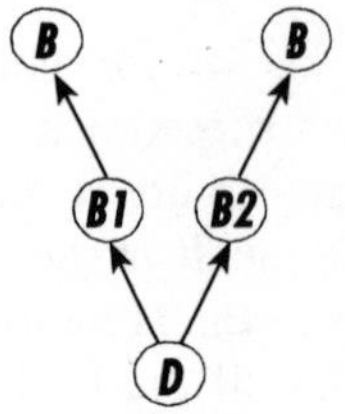

A diagram for a family of classes related by single inheritance always resembles a tree. In single inheritance, a single path always leads from a derived class back to an ultimate root class. Multiple inheritance destroys the resemblance of a class family diagram to a tree. A diagram of classes related by multiple inheritance can resemble the family trees of the crown princes of Europe. The current crown prince of some principality might have two or three separate lines of inheritance leading back, say, to Bismarck. The same can be true for classes. A class might be derived from a given class by means of several paths.

The first potential problem that might spring to mind is naming, but conventional use of the scope resolution operator can manage most naming problems. The real problem is controlling the number of copies of a multiple ancestor present in a derived class. If class *B* is derived from class *A* by means of two separate paths, should there be two copies of *A* inside *B* or only one?

Consider this simple class hierarchy, in which *D* is derived from *A* along two separate paths:

```
class A {
    public:
        double d;
};
class B1 : public A {
    public:
        double d;
};
class B2 : public A {
    public:
        double d;
};
class D: public B1, public B2 {
    public:
        double d;
};
```

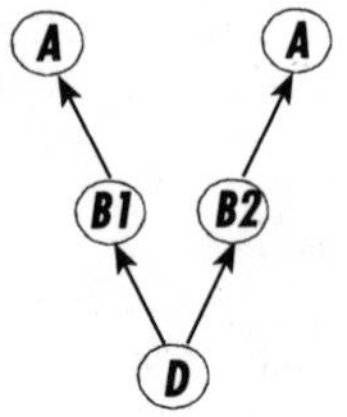

The layout in memory that we might expect for *D* objects is shown in Figure 9-4.

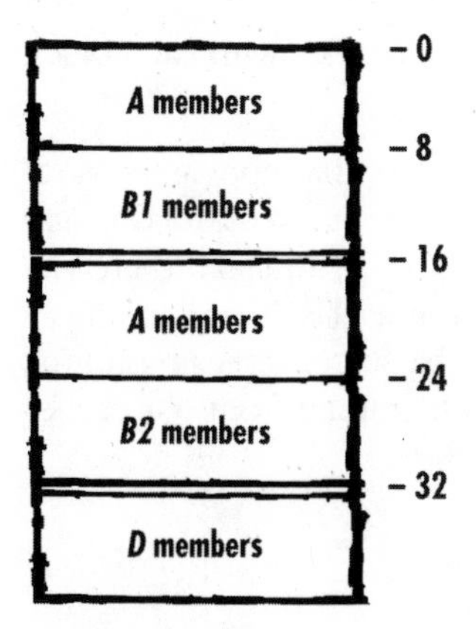

Figure 9-4.
Class D *is shown inheriting twice from class* A, *by means of class* B1 *and of class* B2.

The class *A* member should appear twice because class *D* has two derivation paths to *A*. We can verify that the expected layout is actually used with the following simple test program. This program also shows us how to use the scope resolution operator combined with casting to manage the fivefold name conflict—every element is named *d*.

```
#include <iostream.h>
void main()
{
    D der;
    cout << &der <<
        " & D" << endl;
    cout << &((B1 *)(&der))->A::d <<
        " & d member of A base of B1 base of D" << endl;
    cout << &der.B1::d <<
        " & d member of B1 base of D" << endl;
    cout << &((B2 *)(&der))->A::d <<
        " & d member of A base of B2 base of D" << endl;
    cout << &der.B2::d <<
        " & d member of B2 base of D" << endl;
    cout << &der.d <<
        " & d member of D" << endl;
}
```

Here's the output of the program, which prints the address of every element in a *D* object:

```
0x0D00 & D
0x0D00 & d member of A base of B1 base of D
0x0D08 & d member of B1 base of D
0x0D10 & d member of A base of B2 base of D
0x0D18 & d member of B2 base of D
0x0D20 & d member of D
```

Our suspicions are confirmed. The class is simply a stack of blocks, with each block a double.

Sometimes we don't want to have two copies of a base class that appears several times in a class diagram. We want only a single copy. In C++, we can control duplication by using "virtual derivation." When several classes (*B*, *C*, *D*, and so on) are virtually derived from *A*, there will be only one copy of *A* in a class that is multiply derived from *A*'s descendants (*B*, *C*, *D*, and so on). That last sentence is a mouthful, but the example is really quite simple. Here is the class hierarchy from our earlier example, repeated now with virtual derivation:

```
class A {
    public:
        double d;
};
class B1 : public virtual A {
    public:
        double d;
};
class B2 : public virtual A {
    public:
        double d;
};
class D: public B1, public B2 {
    public:
        double d;
};
```

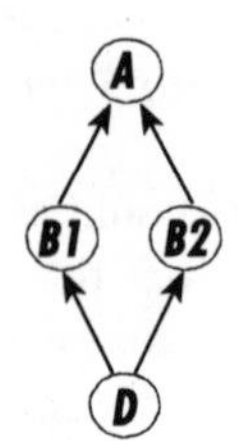

When our earlier address printing program is executed with virtual derivation, in which *B1* and *B2* are virtually derived from *A*, the output looks like this:

```
0x0D14 & D
0x0D30 & d member of A base of B1 base of D
0x0D16 & d member of B1 base of D
0x0D30 & d member of A base of B2 base of D
0x0D20 & d member of B2 base of D
0x0D28 & d member of D
```

There are no longer two copies of *A*. Instead, there is a single *A* group of members at the end of *D*. The virtual inheritance of *A* leads to the layout of *D* shown in Figure 9-5.

The other thing to notice is that the sizes of both *B1* and *B2* have grown to 10 bytes from their previous 8. The extra 2 bytes are for a pointer to an *A*, which is needed because the *A* part of classes that are virtually derived from *A* (for example, *B1* and *B2*) can be almost anywhere.

I've already mentioned that when a class is virtually derived from a base class, the derived class contains a pointer to its virtual base class, which allows the derived class to access its base class elements and which is used when the derived class is converted to or cast to its virtual base type. However, the reverse isn't true; a virtual

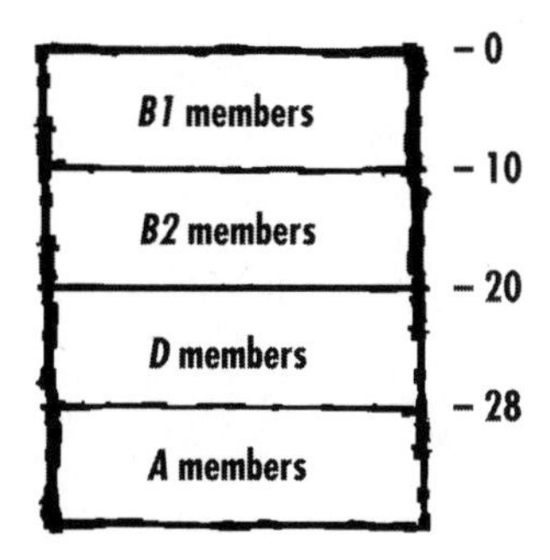

Figure 9-5.
Virtual inheritance. Because class B1 *and class* B2 *are virtually derived from class* A, *the members they inherit from class* A *are not duplicated in the derived class* D.

base class object doesn't contain a pointer to the derived class object. The main practical result of this is that it is impossible, no matter what casting magic you try, to convert a virtual base class object to a derived class object type. The issue isn't casting; the issue is that a virtual base class object simply doesn't know where the rest of the derived class object members are stored, and it has no way to find out. This is illustrated in the next example, which reuses *B1* and *A* from our earlier examples.

```
void main(void)
{
    B1 b;
    A a;

    a = b;               // OK; a B1 is an A
    A *pa = new B1;      // OK; a B1* is an A*
    b = *(B1 *)pa;       // no good; impossible to cast up
                         //  from virtual base
}
```

Initialization and Constructors

One major virtue of C++ programs is reliability, and a major tool for achieving reliability is the constructor member function. The constructor initializes the class objects. It turns raw, uninitialized memory into an object that has the class's properties and characteristic behavior. In this chapter, we'll look at a number of C++ rules pertaining to initialization, constructors, and derivation. We'll look at other aspects of constructors in Chapter 10.

Stand-Alone Class Constructors

When a class is created without derivation, there are only two kinds of constructors to consider: the constructor for the class itself and the constructors for the class members. The rule is that the members are constructed first and then the class constructor is executed. The simple example on the next page illustrates the rule.

```
#include <iostream.h>

class A {
    public:
        A() { cout << "A constructor\n"; }
};
class B {
    public:
        B() { cout << "B constructor\n"; }
};
class C {
    public:
        A a;            // A member object
        B b;            // B member object
        C() { cout << "C constructor\n"; }
};
C c;    // create a C object
```

When the object named *c* is constructed, this series of messages is displayed:

```
A constructor
B constructor
C constructor
```

This confirms the rule: Members of a class are constructed before the class constructor is executed. This is important because it means that inside the class constructor you can rely on class members to be full-fledged, working objects. If members weren't constructed first, it would be problematic for a constructor to access members.

Derived Class Constructors

When one class is derived from another, the order of construction allows for construction of the base class first:

1. Base class constructors
2. Member constructors
3. The class's own constructor

The rule is illustrated by this example:

```
class A {
    public:
        A() { cout << "A constructor\n"; }
};
class B {
    public:
        B() { cout << "B constructor\n"; }
};
```

```
class C {
    public:
        C() { cout << "C constructor\n"; }
};
class D : A {       // D is derived from A
    public:
        B c;        // B member object
        C c;        // C member object
        D() { cout << "D constructor\n"; }
};
D d;      // create a D object
```

When the *D* object *d* is created, these messages appear:

```
A constructor
B constructor
C constructor
D constructor
```

This demonstrates the rule for derived classes: base construction first, then member construction, and then finally class construction.

In the section of Chapter 8 on constructors and destructors, we looked at the syntax for initializing the members of a class by putting an initialization list after the constructor header. Here is the *D* constructor from our example above, rewritten to explicitly construct its *B* and *C* members by means of an initialization list:

```
D::D() :
    b(),      // b member object default constructor
    c()       // c member object default constructor
{
    cout << "D constructor\n";
}
```

But constructor initialization lists aren't just for members; they are also for base classes. The one small difficulty is that the base class part of a derived object doesn't have a name as members do. Therefore, when you use an initialization list to pass arguments to a base class constructor, the base class's name is used in the initialization list. Here is the example with a richer set of constructors, and also with more explicit invocation of the constructors:

```
class A {
    public:
        A()        { cout << "A default constructor\n"; }
        A(char *p) { cout << "A (char *) constructor\n"; }
};
class B {
    public:
        B()       { cout << "B default constructor\n"; }
        B(int i)  { cout << "B (int) constructor\n"; }
};
```

```
class D : B {
    public:
        A aone, atwo;
        D();            // D default constructor
        D(char *p);     // D (char *) constructor
        D(int i);       // D (int) constructor
};
```

This example shows the constructors for classes *A* and *B* but not those for *D*. Class *A* has two constructors: a default constructor and a constructor that takes a *char ** parameter. An *A* constructor taking a *char ** parameter is often referred to as an *A (char *)* constructor. Class *B* also has two constructors: a default constructor and a constructor that takes an *int* parameter, a *B (int)* constructor.

When you declare an ordinary class *A* object, you can invoke either of the constructors:[5]

```
A x;                // construct an A object using default constructor
A y("string");      // construct an A object using A (char *) constructor
```

But when you declare an *A* member object in another class, the choice of the *A* constructor occurs not when the *A* object is mentioned in the class definition but in the initialization list of the derived class's constructor. (If the derived class doesn't have a constructor, each object class must have a default constructor.) This is best illustrated by the definition of the *D* default constructor:

```
// D default constructor
D::D() :
    aone(),         // A default constructor for aone member
    atwo("kari"),   // A (char *) constructor for atwo member
    B(0)            // base class B (int) constructor
{ cout << "D default constructor\n"; }
```

The initialization list for the *D* default constructor initializes both members of *D* and the base part of *D*: The member object *aone* is initialized using the default class *A* constructor, the member object *atwo* is initialized using the *A (char *)* constructor, and the *B* base part of *D* is initialized using the *B (int)* constructor.

When the definition is executed:

```
D d1;
```

these messages are printed:

---

5. Note that the declaration *A x();* specifies that *x* is a function taking no arguments that returns an *A* object; it does not create an *A* object named *x* using the default constructor. Use the declaration *A x;* to create an *A* object named *x* using the default constructor.

```
B (int) constructor
A default constructor
A (char *) constructor
D default constructor
```

Here are the definitions of the remaining two *D* constructors:

```
D::D(char *p) :        // D (char *) constructor
    aone(),            // class A default constructor for aone member
    atwo(p),           // class A (char *) constructor for atwo member
    B()                // base class default constructor
{ cout << "D (char *) constructor\n"; }

D::D(int i) :          // D (int) constructor
    aone(),            // class A default constructor for aone member
    atwo("i*2"),       // class A (char *) constructor for atwo member
    B(i*2)             // base class B (int) constructor
{ cout << "D (int) constructor\n"; }
```

You should examine the constructors above so that you understand the interaction between these constructors and the member and base class constructors.

When the two class *D* objects are created:

```
D d2("reed");
D d3(0);
```

these messages are displayed:

```
B default constructor
A default constructor
A (char *) constructor
D (char *) constructor

B (int) constructor
A default constructor
A (char *) constructor
D (int) constructor
```

C++'s rules for the order of initialization are actually somewhat more complex than our brief survey indicates. The point of having precise rules is to allow you to write code that relies on the order of initialization. The technique of relying on the order of initialization is subtle. When you write code that relies on the order of initialization, you need to be careful to explain your assumptions, in comments. Wherever possible, create classes that are insensitive to the order of initialization. For the occasional situation in which you must rely on initialization order, here it is exactly, from first to last:

1. Virtual base classes, as encountered on a depth-first, left-to-right evaluation of the inheritance graph

2. Base classes, in left-to-right order

3. Member objects, in the order of their declarations in the class definition
4. The class constructor

Notice that this list doesn't mention the order of the initializers in the class constructor. That order is irrelevant; only the order of member object declarations in the class definition and the order of base class declarations in the class definition are used. This makes it possible to ensure that class destructors are always called in an order opposite the constructors' order.

Another, somewhat esoteric, rule governs virtual member functions. It is permissible to invoke virtual member functions from a constructor, but you will always get the base class's own version of the function, not the derived class's version of the function, because base classes are constructed first. When a virtual member function is called from a constructor, only the base class's own members are guaranteed present and operational.

Access Declarations

You can relax the access rules for private base classes by using "access declarations." When class *D* is privately derived from class *B*, the protected and public members of *B* become private members of *D*. That's the whole point of private derivation: to severely restrict access to the base class members.

An access declaration has but a single role, to restore the original protected or public access privilege to a selected member of a privately derived class. Two other likely seeming roles for access declarations are not legal: An access declaration cannot be used to reduce the accessibility of any member; nor can an access declaration be used to increase the visibility of a private or inaccessible base class member—only the visibility of protected or public base class members.

Caveat

My inclination is to avoid access declarations in favor of using public base class members. To me, access declarations seem to be an excessive fine-tuning of a system that already allows tight control of accessibility. For much the same reason, I rarely use private derivation. The original class definition seems like the correct place in which to specify how the class's members can be accessed, and when I make those decisions, I always assume that derived classes will be publicly derived. Don't use private derivation to control access; rather, make members in the base class protected and private as necessary to ensure the class operation you want.

To write an access declaration, write the fully qualified name of the base class member in the protected or public section of the derived class. You can't specify a type, and that prevents an access declaration from looking like an ordinary declaration. This example shows how two members of base class *B* are restored to their original accessibility inside privately derived class *D*:

```
class B {
    protected:
        int pro1, pro2;
    public:
        int pub1, pub2;
        int pubfn(int);
};

class D : private B {
    protected:
        B::pro1;  // access declaration; make pro1 protected
    public:
        B::pub1;  // access declaration; make pub1 public
        B::pubfn; // access declaration; make pubfn() public
        // pro2 and pub2 are not mentioned, hence are private
};
```

Inside class *D*, base class members *pro2* and *pub2* are private because *B* is a private base class. But because of the two access declarations in *D*, base class member *pro1* is restored to protected status, and *pub1* is restored to public status.

The new accessibilities are demonstrated in this code:

```
void main(void)
{
    D d;
    d.pub1 = 1;     // OK; declared accessible
    d.pubfn(1);     // OK; declared accessible
    d.pub2 = 1;     // no good; member of private base class
}
```

There is a strong temptation to mention types in an access declaration. It is seductive, but wrong, to write the access declarations in this style:

```
class D : private B {
    protected:
        int B::pro1;        // wrong; don't mention type
    public:
        int B::pub1;        // wrong; don't mention type
        int B::pubfn(int);  // wrong; don't mention type
};
```

Access declarations can't be used when overloaded functions have different original accessibilities because at least one of the access restorations will be incorrect. For essentially the same reason, access declarations also can't be applied when a derived class name hides a base class name.

10

Constructors and Destructors

Constructors and destructors are key players in C++. They give you control as objects are created and destroyed, in the sense that you can rely on the behavior of your objects. Without constructors and destructors, it would be impossible for a class to guarantee the behavior of its objects. It would be easy to forget to perform necessary initializations and cleanup. Constructors and destructors are written as class member functions, and in a literal sense, they are optional. Classes are not required to have either constructors or destructors, but it is hard to imagine a class that would be useful for object-oriented programming that wouldn't have at least a constructor.

Constructors and destructors fully observe the C++ member access control system, and you should pay careful attention to the accessibility of constructors and destructors; reducing accessibility gives you even greater control over how and when objects are created. However, because of their special roles, constructors and destructors don't obey exactly the same rules that other member functions do. Appendix E presents the constructor activation order, some of the caveats for constructors and destructors, and the various forms of constructor usage.

A constructor turns raw, uninitialized memory into an object. When the body of a constructor starts to execute, memory has been allocated for the object, and like other member functions, the constructor is passed a *this* pointer. But the constructor's *this* pointer is pointing at raw memory, not at a fully formed object whose behavior is the same as the behavior of a finished object. The constructor goes on to initialize members, allocate additional memory, and so forth, in order to create the relationships among the members that differentiate an object from a storage region.

Classes can, and usually do, have multiple constructors. One reason for having multiple constructors is to allow different types to be used to initialize an object. For example, a complex number class might define a trio of constructors so that it could be initialized by a *double* (the real part), or by a pair of *double*s (the real and imaginary parts), or by another complex number.

Yet another reason for having multiple constructors is that certain constructors have specialized roles. For example, a "default constructor," a constructor that doesn't have any arguments, is needed for a variety of situations in which objects are created but their initial values aren't specified explicitly. Similarly, a "copy constructor," a constructor that makes a copy of an existing object, is used when an object is initialized by an existing object of the same type, when an object is passed by value to a function, and when an object is returned from a function.

Default Constructors

The simplest initialization of an object is performed by the "default constructor," which answers the question, "What value should an object have when the user doesn't specify a value?" If class *X* has a default constructor, this declaration will use it to create and initialize an *X* object:

```
X x;
```

The initial state of *x* is determined by the default constructor.

The default constructor is also used in these situations:

- An object is dynamically allocated without the specification of arguments for the constructor.
- An array of objects is dynamically allocated. (The default constructor is invoked for each element of the array.)
- An array of objects is statically allocated, but there are too few initializers (in which case the default constructor is used for the elements that aren't explicitly initialized).
- A base class isn't explicitly initialized in the initialization list of a derived class's constructor.
- A member object isn't explicitly initialized in the initialization list of a class's constructor.

Somewhat paradoxically, a default constructor is allowed to have default arguments:

```
class X {
    // . . .
    X(int n = 0);  // default constructor with default argument
    // . . .
};
```

This constructor is considered a default constructor because it can be invoked without arguments, but it can also be invoked with a single *int* argument. Default arguments can be pointers to members, which makes your job very interesting.

Copy Constructors

A constructor for a class *X* that takes an *X&* argument (a reference to an *X*) is called a "copy constructor." In the following example, object *o1* is created by a default constructor, and then a reference to *o1* is passed to a copy constructor that creates object *o2*:

```
X o1;          // use default constructor to construct o1
X o2 = o1;     // use copy constructor to construct o2
```

The second line could also be written

```
X o2(o1);      // use copy constructor to construct o2
```

When the compiler sees the declaration of *o2*, it searches for a user-written constructor that takes an *X&* argument. If the compiler fails to find one, it builds one for you! Need I say it again? If you don't do it, somebody else (the compiler) will. In either case, the *X&* constructor is used to build a new *X* object from an existing *X* object.

A copy constructor is used in these situations:

- A new object is initialized by an existing object of the same type.
- An object is passed by value to a function.
- An object is returned from a function.

When the compiler creates a copy constructor, it follows these rules:

- The copy constructor is public.
- The copy constructor performs a memberwise initialization, meaning that each member of the new object is initialized by the corresponding member of the existing object.

Consider a class named *A* that has four members named *w*, *x*, *y*, and *z*. If you don't write a copy constructor for *A* but you do write code that would invoke a copy constructor, the compiler will generate a public copy constructor like this one:

```
// copy constructor for class A, whose members are w, x, y, and z
A::A(A &src) :
    w(src.w),     // initialize w
    x(src.x),     // initialize x
    y(src.y),     // initialize y
    z(src.z)      // initialize z
{ }
```

Note that each member, *w*, *x*, *y*, and *z*, will be initialized by its own copy constructor, and so forth, until the end of the chain is reached.

You might choose to override the compiler's copy constructor and instead write your own for any one of three reasons.

- You want a private or protected copy constructor.
- You want something other than memberwise initialization.
- You want to pass additional arguments to a copy constructor.

A copy constructor is closely related to *operator=()* because both are used to give one object the "same" value as another. The difference is that a copy constructor is part of the initialization process but *operator=()* is used for assignment. I put the word "same" in quotation marks because different classes have different notions of similarity. Although having an identical bit pattern in memory is one obvious definition of "same," it is not the only possibility. This whole issue, which is referred to as "deep copy vs. shallow copy," is discussed thoroughly in Chapter 11.

Conversion Constructors

A "conversion constructor" is a constructor that builds an object of one type from an object of another type. It allows us to specify how conversion operations are performed. We've already seen conversion constructors used to create and initialize objects. In the circular number example in Chapter 3, there was a constructor that created a circular number object from an integer. This *int* to circular number constructor can be used to create *Circnum* objects:

```
Circnum c = 90;
Circnum d = Circnum(180);
Circnum e(360);
```

When you declare data, you can use all three forms. What we haven't seen is that the *int* to *Circnum* constructor can also be used in expressions to specify conversions. For example, the following creates two *Circnum* object temporaries, which are then compared using the *Circnum* class's *operator<()* member function.

```
if (Circnum(90) < Circnum(360))     // use Circnum::operator<()
    // action
```

You might remember that in Chapter 3's example *90* lies in the counterclockwise direction from *360* (shortest path), so the result of the expression is *false*. Without the explicit conversions from *int* to *Circnum*, the built-in *int* comparison would generate the opposite result.

Let's look at the mechanics of an expression that involves explicit conversions. When the C++ compiler generates the code for the conversion, it performs these steps:

```
Circnum tmp1 = Circnum(90)     // constructor
Circnum tmp2 = Circnum(360)    // constructor
if (tmp1.operator< (tmp2))      // comparison
    // action
tmp1.~Circnum()                // destructor
tmp2.~Circnum()                // destructor
```

Circular Whole Numbering System

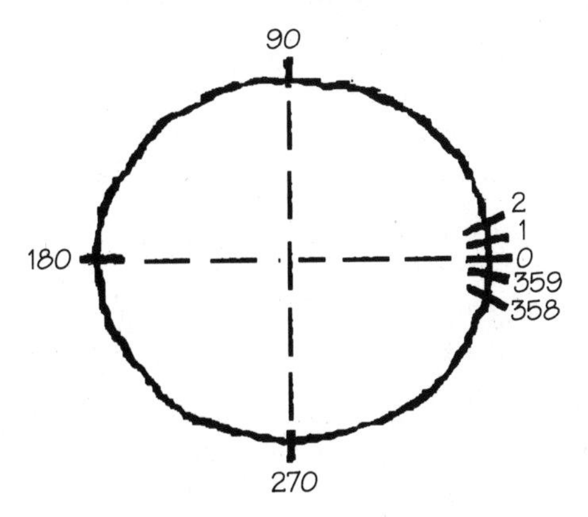

Because the temporaries must be constructed and then destroyed, potentially this is a high-overhead operation. The whole point of C++ is to facilitate operations on objects, such as the comparison of two *Circnum* constants. But when you are designing objects, you have to consider the overhead of common operations.

Let's push this point one step further. The comparisons above could be used to determine which quadrant (which quarter of the unit circle) contains a given *Circnum* object:

```
Circnum c;
. . .    // c attains some value
if (c >= Circnum(0) && c < Circnum(90))
    // first quadrant action
else if (c >= Circnum(90) && c < Circnum(180))
    // second quadrant action
// and so on
```

As you might imagine, the code for the cascaded *if* sketched out above will be monumentally inefficient, even with inline expansion of the constructors and the comparisons. If quadrant testing were to be an important use of circular numbers, it would be better written as a fundamental operation of the *Circnum* class. Or you could derive a new class from *Circnum* that supported the notion of quadrants. Either alternative would allow for a far more efficient and reliable implementation of quadrant testing.

Destructors

A destructor is a class member function that is invoked each time an object goes out of scope. A destructor is the reverse of a constructor. The destructor gives you control over the disassembly of an object. Typical destructor chores are to deallocate memory, to decrease reference counts, to uninstall interrupt handlers, to output messages, to save data in files, and the like. Although some simple and useful classes don't require destructors, most elaborate and tightly controlled classes do rely on destructors.

There is only a single destructor for a class. Destructors cannot be overloaded, they cannot be given arguments, and they cannot return a value. In C++, a destructor for a class named *X* is created by writing a class member function whose name is *~X()*.

But having only a single destructor for a class doesn't mean that only one destructor is invoked when an object is destroyed. The destruction of an object implies the destruction of its class's base class and its class's member objects, always in exact reverse of the order of construction. (See Appendix B for the order of construction.)

Destructors are similar to constructors in that they don't need to worry about memory deallocation for the object itself. That is taken care of automatically unless you choose to override *operator delete()* for the class. Each destructor is given a valid *this* pointer, and at the time that each destructor is invoked, the class's base class and all of the class's member objects have not yet been destroyed.

Destructors aren't usually invoked explicitly, although that is permitted. The usual reason a destructor is invoked is that the compiler notices that an object (of a class with a destructor) is going out of scope. This happens in several different ways:

- A dynamically allocated object is deleted.
- A local object goes out of scope because a block or function is exited.
- The program completes execution, which causes all of its global objects to go out of scope.
- A compiler-generated temporary object is no longer needed.

Note that a dynamically allocated object that isn't deleted is never destroyed. To require the compiler to implement the destruction of dynamically allocated objects would force it to keep much more detailed information about memory allocation than it currently keeps. If you need to ensure that dynamically allocated objects of a given class are always deleted when the program exits, you must write the code for that yourself. You might create a simple helper class (*Xhelper*, for example) that maintains a list of undeleted *X* objects. The *X* constructors and destructor must of course cooperate by notifying *Xhelper* as *X* objects are created and destroyed. When the program starts to exit, the *Xhelper* destructor would automatically go through its list, invoking *X* destructors as needed.

Virtual Destructors

The whole premise that underlies having a single destructor for a class is that at the time of destruction, everything is well known and it is up to the destructor to figure out exactly what needs to be done to clean up. An aspect of class design for some classes involves figuring out what information needs to be retained so that a destructor can do its job.

This idea is sound but for one major flaw, which is illustrated in this example:

```
#include <iostream.h>
class B {
    protected:
        B() { cout << "B constructor\n"; }
        ~B() { cout << "B destructor\n"; }
};
class D : public B{
    private:
        char *buf;
    public:
        D() :     // D constructor; allocate buffer
            buf(new char[1000])
        {
            cout << "D constructor\n";
        }
        ~D()      // D destructor; deallocate buffer
        {
            delete buf;
            cout << "D destructor\n";
        }
};

void main()
{
    B *ptr = new D;
    cout << "main\n";
    delete ptr;
}
```

When the program is executed, these messages are printed:

```
B constructor
D constructor
main
B destructor
```

Notice that a 1000-byte buffer was allocated in *D*'s constructor but never deallocated because *D*'s destructor was never invoked.

A commonly suggested solution for this difficulty is to explicitly call *D*'s destructor inside *B*'s destructor, but that is wrong, wrong, wrong. A base class should never (or almost never) have any knowledge of, or interaction with, its derived class.

The problem, stated as clearly as possible, is this: The correct destructor isn't invoked because a pointer to base is used to delete a derived object.

In other situations in which a pointer to base is used to access variant behavior in a derived object, we have used virtual member functions. They are the accepted C++

method for accessing derived class functionality by means of a base class pointer. Thus, to make the example above work the way we'd like, we'd change the base class definition:

```
class B {
    protected:
        B() { cout << "B constructor\n"; }
        virtual ~B() { cout << "B destructor\n"; }
};
```

Making the base class destructor virtual ensures that the derived class destructor is invoked when the object is deleted. In turn, the derived class destructor is guaranteed, by the compiler, to activate destructors for its base class and all of its member objects. When the revised version of the program above is executed, it produces this output:

```
B constructor
D constructor
main
D destructor
B destructor
```

This is the behavior we want. In fact, it is the behavior we almost always want. Nearly all of your destructors should be declared as virtual, so that the correct destructor is always called. You should try to keep in mind this asymmetry of C++:

- Constructors cannot be virtual; nor do they have any reason to be virtual.
- Destructors can be virtual; and they usually should be virtual.

The main reason for making a destructor nonvirtual is to control the layout of a class. Remember that when a class acquires virtual members, it also acquires a hidden pointer to a virtual function dispatch table. Classes that must have a specified size or shape generally shouldn't have virtual members and probably also shouldn't be base classes. If classes with externally imposed layouts do have virtual member functions, you need to be careful—and to realize that what you are doing is very compiler and system dependent.

11

Operator Functions

Most languages, including C, use algebraic notation to express mathematical or computational operations. Two basic ideas enable programming languages to make use of algebraic notation: the notion of the type, which governs the representation of variable operands and intermediate results, and the notion of the operator, a symbol that specifies a certain operation.

In C++, operators are typically "overloaded," so that a single operator symbol can be used to express the same operation on various types. If *a* and *b* are *doubles*, the expression *a+b* is interpreted to mean addition of *doubles*, which might be performed by calling a library routine. But if *i* and *j* are *ints*, the expression *i+j* is interpreted to mean addition of *ints*, which would probably be coded by the compiler directly.

Unary and Binary Operators

In C++, operators can be both unary and binary. A unary operator, such as ++, works with a single operand. A binary operator, such as +, works with two operands.[1] Some operators work with both unary and binary operands, and the same operator symbol can signify different operations depending on whether it's unary or binary. The symbol & means "address of" when it's used as a unary operator but "bitwise AND" when used as a binary operator.

Operator Precedence and Associativity

The other pieces in the operator puzzle are precedence and associativity.

Precedence

Precedence governs the order in which subexpressions will be evaluated. We all learned in school about the precedence of multiplication before addition. The expression *2+3*4* is always interpreted as *2+(3*4)*, or *14*. This is as true in C as it was in grade school.

1. C also accommodates the ?: ternary operator, which takes three operands. The ternary operator is really a control mechanism written as an operator, but because it can't be overloaded, it doesn't concern us here.

Associativity

Associativity governs the order in which subexpressions will be evaluated when they contain operators of equal precedence. Operators commonly have left-to-right associativity but can have right-to-left. Because the subtraction operator has left-to-right associativity, the expression *3–2–1* is interpreted as *(3–2)–1*, or *0*. (If subtraction had right-to-left associativity, the expression *3–2–1* would be interpreted as *3–(2–1)* and evaluate to *2*.)

The Overloadable Operators

Overloading of the built-in operators is so natural that it is useful to step back slightly and think about what the compiler does to create this facility. As the compiler is analyzing an expression, it encounters a series of values (variables and constants) intermixed with operator symbols. When the compiler comes upon an operator, it first determines whether the operator is being used as a unary operator or as a binary operator. Then the compiler attends to precedence and associativity, grouping operators and operands correctly. Finally the compiler determines the types of the operands. Only then does the compiler know whether the expression is legal and, if it is, what code it should generate.

In C, operators work with variables and constants of only the built-in types, and the operator meanings are fixed. In C++, you can define your own meanings for operators and use algebraic notation to express operations on objects of user-defined classes. You can't redefine the meaning of an operator if it's working with only built-in operand types; at least one operand must be an object before you can redefine the meaning of the operator. This restriction prevents you from fundamentally altering the meaning of C++. Another caveat is that the compiler will complain if you neglect to overload an operator and then try to use the operator on an object.

Nearly all of C++'s rich set of operators can be overloaded, including both the unary and the binary forms of operators and the prefix and postfix forms of the increment operators. Appendix B shows all the C++ operators that can be overloaded and the few that can't be.

You might find a few of the overloadable "operators" somewhat surprising:

`()`	Because the function call is overloadable, you can use something resembling function call syntax to perform operations on classes.
`[]`	Because subscripting is overloadable, you can use element-of-array notation to implement operations such as bounds-checked array accesses.
`-> ->*`	Because the indirection operators are overloadable, you can, among other things, use smart pointers that perform more checking than ordinary pointers do.
`new delete`	Because *new* and *delete* are overloadable, you can control storage allocation for a class.

`(type)` You can specify type conversions explicitly. Technically, this is not operator overloading, but explicit type conversions use operator functions and are specified in much the same way as true operator overloading.

`,` The sequential evaluation operator is overloadable.

`=` The assignment operator is overloadable, so you can control object copying.

These operators can't be overloaded:

`?:` The ternary operator can't be overloaded because there is no syntax in C++ for defining a ternary operator.

`.` The member-of operator can't be overloaded. It was thought important to retain its meaning for accessing members.

`.*` The member pointer operator can't be overloaded, primarily because the member-of operator can't be overloaded.

`::` The scope resolution operator can't be overloaded. Syntactically, the scope resolution operator resembles an ordinary operator, but its left operand, when present, is a type name, not an expression.

`sizeof` The *sizeof* operator can't be overloaded. *sizeof* is like the scope resolution operator in that it is an operator in name only.

Various other symbols, such as the preprocessing symbols (# and ##), curly braces, semicolons, and parentheses when they're used to group subexpressions, have been unsuccessfully suggested as overloadable operators.

The major limitation of C++'s operator overloading scheme is that it allows only the existing operators to be overloaded and they retain their historical precedence and associativity. We might imagine a more flexible language, one that would allow user-defined operators and user-defined operator precedence, but C++ is not that imaginary language.

Most operator functions can be defined either as class member functions or as ordinary functions. One difference between class member operator functions and stand-alone operator functions lies in the way each accesses its operands. Figure 11-1 on the next page points up this difference in both unary and binary operator functions.

We'll look at other differences between class member operator functions and stand-alone operator functions later in this chapter, when we consider operator functions as friends. When defined as ordinary stand-alone functions, operator functions are often made friends of a class so that they can access the private and protected members of the class.

UNARY OPERATOR FUNCTIONS

	Member Operator Function	*Stand-Alone Operator Function*
Single operand:	*this* pointer	first argument

BINARY OPERATOR FUNCTIONS

	Member Operator Function	*Stand-Alone Operator Function*
Left operand:	*this* pointer	first argument
Right operand:	first argument	second argument

Figure 11-1.
Delivering operands to operator functions.

Example: Fixed Point Numbers

We can see the basics of operator functions in a simple yet practical example. In many graphics applications, we need numbers that have both a whole part and a fractional part, but in some situations the overhead of floating point operations is unacceptable. An easy solution is to use 32-bit *long* arithmetic, in which the fraction is stored in the lower 16 bits and the whole part of the number is stored in the upper 16 bits. Such numbers have sufficient resolution for most applications, are easy to implement, and operate significantly faster than floating point numbers do.[2]

To develop this solution, I created a *FIXED* class that implements fixed point arithmetic. It contains conversions to and from fixed point numbers, and operator functions for manipulating fixed point numbers. All the member functions of the *FIXED* class are inline, to maximize speed. In the following examples, some features of *FIXED* are omitted so that we can focus on one thing at a time. The *FIXED* class is shown in Figure 11-2.

The FIXED Class

```
//
// Class for fixed point arithmetic
// This scheme uses a 32-bit long for 16:16 fixed point representation
//
#include <math.h>
```

Figure 11-2.
The FIXED *class.*

(continued)

2. On a 386 with a 387 numeric coprocessor, *long* arithmetic is about twice as fast as floating point arithmetic. On a system without a coprocessor, the difference is even greater.

Figure 11-2. *continued*

```
class FIXED {
private:
    enum FIXEDconsts { Fraction, Whole };   // byte order
    union {   // anonymous
        long complete;
        short parts[2];
    };
public:
    // constructors, conversions to FIXED
    FIXED() { complete = 0; }
    FIXED(double d);
    FIXED(int i) { parts[Fraction] = 0; parts[Whole] = i; }

    // conversions from FIXED to ...
    double FractPart();
    operator int()    { return parts[Whole]; }    // ignore fraction
    operator double() { return double(complete)/65536.0; }

    FIXED operator-() {                          // unary minus
        FIXED result;
        result.complete = - complete;
        return result;
    }
    FIXED operator+(const FIXED& f) {             // addition
        FIXED result;
        result.complete = complete + f.complete;
        return result;
    }
    FIXED operator-(const FIXED& f) {             // subtraction
        FIXED result;
        result.complete = complete - f.complete;
        return result;
    }
    void operator+=(const FIXED& f) {             //  assign sum
        complete += f.complete;
    }
    void operator-=(const FIXED& f) {             // assign difference
        complete -= f.complete;
    }
    void operator=(const FIXED& f) {
        complete = f.complete;
    }
    FIXED operator++() {                      // prefix increment
        parts[Whole]++;
        return *this;
    }

    FIXED operator++(int) {                   // postfix increment
        FIXED tmp = *this;                    // save original state
```

(continued)

Figure 11-2. *continued*

```
        parts[Whole]++;                          // increment
        return tmp;                              // return saved value
    }
    int operator<(const FIXED& f) { return complete < f.complete; }
    int operator>(const FIXED& f) { return complete > f.complete; }
    int operator<=(const FIXED& f) { return complete <= f.complete; }
    int operator>=(const FIXED& f) { return complete >= f.complete; }
};
// double to fixed
// try to get closest
FIXED::FIXED(double d)
{
    long l2 = d * 65536.0;    // naive result
    long l1 = l2-1;
    long l3 = l2+1;
    // check the errors
    double d1 = fabs(d - ((double)(l1) / 65536.0));
    double d2 = fabs(d - ((double)(l2) / 65536.0));
    double d3 = fabs(d - ((double)(l3) / 65536.0));
    complete = l2;
    if (d1 < d2) {
        d2 = d1;   // to make following if work
        complete = l1;
    }
    if (d3 < d2)
        complete = l3;
}
// return fractional part
double FIXED::FractPart()
{
    if (complete < 0) {
        if (parts[Fraction])
            return((unsigned)parts[Fraction] / 65536.0)-1.0;
        else
            return 0.0;
    }else
        return (unsigned)parts[Fraction] / 65536.0;
}
// stand-alone operator function
ostream& operator<<(ostream& s, const FIXED &f)
{
    s << (double)f;
    return s;
}
```

There isn't a single best representation for fixed point numbers. In the class that I developed, I used 16 bits for the whole part and 16 bits for the fraction, which is sometimes referred to as 16:16 representation. Other common representations are 8:8 and 24:8. I tried to think of a way to create a family of classes for fixed point numbers that would allow the creation of a new fixed point number class by means of derivation. Unfortunately, there is little common, representation-independent code required in the various approaches, and I decided against using derivation to achieve the goal of a family of fixed number types.

The data storage part of a *FIXED* object is a private anonymous union containing a *long* named *complete* and an array of two *shorts* named *parts*. On typical Intel 80x86 architecture CPUs, a *long* will be housed in 32 bits and a *short* in 16, so the two elements of the union will occupy the same space. This allows us to use the *shorts* to access either the fractional part or the whole part of the value while using the *long* for performing efficient arithmetic. On Intel architecture CPUs, *parts[0]* contains the fraction and *parts[1]* contains the whole part. To avoid scattering *0*s and *1*s throughout the code, we use an enumeration to define the symbolic constants *Fraction* and *Whole* for *0* and *1*, respectively. The *FIXED* class could be adapted to machines using the opposite byte order if we reversed the enumeration constants.

The public part of *FIXED* contains constructors to create *FIXED* objects from integers or floating point numbers; arithmetic operators; and type conversion operators to convert *FIXED* numbers to integer or floating point numbers. It is crucial that the arithmetic operations and the conversion to integer be extremely efficient because these operations will be used in inner loops of time-critical graphics code.

FIXED's constructors are unremarkable. Both the default constructor and the *FIXED(double)* constructor use initialization to access the *complete* member of the anonymous union. The *FIXED(int)* constructor is forced to use assignment to specify the initial values of the *parts* array. *FIXED* doesn't contain a copy constructor; one will be generated by the compiler if it is needed.

Normal use of the += (assign sum) operator is in expressions like this one:

```
lval += expr
```

where *lval* is an lvalue,[3] and *expr* is any expression. The *operator+=()* function in *FIXED* is defined as taking a reference to a *FIXED* named *f*. When *FIXED*'s *operator+=()* function is invoked, its *this* pointer is pointing at the left operand, which was called *lval* above, and *f* is referencing its right operand, which was called *expr* above. The body of *FIXED*'s *operator+=()* function reflects the way in which the left and right operands are made accessible:

```
void FIXED::operator+=(FIXED& f) { complete += f.complete; }
```

---

3. As Stroustrup notes in *The C++ Programming Language,* 2d ed., the word "lvalue" originally designated an expression that can be on the left side of an assignment statement, and in C++ an lvalue is a modifiable expression referring to an object or function that can be on the left side of an assignment statement. Stroustrup points out that not every lvalue can be used on the left side of an assignment statement, that an lvalue can refer to a constant.

FIXED's *operator+=()* function doesn't return a value, which is fine for the way in which it will be used. But in many cases you do want operator functions to return values so that you can write arbitrary expressions. Except for conversion operator functions, you can specify any return type you want.

The last part of the *FIXED* class contains three conversion routines that convert *FIXED* to *int* and *double*. One of these routines, *FractPart()*, is an ordinary (nonoperator) member function that simply returns the fractional part of the value. The other two conversion routines are operator functions that convert a *FIXED* object to *int* and *double*. The compiler will automatically use conversion routines when they can help resolve a type mismatch, and they can also be invoked explicitly by means of a cast expression.

The following short program exercises some facilities of the *FIXED* class. It creates a pair of *FIXED* objects and then uses the *operator+=()* function to add them.

```
#include <iostream.h>

void main(void)
{
    FIXED a = 20;          // FIXED(int) constructor
    FIXED b;               // FIXED default constructor

    b = 1.0/3.0;           // FIXED(double) constructor; then operator=
    while((int)a < 23) {
        cout << "a: " << double(a) << '\n';
        a += b;
    }
}
```

Even a simple example such as this one requires most of the facilities of the *FIXED* class. The first two lines of *main()* create two *FIXED* objects: *a* is created using the *FIXED(int)* constructor, and *b* is created using the default constructor. Assigning the value *1/3* to *b* is a two-step process. First the *FIXED(double)* constructor builds a temporary *FIXED* object using the value *1/3*. Then an assignment operator is used to assign the temporary *FIXED* object to *b*.

The test expression in the *while* loop uses a cast to explicitly convert *a* to an *int*, so that it can be compared with the value *23*. The cast to *int* is necessary because the compiler could also convert *a* to a *double* before performing the comparison. We might expect the compiler to recognize that converting *a* to an *int* and comparing it with *23* is easier than converting *a* to a *double* and then comparing that to *double(23)*. But the compiler looks at it a bit differently; it sees the *FIXED* type followed by the < operator, so it wants to convert the *FIXED* to something it can use with <, which means either an *int* or a *double*. Thus, the explicit cast is necessary to resolve the ambiguity.

The body of the *while* loop uses an explicit cast to convert *a* to a *double* so that it can be printed by means of the iostream library. Again, the cast is necessary because the iostream library can print both *double*s and *int*s, and the compiler has no way of knowing which we prefer. In this case, I used a conversion to *double* so that the fractional part would be visible. (Remember that *FIXED*'s conversion to *int* truncates the fraction.) When we look at the *operator++()* and the *operator--()* functions later in this chapter, *FIXED* will be expanded so that a *FIXED* object can be printed directly, without conversion, by means of the iostream library.

The second line of the *while* loop body uses the assign sum operator function to add *b* to *a*. Because the assign sum operator function was written as an inline member, this operation has no more overhead than an ordinary addition of one *long* to another. Here's the output of the program:

```
a: 20
a: 20.3333
a: 20.6667
a: 21
a: 21.3333
a: 21.6666
a: 22
a: 22.3333
a: 22.6666
a: 23
```

Although it isn't a common practice, operator functions can be invoked explicitly instead of by writing algebraic expressions. Here is the *while* loop from our example, rewritten using explicit operator function calls:

```
while(a.operator int() < 23) {
    cout << "a: " << a.operator double() << '\n';
    a.operator+=(b);
}
```

Member Operator Functions and Freestanding Operator Functions

Although operator functions are often written as class member functions, as in the previous section, they aren't required to be member functions. For example, the following freestanding operator function implements an addition operation on pairs of *FIXED* numbers:

```
FIXED operator+(const FIXED& lhs, const FIXED& rhs)
{
    FIXED result = lhs;       // FIXED(FIXED&) copy constructor
    result += rhs;
    return result;
}
```

The first line of this function uses a compiler generated copy constructor to create *result* initialized to the value of *lhs*. Then the *FIXED* class *operator+=* operator function is invoked to add *rhs* to *result*, and a copy of *result* is returned.

Because this freestanding *operator+()* function uses only public members of the *FIXED* class, it doesn't even need to be a friend of the class. Many a freestanding operator function, however, needs to be a friend in order to access private and protected parts of a class. Let's look at an equivalent freestanding *operator+()* function that is a friend of *FIXED* so that it can access private *FIXED* members. Here is the friend declaration that needs to be inserted into the *FIXED* class definition:

```
friend FIXED operator+(const FIXED& lhs, const FIXED& rhs);
```

Here is the alternative version of *operator+()*, which uses private members of *FIXED*:

```
FIXED operator+(const FIXED& lhs, const FIXED& rhs)
{
    FIXED result;       // default constructor
    result.complete = lhs.complete + rhs.complete;
    return result;
}
```

In this simple example, there is little difference between the two approaches. But in more complicated situations, the first version of *operator+()* is likely to remain simple because it reuses the code in *FIXED*'s *operator+=()* function. The second version is likely to be complicated.

Written as a member function, *operator+()* has a single argument for its right operand; the left operand is implicitly accessible (via *this*). Here's how *operator+()* would be defined as a member of *FIXED*:

```
class FIXED {
    // . . . other FIXED members
    FIXED operator+(const FIXED& f)
    {
        FIXED result
        result.complete = complete + f.complete;
        return result;
    }
    // . . . other FIXED members
};
```

Member operator functions and freestanding operator functions involve these tradeoffs, which you should consider as you design classes:

- A member operator function can always access private and protected class members.
- A member operator function can be virtual and is inherited.[4]
- A member operator function is assured that its left operand is a class object; the left operand won't be altered or converted by the standard conversions

4. The *operator=()* member operator function is not inherited.

used by the compiler to form function operands. This immutability is a desirable trait for an operator, such as an assignment operator, whose left operand should be an lvalue.

- A member operator function must be used for *operator type()*, *operator=()*, *operator()()*, *operator[]()*, *operator->()*, *operator new()*, and *operator delete()*.
- A freestanding operator function must be declared as a friend if it is to access private and protected class members.
- A freestanding operator function has its left operand delivered as a function argument. Like all function arguments, the left operand is subject to the usual conversions. This is a very desirable feature for symmetrical binary operators, such as the addition operator.
- A freestanding operator function is often ideal when one operand is one type and the other operand is a second type, especially if those two operands can appear in either order.
- A freestanding operator function can be created for a class that you can't modify.

It is easy to be confused by the different ways that the left operand is treated in member operator functions and in freestanding operator functions. A member operator function's left operand must be a class object. Type conversions aren't applied by the compiler. A freestanding operator function's left operand is just an argument for a function, which needn't be an object. And the left argument of a freestanding operator function is subject to ordinary conversions, which the compiler applies to coerce the actual argument type to a type suitable for the function.

The fundamental reason that freestanding operator functions are preferred for "symmetrical" operators is that they behave symmetrically. I personally consider this to be a minor flaw in the C++ language. I would prefer to have operator functions that are clearly vital parts of a class to actually be members of that class—even when they should behave symmetrically.

operator=()

One unusual but successful feature of C is its treatment of assignment. In many programming languages, assignment is a statement, but in C and C++, assignment is handled as part of the expression syntax. This treatment has many consequences because it allows an assignment to be performed anywhere an expression is valid. For example, the following C cliche is a loop that reads in characters, stores them in a variable, and continuously tests for end of file—all in the expression of a *while* statement:

```
while ((c = getchar()) != EOF) { /*body*/ }
```

This is hardly C's worst excess, but it has been widely criticized and is one of the four or five aspects of C that stump most novice C programmers.

C's flexible, expression-based syntax has served well in the transition to C++, and the assignment operator is one of the best examples of this. In many ways, assignment is simply a binary operator, with the proviso that the left operand be an lvalue. But assignment also has much in common with initialization, and C++'s assignment operator function has, as you would expect, many traits in common with copy constructors:

- An assignment operator function must be a class member function. Freestanding assignment operator functions are not allowed.
- An assignment operator function cannot be inherited.
- An assignment operator function is generated automatically by the compiler as needed if you don't write your own. A compiler-generated assignment operator function performs memberwise assignment, is public, and returns a reference to the assigned-to object.

But assignment operator functions also differ from copy constructors:

- An assignment operator function can be virtual. A constructor cannot be virtual.
- An assignment operator function can have a return value. A constructor cannot have a return value.
- A copy constructor's first argument is always, by definition, an *X&* for class *X*, and it can have multiple arguments. An *operator=()* function can have any type for its first, and only, argument.

The standard assignment operator function, which is the only one that can be generated automatically by the compiler, assigns one object to another, where both objects are from the same class. It is usually declared this way:

```
class X {
    X& operator=(X&);
};
```

You can define assignment conversions from foreign types using operator functions. For example, our class *X* might also have an assignment operator function that would allow *doubles* to be assigned to *X* objects:

```
class X {
    X& operator=(X&);
    X& operator=(double);
};
```

The usual return type for an assignment operator function is a reference to the class object. This allows you to write traditional embedded assignments—and to write chains of assignments:

```
class X {
public:
    X& operator=(X&);
    void fn(void);
};

void top(void)
{
    X x, y, z;

    x = y = z;       // assign z to y, and then y to x
    (x=y).fn();      // assign y to x, and then call x.fn()
}
```

The two commented statements in *top()* are possible only because the *X* assignment operator function returns a reference to an *X*. If the declaration were changed so that the assignment function return type were *void*, both of the commented statements in *top()* would be in error. Also note that the parentheses are necessary in the statement that calls *fn()*. Without the parentheses, the default operator precedence rules would change the meaning to "Assign *x* the result of calling *y.fn()*." However, the result of *y.fn()* is *void*, so it can't be assigned to *x*.

There are occasional specific reasons for having an assignment operator function return something other than a reference to its class. The most common return type alternative is *void*, which makes it impossible to use the result of an assignment in an expression. This forces users to adopt a somewhat simplified style of expression.

Many programmers are surprised that assignment can't be an inherited member function, a distinction it shares only with constructors and destructors. The reason is twofold. First, all of C++ works on the premise that a base class doesn't know about its derived classes, and a base class assignment operator member function could never do the right thing for its derived classes without knowing their details. Second, the compiler treats assignment as special, as it treats constructors and destructors, so that base class assignment operator member functions are used automatically when the compiler builds its own derived class assignment operator.

Let's look at assignment and the way it works with derivation in more detail:

```
#include <iostream.h>

class X {
public:
    X& operator=(X&) {
        cout << "X assignment\n";
        return *this;
    }
};
```

```
class Y : public X {
public:
    // no assignment operator; compiler will generate
    //  memberwise assignment
};
```

In this simple set of classes, base class *X* contains an assignment operator member function but derived class *Y* doesn't have an assignment operator function. When an assignment of one *Y* to another *Y* is needed, the compiler generates a memberwise assignment operator function, which means that the base class assignment operator will be used to assign the base part of *Y*:

```
void v(void)
{
    Y a, b;
    a = b;    // use compiler generated memberwise assignment
}
```

The output is

```
X assignment
```

which verifies that the compiler generated *Y* assignment operator function does indeed call its base class assignment operator to handle the base part.

If class *Y* is changed to include its own assignment operator, the user-supplied assignment operator of *Y* assumes full responsibility for assignment of *Y* objects; the base class assignment operator function won't be called automatically.[5] This is shown in the following, slightly modified, *Y* class:

```
class Y : public X {
public:
    // Y assignment operator
    Y& operator=(Y&) {
        cout << "Y assignment\n";
        return *this;
    }
};
```

When the program is executed, the output is

```
Y assignment
```

which indicates that the base class assignment operator hasn't been invoked. However, most derived class assignment operator functions do want to ensure that the

---

5. This differs from the way constructors work. A user-supplied constructor for a derived class can't supersede a base class constructor; the compiler will see that the base class constructor is always called.

base class part participates in assignment. Here is a third version of the *Y* class, showing one way that can be accomplished:

```
class Y : public X {
public:
    Y& operator=(Y& y) {
        this->X::operator=(y);   // base class assignment
        cout << "Y assignment\n";
        return *this;
    }
};
```

In this version of *Y::operator=()*, the *this* pointer and the *X::* scope resolution expression are used to explicitly invoke the *X* class's assignment operator. With this revision of the class definition, these messages are printed by the program:

```
X assignment
Y assignment
```

The messages show that the base class assignment operator function is indeed invoked by the derived class assignment operator function.

Another way to invoke the base class assignment operator is to cast the *this* pointer inside *Y*'s *operator=()* function, which is originally a *Y**, to *X**. Thus, the following line could be substituted in *Y*'s *operator=()* function as an alternative way to invoke the base class assignment operator function:

```
*((X *)this) = y;         // base class assignment
```

A derived class object can be assigned to a base class object, but only the base part of the derived class object will be used. This is a consequence of being able to use a derived class object anywhere you can use a base class object:

```
X x;       // base class object
Y y;       // derived class object
x = y;     // assign base class part of y object to x object
```

But the opposite, assigning a base class object to a derived class object, is not allowed:

```
y = x;     // no good; a base class object can't be assigned to a derived
           //  class object
```

When you want to assign a base class object to the base part of a derived class object, you can do it using a cast:

```
(X&)y = x;     // OK; an X object can be assigned to a Y object cast to an X
```

The *X&* cast effectively converts the *y* object to an *X* object, and then the assignment of one *X* object to another proceeds normally.

operator++() and *operator−−()*

Increment and decrement are unary operators used to increase or decrease the values of their single operands. When applied to a pointer, increment and decrement nudge the pointer enough that it points at the next or previous element in a list of like elements. When applied to a numeric type, the increment and decrement operators increase or decrease the value by 1.

Prefix and Postfix Operators

In one way, increment and decrement are unlike any other of C's unary operators. All other unary operators in C are prefix operators; they come before the operand. Increment and decrement can be either prefix or postfix; they can come either before or after the operand. In use, the difference between prefix application and postfix application of the operators lies in the value delivered to other parts of an expression.

The following example shows the difference. Let's look first at a postfix application of the increment operator. When increment (or decrement) is applied as a postfix operator, the original value of the operand is used in the expression, and then, after use, the operand of the increment (or decrement) operator is changed:

```
int x = 10;
int y;
y = x++;        // postfix increment: y becomes 10; then x becomes 11
```

Prefix increment (or decrement) works the opposite way. First the operand is incremented (or decremented), and then the new value is used in its surrounding expression:

```
int x = 10;
int y;
y = ++x;        // prefix increment: x becomes 11; then y becomes 11
```

Unary and Binary Operators

C has a number of operators that behave one way as unary operators and another way as binary operators. C++ unary and binary operator functions are easy to distinguish by how many arguments are supplied. A unary stand-alone operator function takes a single explicit argument, and a unary member operator function doesn't take any explicit argument, although it does have an implicit *this* argument. A binary stand-alone operator function takes two explicit arguments, and a binary member operator function takes a single explicit argument and an implicit *this* argument. Here are declarations for unary and binary stand-alone and member operator functions:

```
// stand-alone operator functions
E& operator+(E&);             // unary plus
E& operator+(E&, E&);         // binary plus

class E {
    // member operator functions
    E& operator-();           // unary minus (negation)
    E& operator-(E&);         // binary minus (subtraction)
};
```

Early versions of C++ couldn't distinguish between prefix and postfix applications of the increment and decrement operators. This proved to be a serious problem because programmer habits that were deeply entrenched from years of C expression writing weren't serviceable for writing C++ expressions. In later versions of C++, this failing has been fixed, although in a somewhat surprising way.

When *operator++()* (or *operator--()*) is declared in the usual way, which means with one argument for a stand-alone version or with no arguments for a member function version, it is, like other unary operators, a prefix operator. When you want to create a postfix increment (or decrement) operator function, you must supply a dummy extra argument.

Here is an example from the *FIXED* class we've already seen. So that we can focus on the increment (or decrement) operator functions, most of the features of *FIXED* that we've already looked at are omitted:

```
class FIXED {
    enum FIXEDconst { Fraction, Whole };
    union {   // anonymous
        long complete;
        short parts[2];
    };
public:
    // constructors, conversions to FIXED
    FIXED() { complete = 0; }
    :
    // operator functions
    FIXED operator++() {       // prefix increment operator function
        parts[Whole]++;
        return *this;
    }
    FIXED operator++(int) {  // postfix increment operator function
        FIXED tmp = *this;   // save original state
        parts[Whole]++;      // increment
        return tmp;          // return saved value
    }
};
```

C++ distinguishes syntactically between prefix and postfix invocations of increment and decrement operators, but it is up to you to implement them according to your needs. C++ doesn't do anything differently for the prefix and postfix versions of the increment operator, for instance, other than invoke the appropriate member function. If *a* and *b* are class objects for which both increment operators are defined, the expression *a=++b* will be compiled into this sequence of operator functions:

```
a.operator=(b.operator++());        // prefix operator++
```

The same *a* and *b* in the expression *a=b++* will be compiled into this sequence of operator functions:

```
a.operator=(b.operator++(1));       // postfix operator++
```

As you can see, the value that the *operator=()* function receives depends solely on the logic inside the two versions of *operator++()*.

In the fragment of *FIXED* we've just looked at, the prefix version of *operator++()* simply increments the object *b*'s value and then returns a copy. The postfix version is more complicated. It first constructs a new *FIXED* object named *tmp*, which is initialized by **this*, the current value of the object. Next it increments the value, and then finally it returns *tmp*. This simple subterfuge implements the postfix version of *operator++()*.

Here is a simple test function that verifies the operation of the increment functions we've just looked at:

```
void main(void)
{
    FIXED x = 1.5;
    FIXED y = 0;
    cout << x << " " << y << "\n";
    y = x++;        // postfix increment: y becomes 1.5; then x becomes 2.5
    cout << x << " " << y << "\n";
    y = ++x;        // prefix increment: x becomes 3.5; then y becomes 3.5
    cout << x << " " << y << "\n";
}
```

Here is the output of the test:

```
1.5 0
2.5 1.5
3.5 3.5
```

You might have noticed that I'm using the iostream library to print the *FIXED* object directly, without the casts that have been used in previous examples to convert *FIXED* objects to *doubles* so that they can be printed by the stream I/O library. This was done by creating an *operator<<()* of the correct type for use with the iostream library. Here is that function; the details of extending the stream I/O library to work with your own data types will be discussed further in Chapter 12.

```
#include <iostream.h>
ostream& operator<<(ostream& s, const FIXED &f)
{
    s << (double)f;
    return s;
}
```

The operator function overloads the << operator, which is the traditional "shift left" operator, to create a stream output function. The operands of the *operator<<()* function must be a reference to a stream type (*ostream&* for an output stream; *istream&* for an input stream) and a user-defined type, which is usually a class object. The function's return type should be a reference to a stream, and its return value should be that of the stream that was supplied as the left operand. The body of the function contains stream output logic, which in the example above is trivial.

If you want to disallow either prefix or postfix increment operations, simply omit the appropriate one of the two definitions. If you want them to behave the same way, which is contrary to usual C semantics, you can simply define one to call the other. The following, for example, could replace the postfix version of *operator++()* we used in the *FIXED* class above:

```
FIXED operator++(int) { return ++*this; }
```

Notice that the increment operators in class *FIXED* all return *FIXED* objects, not references to (or pointers to) *FIXED* objects. See the discussion of operator function return types toward the end of this chapter.

operator[]()

The subscripting operator's traditional use in C is to access elements of an array. Despite its notation, the subscripting operator is considered a binary operator, whose left operand traditionally indicates a specific array and whose right operand is an index expression. Other binary operators sit smoothly between their operands, but *operator[]()* is split into two parts: the left bracket between the operands, the right bracket to the right of the right operand.

When *operator[]()* is used traditionally, that is, with built-in types, these two caveats apply to its operands:

- The left operand of *operator[]()* must be a pointer type. Remember that if you declare an array named *x*, *x* itself is a pointer to the first element of the array.
- The right operand of *operator[]()*, which is the operand between the square brackets, must be a numeric expression that indicates a particular element in the array.[6]

---

6. Although C has never checked array element expressions, stepping outside an array's bounds has always been erroneous. The prohibition against stepping outside an array's bounds doesn't prohibit negative index expressions; they are prohibited only when the left operand of *[]* indicates the beginning of an array.

When you overload the *[]* operator for a class object, both of these restrictions are removed and are replaced with these restrictions:

- The left operand must be a class object.
- The right operand must be a type that is compatible with the types that are allowed for that class's *operator[]()* member functions.
- *operator[]()* can be written only as a class member function. It can have a single argument of any type, which is its right operand, and its return can be of any type.

It is thus easy to provide bounds-checked arrays, sparse arrays, virtual (mostly disk resident) arrays, associative arrays, dynamically sized arrays, and the like.

In my work at the Rockefeller University, I recently created a software system that allows experimenters to specify the course of an experiment by creating a state table. The state table contains a description of what should be done in each named state and what conditions will cause a transition to the next state. For this project, I created a small compiler that turns user-written state tables into C++ programs. And for this compiler, I needed what compiler writers have always needed: a convenient way to store strings.

To meet that need, I created a *STRLIST* class. *STRLIST* supports only three operations: adding a new character string to an existing list of strings, returning a pointer to a string given an index number, and returning an index number given a pointer to a string. This last characteristic makes *STRLIST* an "associative array," an array that can be "indexed" by its values.

For more specialized needs, I have derived several classes from *STRLIST*. In some cases, I created a new class because I wanted to store more information than simply a string. For example, one of my derived classes stores both the names of parameters and a key to the type of each parameter. Over time I have used the trivially simple *STRLIST* class in several unexpected ways—to me, a sign that the original design was good.[7]

Efficiency wasn't a paramount concern in the design of *STRLIST*. Most state tables are relatively short—the whole state table approach starts to break down when a state table gets too large. The current version of *STRLIST*, which contains no optimizations of any kind, works well for my purposes. It would not work well for a more demanding situation in which high-efficiency string retrieval was important.

---

7. My state table compiler and the *STRLIST* class predate the Microsoft Foundation Class library, which contains several flexible classes that can manage lists of strings. In a new design, I would probably use MFC library classes rather than the *STRLIST* class family.

Here is the header file strlist.h:

```
//
// a list of strings
//
#include <string.h>

class STRLIST {
    typedef char *charptr;
protected:
    charptr *const p;           // the list of pointers
    const int maxstrings;       // how many can be in the list
    int nstrings;               // how many now
public:
    STRLIST(int n) :            // constructor--how big a list
        maxstrings(n),
        nstrings(0),
        p(new charptr[n])
    {
        if (!p)
            return;
        memset(p, 0, n * sizeof(charptr));
    }
    // operator functions
    virtual void operator+=(charptr pc); // add a string to the list
    char *operator[](int i);             // fetch a pointer to a string,
                                         //  given an index
    int operator[](charptr pc);          // fetch an index, given a
                                         //  pointer to a string
    int count() { return nstrings; }     // how many strings in the list
};
```

The single constructor of *STRLIST* simply creates and then zeroes an array of pointers. Its argument specifies how many pointers can be stored in the array, which is the same as how many strings can be in the list. The *STRLIST* class has three operator functions: an *operator+=()* function for adding strings to the list and two *operator[]()* functions for accessing the list. Using *operator+=()* for adding strings is a somewhat iffy choice. Numerics spring to mind when we see +=, but a list of strings isn't a numeric entity. Even so, adding a string to a list of strings is, in a sense, similar to adding some value to a variable. Using the *[]* operator to access elements in the array is a much more conventional use of an operator function.

Let's look more closely at the three operator functions at work here. The *operator+=()* function is interesting primarily because it uses *operator[]()* to ensure that the new string isn't already in the list. Here is *operator+=()*:

```
// add a string to the list
void STRLIST::operator+=(charptr pc)
{
```

```
        if (!p)
            return;
        // check for string already in the list
        if ((*this)[pc] != -1)
            return;    // already in the list
        // add to end of list
        if (nstrings < maxstrings) {
            p[nstrings] = new char[strlen(pc) + 1];
            if (p[nstrings]) {
                strcpy(p[nstrings], pc);
                nstrings++;
            } else
                ; // allocation failed
        } else
            ;    // list full
    }
```

Note the use of *this* to call up *STRLIST*'s *operator[]()* member function. In the body of *operator+=()*, the new operator is used to get space to store a string, and then the string is copied into that space. Two errors are possible: running out of free storage and running out of positions in the list. Neither of these errors is signaled by *operator+=()*. A more robust version would be careful to manage these errors.

There are two *operator[]()* member functions. The simpler takes an *int* index and returns a pointer to that string. It is useful, for example, in printing out the full list of strings.

```
    // return a pointer to the ith string in the list
    char *STRLIST::operator[](int i)
    {
        if (i >= 0 && i < nstrings)
            return p[i];
        else
            return 0;
    }
```

The second *operator[]()* returns the index of a given string. It is used in the *operator+=()* function to avoid placing duplicates in the list:

```
    // if a given string isn't in the list,
    // return index or -1 for failure
    int STRLIST::operator[](charptr pc)
    {
        for(int i = 0; i < nstrings; i++)
            if (!strcmp(p[i], pc))
                return i; // already in list
        return -1;
    }
```

Here is a simple test program to demonstrate the *STRLIST* class. The first part of *main()* creates a *STRLIST* object and then pours in three strings. The middle part prints the list using the *operator[](int)* member function, and the last part of *main()* shows how the *operator[](char *)* member function is used to find a string in the list.

```
#include <iostream.h>

void main()
{
    STRLIST s(10);      // create a list big enough for ten strings

    // put some strings in the list
    s += "Kari";
    s += "Arli";
    s += "Reed";

    // print full list
    int i = 0;
    char *p = s[i++];
    while(p) {
        cout << p << " ";
        p = s[i++];
    }
    cout << '\n';

    // print index of "Kari" in the list
    cout << "Kari: " << s["Kari"] << '\n';
}
```

Here's the output of this test program:

```
Kari Arli Reed
Kari: 0
```

operator->()

The member access operator gives you a way to control and monitor access to some resource. There are a variety of rationales for using *operator->()*, but they all boil down to a need to perform some operation automatically each time an object is accessed.

In traditional C usage, -> requires a pointer to a struct or to a union as its left operand and the name of a member of that struct or union as its right operand. Well, perhaps I shouldn't call the thing on the right an "operand" because in C++, the -> operator is considered a unary operator of its left operand. The result of applying -> to its left operand must be something that can point at its right operand—either a true class, struct, or union pointer, or a class object for which *operator->()* is defined. Yes, this needs more explanation.

If *a* is a class object for which *operator->()* is defined, the expression

```
a->x
```

has the following interpretation:

```
( a.operator->() ) -> x
```

In order for this to make sense, *a.operator->()* must return something that can appear to the left of the -> operator. In C++, only two items can appear to the left of a -> operator:

- A class object for which *operator->()* is defined.
- A true pointer to a class, struct, or union. In this case, the name to the right of -> must be the name of an accessible member of that class, struct, or union.

The other rule for the member access operator is that it must be a class member function; it cannot be a stand-alone function.

The following example of *operator->()*, like any such example, contains a pair of classes. The first class, named *X*, contains some data members. It has a private constructor; hence it can be constructed only by a friend or a member.[8] Its only friend is *PX*, a smart pointer class. Here is the simple *X* class:

```
class X {
    friend class PX;
    private:
        // constructor
        X() : a(0), b(0), c(0) {}
    public:
        // data members
        int a, b, c;
};
```

The smart pointer class *PX* contains two pointers to *X* objects named *p* and *q*. Each time a *PX* object is created, two *X* objects are created and *p* and *q* are pointed at those objects. The only public member of *PX*, other than its constructor, is an *operator->()* function. Each time *operator->()* is used, it increments a reference counter in such a way that it grants two accesses to *p*'s object and then two accesses to *q*'s, and then to *p*'s, and so on.

```
class PX {
        X *p, *q;
        int cnt;
public:
    X *operator->() {          // smart pointer to an X
        if (cnt++ % 4 < 2)     // two of p, two of q
            return p;
        else
```

8. Not even a derived class can access a base class's private constructor; only a friend class member function, a friend function, or one of the class's own member functions can access a private member.

```
            return q;
        }
        PX() : p(new X), q(new X), cnt(0) {}
};
```

Here is a simple example that exercises this class. It simply creates a *PX* object and then uses it to increment the *a* member of *X*.

```
#include <iostream.h>
void main()
{
    PX x;
    int i;
    for(i=0;i<8;i++)
        cout << x->a++ << "\n";
}
```

The first two accesses increment the *a* of one *X* object, the next two accesses increment the *a* of the other, and so forth, producing the following output:

```
0
1
0
1
2
3
2
3
```

operator()()

The function call operator lets you use function call syntax to access a class operator function. Function call is an odd operator whose left operand must be a class object and whose right operand is a set of expressions. For example, if *a* is an object of a class with an *operator()(int, double, int)*, the expression

```
a(5, 1.0, 3)
```

is shorthand for

```
a.operator()(5, 1.0, 3)
```

Considered a binary operator, *operator()()* is the only operator function that can take multiple "right-hand" operands. This gives it great flexibility but with the caveat that the syntax makes every use of *operator()()* look like a traditional function call. This feature of *operator()()* makes it unclear to me why it is better to use *operator()()* instead of using a traditional named member function. Stroustrup says that it is useful mainly for defining types with only a single operation or types that have a predominant operation.

Here is an example of using *operator()()* to create objects containing name and value pairs, somewhat like the name/value pairs that form the DOS environment. For example, in your DOS system's autoexec.bat file, you probably have a line like this:

```
set lib=c:\C700\lib
```

The string "lib" is the name, and the string "c:\C700\lib" is the value of this entry in the DOS environment.

To manage a collection of name/value pairs, I created an *NVPAIR* class. It relies on the previously introduced *STRLIST* class to handle the name/value strings. However, *STRLIST* has one shortcoming from the perspective of current use. It is desirable to be able to change the value of a name, which is not a feature of *STRLIST*. Accordingly, I derived a class from *STRLIST* whose only new feature is the ability to change the value of an entry. Before we go to the new *NVPAIR* class, let's take a brief look at this enhanced *STRLIST* class:

```
// rewritable stringlist
class STRLIST_rewrite : public STRLIST {
public:
    // constructor--invoke STRLIST constructor
    STRLIST_rewrite(int n) : STRLIST(n) {}
    // change an entry, given an index number
    void rewrite(int n, char *newval);
};
```

The public members of *STRLIST_rewrite* are its constructor, which simply invokes its base class constructor, and *rewrite()*, which puts a new string value in the *n*th entry of the list. The definition of the *rewrite()* procedure is shown below:

```
// rewrite entry n in a list of strings
void STRLIST_rewrite::rewrite(int n, char *newval)
{
    if (n >= 0 && n < nstrings) {
        delete p[n];
        p[n] = new char[strlen(newval) + 1];
        if (p[n])
            strcpy(p[n], newval);
        else
            ;     // allocation failure
    }
}
```

Because *p* and *nstrings* are protected members of *STRLIST*, and because *STRLIST_rewrite* is publicly derived from *STRLIST*, *p* and *nstrings* are accessible in the *rewrite()* procedure.

I could have implemented the rewrite facility by adding it to *STRLIST* instead of deriving a new class from *STRLIST* for the sole purpose of adding this feature. Had I thought about rewriting at the outset, I probably would have included that feature in

STRLIST. But by the time I had decided that I needed to rewrite *STRLIST*, I had already been using it for many months, I had already derived several classes from it, and I simply didn't want to disturb this stable, established class. Also, by building a separate class I have created two flavors of *STRLIST*: the original, immutable kind, and the new, rewritable kind. This duality is useful, as we will see shortly.

Now back to the original goal, a class for managing name/value string pairs. The *NVPAIR* class contains a pair of *STRLIST* objects (actually a *STRLIST* object for storing names and a *STRLIST_rewrite* object for storing values) and a pair of *operator()()* functions:

- *char *operator()(char *nm)* looks up *nm* and returns its value.
- *void operator()(char *name, char *val)* creates (or updates) a name/value pair using *name* as the name and *val* as the value.

Note that the two *operator()()* functions return different types.

Here is the *NVPAIR* class definition:

```
// a collection of name/value pairs
class NVPAIR {
    STRLIST nm;                         // name storage
    STRLIST_rewrite val;                // value storage
public:
    NVPAIR(int i) : nm(i), val(i) {}    // constructor
    // return value, given name
    char *operator()(char *name);
    // create (or update) a name/value pair
    void operator()(char *name, char* val);
};
```

The single argument *operator()()* function looks up its name in the *nm STRLIST*. If the name is found, the function returns the corresponding value of *val*; otherwise, it returns a pointer to a null string.

```
// return value, given name
char *NVPAIR::operator()(char *name)
{
    int index = nm[name];      // look up name
    if (index != -1)
        return val[index];
    else
        return "";             // empty string for a missing name
}
```

Creating a name/value pair is a bit more complex. The first step is to look up the given name in the list to see whether it is there already. If it is, *rewrite()* is called to install the new value; otherwise, both the *name* string and the *value* string are tacked onto the ends of the respective lists.

```
// create a new name/value pair
void NVPAIR::operator()(char *name, char* value)
{
    int index = nm[name];
    if (index == -1) { // not there already
        nm += name;
        val += value;
    } else
        val.rewrite(index, value);
}
```

Here is a simple test program that exercises most of the features of the *NVPAIR* class:

```
#include <iostream.h>

void main()
{
    NVPAIR pairs(50);

    pairs("Kari", "Age 10");
    pairs("Arli", "Age 8");
    cout << "Kari " << pairs("Kari") << '\n';
    pairs("Kari", "A Perfect 10");
    cout << "Kari " << pairs("Kari") << '\n';
}
```

The test program creates an *NVPAIR* object and then stores two name/value pairs using the *operator()(char *, char*)* function. Next the *operator()(char *)* function is used to print a value, the value is updated, and then it is printed again. The program produces this output:

```
Kari Age 10
Kari A Perfect 10
```

If you strip away the declarations and such, the *NVPAIR* class contains just 11 lines of C++ code yet manages to do something quite useful. That's why programmers are so excited about object-oriented programming.

operator type()

Type conversion has always been a key aspect of C. Insofar as built-in types are concerned, most C programmers take it for granted that

```
'\t' == 9
```

is *true*, or that

```
3.14159 + '\t'
```

is *12.14159*! Most languages allow some leeway in using mixed operands, but few are as generous as C, which allows a *char* to be promoted all the way to a *double*.

C++ offers two ways to specify and manage type conversions. The first is to create class constructors. A constructor manages a conversion from a foreign type (or types) to an object's own type. The second is to create conversion operator member functions, which are conversions from an object's own type to some other type.

Back in our look at fixed point numbers earlier in this chapter, we saw two conversion operator functions for the *FIXED* class. Here's a repeat of the conversion operator part of that class definition:

```
class FIXED {
    // . . . data members
public:
    // . . . constructors
    // conversion operations
    operator int();
    operator double();
};
```

The header of a conversion operator function is modeled on the usual operator function syntax except that the operator symbol (the *+=* in *operator+=()*, for instance) is replaced by a type specification. The type specification doesn't have to be a single-word type name such as *int*, *double*, or *char*. It can be a multiple-word description of a type such as *const char **.

These restrictions apply to type conversion functions:

- Conversion operator functions do not take parameters. They are always member functions, and their single, implicit, operand is **this*.
- You cannot specify a return type in the function header. The implicit return type is the conversion type; in the body of the function, a value of the appropriate type must be returned.

A conversion operator function is invoked in one of three ways. The first way, which is probably the most common, is to explicitly code a type cast expression. We saw this means of invoking a conversion early on, in our look at fixed point numbers. A *FIXED* object was explicitly cast to *int* so that it could be compared with an integer constant; and a *FIXED* object was explicitly cast to *double* so that it could be printed:

```
while((int)a < 23) {
    cout << "a: " << double(a) << '\n';
    a += b;
}
```

The second method is to explicitly call the conversion operator function by name, as shown in the last example in this chapter's early discussion of fixed point numbers.

```
while(a.operator int() < 23) {
    cout << "a: " << a.operator double() << '\n';
    a.operator+=(b);
}
```

The third invocation is automatic; the compiler will call a type conversion operator function when it needs to perform a conversion, as in this example:

```
#include <math.h>     // pull in prototype double sin(double);
void f(void)
{
    FIXED f;
    sin(f);           // compiler does sin(double(f)), which is
                      // the same as sin(f.operator double());
}
```

To the compiler, both conversion by constructor and conversion by type conversion operator function are considered user-defined conversions. When the compiler tries to resolve a type mismatch, it looks at all of the known user-defined conversions, trying to come up with a best conversion. When you specify both constructor conversion functions and operator conversion functions, you risk creating ambiguities that must be resolved manually. For example, consider the following simple class:

```
class C {
private:
    double d;
public:
    C(int i) : d(i) {}
    void operator+(C& c) { }
};
```

Given the above, the compiler has no trouble with the following:

```
void main(void)
{
    C c(1);
    c+2;        // compiler codes c.operator+(C(2));
}
```

Because the compiler has seen the *operator+()* function, it automatically invokes a constructor to make the conversion shown in the comment. But consider how things change if this conversion operator is added to the public part of class C:

```
operator int() { return (int)d; }
```

The compiler suddenly has two equally valid conversion operations that can be applied to the resolutions of a type mismatch:

```
c+2;        // either c.operator+(C(2)) or c.operator int(c)+2
```

By adding functionality to a class, we have introduced ambiguity. The solution is to make our needs explicit by writing a cast. The *c+2* expression should be written either

```
(int)c+2
```

or

```
c+C(2)
```

In general, I don't recommend relying on the compiler to invoke object conversions automatically. The effect can be very subtle. I prefer to see a written program that tells me, forthrightly, just what is going on. And relying on automatic conversions can be hazardous because the compiler's notion of "best" conversion can change mysteriously when you make seemingly unrelated changes to the class definition.

operator new() and *operator delete()*

It takes a while to get used to the idea that memory is allocated by an operator. The *operator new()* and *operator delete()* functions are like several of the "operators" we've already looked at in that they are "flag-of-convenience operators." Two main benefits come from using operators for memory allocation. One is that using operators makes memory allocation a more central feature of the language, a plus because constructors and destructors will be called automatically as objects are dynamically created and destroyed. The second benefit is that you can overload *new()* and *delete()* to fine-tune memory allocation to meet the needs of individual classes.

When you dynamically create an *X* object, the compiler first checks to see whether there is an *X::operator new()* function. If there is, it is used; otherwise, the global *::operator new()* function is used. Class-specific *operator new()* and *operator delete()* are used only when individual objects are allocated dynamically. They are not used when arrays of objects are allocated, when auto objects are allocated on the stack, or when static global objects are created. Thus, *X::operator new()* is called only when you write *new X*, or when you use *new* to allocate an object derived from *X*. The *X::operator new()* function is not used to construct a class that merely contains an *X* member object.

Uses for the Allocation Operator

There are a variety of common reasons for implementing a class-specific memory allocation operator:

- For keeping a list of dynamic objects so that they can be deleted reliably. Without manual intervention, dynamic objects are never deleted, unlike global objects and auto objects.
- For debugging. The ability to gain control during dynamic object creation enables various debugging and record-keeping strategies.

- For efficiency. A class-specific allocator can sometimes operate much more efficiently than a generic allocator because it knows more about the size of the object that will be allocated, and how and when it will be deleted.
- For control. A class-specific allocator can place an object in a specific location, such as shared memory.

A language that has both constructors and class-specific *operator new()* memory allocation can be confusing. Both facilities are involved in object creation, but their roles are separate. A constructor initializes; it converts a region of storage to an object by assigning values to members and performing other "let's get started" chores. The function *operator new()* has no role in initializing members of an object; its only mandated role is to return a pointer to adequate storage for the object.

Restrictions on the Allocation and Deallocation Operators

As you might expect, *operator new()* and *operator delete()* come with plenty of restrictions:

- Class-specific *operator new()* and *operator delete()* are always member functions. They cannot be ordinary, freestanding functions, although you can redefine the global *operator new()* and *operator delete()* functions.
- *operator new()* and *operator delete()* are always static member functions, although you do not need to use the keyword *static* in the class definition. They cannot be made virtual.
- *operator new()* is given a *size_t* operand[9] that specifies the size of memory the object needs, and it must return a *void ** pointer to the allocated storage. If C++ didn't have class derivation, the size argument would be redundant because *operator new()* for class *X* would always need to allocate exactly *sizeof(X)* bytes. But class derivation breaks this relationship; always allocate the number of bytes specified by *operator new()*'s argument.
- *operator new()* can be overloaded by using additional arguments, called "placement arguments." These arguments are passed to *operator new()* in parentheses immediately following the *new* keyword:

  ```
  X *x = new (placement args) X(constructor args);
  ```

  Don't confuse placement arguments, which are seldom used, with the far more common constructor arguments, which are routinely used. If you do use placement arguments, the class must have an *operator new()* function whose signature matches the types of the placement arguments.

---

9. *size_t* is an integral *typedef* that is defined in the include file <stddef.h>.

- *operator delete()* can be defined to take either one or two arguments. The first argument is always a *void ** pointer to the object to be deleted. The second, optional, argument is the size of the object to be deleted. You should define only one of these two versions of *operator delete()*. An *operator delete()* must return type *void*, that is, nothing. If your *operator delete()* relies on the object size information, the class should also contain a virtual destructor, to ensure that the correct destructor will always be called. This will in turn ensure that the correct size will be passed to *operator delete()*.

Access and the Allocation and Deallocation Operators

The functions *operator new()* and *operator delete()* obey the same access rules as other class member functions:

- If *D* is publicly derived from *B* and *B* contains an accessible *operator new()*, *B*'s *operator new()* is used to allocate space for *D* unless *D* has its own *operator new()*.
- If *D* is privately derived from *B* and *B* contains an *operator new()*, *B*'s *operator new()* is inaccessible and *D* objects can't be dynamically allocated unless *D* contains an *operator new()*.

Here is a class that contains its own *operator new()* and its own private memory pool from which dynamic objects are allocated. This class has an *operator delete()*, so deleting an object won't invoke the global *operator delete()*.

```
#include <stddef.h>                          // drag in size_t type

class A {
private:
    enum Aconst { Abufsize = 1000 };
    static char buf[Abufsize];       // storage for A objects
    int a;
public:
    void *operator new(size_t t);    // allocate A objects from buf[]
                                     // avoid ::operator delete
    void operator delete(void *v, size_t t) {}
    virtual ~A() {}                  // ensure correct destructor
};
```

Here is the *operator new()* from *A*.

```
void * A::operator new(size_t t)
{
    static char *freebase = buf;          // freebase private to
                                          //  operator new()
    char *val = freebase;
    freebase += t;
    if (t == 0) return 0;
    return ((val+t) <= (buf+Abufsize)) ? val : 0;
}
```

This allocator doesn't keep track of allocations. There is thus no way to write a corresponding deallocation function. In general, this is a very bad idea, although there are some situations in which the user only adds to a list and never removes items for which it would be suitable.

Shallow Copy, Deep Copy

Some important classes, such as the *FIXED* class, are self contained. They don't reference any memory outside the bounds of the initial chunk of memory that was allocated to hold the object. Making a copy of an object of such a class, or comparing two objects of such a class, is relatively easy.

However, most classes are not self contained; they instead contain references and pointers to data stored elsewhere. For example, the *STRLIST* class that illustrated use of *operator[]()* earlier in this chapter contains a dynamically allocated array of pointers to dynamically allocated strings. When you allocate a *STRLIST* object, *new* sets aside only a few bytes of storage for the three data members of *STRLIST*. But the constructor of *STRLIST* immediately sets aside much more storage by allocating an array of *char** pointers. Then as character strings are deposited in the list, each is stored in a separately allocated buffer. Thus, a full *STRLIST* object with a capacity of 50 strings would occupy 52 separate storage regions: the few bytes of storage for the object; the storage for the array of string pointers, which would be *50 * sizeof(char*)*; and 50 separate storage sites (of various sizes) for the strings.

Let's think about what it might mean to make a copy of a *STRLIST* object:

- *Shallow copy.* Copy only the object itself, which is what the C++ compiler would do if it built its own *operator=* or copy constructor. This could cause problems in the *STRLIST* class because of the way strings are added to the list. Both the original object and the copy would assume it had "ownership" of the list of string pointers, and the copy might make changes that would overwrite changes made by the original object.

- *Intermediate copy.* Copy the object and the list of string pointers, but don't copy the individual strings. This would work well, provided existing strings aren't deleted or modified. There are often several ways to perform an intermediate copy.

- *Deep copy.* Copy everything: the object, the array of string pointers, and every extant string. This is the safest, but by far the most time-consuming, option.

Shallow copies are simple but often inadequate. Deep copies are often too onerous, especially for large objects. In between lies treacherous territory, in which you must make difficult trade-offs among considerations of space, time, and complexity. Be careful: These decisions can have a profound influence on the meaning of your abstraction, on the usability of your classes, and on the performance of your design.

Let's examine the different copy depths by means of a simple example, a copy constructor for the *STRLIST* class. Here's the declaration of the copy constructor, which must appear in the public part of the *STRLIST* class definition:

```
STRLIST(strlist &);       // copy constructor
```

Shallow Copy

Here is the all-but-useless shallow copy constructor, which is what the compiler will generate if you don't create your own copy constructor:

```
STRLIST::STRLIST(strlist &rhs) :    // shallow copy constructor
    p(rhs.p),
    nstrings(rhs.nstrings) ,
    maxstrings(rhs.maxstrings)
{ }
```

Intermediate Copy

Now let's look at the intermediate version, which makes a copy of the table of pointers but doesn't copy the individual strings:

```
STRLIST::STRLIST(strlist &rhs) :    // intermediate copy constructor
    p(new charptr[rhs.maxstrings]),
    nstrings(rhs.nstrings),
    maxstrings(rhs.maxstrings)
{
    if (!p)
        return;
    memcpy(p, rhs.p, rhs.maxstrings * sizeof(charptr));
}
```

Once the intermediate copy constructor has copied a *STRLIST* object, there are two pointers to each stored string. As long as the strings and their pointers are treated as "read-only," everything will be fine; but if one object starts modifying the strings the original and the copy have in common, the other object will quickly trip over those changes.

Deep Copy

The deep copy constructor is the safest, the slowest, and the most complex:

```
STRLIST::STRLIST(strlist &rhs) :    // deep copy constructor
    p(new charptr[rhs.maxstrings]),
    nstrings(rhs.nstrings),
    maxstrings(rhs.maxstrings)
{
```

```
        if (!p)        // allocation failure
            return;
        // clear pointer array
        memset(p, 0, maxstrings * sizeof(charptr));
        // copy individual strings
        int i;
        for(i=0; i<nstrings; i++) {
            p[i] = new char[strlen(rhs.p[i]) + 1];
            if (p[i])
                strcpy(p[i], rhs.p[i]);
        }
    }
```

We've looked at examples for copy constructors, but the same principle applies to *operator=()* and to all the comparison operators.

Operator Function Return Types

One of the most exacting areas of object-oriented design is choosing appropriate return types for class member functions and for operator functions. You need to consider several, sometimes conflicting, factors that were of much less importance in the pre-object era.

One consideration is that function return types shouldn't violate the encapsulation of an object. This principle argues for value returns and against pointer and reference returns. By returning a copy of a member datum, the object's member functions retain control. By returning a pointer or a reference, the object's member functions lose all control over a member datum. If you were using classes to mediate access to a large, shared data structure, it would be inconceivable to return a pointer to the shared reference count, but it might be very reasonable to return a pointer to an element of the shared data structure.

Another consideration in choosing function return types is efficiency. Returning references and pointers is efficient; they should be used wherever appropriate to avoid wearing out the stack. Returning whole objects can be very inefficient—even impossible for large objects on machines with fixed stacks.

A third consideration is the creation of temporaries. When you use operator functions, you invariably produce situations in which the compiler is forced to create temporary objects. For example, if *a*, *b*, and *c* are objects of class *E* and *E* has an *operator+()* function, the compiler will probably implement the expression *a+b+c* by assigning *a+b* to a temporary object and then adding that temporary object to *c*. Clearly, *operator+()* must return either an *E* object or a reference to an *E* object; otherwise, you'd have trouble adding the temp to *c*. If *operator+()* returns a reference, then a reference to what?

- Certainly not a reference to one of its own arguments; the usual meaning of *operator+()* forbids changes to the operands.

- Certainly not a reference to a local object; that would be destroyed when the operator function exited.
- Certainly not a reference to a static (global) object; that could be overwritten by a subsequent call to *operator+()* before it was used.
- Certainly not a reference to a dynamically allocated object; that would never be deleted.

The only simple and safe return for an operator such as *operator+()* that needs to return something that has been formed from its operands is to return an object.

Reference returns, which sound like a great return type because they are efficient, are typically used in these situations:

- To return references to arguments. For example, the iostream library output and input functions all receive a *stream&* argument, which by convention is both used for I/O operations and returned, by reference, as the function return value. This convention facilitates cascading I/O expressions such as this:

  ```
  cout << "message " << 10 << '\n';
  ```

- To return references to members of the object. For example, a bounds-checked array class would be likely to have an *operator[]()* function that returned a reference to an element of the member array.

Designers of classes for representing large objects that need to be manipulated by operator functions, such as matrices, vectors, and databases, face particularly difficult challenges. Copying each time a temporary object is created is usually impractical. Several solutions are available. One strategy is to implement only the operator *op=()* operators, which forces users to adopt a restrictive coding style. For example, the expression

```
a = b + c;
```

could be recoded as

```
a = b;
a += c;
```

to avoid creation of temporaries.

Another solution is to recognize and manage the creation of temporaries. Consider

```
x = a + b + c
```

The first step would be for *operator+()* to add *a* and *b*, place the result in a temporary, and then return a reference to that temporary. In the next step, a second invocation of *operator+()* would add the temporary to *c*. This time, the operator function would notice that one operand was a temporary, reuse it, and then return a reference to it. Finally, *operator=()* would notice that its right operand was a temporary and handle it specially, avoiding a massive copy. This technique is difficult but rewarding.

Let's draw some admittedly overgeneralized conclusions from all of this. When operator functions are used in algebraic settings, in classes for matrix or vector operations and so forth, they can either take the simplest tack and return objects or sacrifice simplicity in order to gain efficiency. When operator functions are used for other purposes—to access class members, to perform I/O, to provide an alternative to the syntax for calling member functions—it is often convenient and efficient to have them return references.

12

I/O Streams

C is notable for its approach to input and output. Unlike I/O systems in most computer languages, the C I/O system is supplied as a separate library; it isn't a part of the language proper. You're probably familiar with the pros and cons of the library approach. The advantages of supplying essential I/O in a separate library are that it simplifies the compiler and that such a division makes it possible, at least in theory, for alternative I/O systems to be developed. The disadvantage is that C I/O is, somewhat in the spirit of C itself, powerful and flexible, but ugly and unsafe.

The C standard I/O library (stdio) contains two related facilities. The first is a buffered I/O system that contains character-at-a-time and bulk I/O routines: *getc()*, *putc()*, *fread()*, and *fwrite()*. On top of the buffered I/O facility are a text conversion facility that uses *printf()* to convert built-in data types to text and a comparable input facility that uses *scanf()* to convert text to the host computer's binary format.

To many programmers, the awkward format codes in *printf()*'s format string—*%-8.2g*, for example—and the complete lack of argument type checking are serious drawbacks. Among the modern computer languages, only C accepts utter nonsense output statements:

```
printf("%s %f %c\n", 1.0, '2', "3");
```

To other programmers, especially to people like me, who have grown accustomed to the scheme, the C I/O system has become second nature: an austere and unforgiving but reliable companion.

The migration from C to C++ created an opportunity to develop a totally new approach to I/O. The main goals of the new approach, which has evolved into the iostream library described in this chapter, are to create an I/O system that is both type safe and extensible. A type-safe I/O system is one in which the compiler prevents such I/O absurdities as the *printf()* statement we just saw. An ideal extensible I/O system is one that can be extended in two ways: first to encompass user-defined data types and second to accommodate new I/O paradigms such as I/O using shared memory, I/O by means of network communication links, and I/O to and from graphical windowing systems.

Although the C++ iostream library is a totally new I/O system, it has much in common with C's stdio library in that it is based on the concept of the stream, an infinitely long sequence of characters that are accessed sequentially. And like stdio, the iostream library introduces refinements to the stream concept to allow file operations, such as seeking from one position to another. The basic stream concept works well with plain text data, such as data being sent to files or to dumb terminals. With the addition of manipulators, the stream concept is also applicable to richer environments in which "text" has characteristics such as size, font, color, and position.

In earlier parts of the book, we've seen examples that incidentally featured simple examples of iostream library use. The basics are indeed simple. Several predefined iostream connections, such as *cout* and *cin*, combined with insertion and extraction operators, facilitate output and input in MS-DOS programs. Built-in data types can be output using an insertion operator:

```
cout << 1.0 << '2' << "3" << "\n";
```

Similarly, values can be input from a stream using an extraction operator:

```
double d;
cin >> d;
```

Later in this chapter, we'll look in much more detail at using and extending the iostream library. But first we'll look at the overall organization and design of the iostream library—in itself a valuable lesson in object-oriented design.

I/O Options

Nearly all useful programs need to enter and display text. The question is By what means? C++ already includes all of C's I/O possibilities in the C stdio library and adds to those options the C++ iostream library. And C compilers on the PC have always included low-level MS-DOS and BIOS I/O facilities. Finally, let's not forget Windows, which has its own unique ideas about I/O. For most programs, you need to pick an I/O system and stick with it. Mixing and matching is not a good idea.

If you're writing Windows software, stick with the Windows I/O paradigm, using *wsprintf()* to load values into strings and *TextOut()* to write those strings to a window. As a quick start to Windows, some programmers choose to use the QuickWin library, a simplistic way to transform DOS programs into Windows programs. You can use the C++ iostream library with the QuickWin library, but don't put too much effort into QuickWin. View it as a transition aid, not as a long-term solution.

If you're writing DOS applications, you might want to stick with the tried-and-true C stdio library, especially if you are already familiar with it or if some of a program's code is C code that currently uses C stdio. Many programs that use third-party libraries will be tied to C stdio—even if some of the newer parts of the programs are developed in C++.

If raw performance is critical to your application, you might need to use the low-level DOS and BIOS facilities. On old 8088 PCs and slow 80286 PCs, the low-level I/O routines are far faster at sending data to the screen than C stdio or C++ iostream operations. On most newer machines, the performance difference is imperceptible.

If portability is a prime concern, you should try to use either the C stdio library or the iostream library. I have a strong preference for the iostream library, mostly because it is type safe. I was once a *printf()* enthusiast, and for a while I used C++ but avoided the iostream library. I thought the iostream library was clumsy and that it required too much verbiage (too many keystrokes). But I changed my mind as I began to realize that the only "stupid" mistakes that were getting past the compiler were related to *printf()*. Since switching to the iostream library, I've had no regrets. Output statements do take more keystrokes than their equivalents in C stdio, but they are more likely to work correctly, and for me that's more than enough reason to use the iostream library.

Organization of the iostream Library

The iostream class library hierarchies are not particularly hard to understand, but it is certainly useful at the outset to stand back and look at the big picture. Figure 12-1 on the next page shows a fleshed-out but still slightly simplified diagram of the iostream class hierarchy we looked at briefly in Chapter 4 as an illustration of multiple inheritance.[1]

Perhaps the most striking aspect of the iostream library, an aspect easily seen in Figure 12-1, is its complexity. The iostream library contains about as many classes as the stdio library contains functions. But with the iostream library, you get what you pay for. The iostream library is far more capable than stdio, and with a bit of effort you'll soon know where to look when you need to find a particular capability.

The iostream library contains two separate class hierarchies. The more complex family of classes, the one for formatted I/O, is based on the *ios* class and contains capabilities roughly analogous to those of stdio's *printf()* and *scanf()* functions. The "Pure Streams" classes perform the functions of *printf()* and *scanf()*; they are concerned with conversion to and from text.

The "File I/O Streams" classes take the place of *fprintf()* and *fscanf()*, and the "In-Core I/O Streams" classes are analogous to *sprintf()* and *sscanf()*.

The simpler family of classes, the one for unformatted I/O, is based on the *streambuf* class and implements the stream concept. This family of classes is concerned with data movement, not with conversion to and from text. The *streambuf* base class is the purest expression of the stream idea, the *filebuf* derived class adapts streams to files, and the *strstreambuf* class, also derived from *streambuf*, adapts *streambuf* objects to in-memory operation.

1. I've omitted a few implementation-dependent details that shouldn't be relied on in application programs.

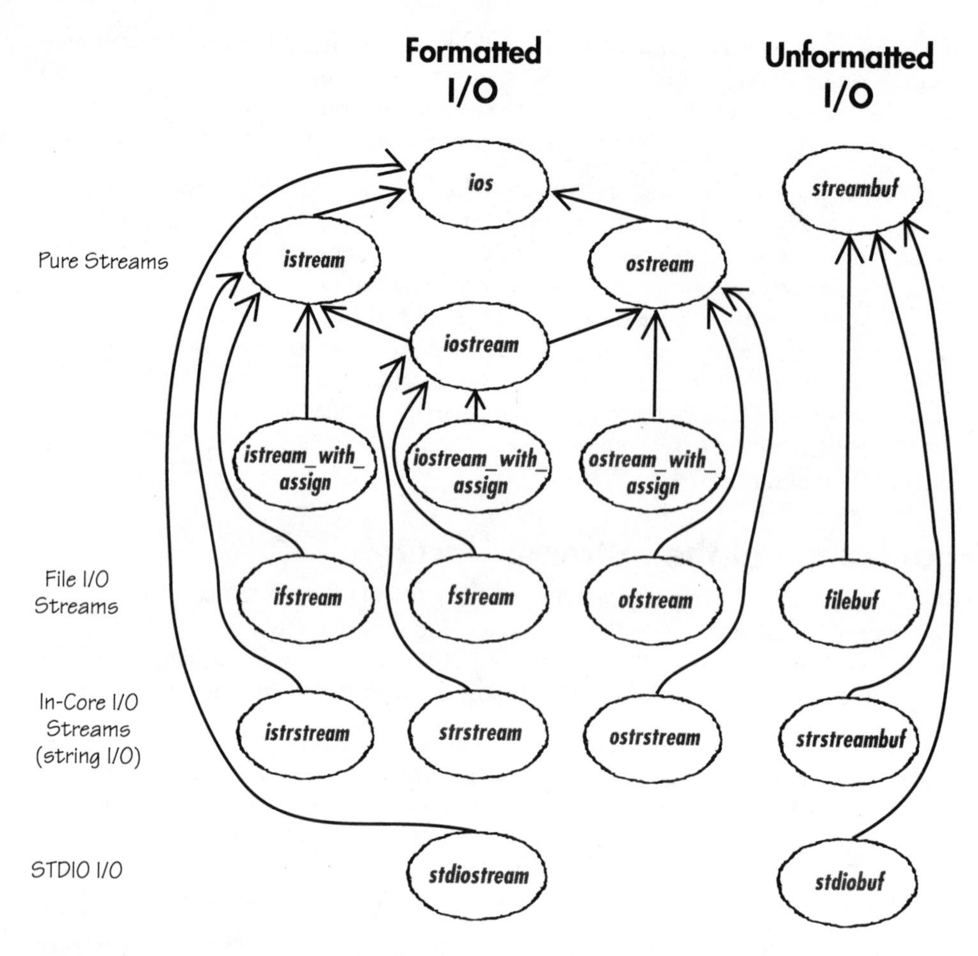

Figure 12-1.
The iostream class library hierarchies.

The connection between the *ios* family of classes and the *streambuf* family is that the *ios* base class uses a *streambuf* object to perform its I/O. Notice that I said that *ios* "uses" a *streambuf* object; it contains a pointer to a *streambuf* object. An *ios* object *is* not *a streambuf*; its class is not derived from the *streambuf* class.

Polymorphism is important to the functioning of objects in the *ios* class hierarchy. All of the I/O performed by *istream* and *ostream* objects is accomplished by means of a *streambuf* object—any kind of *streambuf* object. When you create an *ifstream* object, you automatically create a *filebuf* object to take care of the unformatted I/O, and a pointer to the *filebuf* object is passed to the *ios* object constructor. Thus, when you extract from the *ifstream* object, you're using the *filebuf* object to deliver the raw data and you're using the *istream* object to convert the data. Similarly, when you create an *istrstream* object, you automatically create a *strstreambuf* object to do the

I/O. At the level of the *istream* class, it doesn't matter what kind of *streambuf* object is being used.

The Classes Themselves, in Brief

Before we delve into more detailed examinations of the classes and their relationships, let's take a quick tour of the hierarchy, with plenty of reference to Figure 12-1.

Formatted I/O classes

ios is the base class for the hierarchy. It contains status flags, format flags, operator functions to test the state of the stream, status functions, and a pointer to a *streambuf* object.

istream is derived from *ios*. It contains extractors (*operator>>()* member functions) for all the built-in data types, simple unformatted input functions, and routines to move the *get (read)* pointer.

ostream is derived from *ios*. It contains inserters (*operator<<()* member functions) for all the built-in data types, simple unformatted output functions, and routines to move the *put (write)* pointer.

iostream is derived from both *istream* and *ostream*. It implements a read/write I/O connection.

istream_with_assign, *ostream_with_assign*, and *iostream_with_assign* are the *with_assign* versions, respectively, of *istream*, *ostream*, and *iostream*. Each implements an *operator=()* member function. This means that each can be assigned a new stream, which changes the I/O connection. *cin* is an *istream_with_assign* object, and *cout*, *cerr*, and *clog* are *ostream_with_assign* objects.

ifstream, *ofstream*, and *fstream* are also derived, respectively, from *istream*, *ostream*, and *iostream*. These three classes implement stream connections to and from a file. They add file open and close routines to the extractors and inserters provided by their base classes.

istrstream, *ostrstream*, and *strstream* are derived from *istream*, *ostream*, and *iostream* and implement stream connections to and from memory regions. They add a routine to return a pointer to the string.

stdiostream is derived from *ios*. It implements a stream connection that uses a *FILE ** (from stdio) connection. Note that no insertion or extraction operations are available for *stdiostream* objects.

Unformatted I/O classes

streambuf is the base class for the *streambuf* hierarchy. It implements a stream connection containing an I/O buffer, read and write pointers, simple input and output functions, functions to move the read and write pointers, and functions for simple status and error reporting.

filebuf is derived from *streambuf*. It adds file open and close routines to *streambuf*'s functionality.

strstreambuf is derived from *streambuf*. It adds buffer management functions to *streambuf*'s functionality.

stdiobuf is derived from *streambuf*. It adapts *streambuf* to use *FILE* * (from stdio) connections.

Practical File Considerations

In order to use the iostream library, you need to include some files in your program's source code files. The fundamental include file for the iostream library is iostream.h (iostream.hpp with some compilers). It details the classes depicted as "Pure Streams" in Figure 12-1. This is the only include file you'll need in order to use the standard streams (*cin*, *cout*, *cerr*, and *clog*).

For iostream file operations, you should instead include fstream.h (sometimes called fstream.hpp).

For iostream in-core (string) operations, you should instead include strstream.h (also called strstream.hpp, sstream.hpp, or sstream.h). (Both fstream.h and strstream.h include iostream.h, so you don't need to include iostream.h additionally.)

The iostream manipulators, which are used to control formatting, are declared in iomanip.h (or iomanip.hpp), which includes iostream.h.

The *streambuf* Class Hierarchy

The *streambuf* class outlines the shape of a generalized buffering class. Its fundamental operations are *get()* to retrieve data from the buffer and *put()* to store data into the buffer. *streambuf* contains versions of *get()* and *put()* to transfer either single or multiple characters at one time. It also contains status routines and prototype seek routines.

Each *streambuf* object has a buffer, plus *get* and *put* pointers to that buffer. In a pure *streambuf* object, the *get* and *put* pointers operate in separate parts of the buffer; thus, out of the box, a *streambuf* is bidirectional. Classes derived from *streambuf* are able to alter the details of the way the *get* and *put* pointers are used, which makes it easy to implement circular buffers, input buffers, or output buffers.

The most surprising aspect of the *streambuf* class is that it isn't intended to be used directly; rather, it is intended to be used as a base for more specialized classes. The iostream library supplies three such specialized descendants of *streambuf*: *filebuf* for file operations, *strstreambuf* for string (in-core) operations, and *stdiobuf* for I/O using C's standard I/O library. For compatibility with the original C++ stream library, *streambuf*'s constructor is public, but you should consider the constructor to be protected in that you should refrain from creating any *streambuf* objects.

The *streambuf* Public Member Functions

int sgetc() returns the next character from the *get* buffer, or *EOF* if no character is available. The *get* pointer is not moved.

*int sgetn(char *buf, int n)* fills the buffer with the next *n* characters from the *get* buffer. The return value is the number of acquired characters—which might be less than *n* if fewer than *n* were available—or *EOF* if no character is available. The *get* pointer is moved past the fetched characters.

int snextc() moves the *get* pointer forward one character and then returns the next character.

int stossc() moves the *get* pointer forward. No error is generated if the *get* pointer is already at the end of the input.

int sbumpc() returns the current character from the buffer, or *EOF* if no character is available. The *get* pointer is moved forward one character.

int sputbackc(char c) returns the last-fetched character to the buffer. Note that *c* must be the last-fetched character; the function is not defined to put back something different. The return value is *0* for success and *EOF* for failure.

int in_avail() returns the number of characters that can be fetched without delay or error.

int sputc(int c) stores *c* in the *put* buffer and moves the *put* pointer forward. The return value is *1* for success and *EOF* for failure.

*int sputn(const char *buf, int len)* stores *len* characters from *buf* in the *put* buffer and moves the *put* pointer forward *len*. The return value is the number of characters stored for success and *EOF* for failure.

int out_waiting() returns the number of characters waiting in the *put* buffer.

virtual streampos seekpos(streampos p, int m = ios::in | ios::out) seeks to position *p*. The mode *m* specifies whether the *put* pointer, the *get* pointer, or both (the default) should be moved. The return value is the new position of the stream.

virtual streampos seekoff(streamoff p, seek_dir d, int m = ios::in | ios::out) seeks to the specified relative position. The *seek_dir*, an enumeration defined in *ios*, is either *beg*, *cur*, or *end*, and the mode *m* specifies whether the *put* pointer, the *get* pointer, or both (the default) should be moved. The return value is the new position of the stream.

virtual int sync() synchronizes the buffer state with the ultimate producer or consumer, which is a flush operation for *filebuf*s.

Note that *streambuf* also contains public constructors and a virtual public *setbuf()* function, but we won't look at them in detail here. They should be used as if they were protected, that is, used only in derived classes.

Even though you shouldn't create any *streambuf* objects, you need to know about *streambuf*'s capabilities because they are useful whenever you create a *filebuf* object, a *strstreambuf* object, or an object of any of the classes derived from *ios* that use *filebuf*s or *strstreambuf*s.

From the perspective of someone planning to derive a class from *streambuf*, the brief survey of the *streambuf* public member functions in our sidebar is inadequate because it doesn't mention the *streambuf* protected member functions. This is a large omission because the protected *streambuf* member functions, which are primarily virtual member functions, are the locus of activity for extending the class. Most of the public *streambuf* member functions are simple. It's the protected *streambuf* member functions that tend to the work. For example, the public *sputc()* places a character in the buffer if there is room; otherwise, it calls the protected virtual *overflow()* member function. *overflow()*, which is redefined in both *filebuf* and *strstreambuf*, is charged with the task of making room. In *filebuf*, *overflow()* will flush the existing buffer to the file and then reset the *put* pointer to the start of the buffer. In *strstreambuf*, *overflow()* is likely to allocate more space.

The Derived *filebuf* Class

A *filebuf* is a *streambuf* object that is specialized for file I/O. It adds file open, close, and attach routines to the set of standard *streambuf* routines. A *filebuf* also has several public constructors and a public interface that lets you control the buffering.

Let's look at a simple program that uses a *filebuf*. The program is a replacement for cat, an early Unix utility that catenates (combines) its input files. The version of cat found on recent Unix systems contains several command line option flags for variants; the substitute for cat we'll look at here is much more like the earlier, mid-seventies incarnation of cat, which had no command line options.

```
#include <fstream.h>

// cat--catenate files specified on the command line
void main(int argc, char **argv)
{
    filebuf f;
    while(--argc) {
```

The *filebuf* Public Constructors

filebuf() creates a *filebuf* object, one that is not attached to an open file.

filebuf(int fd) creates a *filebuf* object that is attached to *fd*, which is a file descriptor returned by a successful *open()* or *create()*.

*filebuf(int fd, char *buf, int buflen)* also creates a *filebuf* object that is attached to *fd*, the file descriptor returned by a successful *open()* or *create()*. The *buf* and *buflen* arguments are used to control buffering.

```
        f.open(*++argv, ios::in);
        if (f.is_open())
            cout << &f;
        f.close();
    }
}
```

The example above revolves around a *filebuf* named *f*. Each command line argument is presumed to be a file, and the program tries to open each file and attach it to the *filebuf* object. As in Unix's original cat, error messages aren't displayed when a file open fails, although this feature would be easy to add. If the file open is successful, the file buffer is output by means of the predefined *cout* stream and then the file is closed. (The processing of the program's command line arguments using *argc* and *argv* is standard—refer to any C text.)

The *filebuf* Public Interface Member Functions

*filebuf *open(char *name, int mode, int prot = openprot)* opens the file *name*. The *mode* argument is an OR of the *open_mode* enumeration constants defined in the *ios* class we'll look at shortly. The *prot* argument specifies the protection status of the file. In MS-DOS, you can construct the protection bitmask by ORing the *S_IREAD* and *S_IWRITE* constants from sys/stat.h.

*filebuf *attach(int fd)* connects the *filebuf* object to *fd*, the file descriptor returned by a successful *open()* or *create()*.

*filebuf *close()* closes the file that is attached to the *filebuf*. The *close()* function returns the address of the *filebuf* for success and *0* for failure. The function returns NULL if the stream is already attached; otherwise, it returns its own address.

int is_open() returns nonzero if the *filebuf* is attached to a file; *0* otherwise.

streampos seekoff(streampos p, seek_dir d, int mode) overrides the *seekoff()* function of the *streambuf* class.

int fd() returns the file descriptor of the file that is attached to the *filebuf* and *EOF* if no file is attached.

*streambuf *setbuf(char *buf, int buflen)* controls the buffering. If *buf* is null or *buflen* is *0*, it turns off buffering; otherwise, it uses *buf*, whose length is *buflen*. The *setbuf()* function is effective only before a file has been attached to the *filebuf*. If buffering can be specified, the return value is the address of the *filebuf*; otherwise, *0* is returned.

The Derived *strstreambuf* Class

A *strstreambuf* is a *streambuf* optimized for in-memory operation. Objects of the *strstreambuf* class are intended primarily for use with the string-based *ios* classes (*istrstream*, *ostrstream*, and *strstream*), but they can also be used independently.

A *strstreambuf* is simply an object that is fully memory resident yet follows the blueprint of the *streambuf* class. Thus, it has get, put, and seek operations, as any *streambuf* does.

A *strstreambuf* can operate in dynamic allocation mode, in which sufficient memory is allocated as needed, or in fixed mode, in which a fixed size buffer is used. If you supply a buffer to the constructor, you implicitly specify a *strstreambuf* of a fixed size; otherwise, you create a dynamic *strstreambuf*. In dynamic allocation mode, the get and put areas overlap, as each is the full size of the buffer, whereas the get and put areas are separate for fixed size *strstreambuf*s.

Despite the *str* prefix, *strstreambuf*s aren't solely for storing strings and therefore don't necessarily follow C's convention for terminating strings with nulls. A *strstreambuf* can store anything, which certainly includes nulls. But if you place some text into a *strstreambuf* and then want to use it as a normal C string, you must remember to add the trailing null.

When you first create a *strstreambuf*, it is active, which gives it two characteristics. The first and more obvious is that the *strstreambuf* is ready for use. The second is that it owns its buffer region. A *strstreambuf* object is in charge of allocation and deallocation for a dynamic buffer, and it assumes that you won't deallocate or move

The *strstreambuf* Constructors

strstreambuf() creates an empty *strstreambuf*. Buffer space will be allocated automatically as needed by means of *new* and *delete*. Allocation details can be specified using *strstreambuf*'s *setbuf()* member function.

strstreambuf(int n) is the same as the default constructor except that an initial space of *n* bytes is allocated.

*strstreambuf(void *(*salloc)(long), void (*sfree)(void *))* creates an empty *strstreambuf*. Buffer space will be allocated automatically as needed by means of **salloc()* and freed by means of **sfree()*. The **salloc()* function will be called with a *long* denoting the allocation size, and **sfree()* will be called with a pointer to a previously allocated buffer. If the **salloc()* pointer is null, *new* will be used; if the **sfree()* pointer is null, *delete* will be used.

*strstreambuf(char *buf, int n, char *pstart = 0)* creates a *strstreambuf* using *buf* for the storage buffer. No further buffer space will be allocated. If *n* is positive, it is the size of *buf*; if *n* is *0*, *buf* is assumed to contain a null terminated string, with the null marking the end of the buffer; if *n* is negative, the buffer is assumed to continue indefinitely. The *get* pointer is initialized to *buf*; the *put* pointer is initialized to *pstart*. If *pstart* is null, puts are erroneous and the get buffer is the entire array; if *pstart* is nonnull, the get buffer is from *buf* to *pstart–1* and the put buffer is from *pstart* to the end of the buffer. Because the default value of *pstart* is *0*, the default initialized *strstreambuf* is a read-only buffer.

a static buffer. Executing the *str()* or *freeze()* member function freezes the buffer, which means that you shouldn't deposit additional data, and which also means that you now own the buffer. If you delete a frozen *strstreambuf,* you must also be sure to delete its buffer region if it is dynamic.

The next example we'll look at reverses a string. In this example, the *strstreambuf* constructor is given the string to be reversed, although you could also move a string into a *strstreambuf* using the base class *streambuf*'s *sputc()* or *sputn()* and then reverse the string. The second constructor argument, *0,* tells the constructor to use the length of the null terminated string argument as the size of the buffer.

```
// in-core string reversal
#include <strstrea.h>
void main()
{
    strstreambuf s("The rain in Spain falls mainly on the plain.", 0);

    s.seekoff(0, ios::end, ios::in);             // seek to end
    while(s.seekoff(-1, ios::cur, ios::in) >= 0) // move backward
        cout << (char)s.sgetc();                 // output a character
    cout << endl;
}
```

The logic of the string reversal is performed by means of the *seekoff()* member function from the *streambuf* base class. The *seekoff()* just above the *while* loop moves to the end of the string, and then the *seekoff()* in the test expression of the *while* loop continually moves backward until the beginning of the string is encountered. The output of *sgetc()* is cast to *char* so that the *cout* stream will print a character.

The *strstreambuf* Public Member Functions

*char *str()* returns a pointer to the *strstreambuf* buffer and freezes the buffer. When frozen, the buffer becomes the client's responsibility, which means that a dynamically allocated buffer won't be deallocated automatically by the *strstreambuf* destructor. Also, you shouldn't deposit to or withdraw from a frozen *strstreambuf.* Note that *str()* can return null if the buffer has not yet been used.

void freeze(int n = 1) freezes or thaws a *strstreambuf.* Thawing is accomplished by means of a *0* argument. Freezing is accomplished by omitting the argument or by using the argument *1.*

*streambuf *setbuf(char *unused, int granularity)* sets the allocation granularity. The first parameter to *setbuf()* is present only for compatibility with the *setbuf()* function in the *streambuf* base class; it should always be specified as *0.* The *granularity* value determines how much additional storage is allocated whenever additional space is needed.

Remember that *sgetc()* would otherwise return an *int*, which by default would be output numerically. Here's the output of the program:

```
.nialp eht no ylniam sllaf niapS ni niar ehT
```

The Derived *stdiobuf* Class

A *stdiobuf is a streambuf* that uses a *FILE ** (from the C stdio library) I/O connection. It is useful primarily when you are adding C++ code to a C application that already uses the C standard I/O library for file operations.

> **The *stdiobuf* Public Constructor**
>
> *stdiobuf* has only one public constructor. *stdiobuf(FILE *f)* creates a *stdiodbuf* object using the specified *FILE** file connection for input and output.

Using a *stdiobuf*, you can move to *streambuf* operations without discarding existing code. In newer code that doesn't need to coexist with old C stdio code, avoid *stdiobuf*s (and *stdiostreams*).

> **The *stdiobuf* Public Member Function**
>
> *stdiobuf* has only one public member function. *FILE *stdiofile()* returns the FILE * pointer that is being used for I/O.

The *ios* Class Hierarchy

The *ios* class is the base class for the iostream library's hierarchy of classes for formatted I/O. It establishes the rules and the shape of the iostream class hierarchy. Like so many powerful base classes, *ios* by itself can't be used to create a useful object. Instead, *ios* facilities are accessed by its derived classes, principally *istream* and *ostream*. Note that every object created in a class derived from *ios* uses a *streambuf* for the actual I/O.

ios is concerned with two separate tasks. The first task is to control and manage the status of an iostream connection. To manage the status of an iostream connection, *ios* has member functions to return status information, to reset status information, to return a pointer to the stream's *streambuf* connection, and to tie one stream to another so that input and output are synchronized. The ios class's other task is to establish a framework for formatted I/O operations.

The *ios* Public Member Functions for Status

int rdstate() returns the current state of the stream. The bits in the return value should be interpreted by means of the *io_state* enumeration.

int bad() returns *true* if the stream is in the bad state, meaning that it is unusable.

int fail() returns *true* if the stream is in either the bad or the fail state; if the stream is only in the fail state (*fail() && !bad()*), the stream is usable, although an insertion or an extraction has failed.

int eof() returns *true* if the stream is at the end of the file.

int good() returns *true* if the stream is not in any error state.

int clear(int state = 0) sets the stream state bits. By default, the state is set to *0* (*ios::good()*), but a more specific state can be specified by means of the optional argument.

int operator!() returns *true* if the stream is in either the fail or the bad state. This is usually written

```
if (!cout) failure();
```

where *failure()* is a function that takes care of the problem.

operator void()* returns *0* if the stream is in either the fail or the bad state. This is usually written

```
if (cout >> a) success();
```

where *success()* is a function that is called for a successful operation.

*streambuf *rdbuf()* returns a pointer to the stream's *streambuf* object.

static void sync_with_stdio() causes the predefined streams *cin, cout, cerr,* and *clog* to operate by means of the C standard I/O connections *stdin, stdout,* and *stderr*; and it also implies unit buffering. This is useful when you are mixing C stdio code with C++ stream code but is not recommended otherwise.

*ostream *tie()* returns a pointer to the tied stream.

*ostream *tie(ostream *)* ties the current stream to the specified *ostream,* which is called the "tied stream." For an *istream,* this means that the tied stream will be flushed whenever the *istream* needs input; for an *ostream,* this means that the tied stream will be flushed whenever the *ostream* is flushed. By default, *cin* is tied to *cout, cout* is tied to *cerr,* and *cerr* is tied to *clog.* Tying streams forces *ostreams* to output their contents, such as prompts for input, before input operations.

The motivation for having separate classes for input and output is obvious; there are many more differences between input and output than the direction in which the data travels. But input and output also have much in common, such as the base for numeric conversions and the format of floating point conversions. The features that input and output have in common are addressed by an *ios* pool of format conversion flags. Fifteen conversion flags, such as *hex* to specify hexadecimal input or output, are predefined, and additional flags can be allocated to meet the needs of user-defined types.

The *ios* format control flags can be controlled in two ways. The first way is simply to set or unset the flags using the *setf()* and *unsetf()* member functions, as in this *hex* flag example:

```
cout.setf(ios::hex);
```

The *ios* Public Member Functions for Formatting

The *ios* class clearly anticipates the needs of its *istream* and *ostream* offspring with several public member functions for formatting.

long flags() returns the current format flags.

long flags(long newflags) sets the format flags to *newflags* and returns the previous settings:

```
flags = newflags;
```

long setf(long bits) sets the logical OR *bits* with the current format flags and then returns the previous setting:

```
flags |= bits;
```

long setf(long bits, long field) sets the format flags whose corresponding bits are set in *field* to *bits* and then returns the previous setting. Flags corresponding to *0* bits in *field* are not altered:

```
flags = (flags & ~field) | (bits & field);
```

long unsetf(long bits) unsets the format flags whose bits are set in *bits* and then returns the previous setting:

```
flags &= ~bits;
```

static long bitalloc() allocates a format flag bit and returns a bitmask for that bit.

static int xalloc() allocates a format word from a small pool of format control words and returns the index of that word. The index should be used subsequently in *iword()* or *pword()* to get a reference to the word.

The drawback is that this statement can't be used in the midst of an iostream insertion expression. Thus, to output a numeric variable named *val* in decimal, octal, and hexadecimal notation would require the following elaborate sequence of statements:

```
cout.setf(ios::dec);
cout << val << " ";
cout.unsetf(ios::dec);
cout.setf(ios::oct);
cout << val << " ";
cout.unsetf(ios::oct);
cout.setf(ios::hex);
cout << val << endl;
cout.unsetf(ios::hex);
```

The iostream library has been justly criticized for its wordiness, but this is too chatty even for iostream! The solution is to use a "manipulator" function, a function that

long& iword(int index) const returns a reference to a previously allocated format control word, given that word's index.

*void *& pword(int index) const* returns a reference to a previously allocated format control pointer, given that pointer's index. The only difference between *iword()* and *pword()* is that *iword()* returns a reference to a *long* and *pword()* returns a reference to a generic pointer.

char fill(char fillch) sets the output fill character to *fillch*.

int precision() const returns the precision setting.

int precision(int val) sets the precision setting to *val*. The precision setting governs the number of significant digits output by the floating point inserters.

int width() const returns the current setting of the field-width format variable.

int width(int val) sets the field-width format variable to *val*. For output, the field width is the minimum number of characters to be output. If necessary, fill characters will pad the output to the specified width. Note that numeric and string inserters don't truncate; they may thus output more-than-width characters.

For input, the field width is the length of the buffer for string extractions. For both input and output, the field width is reset to *0* after every insertion or extraction. The *setw()* parameterized manipulator can be used to set the width format parameter.

can work in the midst of an iostream expression. Here's how manipulators can condense our wordy example:

```
cout << dec << val << " " << oct << val << " " << hex << val << endl;
cout.unsetf(hex);
```

The names *dec*, *oct*, and *hex* refer to manipulator functions that are invoked, by overloaded *operator<<()*, to change the I/O flags. At first glance, you might think that *dec*, *oct*, and *hex* refer to the *format_mode* enumeration constants that are defined in the *ios* class. This is a tempting but incorrect conclusion. Remember that to refer to a type name or an enumeration constant defined within a class, you must use the scope resolution operator. Thus, if you wanted to output the *dec*, *oct*, and *hex* enumeration constants, you would write

```
cout << (int)ios::dec << endl;
cout << (int)ios::oct << endl;
cout << (int)ios::hex << endl;
```

The output would be the values *16*, *32*, and *64*, which correspond to the values of the constants that are defined in the *format_mode* enumeration. Let's take a look at the *ios* class enumerations before we move on to a detailed consideration of its derived *ostream* and *istream* classes—and of manipulator functions.

The *ios* class enumerations

The *ios* class has public *io_state* and format mode enumerations.

```
enum io_state {
```

`goodbit,`	Everything is fine—no problems.
`eofbit,`	Stream is at end of file.
`failbit,`	The stream's last I/O operation has failed—which often means that an unexpected input value was encountered—but the stream is still operational.
`badbit`	A serious error has occurred, and the stream is unusable.

```
};
```

and

```
enum {
```

`skipws,`	Input: White space (including spaces, tabs, carriage returns, and newlines) in the input is skipped before extractions of numeric or string values.
`left, right,`	Output: Left-adjust or right-adjust output.
`internal,`	Output: For numeric values, the initial sign (+ or –) and the base indicator (*0* or *0x*) is left adjusted, followed by the fill characters, followed by a right-adjusted value.

`dec, oct, hex,`	Output: Integral values are inserted in decimal (base 10), octal (base 8), or hexadecimal (base 16) notation. Input: Integral values are extracted in decimal, octal, or hexadecimal notation. If none of these flags are set, output is in decimal notation and input follows standard C++ lexical conventions based on the value's first digits: *1* through *9* implies decimal input, *0x* implies hexadecimal input, and *0* implies octal input.
`showbase,`	Output: Integral values will be inserted with a leading *0* for octal insertions or with a leading *0x* for hexadecimal insertions.
`showpoint,`	Output: Floating point output will always contain a decimal point and trailing zeros.
`uppercase,`	Output: Uppercase indicators will be used for hexadecimal (0X*nnn*) and scientific (*n.nnn*E*nn*) insertions.
`showpos,`	Output: Decimal insertions of positive integral values will be inserted with an initial + symbol.
`scientific,` `fixed,`	Output: *scientific* implies the format *n.mmmenn*; *fixed* implies the format *nnn.mmm*. The number of digits *m* after the decimal point is governed by the *ios* class's *precision()* member function. If neither is set, output will be in scientific format if the exponent is less than *–4* or greater than the precision and in fixed format otherwise.
`unitbuf,`	Output: The buffer is flushed after each insertion.
`stdio`	Output: The C standard I/O library's *stdout* and *stderr* are flushed after each insertion.

```
};
```

The *ios* class also contains the *open_mode* and *seek_dir* enumerations.

```
enum open_mode {
```

`in,`	Open the file for input (read).
`out,`	Open the file for output (write).
`ate,`	Seek to the end when the file is opened. The abbreviation is for "automatic to end."
`app,`	Open the file in append mode, meaning that all write operations will occur at the end of the file.
`trunc,`	Truncate the file if it already exists.

`nocreate,`	Don't create the file; the open will fail unless the file exists.
`noreplace,`	Don't replace the file; the open will fail if the file exists.
`binary`	Open the file in binary mode; otherwise, CR/LF is translated to LF on input, and LF is translated to CR/LF on output. This is Microsoft C7 specific.

```
};
```

and

```
enum seek_dir {
```

`beg,`	Seek relative to the beginning of the file.
`cur,`	Seek relative to the current position.
`end`	Seek relative to the end of the file.

```
};
```

Note that the *seek_dir* enumeration is misleadingly named; either *seek_pos* or *seek_relative_to* would reveal more.

The *ostream* Class—Insertion

"Insertion" is a newly coined term for sending output to an output stream connection. It is implemented by the *ostream* class, which is primarily concerned with the conversion of binary values to text. *ostream* is derived from *ios*, so all of the public facilities of *ios* are available to it.

Several specialized classes are derived from *ostream*: the class *iostream* for generic input/output streams, the class *ofstream* for output streams directed to files, and the class *ostrstream* for output streams directed to strings.

The C++ insertion mechanism is based on overloading the left shift (<<) operator:

```
cout << '1' << 2 << 3.0 << endl;
```

When the compiler encounters such an expression, it performs the same analysis as for any expression. Its first step is to investigate the precedence and associativity of the operators. The compiler thus quickly realizes that the expression is equivalent to

```
(((cout << '1') << 2) << 3.0) << endl;
```

The innermost expression prompts the compiler to look for an *operator<<()* function whose left operand is an *ostream* (*cout*) and whose right operand is a *char* (the *'1'*). Finding such a function in the *ostream* class, we can transform the expression:

```
((cout.operator<<('1') << 2) << 3.0) << endl;
```

Because *operator<<()* returns a reference to an *ostream*, the next task of the compiler is to find an *operator<<()* function whose left operand is an *ostream* and whose right operand is an *int* (the *2*). Following this chain of logic leads us to this equivalent expression:

```
cout.operator<<('1').operator<<(2).operator<<(3.0).operator<<(endl);
```

The important point is not this horrendous expression. Rather, it is that the compiler uses standard rules of precedence, associativity, and overloading to resolve *iostream* statements. Thus, you can anticipate trouble when, for example, each item to be output is an expression rather than a simple value. If you want to output the value of *a* (an *int*) bitwise *OR*'d with *b* (also an *int*), you must write

```
cout << (a | b) << endl;
```

It's wise to parenthesize numeric expressions entwined in iostream statements. If you prefer to flaunt your virtuosity, remember that unary, multiplicative, and additive

The *ostream* Inserters

*char **, *signed char **, and *unsigned char ** all output a string. The individual characters of the string aren't converted, and the trailing null is not output. Padding will be inserted if necessary, but the string will not be truncated to the *width* format setting.

*void ** inserts a pointer in hexadecimal notation, as if the *showbase* flag were set.

char, *signed char*, and *unsigned char* all insert a single character, without conversion.

short, *int*, *long*, *unsigned short*, *unsigned int*, and *unsigned long* all convert the value to text and then insert it. The format is controlled by the *dec*, *oct*, *hex*, *showpos*, *showbase*, and *uppercase* flags. Padding will be inserted if necessary, but the value will not be truncated to fit the *width* format setting.

float and *double* convert the value to text and then insert it. The format is controlled by the *scientific*, *fixed*, and *uppercase* flags and by the *precision()* setting.

*streambuf ** extracts from a stream buffer and inserts. No formatting, such as padding, is performed.

*ostream &(*fn)(ostream&)* and *ios& (*fn)(ios&)* call the I/O manipulation function *fn()*. The function must take a reference to an *ostream* or an *ios* and must return its argument. The supplied I/O manipulators for *ostreams* are *endl*, *ends*, *flush*, *dec*, *hex*, and *oct*.

operators have higher precedence than the shift operator, which means they don't need to be parenthesized when used in an iostream statement. Logical, relational, bitwise, and assignment operators all have less precedence than shift; thus, expressions using these operators must be parenthesized in an iostream statement.

The *ostream* class has two seek functions named *seekp()*. The letter *p* is for "put," because seeks in an *ostream* move the *ios* object's put pointer. The two seek flavors are seek to an absolute position and do a relative seek. When you call *seekp()* with a single *streampos* argument, you will move to that point in the stream, but when you call *seekp()* with both a *streamoff* argument and a *seek_dir* argument, you will perform a relative seek. Both member functions return the absolute position in the stream.

The *ostream* Constructor and Public Member Functions

*ostream(streambuf *b)* creates an *ostream* object that will output by means of the supplied *streambuf*.

ostream& flush() sends all pending data to its final destination.

ostream& seekp(streampos) moves to the specified absolute location.

ostream& seekp(streamoff, seek_dir) moves by the specified amount. *seek_dir* is the enumeration defined in *ios* that has the values *beg*, *cur*, and *end*.

streampos tellp() reports the current position of a stream.

ostream& put(char) outputs a single character, without conversion, to a stream.

*ostream& write(char *buf, int len)* outputs a region of memory, without conversion, to a stream. The *int* parameter is the length of the buffer. (*buf* can be either *char ** or *unsigned char **.)

int opfx() and *void osfx()* output prefix and suffix routines that are used in user-written inserters.

The *istream* Class—Extraction

The *istream* class is the blueprint for input from streams. Its primary role is to implement "extraction" operations, reading data from a stream. The C++ extraction mechanism is implemented by overloading *operator>>()*. Like *ostream*, the *istream* class uses the format flags and status mechanisms of the *ios* base class. The primary difference between *istream* and *ostream* is one of orientation. To *istream*, the format flags generally specify what input is expected, and to *ostream*, the format flags specify what output should be produced.

As in *ostream*, simple operations are straightforward:

```
double dval;
int ival;
cin >> dval >> ival;
```

If the input stream contains the text *1.5 10*, this routine will assign the value *1.5* to *dval* and then assign the value *10* to *ival.*

As with an *ostream*, understanding the type of the variables is the key to understanding an expression. In the above, a *double* value and an *int* were extracted from the *cin* stream. But we could also extract the same input into different types of variables:

```
int a, b, c;
char ch;
cin >> a >> ch >> b >> c;
```

Given the same input as in the previous example, *1.5 10*, the extraction will produce very different results: *a* is assigned the value *1*, *ch* is assigned the character . (the period character), *b* is assigned *5*, and *c* is assigned *10.*

The *istream* Class Extractors

*char **, *signed char **, and *unsigned char ** all extract a white-space–delimited string into a character array. Before extracting into a character array, you should always specify the size of the array by means of the *setw()* manipulator or the *width()* member function. If the *ios::skipws* flag is set, leading white space will be skipped. Insertion terminates when white space is encountered.

char, *signed char*, and *unsigned char* all extract a single character. If the *ios::skipws format_mode* flag is set, white space will be skipped and the next non-white-space character will be fetched; otherwise, the current character will be fetched.

short, *int*, *long*, *unsigned short*, *unsigned int*, and *unsigned long* all extract a numeric value. If the *ios::skipws format_mode* flag is set, leading white space will be skipped. The numeric input will be governed by the settings of the *ios::dec*, *ios::oct*, and *ios::hex* flags. If none of these flags are set, the C prefix conventions will be followed. (A leading nonzero digit implies the decimal radix, a leading *0* implies octal, and a leading *0x* implies hexadecimal.)

float and *double* extract a floating point value. The number can be in either *scientific* or *fixed* format.

*streambuf ** extracts into a *streambuf* until end of file.

*istream& (*fn)(istream&)* and *ios& (*fn)(ios&)* call an *ios* manipulator.

Format flags from the *ios* base class specify what form of input is expected. In this example, the integral input is specified in the hexadecimal radix (using the *hex* manipulator):

```
cin >> dval >> hex >> ival;
```

The *istream* Public Member Functions

int get() gets and returns a single character.

istream& get(char &c) gets a single character and stores it in *c*.

istream& get(streambuf& sb, char delim = '\n') extracts and stores in the *streambuf& sb* until the delimiter character is encountered. The delimiter becomes the current character in the input stream.

*istream& get(char *ptr, int len, char delim = '\n')* extracts and stores in the buffer at address *ptr*. The buffer length is *len*, and extraction stops when the delimiter is encountered. After extraction, a null will be appended to the buffer. The delimiter becomes the current character in the input stream.

*istream& getline(char *ptr, int len, char delim = '\n')* is the same as *get(ptr, len, delim)* above except that the delimiter is copied into the buffer if there is sufficient space.

int peek() returns the next character in the stream without moving the stream pointer.

istream& ignore(int len = 1; int delim = EOF) is like *get(ptr, len, delim)* except that the extracted characters are discarded.

istream& putback(char) returns a character to the stream.

*read(char *buf, int len)* inputs from a stream to a buffer. *len* is the length of the buffer. No conversions are performed.

streampos seekg(streampos p) moves to the specified absolute location.

streampos seekg(streamoff o, seek_dir d) moves by the specified amount. *seek_dir* is the enumeration defined in *ios* that has the values *beg*, *cur*, and *end*.

streampos tellg() reports the current position of a stream.

int ipfx(int need) inputs a prefix routine that is used in user-written extractors. *ipfx()* is responsible for checking the stream's status, flushing tied streams, and skipping white space. Flushing is performed only if *need* is *0* or if fewer than *need* characters are available. White space is skipped only if the *ios::skipws* flag is set. *ipfx()* returns *0* if an error is encountered, nonzero otherwise.

If the input stream again contains the text *1.5 10*, a hexadecimal *10* (*16* in decimal) will be assigned to *ival*.

Using *ostream*, you can insert a generic pointer, but using *istream*, you won't find a built-in method for extracting a generic pointer.

The iostream library is type safe, which means that operand types dictate the conversion operations. The major weakness of this approach is the fact that in C and C++ the type of an array doesn't include information about its length. This can be remedied by using classes to encapsulate arrays, but arrays of characters are pervasive, and extraction into an array of characters should be approached with caution. To avoid overwriting input buffers, you should use the *setw()* manipulator (or the *width()* member function) to specify the size of the buffer:

```
char bufa[20];
char bufb[80];
cin >> setw(sizeof(bufa)) >> bufa >> setw(sizeof(bufb)) >> bufb;
```

When a width is specified, and it should always be specified, a maximum of *width–1* characters will be placed in the buffer, followed by a trailing null.

An explicit width, for either insertion or extraction, applies only to the operation immediately following. It is thus not safe to do the following, because data might flow beyond the end of *bufb*:

```
const BufSize = 50;
char bufa[BufSize], bufb[BufSize];
cin >> setw(BufSize) >> bufa >> bufb;    // NO--might overflow bufb
```

Before each extraction to a character string buffer, you should explicitly set the input width. Although this rule is not enforced by the *istream* class, you should follow it scrupulously.

Extraction into a character string works somewhat the way extraction of a numeric value does. If the *ios::skipws* flag is set, any leading white space is skipped. (Nothing is extracted if the stream is positioned on white space and *ios::skipws* is not set.) Next, characters are fetched from the stream until white space is encountered or until the supply is exhausted. This mode of operation differs from the treatment of string insertion, which ignores white space and inserts an entire null-delimited string. Here is a small example that shows the asymmetry of string extraction and insertion:

```
#include <iomanip.h>
#include <strstrea.h>

void main()
{
    char *msg = "two words";
```

```
        char bufa[20];
        char bufb[20];
        strstream s;

        s << msg;                                        // insert entire string
        s >> setw(20) >> bufa >> setw(20) >> bufb;       // extract words
        cout << bufa << endl << bufb << endl;            // insert strings
    }
```

White-space–delimited extraction is but one of many possibilities; most other needs can be met by using one of the *get()* member functions, or by writing your own extraction operators.

Also note that extraction into a character buffer ignores the type of the character buffer. Extraction into an array of *signed char* or *unsigned char* is the same as extraction into an array of *char*.

File and String Classes

The *ios*, *istream*, and *ostream* classes define the standard set of inserters and extractors, a set of simple utility operations, and a common set of symbolic constants. They don't show how the iostream library is used with files or with strings.

The *fstream*, *ifstream*, and *ofstream* Class Constructors

fstream(), *ifstream()*, and *ofstream()* create a file stream that is not currently attached to a file.

fstream(int fd), *ifstream(int fd)*, and *ofstream(int fd)* create a file stream that is connected to a previously opened file, whose file descriptor is *fd*. The file should have been opened in a mode appropriate for the specified file stream.

*fstream(int fd, char *ptr, int len)*, *ifstream(int fd, char *ptr, int len)*, and *ofstream(int fd, char *ptr, int len)* create a file stream that is connected to a previously opened file whose file descriptor is *fd*. The file should have been opened in a mode appropriate for the specified file stream. The *ptr* and *len* parameters specify the location and length of the buffer; if *len* is less than 1, the access will be unbuffered.

*fstream(const char *filename, int mode, int prot = filebuf::openprot)*, *ifstream(char *filename, int mode = ios::in, int prot = filebuf::openprot)*, and *ofstream(char *filename, int mode = ios::out, int prot = filebuf::openprot)* create a file stream by opening the file whose name is in the string pointed at by *filename*. The optional file access mode parameter should be one of the symbolic *open_mode* enumeration constants from the *ios* class. The optional *prot* parameter specifies the file access mode; it defaults to the value of the *openprot* constant from the *filebuf* class.

Both file streams and string streams come in three variants: a version derived from *iostream* that is for both input and output, a version derived from *istream* for input, and a version derived from *ostream* for output. Buffering in a file stream is handled by the *filebuf* class; for a string stream, by the *strstreambuf* class.

For file streams, the added operations, not surprisingly, support the opening and closing of files. For existing file streams, the *open()* routine opens or creates a file specified by name, and the *attach()* routine associates a file stream with an already opened file, given its file descriptor. There are two forms of file stream constructors. The simpler is the default constructor, which creates a file stream but doesn't associate it with a file. The second form requires a file descriptor parameter for opening a stream and associating it with an already open file.

String streams are used for performing iostream operations by means of buffers in memory. String streams correspond roughly to the functionality provided by the *sprintf()* and *sscanf()* functions in the standard C I/O library. However, there are several important differences between the functionality of string streams and the functionality of *sprintf()* and *sscanf()*. String streams are both type safe and extensible. The third major difference is that string streams can be dynamic; this makes them suitable for applications that *sprintf()* and *sscanf()*, which use fixed size strings, can't tackle.

There are two separate strategies for buffer management in string streams. The first approach is for you to supply a buffer for the string stream. This lets you completely

The *fstream, ifstream,* and *ofstream* Class Public Member Functions

*open(const char *name, int mode, int prot = filebuf::openprot)* opens a file for use by an existing stream. The *mode* should be specified using the flags of the *open_mode* enumeration from *ios*. The mode is often constructed by *OR*ing flags; for example, *ios::out|ios::nocreate* is used to specify a file that is opened for writing but must already exist. For an *ifstream*, the default mode is *ios::in*; for an *ofstream*, the default mode is *ios::out*; for an *fstream*, there is no default mode. The flag bit *ios::failbit* is set if the open fails.

attach(int fd) associates an already opened file with an existing file stream. *fd* is the file descriptor of the file. The flag bit *ios::failbit* is set if the open fails.

close() closes the file associated with the file stream.

filebuf rdbuf()* returns a pointer to the file buffer that is used for I/O by the file stream.

streambuf setbuf(char *buf, int len)* uses the buffer at *buf* whose length is *len* bytes. The function is an entry into the *setbuf()* function of the *filebuf* class.

handle the buffer creation, and the low overhead is appealing. The second approach is to let the *strstreambuf* class allocate the buffer dynamically. This offers the appeal of flexibility because the buffer will grow as necessary, but you also need to remember that dynamic memory allocation is relatively time consuming.

There are only a few additional facilities in string streams. Common to all three varieties of string streams is the *rdbuf()* member function, which returns a pointer to the string stream's *streambuf*. This helps you access *streambuf* functions, such as the *streambuf* member functions that control buffering. The *ostrstream* and *strstream* classes contain a *str()* member function. Be careful with *str()* because it does three things at once: It concludes the stream write operations, it transfers buffer ownership to you, and it returns a pointer to the start of the buffer. Thus, once you call *str()* you can no longer output data to the string stream and you own the buffer, which means that you are responsible for deallocating the buffer.

Another useful facility for string streams is the *ostream ends* manipulator, which writes a null to the stream. This trailing null is vital if you have a stream of text that you want to treat as a valid string. Note that you needn't use *ends* if you are creating a binary stream. If you do create a binary stream, you will be interested in the *ostream pcount()* member function, which tells you how many bytes have been written to the stream.

The *strstream, istrstream,* and *ostrstream* Class Constructors

strstream() creates a string stream for both input and output that will use dynamically allocated storage.

*strstream(char *buf, int buflen, int mode)* creates a string stream for both input and output, using the buffer at *buf* whose length is *buflen* bytes. If either the *ios::ate* or the *ios::app* mode bit is set, *buf* is presumed to point at a null terminated string and write operations will be appended to the string; otherwise, write operations commence at *buf*.

ostrstream() creates an output string stream that will use dynamically allocated storage.

*ostrstream(char *buf, int buflen, int mode = ios::out)* creates a string stream for output, using the buffer at *buf* whose length is *buflen* bytes. The *mode* has a default value of *ios::out*; otherwise, it is handled as the *strstream()* constructor is.

*istrstream(char *s)* creates a string stream for input, using the string indicated by the variable *s*.

*istrstream(char *s, int len)* creates a string stream for input, using the buffer at *s*, whose length is *len*.

The *strstream, istrstream,* and *ostrstream* Class Public Member Functions

*strstreambuf *rdbuf()* returns a pointer to the *streambuf* that is used by the stream.

*char *str()* freezes a string stream and returns a pointer to its starting location in memory. Once the string stream has been frozen, you should not insert further data into the stream. Freezing a stream transfers ownership of the buffer to you, which means that you must free the buffer if it has been dynamically allocated. (This function is available only in *strstream* and *ostrstream* classes.)

int pcount() returns a count of the number of bytes that have been stored in the stream. (This function is available only in the *ostrstream* class.)

Overloading *operator<<()* and *operator>>()*

The iostream library is designed to be extended to handle your own class objects. In some cases, a class is an integral part of your design, and integrating it into the iostream facility is another primary benefit of the object-oriented approach. In other cases, you create a new class expressly to gain control over I/O; the class itself might have little other use.

User-written inserters and extractors should, as much as possible, honor the existing format flags of the iostream library. For example, the justification and width settings should usually be observed if possible in a user-written inserter. But of course, if you were writing an inserter for a currency type, it would rarely (if ever) make sense to honor the *ios::oct* or *ios::hex* flag; few people would understand that *$0xff* is two hundred fifty-five dollars.

One easy way to honor the width and justification settings in an inserter is to perform a single insertion into the final output stream. This technique is actually quite simple. All you need to do is accumulate your output in a temporary string stream and then output the temporary stream in a single chunk. When you use a temporary string stream for either input or output, you might need to set the conversion or other flags of the temporary stream to match those of the user-supplied stream. And when you use a temporary stream, see that dynamic buffers are deallocated.

These techniques are illustrated by an inserter/extractor duo I wrote to make it easier to read large numbers. When CHKDSK reports that I have 41904128 bytes of free disk space, I have to look carefully to discover whether that means 4, 41, or 419 megabytes. I don't have the source code for CHKDSK, so I can't repair that problem, but I can improve the appearance of large numbers in my own software. The only storage in the *legible* class is for a single *long,* and its only operations are conversions to integral numeric types. The class, as you'll see on the next page, is simple.

```
#include <strstrea.h>

// legible whole numbers (containing commas on input and output)
class legible {
    friend ostream& operator<<(ostream &s, legible &rhs);
    friend istream& operator>>(istream &s, legible &rhs);
    protected:
        long value;
    public:
        static char comma;
        legible() { value = 0; }
        legible(long l) { value = l; }
        legible(short s) { value = s; }
        legible(int i) { value = i; }
        operator int() { return value; }
        operator short() { return value; }
        operator long() { return value; }
};
char legible::comma = ',';
```

The interest here is clearly in creating overloaded *operator<<()* and *operator>>()* functions that will output and input legible objects legibly, that is, with commas. Let's consider output, *operator<<()*, first.

Insertion

operator<<() can't be a member function of the *legible* class because its left operand (the first argument) is an *ostream*, not a *legible*. I made *operator<<()* a friend in the class definition so that it could access the protected *value* member variable of *legible*.

I used a three-phase approach to produce legible output inside *operator<<()*. In the first phase, the numeric value is converted to text and stored in a string stream. This lets me take advantage of the conversion facilities of the iostream library. In the second phase, this string is copied into a second temporary string stream as commas are inserted into their proper positions. This operation didn't use any significant capabilities of the iostream library; alternatively, I could have merged the digits and commas into a character buffer. In the third phase, the legible text is inserted into the output stream. Moving the text into the output stream in a single operation lets me use the iostream library's existing facilities for width padding and justification.

```
#include <string.h>
#include <ctype.h>

// insertion of legible whole numbers
ostream& operator<<(ostream &s, legible &rhs)
{
    // convert rhs to text and store in strm; use
    //  numeric flags from s
    ostrstream strm;              // temporary string stream
    strm.setf(s.flags() & ios::basefield, ios::basefield);
```

```
    if (s.flags() & ios::showpos) strm.setf(ios::showpos);
    if (s.flags() & ios::showbase) strm.setf(ios::showbase);
    strm << rhs.value << ends;

    // copy to strm2, adding commas
    ostrstream strm2;
    int sep = s.flags() & ios::hex ? 4 : 3;
    char *p = strm.str();             // freeze
    // first output the beginning of the number
    if (*p == '-' || *p == '+')       // skip leading sign
        strm2 << *p++;
    if (*p == '0')                    // skip base digit
        strm2 << *p++;
    if (*p == 'x' || *p == 'X')       // skip hex base flag
        strm2 << *p++;
    strm2 << *p++;                    // output first true digit

    // now insert digits and commas
    int len = strlen(p);
    do {
        if (*p && !(len-- % sep))
            strm2 << legible::comma;
        strm2 << *p;
    } while(*p++);
    strm2 << ends;

    // output text to s;
    //  s will do opfx() and osfx() and honor
    //  width and left/right justification requests
    s << strm2.str();          // freeze
    strm.rdbuf->freeze(0);     // thaw
    strm2.rdbuf->freeze(0);    // thaw
    return s;
}
```

In the *operator<<()* function, I create two temporary output string streams. Each of these streams will automatically allocate memory, as needed, for string storage. Alternatively, I could have initialized these string streams with a local buffer, to avoid the expense of dynamic memory allocation. For each of the string streams, I first filled the stream using *ostream* inserters, next used the *ends* manipulator to write the trailing null, and finally used *str()* to fetch a pointer to the string buffer. Once you use *str()* with a string stream, you own the buffer, and ownership implies responsibilities. When you own a stream buffer, you must either delete it yourself or hand it back to its original owner. In the *operator<<()* function, I used the *streambuf* class's *freeze()* member function to return the buffers to their original owners.

In Figure 12-2 on the next page, a simple testbed program exercises the *legible* class's insertion function.

Code	Output
`#include <iomanip.h>`	
`void main(){`	
`cout.setf(ios::right);`	
`cout << setw(10) << legible(-1) << endl;`	-1
`cout << setw(10) << legible(12) << endl;`	12
`cout << setw(10) << legible(-123) << endl;`	-123
`cout << setw(10) << legible(1234) << endl;`	1,234
`cout << setw(10) << legible(-12345) << endl;`	-12,345
`cout.setf(ios::showpos);`	
`cout << setw(12) << legible(123456) << endl;`	+123,456
`cout << setw(12) << legible(-1234567) << endl;`	-1,234,567
`cout << setw(12) << legible(12345678) << endl;`	+12,345,678
`cout << setw(12) << legible(-123456789) << endl;`	-123,456,789
`cout << setw(12) << legible(1234567890) << endl;`	+1,234,567,890
`cout.setf(ios::showbase);`	
`cout << hex << legible(0x12345) << endl;`	0x1,2345
`cout << hex << legible(0x12345678) << endl;`	0x1234,5678
`cout << oct << legible(076543210) << endl;`	076,543,210
`}`	

Figure 12-2.
Examples of using the legible *class's inserter. Output is shown on the right.*

The code for *main()* is shown on the left, and the resulting output is shown on the right. Notice how the width, justification, and base manipulators, which are originally defined for the built-in iostream operations, have been made to work with legible numbers.

Extraction

Extraction of a legible number using *operator>>()* is also a multistep process. The first step is to extract the number, character by character, from the input stream. Character-at-a-time extraction is an unfortunate necessity because none of the standard extractors fit the bill. The numeric extractors will stop when a comma is encountered; the string extractor will stop when white space is encountered. I ended up writing a simple "extract while the input is numeric or a comma" loop. Within this loop, the commas are dropped, leaving only the digits. The second step is to use an *istrstream* to convert the text to binary. The conversion flags from the input stream are used to specify the base of the conversion.

```
// macro more or less stolen from <ctype.h>
#define is_ok_char(c, mask)   (_ctype[(c)+1]&(mask))

// extraction of legible whole numbers
istream& operator>>(istream &s, legible &rhs)
{
    // copy digit sequence from s into buf
```

```
    char buf[20];
    char *p = buf;
    if (!s.ipfx()) // skip ws and check stream
        return s;

    int mask = s.flags() & ios::hex ? _HEX : _DIGIT;
    while(p < (buf + sizeof(buf)) && s) {
        *p = s.get();
        if (is_ok_char(*p, mask))
            p++;
        else if (*p == legible::comma)
            ;    // no increment; ignore the input comma
        else {
            s.putback(*p);
            *p = 0;
            break;
        }
    }

    // check for underrun (no valid input) or overrun
    if (p == buf || p == (buf + sizeof(buf))) {
        s.clear(s.rdstate() | ios::failbit);
        return s;
    }

    // convert
    istrstream istrm(buf, 0);
    istrm.setf(s.flags() & ios::basefield, ios::basefield);
    istrm >> rhs.value;
    return s;
}
```

Extractors should always call the *ipfx()* routine, both to check for errors and to skip white space. If *ipfx()* returns *0*, the extractor should proceed with its task. By convention, an extractor should set the *failbit* flag if the input it expects is not present. Careful programmers will check for failure after calling an extractor. When an extraction failure is detected, you can either give up (exit) or reset the stream's failure bit and try to resume.

Here is a simple main program that exercises the *legible* extractor:

```
void main()
{
    legible myvar;
    while (cin) {
        cin >> myvar;
        if (!cin)
            break;
        cout << myvar << "  " << (long)myvar << endl;
    }
}
```

Note that the *while* expression implicitly uses *operator void *()* from the *ios* class and that the *if* expression uses *operator !()*. Both operators test both the *failbit* and the *badbit* status flags of the stream. Extraction ceases when an EOF is encountered or when an input failure occurs.

Manipulators

A manipulator is a function that from inside an insertion or extraction expression operates on an I/O stream. The *hex* manipulator, for example, changes the conversion base to hexadecimal. The iostream library has about 10 predefined manipulators plus a framework for creating your own manipulators.

The iostream Library Manipulators

The bulk of the iostream manipulators come from the *ostream* class. One manipulator comes from *istream*, and six come from the *ios* base class.

The simplest manipulators don't take any parameters. You can create your own parameterless manipulator by creating a function modeled on the following:

```
// insert a tab
ostream& tab(ostream& s)
{
    s << '\t';
    return s;
}
```

The *ios* Manipulators

setiosflags(long flags) sets the flags specified in *flags*.

resetiosflags(long flags) resets the flags specified in *flags*.

dec sets the conversion radix to *10*.

oct sets the conversion radix to *8*.

hex sets the conversion radix to *16*.

setfill(int nfill) sets the stream's fill character.

setprecision(int np) sets the stream's floating point display precision.

setw(int wid) sets the conversion width to *wid*. Insertion: Note that *setw()* specifies a minimum width; the next inserted value might be wider than *wid* if necessary to avoid truncation. The field width is reset to *0* each time something is inserted. Extraction: The *setw()* manipulator should be used before extraction into a string, to specify the length of the string's buffer.

> **The *istream* Manipulator**
>
> *ws* skips white space. It is called by *ipfx()* but can also be called as needed.

This manipulator applies only to the *ostream* class and its descendants. For an *istream* manipulator, you would change *ostream* to *istream*; for a manipulator for any stream, you would change *ostream* to *ios*.

You can use a parameterless manipulator by placing its name in an insertion or extraction expression. Both the *istream* and the *ostream* classes recognize that a function pointer with the signature above is a manipulator, and they call that function. Any other function pointer is treated as a generic pointer (*void **). *ostream* outputs void pointers in hexadecimal; *istream* does not have a built-in operation that applies to void pointers. Here's an example that outputs the address of the *main()* routine, indented by one tab stop:

```
#include <iostream.h>

ostream& tab(ostream& s) { s << '\t'; return s; }

void main()
{
    cout << tab << main << endl;
}
```

The insertion expression contains two function pointers, but they are handled differently because they are different types. Because *tab* is a pointer to a function that takes a reference to an *ostream* and returns a reference to an *ostream*, it is assumed to be a manipulator and is called. But because *main* is a pointer to a function with an unrecognized signature, its value is printed in hexadecimal.

> **The *ostream* Manipulators**
>
> *ends* finishes a string stream by appending a null.
>
> *endl* outputs an end-of-line character sequence.
>
> *flush* flushes the stream.

Other *ostream* Manipulators

The standard collection of output manipulators is too small for my taste. I've therefore created the header file iomanip2.h shown in Figure 12-3 on the next page. That file defines additional manipulators that I've often used in my work.

```
// additional I/O manipulators

#ifndef _INC_IOMANIP
#include <iomanip2.h>
#endif

#ifndef _INC_IOMANIP2
#define _INC_IOMANIP2

// floating point formats
inline ostream& fixed(ostream& s)
    { s.setf(ios::fixed, ios::floatfield); return s; }
inline ostream& scientific(ostream& s)
    { s.setf(ios::scientific, ios::floatfield); return s; }
inline ostream& floating(ostream& s)
    { s.setf(0, ios::floatfield); s.setf(0, ios::showpoint); return s; }
inline ostream& showpoint(ostream& s)
    { s.setf(ios::showpoint); return s; }

// justification formats
inline ostream& leftjust(ostream& s)
    { s.setf(ios::left, ios::adjustfield); return s; }
inline ostream& rightjust(ostream& s)
    { s.setf(ios::right, ios::adjustfield); return s; }
inline ostream& internal(ostream& s)
    { s.setf(ios::internal, ios::adjustfield); return s; }

// whole number formats
inline ostream& showbase(ostream& s)
    { s.setf(ios::showbase); return s; }
inline ostream& showpos(ostream& s)
    { s.setf(ios::showpos); return s; }

#endif          // ! _INC_IOMANIP2
```

Figure 12-3.
Additional output manipulators defined inline in a header file.

Notice that the manipulators in iomanip2.h are functions that are specified in a header file. Placing functions in a header file is usually a bad idea, but I make an exception for tiny functions that are analogous to C's occasionally useful preprocessor macro (*#define*) functions. When you define a function in a header file, make that function either static or inline so that each source module will have a private copy. If your header file functions aren't static (or inline), you are likely to get "multiply defined" errors from the linker.

Even though the functions in iomanip2.h are declared inline, they will rarely be truly inline. When a function is used as a manipulator, only a pointer to the function appears in the output expression, which forces the compiler to build an anonymous version of the function that will be called by the inserter:

```
cout << fixed << 1.234 << endl;
```

The inline version would be used only if you used the manipulator as an ordinary function:

```
fixed(cout);
```

In iomanip2.h, the manipulators are declared inline primarily for the side effect that inline subroutines are static by default and secondarily so that they may be inlined when they are used as ordinary functions.

A manipulator with a parameter is more complicated and works with an entirely different approach. The first clue that something is out of the ordinary is the fact that the file iomanip.h must be included if you want to use any of the standard manipulators, such as *setw()*, that take parameters. The basic trick of manipulators like *setw()* is to create a class that stores a pointer to the manipulator function and that stores the value that should be passed to that function. For that class there is an overloaded *operator>>()* (or *operator<<()*) function whose job is to call the manipulator while supplying the proper value.

Other *ostream* Manipulators

scientific sets the floating point format to scientific.

fixed sets the floating point format to fixed.

showpoint sets the floating point format to always show the decimal point.

floating resets the floating point format to the default, by resetting the *ios::scientific*, *ios::fixed*, and *ios::showpoint* flags.

leftjust specifies left justification.

rightjust specifies right justification.

internal specifies internal justification, which means that white space is added between the numeric prefix (the minus, plus, or base specifier) and the digit sequence.

showbase specifies that the output base should be indicated by the prefix *0* for octal or *0x* for hexadecimal.

showpoint specifies that a decimal point should always be used in the output of a floating point value.

showpos specifies that a + should be used in the output of a positive whole number.

You could, of course, write your own class whose sole purpose is to manipulate an I/O stream, but the job is considerably eased by the macros in the iomanip.h file. iomanip.h is one of those occasional software gems that are easy to use but hard to understand. If you enjoy puzzles, and especially if you enjoy difficult puzzles, you should try to decipher the macros in iomanip.h. If all you want to do is create your own manipulators, read on—iomanip.h makes it easy.

Parameter-taking manipulators come in two pieces: the function that actually performs the manipulation and the function that you use to invoke the manipulation. This seems tortuous, but both functions are usually 99 percent boilerplate. Here is a parameter-taking iostream manipulator that emits an ANSI control sequence to control the color of the text in an ANSI character mode environment:[2]

```
#include <iomanip.h>

enum Colors { Black, Red, Green, Orange, Blue, Purple, Cyan, White };

ostream& color(ostream& s, int color)
{
    c &= 0x7;          // colors 0..7 are OK
    s << (char)033 << '[' << 30+color << ";40m";
    return s;
}

OMANIP(int) color(int val)
{
    OMANIP(int) p(color, val);
    return p;
}
```

As is common practice, the two functions have the same name and are distinguished by their signatures. The first *color()* function is the actual manipulator; it resembles the *tab()* function in the previous example, except that *color()* has an additional parameter. The second *color()* function is the more mysterious. Its return type is *OMANIP(int)*, which has been defined by a macro in iomanip.h to expand to the name of a class. The body of the second *color()* function declares an *OMANIP(int)* object, initialized by a pointer to the first *color()* function and by the value passed to the second *color()* function. Perhaps a recap is in order: The first *color()* function is the actual manipulator, and the second *color()* function creates and returns an object that is used by *operator<<()* to invoke the first *color()* function.

Here is a statement that uses the ANSI color manipulator:

```
cout << color(Orange) << "orange" << endl;
```

---

2. ANSI control sequences are discussed in many references, and I won't go into them in detail here. They will be recognized on a PC only if the statement *DEVICE=ansi.sys* is in the config.sys file. ANSI control sequences are recommended for portable software only; software intended solely for the PC should use BIOS services to manage color.

The expression *color(Orange)* calls the second *color()* function, which creates and then returns an *OMANIP(int)* object. In iomanip.h, an overloaded *operator<<()* function calls the actual manipulator (the first *color()* function) with the specified parameter. Yes, a lot of work for the compiler, and a lot of explanation on my part, but if you model your manipulators on the pair of *color()* functions, you'll find that the facility is easy to use.

Stream manipulators that take parameters other than *int* or *long* require even more work. Here's an example of an *ostream* manipulator that uses ANSI control sequences to move the cursor to a specified position on the screen:

```
// ostream manipulator to move the cursor using ANSI control sequences
#include <iomanip.h>

struct rcpos {       // structure to store a row/column position
    short r, c;
    rcpos(short rr, short cc) : r(rr), c(cc) {}  // initialize
    rcpos() : r(0), c(0) {}                      // default constructor
};
IOMANIPdeclare(rcpos);    // declare a set of classes to support the
                          //  rcpos struct

// manipulator that uses ANSI control sequences to move the cursor
ostream& go(ostream& s, rcpos p)
{
    if (p.c < 0) p.c = 0;     // bounds checking
    if (p.c > 79) p.c = 79;
    if (p.r < 0) p.r = 0;
    if (p.r > 24) p.r = 24;
    // esc [ row ; col H
    // row 1..25, col 1..80 for 80x25 screen
    s << (char)033 << "[" << p.r+1 << ';' << p.c+1 << 'H';
    return s;
}

// function to create an object to invoke the go() manipulator
OMANIP(rcpos) go(short row, short col)
{
    rcpos pos(row, col);
    OMANIP(rcpos) rc(go, pos);
    return rc;
}
```

There are two noteworthy elements in this example. The first is the use of the *rcpos* struct to create a type that encompasses the row and column parameters. Having a single type is important because the facilities in iomanip.h presume that you have only a single type name. (If you're ambitious, you can create your own set of macros, based on the iomanip.h macros, that remedy this shortcoming.) The second noteworthy element is the use of the *IOMANIPdeclare* macro, which actually creates a set of classes tuned for the *rcpos* type. Look at the preprocessor output if you want to fully understand the *IOMANIPdeclare* macro. Note that iomanip.h contains the statements

```
IOMANIPdeclare(int);
```

and

```
IOMANIPdeclare(long);
```

which means that you need to use *IOMANIPdeclare()* only for your own types; it is done for you for *int* and *long* types.

PART 3

THE MICROSOFT FOUNDATION CLASS LIBRARY

Windows. Everybody wants to develop for the Windows environment, but until the Microsoft Foundation Class (MFC) library came along, Windows development was a tough job. In the first four chapters in this part of the book, we'll see for ourselves how easy it can be to write a Windows program using the MFC library. Yes, easy. With MFC, most of the Windows development traps and pitfalls have been eliminated. You can develop for days at a time—imagine—without provoking a UAE. To me, MFC Windows development feels like assembling a fine machine using precision parts. Things either fit, or they don't, and when they don't fit, the compiler tells you that you're doing something wrong.

In Chapter 13, we'll look at the basic recipe for assembling an MFC application for Windows. In Chapter 14, we'll move on to more sophisticated work, using the MFC library to manage menus and dialog boxes. In Chapter 15, we'll go into the rich topic of GDI and see how the MFC library helps a developer manage device contexts. In Chapter 16, the last Windows chapter, we'll see how the MFC library can take over much of the work involved in developing a Multiple Document Interface (MDI) application for Windows. Chapter 16 focuses on the *CObject* class, the root class of the MFC library. *CObject* might appear rather pedestrian at first, but an understanding of *CObject* can make all of your MFC library development more productive. The MFC library isn't only a set of classes for programming applications for Windows. MFC contains facilities for runtime typing, serialization, and managing runtime exceptions and utility classes, such as string, time, and collection classes. We'll take a look at these features of MFC in the final two chapters. In Chapter 17, we'll look at general purpose MFC library classes for runtime class information, saving and restoring information, debugging, and exception handling. In Chapter 18, we'll look at useful classes that ease common chores, such as managing strings, times, and collections.

The MFC library helps you realize the promise of C++. It takes care of common tasks, freeing you to concentrate on the unique, core operations of your application. The potential benefit to you is enormous, but to realize that benefit you must put some effort into understanding the MFC library.

13

MFC Library Programming for Windows

The Microsoft Foundation Class (MFC) library is both a fundamental new way to program for the Windows environment and, paradoxically, more of the same old thing. The delicate balance between these opposing ideas defines the MFC library. Imagine writing a program for Windows that doesn't have a *WinMain()* routine, that doesn't have message switch statements, that doesn't use *MakeProcInstance()*, and that is safe and secure. The MFC library, we should all agree in this light, is a revolution. But also imagine a new Windows interface so familiar that questions can be answered by reference to Charles Petzold's bible *Programming Windows* (Microsoft Press, 1990) or the standard Windows SDK documentation. The MFC library in this light is for programming the Windows operating system as usual.

MFC is a success because it has managed to ameliorate the major problems associated with programming for Windows without obscuring the basic Windows interface. You'll find it easy to start programming for Windows with MFC. If you have never programmed for Windows before, you should work through some of the examples in this book to get a feel for the event-driven model that underlies programming for Windows. Programs for Windows, it has often been said, don't have a traditional thread of control; rather, they have a set of capabilities that are invoked in response to messages from the Windows kernel. Once you are familiar with writing for Windows with MFC applications, you can move on to more ambitious projects, using standard references to learn more about the Windows operating system itself.

If you already have some experience in programming for Windows, learning to use MFC for Windows programming will involve your learning how MFC structures an application. Once the shock of the new method has worn off, you'll find that using the MFC library is far more convenient and reliable than using the old C application programming interface.

In the first three sections of this chapter, we'll look at the key elements of the MFC library, at the general organization of the library's window classes, at the most common base classes in the MFC library, and at the messaging paradigm that underlies MFC programming for Windows. If you prefer to start with a concrete example, skip these sections and go straight to the HelloApp example on page 272, which shows a simple MFC program for Windows in detail, and then come back here to learn more about the MFC basics.

In the second half of the chapter, you'll find sections on the key *CWinApp* and *CWnd* classes, more about message maps, and two simple variations on the HelloApp example. The first variant is like HelloApp, but with a bit more detail, and the second replaces the main window with a dialog box.

MFC Library Classes for Windows Development

The MFC library classes for Windows development tame the troublesome Windows application programming interface. The library classes mediate between you and Windows. They impose little time and space overhead but provide a large benefit in reliability and reusability.

The MFC library architecture reflects the requirements of the Windows API. As the class names in Figure 13-1's diagram of the Windows-specific classes suggest, an MFC library class corresponds to almost every Windows entity.

The five classes in Figure 13-1 descended from *CObject*—*CWinApp*, *CWnd*, *CMenu*, *CGdiObject*, and *CDC*—are primarily interface classes. They regularize and manage the slippery Windows interface, and they take care of many low-level details.

The five classes derived directly from *CObject* are base classes in the MFC Windows family tree; each encapsulates an aspect of the Windows interface. *CWnd*, *CGdiObject*, and *CDC* have offspring that implement more specialized functionality. As you study each specialized derived class, keep in mind the functionality of its base class. It's easy to forget while studying *CFrameWnd*'s few member functions that its parent, *CWnd*, has more than two hundred additional member functions that must be considered. Derivation means *is a*; a *CFrameWnd is a CWnd*.

The three classes in Figure 13-1 that are not descended from *CObject*—*CSize*, *CPoint*, and *CRect*—are value classes that implement basic Windows data structures. Because these classes are used in expressions and returned from functions, they must operate with maximal space and time efficiency. They can't afford even the small overhead that comes with derivation from *CObject*.

Member Functions vs. Windows API Functions

Many member functions of the MFC windows library classes have the same names as traditional Windows API functions. The *CScrollBar* class, for instance, contains the *GetScrollPos()*, *SetScrollPos()*, *GetScrollRange()*, and *SetScrollRange()* member functions. You might already be familiar with these functions as parts of the stan-

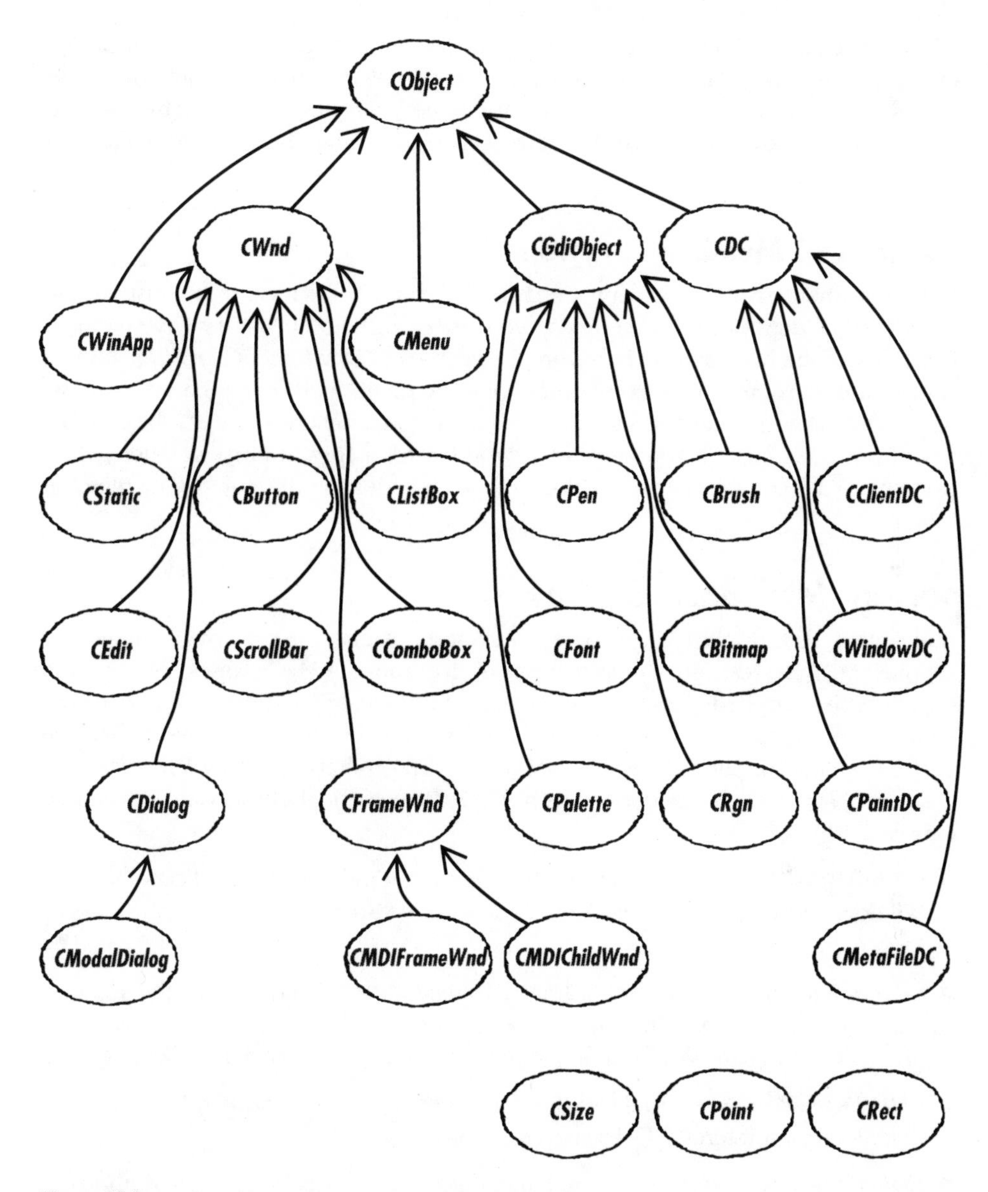

Figure 13-1.
The Microsoft Foundation classes for Windows development.

dard Windows API. When you read code, it's easy to tell the difference because most Windows API functions take *HANDLE* as a first parameter. The other visible difference is that member functions are, well, member functions, which means that they are invoked using *obj.fn()* or *objptr->fn()* notation (unless they are invoked from inside a member function of the same class). You can always refer to a native Windows routine by putting a *::* (scope resolution operator) in front of the function name, as in *::SetScrollPos()*. When not preceded by a class name, the *::* scope resolution operator refers to the global scope, which is where native Windows functions reside. Even when such explicit notation is not strictly necessary because of name duplication, it's a good idea to preface Windows API function names with *::* to make your program easy to read.

Versions of Member Functions

I chose to mention the scroll functions in my example because they illustrate another kind of duplication. Sometimes two classes in the MFC library have member functions of the same name. For example, both the *CWnd* and *CScrollBar* classes contain the four scroll bar member functions I've mentioned. If you have a window with standard horizontal and vertical scroll bars, you should use the scroll bar functions from *CWnd*. But if you're using a scroll bar for a special purpose, such as implementing a color selector in a dialog box, you should use the *CScrollBar* member functions.

Important MFC Base Classes

Building an MFC application involves three sorts of classes: your own classes, the supplied MFC classes, and classes that you derive from the MFC classes. You can find out about the supplied classes in the manual, and I trust you know how to use your own classes. What's most interesting is the middle ground, the classes that you derive from the supplied classes. Although you can profitably use any MFC class as a base class, six MFC classes derived from *CWnd* are particularly serviceable as base classes:

- *CWinApp* is the basis for MFC applications for Windows. All applications for Windows developed with the MFC library derive an application-specific class from *CWinApp*.
- *CFrameWnd* implements an ordinary, framed, titled window like the main window of most applications for Windows. Almost all MFC applications derive classes from *CFrameWnd* that implement an application's basic functionality.
- *CMDIFrameWnd* and *CMDIChildWnd* are used instead of *CFrameWnd* in multiple document interface (MDI) applications.
- *CDialog* and *CModalDialog* implement generic dialog boxes. Applications derive classes from these classes to create more specialized dialog boxes.

CWinApp

CWinApp is the basis of an application-specific class in all MFC applications. In the Hello application we'll look at later in this chapter, the *CHelloApp* class is derived from *CWinApp*. *CWinApp* encapsulates the key aspects of an application for Windows, the aspects that are usually handled by *WinMain()* in a traditional C-language application for Windows. Your derived application class will always override the

InitInstance() member function of *CWinApp* to initialize data, create the application's main window, and perform other startup chores. You must also remember to declare a global instance of your application object, because creation of that object initiates the construction of the entire application. This MFC development convention, supplying a single *CWinApp*-derived object, is somewhat like the convention that you must supply a *main()* routine in an ordinary C program or a *WinMain()* routine in a traditional (non-MFC) program for Windows.

CFrameWnd, CMDIFrameWnd, and CMDIChildWnd

CFrameWnd is the MFC library class that implements a single document interface (SDI) window. Its primary task is to add features for managing an accelerator table, and it has a *Create()* routine that is slightly more convenient than its *CWnd* base class's *Create()* routine. Single document interface MFC applications invariably have an application-specific class derived from *CFrameWnd* so that the application can respond to selected Windows messages. For example, if an application needs to respond to a WM_PAINT message, it should have a class derived from *CFrameWnd* that contains an *OnPaint()* member function to handle the WM_PAINT message.

Many applications are multiple document interface (MDI) applications, not SDI applications, and MDI applications use *CMDIFrameWnd* and *CMDIChildWnd*, instead of *CFrameWnd*, as base classes.

CDialog and CModalDialog

CDialog and *CModalDialog* are the remaining MFC library classes that commonly serve as bases for application-specific classes. Most dialog boxes contain diverse controls, need to respond to messages, and need to exhibit complex behavior. Such dialog boxes are usually implemented by a class derived from the *CDialog* class, the *CModalDialog* class. The derived class will contain member functions that respond to control messages, can contain data members that relate to the controls, and might override some of the member functions of its base class.

A trivially simple dialog box, such as an About dialog box that contains only static controls (text) plus an OK button, can be managed by the *CModalDialog* class.

Message Handling

Windows programs must be designed to respond to messages from the Windows kernel. Readers who are not familiar with the message-handling concept should consult the Windows documentation or Petzold's *Programming Windows*. In traditional programs for Windows written in the C language, you create a message loop to receive the messages from the kernel, and then you use a large switch statement to handle the messages. The message-handling architecture leads to monolithic functions that often contain large numbers of local variables. For messages that you choose not to handle, you must be careful to call *DefWndProc()* to perform standard processing.

The MFC library approach to message handling is vastly superior to the traditional system. MFC applications handle messages by means of polymorphic class member functions. There is no monster switch statement, each individual message-handling function has its own scope, and, if you call the base class, which you should normally do, the default cases are handled automatically. This is a far simpler and more robust message-handling paradigm than the original.

Most standard Windows messages, such as WM_PAINT and WM_SIZE, are handled by one of the *CWnd* class's approximately 100 message-handler member functions. These functions are easily identified because their names begin with *On*: *OnPaint()* and *OnSize()*, for instance. The *CWnd* class's message-handler member functions are commonly overridden, as necessary, in application-specific derived classes. Messages from menu item selections and messages from dialog box controls are handled for the most part by message-handler member functions you write.

Message Maps

When you derive a class from *CFrameWnd* (or from *CMDIFrameWnd*, *CMDIChildWnd*, *CDialog*, or *CModalDialog*) and add your own message-handler member functions, you must also add a "message map" for the class, a table of addresses for the message-handler member functions. There are two parts to a message map. First, in the class declaration, you must place the line

```
DECLARE_MESSAGE_MAP()
```

to declare the data and function members related to the message map. Then you must place the actual message map definition in one of your .cpp files, usually near the class member functions. A message map has one entry for each message that the class handles. For example, here is the short message map from the Hello example we'll look at later in this chapter:

```
BEGIN_MESSAGE_MAP(CMainWindow, CFrameWnd)
    ON_WM_PAINT()
    ON_COMMAND(IDM_ABOUT, OnAbout)
END_MESSAGE_MAP()
```

This message map indicates that the *CMainWindow* class is derived from the MFC *CFrameWnd* class and that its member functions respond to two Windows messages. The first line of the table body indicates that the WM_PAINT message should invoke the *OnPaint()* member function of *CMainWindow*, and the second line indicates that the message IDM_ABOUT should be handled by *CMainWindow*'s *OnAbout()* member function. Message maps are discussed in more detail later in this chapter.

The HelloApp Example

The screen for HelloApp, a simple MFC sample application for Windows that is delivered with Microsoft C/C++ 7.0, is shown in Figure 13-2.

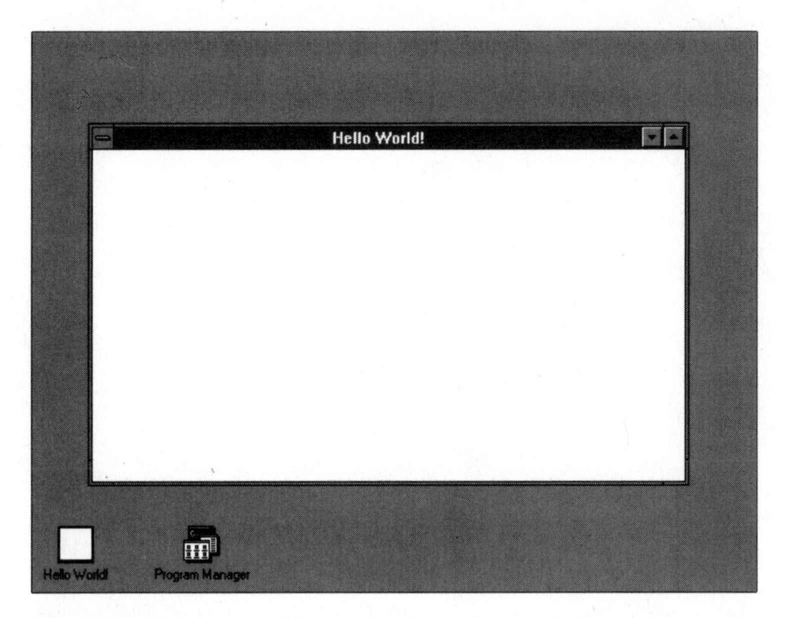

Figure 13-2.
The HelloApp screen.

Actually, this is about as simple a Windows example as you can imagine. It makes a fine introduction to MFC because it shows very clearly the approach used in MFC programming. But it also has serious limitations: It doesn't have a menu, doesn't use dialog boxes, doesn't use a resource file, and doesn't have an icon. We'll get to these clearly necessary features of a program for Windows shortly, but let's leave them aside for a moment. Right now, let's concentrate on understanding a legitimate albeit simple MFC program for Windows.

The HelloApp source code is supplied with C7. If you have installed Microsoft C7 in the default location, HelloApp's files will be in the \c700\mfc\samples\helloapp directory. (Be careful not to look instead in the hello directory; we'll look at the Hello application later in this chapter.) The directory should contain the files helloapp.cpp, helloapp.def, helloapp.mak, and makefile. The .def file is the definition file, and I'll mention it again shortly. The .mak file is the project file for the Microsoft Programmer's Workbench (PWB). If you prefer to work using PWB, you can use this file to build the HelloApp application, but I'm going to ignore the C7 project files in favor of the C7 makefiles, which are much easier to display and understand.

The helloapp.cpp file contains the source for the entire application. Most MFC applications will consist at the least of an .h header file or files and one or more .cpp files. But HelloApp is simple enough for a single file containing both the class declarations and the definitions of the class member functions. The HelloApp program consists of two classes, *CHelloWindow* and *CHelloApp*.

The application's window class, *CHelloWindow*, is derived from *CFrameWnd*. The only member of *CHelloWindow* is an inline constructor. Here is the declaration of *CHelloWindow*, which is taken verbatim from the C7 distribution:

```
#include <afxwin.h>

// Define a window class derived from CFrameWnd
class CHelloWindow : public CFrameWnd
{
public:
    CHelloWindow()
    {
        Create(NULL, "Hello World!", WS_OVERLAPPEDWINDOW, rectDefault);
    }
};
```

An ordinary MFC *CFrameWnd* object is assembled in two steps: First, the constructor, which doesn't take any parameters, is invoked to build the object; then, in a mandatory second step, the *CFrameWnd* class's *Create()* member function is called with parameters that specify the details of the window. The *CHelloWindow* class's constructor combines these two steps into a single step. Creating a *CHelloWindow* object automatically creates the *CFrameWnd* object, and then the body of the *CHelloWindow* constructor automatically calls *Create()* to complete the process.

The parameters supplied to *Create()* indicate, in order, that the window is registered using the default MFC window class; that the window title is "Hello World!"; that the window has the overlapped style; and that the window should be the MFC default size at the default position. (*rectDefault* is a static *CRect* member of *CFrameWnd*.)

CHelloWindow is not representative of a typical application's main window class. It doesn't have a message map, which means that it contains none of its own behavior. It doesn't have an *OnPaint()* member function, which means that it doesn't draw on its own client area. *CHelloWindow* is a useful first example class, period.

The second class in the HelloApp program is *CHelloApp*, which is derived from *CWinApp*. The purpose of *CHelloApp* is to override the *InitInstance()* virtual member function of *CWinApp*. This gives you control over initialization of your application. It's as if you could reach into the *WinMain()* procedure of an ordinary C-language application for Windows and patch in your own initialization and window creation code. Here is HelloApp's *CHelloApp* class:

```
// Define an application class derived from CWinApp
class CHelloApp : public CWinApp
{
public:
    virtual BOOL InitInstance();
};
```

The *InitInstance()* member of *CHelloApp* is responsible for creating the application's main window and for performing any other initialization chores:

```
// Construct the CHelloApp's m_pMainWnd data member
BOOL CHelloApp::InitInstance()
{
    m_pMainWnd = new CHelloWindow();
    m_pMainWnd->ShowWindow(m_nCmdShow);
    m_pMainWnd->UpdateWindow();
    return TRUE;
}
```

The *m_pMainWnd* member of *CWinApp* must be initialized to point at an MFC window object. Most often, the window object is from a class derived from *CFrameWnd* (or from *CMDIFrameWnd*), but other window classes can be used. The second statement in *InitInstance()* invokes the *ShowWindow()* member of the *CWnd* class. The parameter for *ShowWindow()* is *m_nCmdShow*, which indicates to *ShowWindow()* whether the window should initially be iconic. This is the fourth argument that Windows supplies to *WinMain()* when it starts an application. Yes, MFC programs do have a *WinMain()*, but it's hidden away and you needn't think about it much, if at all. The four arguments to *WinMain()* are stored in the *CWinApp* member variables *m_hInstance*, *m_hPrevInstance*, *m_lpCmdLine*, and *m_nCmdShow*. The third line of *InitInstance()* invokes the *UpdateWindow()* member function of *CWnd*, which (finally!) gets some bits twiddled on the screen.

Even though the HelloApp application is trivial, its *CHelloApp* class and that class's *InitInstance()* member function are fairly representative. More complex applications often do have a somewhat more complex application class, but the *CHelloApp* class is a realistic starting point.

As we've noted already, to actually create an MFC application, we must create a *CWinApp* object. Thus, the final line of the helloapp.cpp file is the following, which declares a *CHelloApp* object:

```
CHelloApp HelloApp;  // HelloApp's constructor initializes
                     //  and runs the application
```

Note that we don't have to (that is, shouldn't) statically declare a *CHelloWindow* object; the application's *CHelloWindow* object is created by *CHelloApp*'s *InitInstance()* member function.

To be thoroughgoing in our examination of the HelloApp MFC application, let's turn briefly to the module definition file and to the makefile. Here is the module definition file:

```
NAME         HelloApp
DESCRIPTION  'Hello Microsoft Foundation Classes Windows Application'

EXETYPE      WINDOWS
STUB         'WINSTUB.EXE'
```

```
CODE         PRELOAD MOVEABLE DISCARDABLE
DATA         PRELOAD MOVEABLE MULTIPLE

HEAPSIZE     1024
STACKSIZE    4096
```

The settings in the module definition file are unremarkable, familiar to anyone who has written programs for Windows.

The HelloApp makefile is also unremarkable:

```
# Makefile : Builds the HelloApp application
#
# Usage:     NMAKE helloapp

helloapp.exe: helloapp.obj helloapp.def
    link /NOD /FAR helloapp,,,safxcw libw slibcew,helloapp.def;
    rc /t helloapp.exe

helloapp.obj: helloapp.cpp
    cl /Oxs /c helloapp.cpp

clean:
    -del helloapp.exe
    -del helloapp.obj
```

In the unremarkable face of the HelloApp program, the client area is empty because the program doesn't contain an *OnPaint()* member function. It doesn't have a menu bar because it never loads one. Its icon, which is shown at the bottom of the screen,[1] is an empty rectangle. The "Hello World!" text in the HelloApp main window's title bar comes from the *CHelloWindow* constructor, which passes that string to the *CFrameWnd* class's *Create()* member function.

More on the *CWinApp* Class

In addition to serving as the basis for every MFC application, the *CWinApp* class is a repository of some of the information that is delivered to *WinMain()*, such as the application name and the instance handles. The four arguments to *WinMain()* are stored in these four public members of *CWinApp*:

```
HANDLE m_hInstance

HANDLE m_hPrevInstance

LPSTR m_lpCmdLine

int m_nCmdShow
```

1. Two instances of HelloApp are running: one occupying most of the screen and one that is iconified.

Two other important public members of *CWinApp* are *m_pMainWnd*, which is declared to be a *CWnd** and which should be initialized in the *InitInstance()* function to point at the application's main window object, and *m_pszAppName*, which is a pointer to the name of the application. If the name of the application isn't supplied in the constructor of *CWinApp*, the name defaults to the full pathname of the application's .exe file.

In a class that is designed specifically for use in a single application, such as the *CHelloWindow* class in the HelloApp application, it's easy to get at the information stored in the *CWinApp* object. All you need to know is the name of the *CWinApp* object (*HelloApp* in the HelloApp example) and the name of the member you want to access. But classes designed for broader use need some other method because the name of the application object varies from application to application. MFC has a set of global functions that enable you to access the application's *CWinApp* object and more specific functions for accessing the application's often-needed handles and names:

```
CWinApp* AfxGetApp()

HANDLE AfxGetInstanceHandle()

HANDLE AfxGetResourceHandle()

const char* AfxGetAppName()
```

The *AfxGetApp()* and *AfxGetAppName()* functions are self-explanatory, but the other two need some explanation. In the C7 version of MFC under the Windows 3.0 and 3.1 environments, *AfxGetInstanceHandle()* and *AfxGetResourceHandle()* both return the *hInstance* that was passed by Windows to *WinMain()* and stored in *CWinApp*'s *m_hInstance* member variable. But you should use them as follows. For situations in which a true handle to the current instance is required, as in operations on the window class (the *::GetClassInfo()* Windows function, for example), use *AfxGetInstanceHandle()*. But when you are dealing with resources, as in the *::LoadAccelerators()* and *::LoadString()* Windows functions, use *AfxGetResourceHandle()*. Making this distinction now might save you work in the future.

In traditional C programs for Windows, it is sometimes necessary to perform some special processing for the first instance of an application. This is easy in *WinMain()* because *hPrevInstance* is NULL for the first instance of an application. A similar feature exists in *CWinApp* if you override the *InitApplication()* member function. This member function will be called only when the first instance of an application is loaded, not when a subsequent copy is loaded. (Similar functionality is available in the *InitInstance()* member function simply by means of testing the *m_hInstance* member variable.)

The *CWnd* Class

The *CWnd* class is the center of the MFC library facility for the windowing aspect of Windows. It is the base class for *CFrameWnd*, *CDialog*, *CStatic*, *CButton*, *CListBox*, *CComboBox*, *CEdit* and *CScrollBar*. The *CWnd* documentation is suggested reading for a rainy day, and it is where you should look when you need to do something to a window that isn't mentioned in the manual entry for one of its offspring. It's possible that you will derive your own class from *CWnd*, although it's more likely that you'll derive from one of *CWnd*'s offspring, such as *CFrameWnd* and *CDialog*.

One of *CWnd*'s public data members is *m_hWnd*, a Windows *HWND* for the window. In general, you don't need to use this member because *CWnd* has member functions that allow you to access all the native Windows functions that require an *HWND* first parameter. But sometimes you need to go native, which means using *m_hWnd*.

About half of *CWnd*'s member functions are simple replacements of native Windows functions. These functions have exactly the same names as their Windows counterparts. For example, the *CWnd* member function named *ShowWindow()* has the same functionality as the native Windows *::ShowWindow()*.

The other half of *CWnd*'s member functions are message-handler functions. The name of a message-handler function starts with *On* and ends with a variant of the name of the Windows WM_ message it responds to. For example, the *OnCreate()* member function is activated when a window receives the WM_CREATE message. All of the message-handler functions are protected; you can't access one except in a class that is derived from *CWnd*. Thus, if you have a *CWnd* object named *oCWnd*, you can write *oCWnd.ShowWindow()* anywhere because *ShowWindow()* is public, but you can't write *oCWnd.OnCreate()*, except in a *CWnd* or *CWnd*-offspring member function.

The *CWnd* message-handler member functions are designed to provide a default handler, often by calling *::DefWindowProc()*. Nearly all MFC applications derive a class from *CFrameWnd* (or *CMDIFrameWnd*) so that they can provide their own message handlers. As a general rule, derived class message handlers should call base class message handlers to invoke default behavior. One of the initially surprising aspects of MFC is that the *CWnd* message handlers aren't virtual. There are many *CWnd* message-handler functions, and many types of *CWnd* offspring. Using dozens of virtual tables, each containing hundreds of entries, would have called for too much overhead. Instead, MFC uses message maps, which indicate more precisely which message handlers each class has overridden.

In native Windows, each message is accompanied by two parameters, commonly called *wParam* and *lParam*. These two parameters are part of the worst of Windows design because they force all information pertaining to messages to be typeless and because they force thousands of applications programmers into the bad—no, that's awful—habit of using the *MAKELONG*, *HIWORD*, *LOWORD*, *LOBYTE*, and *HIBYTE* macros. The *CWnd* message-handler functions are a far safer and more convenient interface to Windows messages because they are a strongly typed interface. For example, the *OnKeyDown()* message-handler member function has three parameters: *nChar*, *nRepCnt*, and *nFlags*. Inside *OnKeyDown()*, you can access the key repeat count simply by using the *nRepCnt* parameter; you don't need to consult the Windows function reference to discover that it is stored in the *LOWORD* of *lParam*.

When you override *CWnd* message handlers in your derived class, you need to be careful of three things. First, you need to be sure that your new message-handler member function has exactly the same parameters and return type as the one it replaces. The easiest way to do this is to use your text editor to copy the message-handler declaration from afxwin.h and paste it into your own code. Second, remember to mention your substitute handler in your derived class's message map. Third, find out whether the original *CWnd* member function must be invoked from within your surrogate handler. Some *CWnd* message handlers don't do much; others are vital and must be invoked explicitly from within your own message handler. You can discover which are which by consulting the MFC *Class Libraries User's Guide* or by looking at the MFC code supplied with C7.

The Hello Example

The Hello application delivered with C7 is a more realistic MFC example than the ultra-simplistic HelloApp. Hello, whose screen is shown in Figure 13-3, includes an *OnPaint()* routine to draw in the application's client area, a menu and menu handlers, a dialog box, an icon, a message map, and a resource file.

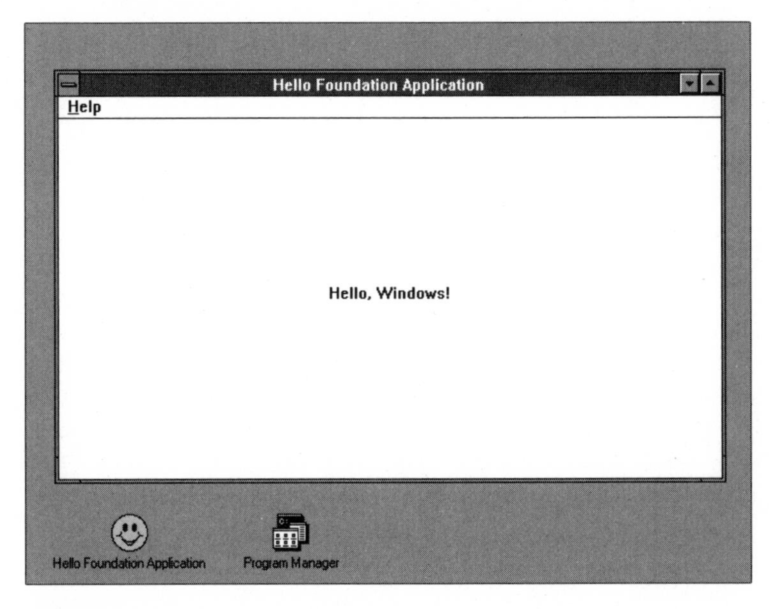

Figure 13-3.
The Hello screen.

Although Hello is also a very simple program, it includes most of the pieces of an MFC application for Windows. When I write an MFC application for Windows, I usually use Hello as a seedling. With your patience and effort, Hello can grow into a full application.

The source code and other listings for the Hello application that are presented here are taken verbatim from the C7 distribution. No changes have been made, except that individual parts are presented in the order most convenient for explanation and a few long comments that introduce some of the routines are omitted. The Hello files can be found in the \c700\mfc\samples\hello directory of your C7 distribution.

The Hello program contains a set of files representative of most MFC applications. Of course, a more complex, more serious MFC program will contain a more heavily laden banquet table, but most of the dishes are present in Hello.

readme.txt	Microsoft's description of the Hello files
hello.h	The header file that declares the *CMainWindow* (derived from *CFrameWnd*) and *CTheApp* (derived from *CWndApp*) classes
resource.h	The header file that defines the resource-related constants, such as the constants related to menus and dialog boxes
hello.cpp	The C++ source code for the *CMainWindow* and *CTheApp* classes, including the *CMainWindow* message map and the declaration of the application object
hello.rc	The Hello resource file, which defines the application's menu and specifies the icon and dialog box files
hello.dlg	The Hello application's About dialog box specification
hello.ico	The Hello application's icon file (binary)
hello.mak	The Hello application's project file, for building Hello using the PWB environment
makefile	The Hello application's makefile, which is used by nmake
hello.def	The Hello module definition file, which is used by the linker

Figure 13-4 shows the declarations from the hello.h file.

Hello contains two specialty classes, *CMainWindow* and *CTheApp*. *CTheApp* is almost identical to the application class we saw in the HelloApp program. *CMainWindow* is a simple example of a typical application's main window. *CMainWindow* is, like most single document application classes for Windows, derived from *CFrameWnd*. And like most MFC application classes, it contains message-handler member functions and a message map. *CMainWindow*'s two message handlers are *OnPaint()* and *OnAbout()*. Notice that in the *CMainWindow* declaration, the message map is merely declared; it is fully defined in the hello.cpp file.

```
// hello.h : Declares the class interfaces for the application.
//          Hello is a simple program which consists of a main window
//          and an "About" dialog which can be invoked by a menu choice.
//          It is intended to serve as a starting-point for new
//          applications.
//
// This is a part of the Microsoft Foundation Classes C++ library.
// Copyright (C) 1992 Microsoft Corporation
// All rights reserved.

#ifndef __HELLO_H__
#define __HELLO_H__

/////////////////////////////////////////////////////////////////////////

// CMainWindow:
// See hello.cpp for the code to the member functions and the message map.
//
class CMainWindow : public CFrameWnd
{
public:
    CMainWindow();

    afx_msg void OnPaint();
    afx_msg void OnAbout();

    DECLARE_MESSAGE_MAP()
};

/////////////////////////////////////////////////////////////////////////

// CTheApp:
// See hello.cpp for the code to the InitInstance member function.
//
class CTheApp : public CWinApp
{
public:
    BOOL InitInstance();
};

/////////////////////////////////////////////////////////////////////////

#endif // __HELLO_H__
```

Figure 13-4.
The hello.h file class declarations.

The Hello application contains a trivial menu; its only option is to display the About dialog box shown in Figure 13-5 on the next page.

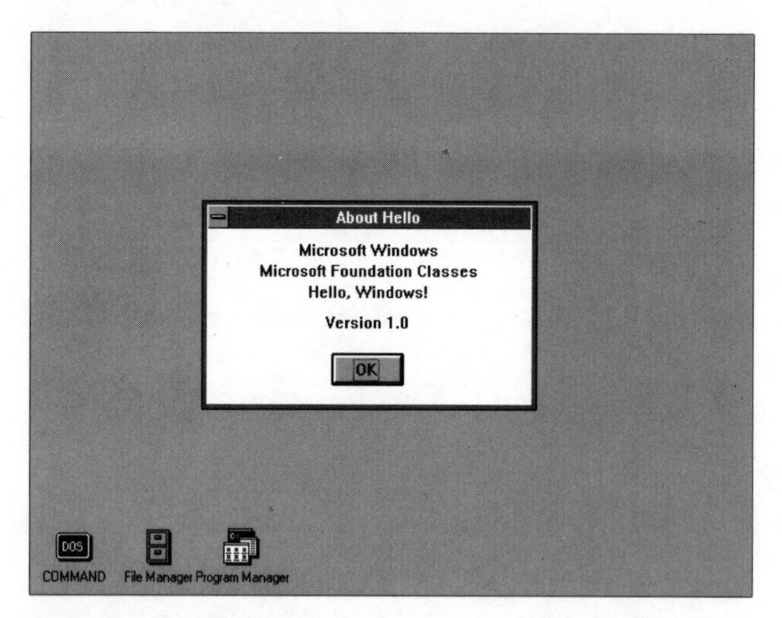

Figure 13-5.
The About Hello dialog box.

Here's the menu definition from the Hello resource file, hello.rc:

```
MainMenu MENU
{
    POPUP       "&Help"
    {
        MENUITEM "&About Hello...\tF1", IDM_ABOUT
    }
}
```

The symbol IDM_ABOUT is defined as 100 in resource.h, which is included into hello.rc. The full listing of hello.rc appears in Figure 13-6.

When the user opens the Hello application's Help menu and selects About Hello, the Hello application's *CMainWindow* object receives the IDM_ABOUT message. In a traditional C program for Windows, you would have a *WM_COMMAND* case in the main message loop, and then within that case you would switch on *wParam* to handle individual messages such as IDM_ABOUT. But in MFC applications, the requirement is different: You must have a message-handler member function to process each message. For the Hello application's IDM_ABOUT message, the message-handler function is *OnAbout()*.

CMainWindow's message map makes the connection between the IDM_ABOUT message and the *OnAbout()* member function. Here is the message map definition from the hello.cpp file that we looked at briefly earlier in this chapter:

```
BEGIN_MESSAGE_MAP(CMainWindow, CFrameWnd)
    ON_WM_PAINT()
    ON_COMMAND(IDM_ABOUT, OnAbout)
END_MESSAGE_MAP()
```

This message map states three principal facts:

- This is a message map declaration for the *CMainWindow* class, which is derived from *CFrameWnd.*
- The *CMainWindow* class contains an *OnPaint()* member function to handle WM_PAINT messages.
- The *CMainWindow* class contains an *OnAbout()* member function to handle the IDM_ABOUT version of the WM_COMMAND message.

```
/* hello.rc : Defines the resources for the Hello application.
//
// This is a part of the Microsoft Foundation Classes C++ library.
// Copyright (C) 1992 Microsoft Corporation
// All rights reserved.
//
// This source code is only intended as a supplement to the
// Microsoft Foundation Classes Reference and Microsoft
// QuickHelp documentation provided with the library.
// See these sources for detailed information regarding the
// Microsoft Foundation Classes product.
*/

#include <windows.h>
#include <afxres.h>
#include "resource.h"

AFX_IDI_STD_FRAME   ICON    hello.ico

MainMenu MENU
{
    POPUP       "&Help"
    {
        MENUITEM "&About Hello...\tF1", IDM_ABOUT
    }
}

MainAccelTable ACCELERATORS
{
    VK_F1,      IDM_ABOUT,  VIRTKEY
}

rcinclude hello.dlg
```

Figure 13-6.
The hello.rc file resource definitions.

MFC requires that each message handler take specified arguments and return a specified type. In the case of a message handler for menu and accelerator messages, the function must not take any arguments and must declare the return type *afx_msg void.* At present, the *afx_msg* designator is a visual clue that the function is a message handler, but the designator might play a more important role in the future. The member function signature for WM_COMMAND messages, like all low-level information about message maps, can be discovered in the afxmsg.h header file, which is automatically included into all MFC programs for Windows when you include afxwin.h. We'll look at using afxmsg.h to answer questions about message maps shortly; for now, take on faith the fact that a handler for a WM_COMMAND message must be a member of the *CWnd* class or a member of a class derived from *CWnd* and that it must have the following type:

```
afx_msg void fn(void);
```

Here is the *OnAbout()* member function of the *CMainWindow* class:

```
void CMainWindow::OnAbout()
{
    CModalDialog about( "AboutBox", this );
    about.DoModal();
}
```

The *OnAbout()* function is a complete handler for a simple dialog box. Its virtue is its straightforwardness. It approaches the task of creating a dialog box directly, by creating a *CModalDialog* object. The *CModalDialog()* constructor requires two parameters: the name used in the resource file to identify the dialog box and a pointer to the dialog box's parent *CWnd* object. The hello.dlg file, which contains the AboutBox dialog box, is shown in Figure 13-7.

```
DLGINCLUDE RCDATA DISCARDABLE
BEGIN
    "RESOURCE.H\0"
END

ABOUTBOX DIALOG 34, 22, 144, 75
STYLE DS_MODALFRAME | WS_CAPTION | WS_SYSMENU
CAPTION "About Hello"
BEGIN
    CTEXT           "Microsoft Windows", -1, 0, 5, 144, 8
    CTEXT           "Microsoft Foundation Classes", -1, 0, 14, 144, 8
    CTEXT           "Hello, Windows!", -1, 0, 23, 144, 8
    CTEXT           "Version 1.0", -1, 0, 36, 144, 8
    DEFPUSHBUTTON   "OK", IDOK, 56, 53, 32, 14, WS_GROUP
END
```

Figure 13-7.
The hello.dlg file.

Creating a *CModalDialog* object doesn't actually bring up the dialog box because MFC provides several opportunities for you to step in and modify the default operation. To actually display the About dialog box on the screen, you need to call the *DoModal()* member function of the *CModalDialog* class. *DoModal()* returns when the OK button is clicked, which terminates the execution of the *OnAbout()* member function. Note that the *about* object was created locally, which means that it will be destroyed automatically when *OnAbout()* returns.

It's easy to read the description of handling a dialog box without noticing how much Windows detail has been hidden by the MFC library. In MFC applications, you can create a dialog box without callback functions, without using *MakeProcInstance()*, without export statements in the .def file, and without creating a message loop in the dialog box handler.

The heart of the Hello application, if such a simple program can be said to have a heart, is its *OnPaint()* member function. The *OnPaint()* function is connected to the WM_PAINT message by the message map and writes a single text string to the center of the client area:

```
void CMainWindow::OnPaint()
{
    CString s = "Hello, Windows!";
    CPaintDC dc( this );
    CRect rect;

    GetClientRect( rect );
    dc.SetTextAlign( TA_BASELINE | TA_CENTER );
    dc.SetBkMode( TRANSPARENT );
    dc.TextOut( (rect.right / 2), (rect.bottom / 2),
                s, s.GetLength() );
}
```

OnPaint() creates three MFC objects: a *CString* object *s* initialized with the message, a *CPaintDC* device context object *dc*, and a *CRect* object *rect*. The *CPaintDC* class implements a device context object that is tuned for painting. The class is derived from *CDC*, which is MFC's generic device context class. A *CPaintDC* object should be created only in response to a WM_PAINT message, usually inside an *OnPaint()* member function. The chief difference between a *CPaintDC* object and a *CDC* object is that the *CPaintDC* object automatically performs the *BeginPaint()* and *EndPaint()* operations.

The body of *OnPaint()* loads the current client area coordinates into the *rect* object (using *CWnd*'s *GetClientRect()* member function) and then uses the *dc* object to set the output modes and to actually output the text.

The remaining element of Hello's *CMainWindow* class is the constructor. The Hello constructor has two chores beyond those faced by the HelloApp constructor: It must load the keyboard accelerator table, and it must initialize the menu. Here is the *CMainWindow* constructor:

```
// CMainWindow constructor:
// Create the window with the appropriate style, size, menu, etc.
//
CMainWindow::CMainWindow()
{
    LoadAccelTable( "MainAccelTable" );
    Create( NULL, "Hello Foundation Application",
        WS_OVERLAPPEDWINDOW, rectDefault, NULL, "MainMenu" );
}
```

A quick look at the hello.rc file shown in Figure 13-6 on page 283 tells you that the accelerator table is named *MainAccelTable* and that the menu is named *MainMenu*. These names are passed as strings to *CFrameWnd*'s *LoadAccelTable()* and *Create()* member functions to enable these aspects of the Hello application.

The last piece of the Hello application is its application object. The Hello application is defined by the *CTheApp* class, which is derived from *CWinApp* and which has been declared in hello.h (shown in Figure 13-4 on page 281):

```
// CTheApp
// InitInstance:
// Returns TRUE if the initialization is successful.
//
BOOL CTheApp::InitInstance()
{
    TRACE( "HELLO WORLD\n" );

    m_pMainWnd = new CMainWindow();
    m_pMainWnd->ShowWindow( m_nCmdShow );
    m_pMainWnd->UpdateWindow();

    return TRUE;
}
```

The logic of *CTheApp*'s *InitInstance()* member function is the same as *CHelloApp*'s. The only additional element is the *TRACE* macro, a useful debugging aid we'll look at in a later chapter. The Hello application is managed by means of its application object, which is declared in hello.cpp:

```
// theApp:
// Just creating this application object runs the whole application.
//
CTheApp theApp;
```

Figure 13-8 shows the hello.cpp file in its entirety.

```
// hello.cpp : Defines the class behaviors for the application.
//          Hello is a simple program which consists of a main window
//          and an "About" dialog which can be invoked by a menu choice.
//          It is intended to serve as a starting-point for new
//          applications.
//
// This is a part of the Microsoft Foundation Classes C++ library.
// Copyright (C) 1992 Microsoft Corporation
// All rights reserved.
//
// This source code is only intended as a supplement to the
// Microsoft Foundation Classes Reference and Microsoft
// QuickHelp documentation provided with the library.
// See these sources for detailed information regarding the
// Microsoft Foundation Classes product.

#include <afxwin.h>
#include "resource.h"

#include "hello.h"

/////////////////////////////////////////////////////////////////////////

// theApp:
// Just creating this application object runs the whole application.
//
CTheApp theApp;

/////////////////////////////////////////////////////////////////////////

// CMainWindow constructor:
// Create the window with the appropriate style, size, menu, etc.
//
CMainWindow::CMainWindow()
{
    LoadAccelTable( "MainAccelTable" );
    Create( NULL, "Hello Foundation Application",
        WS_OVERLAPPEDWINDOW, rectDefault, NULL, "MainMenu" );
}

// OnPaint:
// This routine draws the string "Hello, Windows!" in the center of the
// client area.  It is called whenever Windows sends a WM_PAINT message.
// Note that creating a CPaintDC automatically does a BeginPaint and
// an EndPaint call is done when it is destroyed at the end of this
// function.  CPaintDC's constructor needs the window (this).
//
void CMainWindow::OnPaint()
{
```

Figure 13-8.
The hello.cpp file.

(continued)

Figure 13-8. *continued*

```
    CString s = "Hello, Windows!";
    CPaintDC dc( this );
    CRect rect;

    GetClientRect( rect );
    dc.SetTextAlign( TA_BASELINE | TA_CENTER );
    dc.SetBkMode(TRANSPARENT);
    dc.TextOut( ( rect.right / 2 ), ( rect.bottom / 2 ),
                s, s.GetLength() );
}

// OnAbout:
// This member function is called when a WM_COMMAND message with an
// IDM_ABOUT code is received by the CMainWindow class object.  The
// message map below is responsible for this routing.
//
// We create a CModalDialog object using the "AboutBox" resource (see
// hello.rc), and invoke it.
//
void CMainWindow::OnAbout()
{
    CModalDialog about( "AboutBox", this );
    about.DoModal();
}

// CMainWindow message map:
// Associate messages with member functions.
//
// It is implied that the ON_WM_PAINT macro expects a member function
// "void OnPaint()".
//
// It is implied that members connected with the ON_COMMAND macro
// receive no arguments and are void of return type, e.g.,
// "void OnAbout()".
//
BEGIN_MESSAGE_MAP( CMainWindow, CFrameWnd )
    ON_WM_PAINT()
    ON_COMMAND( IDM_ABOUT, OnAbout )
END_MESSAGE_MAP()

/////////////////////////////////////////////////////////////////////////////
// CTheApp
// InitInstance:
// When any CTheApp object is created, this member function is
// automatically called.  Any data may be set up at this point.
//
// Also, the main window of the application should be created
// and shown here.
// Returns TRUE if the initialization is successful.
//
```

(continued)

Figure 13-8. *continued*

```
BOOL CTheApp::InitInstance()
{
    TRACE( "HELLO WORLD\n" );

    m_pMainWnd = new CMainWindow();
    m_pMainWnd->ShowWindow( m_nCmdShow );
    m_pMainWnd->UpdateWindow();

    return TRUE;
}
```

Message Maps

Message maps are central to MFC applications. They dictate how a window will respond to the rich collection of Windows messages. The *CWnd* class is the basis of the MFC messaging paradigm. Classes derived from *CWnd*, such as *CModalDialog*, can have their own message maps that augment the *CWnd* map. Of the MFC library classes that are derived from *CWnd*, only *CModalDialog* and *CMDIFrameWnd* have their own message maps. The other MFC offspring of *CWnd* use the standard *CWnd* map. But when you derive a window class, usually from *CFrameWnd*, *CDialog*, *CModalDialog*, *CMDIFrameWnd*, or *CMDIChildWnd*, you will almost certainly want to include a message map.

We've already looked briefly at the Hello application's message map, which contains two of the four types of message map entries:

```
BEGIN_MESSAGE_MAP( CMainWindow, CFrameWnd )
    ON_WM_PAINT()
    ON_COMMAND( IDM_ABOUT, OnAbout )
END_MESSAGE_MAP()
```

Entry for a Constant Message

The first type of entry in the table is for one of Windows' constant messages. These entries are the easiest to use. As we've seen, for every *On...()* member function of the *CWnd* class there is a corresponding *ON_...* message map entry that is defined in afxmsg.h. The naming convention is consistent. For a given Windows message, the corresponding *CWnd* member function is named in mixed case with the *On* prefix and no underscore, and the message map entry is named in uppercase with the *ON_* prefix and underscore. Thus, the *CWnd* class's handler for the WM_PAINT message is the *OnPaint()* member function, and the *CWnd* message map entry is the *ON_WM_PAINT()* macro.

Placing an *ON_WM_PAINT()* entry in a class's message map implies that you have an *OnPaint()* member function for that class. Furthermore, your *OnPaint()* member function must have exactly the same parameters and return value as the *OnPaint()*

member function of *CWnd.* You will get compilation errors from the message entry macros if your member function is incorrectly declared.

Entry for a WM_COMMAND Message

The second type of entry in the Hello application's message map is an entry for a WM_COMMAND message, whose *wParam* value is *IDM_ABOUT.* WM_COMMAND messages are generated primarily from menus and accelerator keys. The message handlers must take no arguments and return no value.

You can use a single message handler to manage several related messages. The obvious part of this task is to specify the same handler for several messages. For example, here is part of a message map that specifies that the *OnYscale()* member function should be invoked for four separate messages:

```
ON_COMMAND(IDM_Gain_1, OnYscale)
ON_COMMAND(IDM_Gain_2, OnYscale)
ON_COMMAND(IDM_Gain_5, OnYscale)
ON_COMMAND(IDM_Gain_10, OnYscale)
```

Inside the *OnYscale()* member function, you have to determine which of the four menu selections was actually invoked. The trick is to use the *GetCurrentMessage()* member function of *CWnd,* which returns a pointer to an *MSG* struct. The *MSG* struct is defined in windows.h this way:

```
typedef struct tagMSG
    {
        HWND    hwnd;
        WORD    message;
        WORD    wParam;
        LONG    lParam;
        DWORD   time;
        POINT   pt;
    }   MSG;
```

The actual code in *OnYscale()* that retrieves the specific menu selection ID is

```
WORD iYScale = GetCurrentMessage()->wParam;
```

The expected values for *iYScale* are *IDM_Gain_1, IDM_Gain_2, IDM_Gain_5,* and *IDM_Gain_10.*

Entry for a Control Message

The third type of message map entry is for control messages, of which there are four types:

ON_EN_...	Edit notifications
ON_BN_...	Button notifications
ON_LBN_...	List box notifications
ON_CBN_...	Combo box notifications

The control messages that can be handled correspond to the control messages that are listed in the Windows reference. The specific control message macro names for use in message maps are listed in afxmsg.h. Each control message macro requires two parameters: the ID of the control, which is the same ID that you use in your resource file, and the name of the message-handler function:

```
ON_BN_CLICKED(IDD_FORTUNE, OnBtnFortune)
ON_LBN_SELCHANGE(IDD_FOOD, OnLbnFortune)
```

Control notification message-handler member functions should be declared to take no arguments and return no value.

Entry for a Registered Windows Message

The fourth and final type of message map entry is for registered Windows messages. You can register a new Windows message using the *::RegisterWindowsMessage()* function. A handler for a user message should be declared by means of *ON_REGISTERED_MESSAGE()*. The first parameter is the name of a *WORD* variable that will store the result of the *::RegisterWindowsMessage()* function—a variable, not a constant, because you can't know in advance what message number will be assigned by Windows; the second parameter must be the name of the message handler:

```
ON_REGISTERED_MESSAGE(nMyMessage, OnMyMessage)
```

The message handler for a registered Windows message must take two parameters, a *UINT* and a *LONG*, which correspond to the *wParam* and *lParam* values that are passed by Windows along with all messages.

For a standard Windows message

Similarly, you build a message map entry to handle a standard Windows message using the *ON_MESSAGE()* macro. The first parameter is the ID of the message, and the second is the name of a handler member function that takes a *UINT* and a *LONG*.

The HelloDlg Example

Some Windows programs don't need a full top-level window; such a program might consist of a single dialog box. The Calc program in the Petzold bible is one example, and anyone who has sampled the rich collection of Windows utilities and games has come across many others.

The C7 distribution doesn't contain a program that consists of a single dialog box, but it is easy to build one from the Hello program. To build your own HelloDialog example:

1. Copy all the Hello files into a directory called hellodlg. In the hellodlg directory, delete resource.h.

2. Edit hello.rc to remove the menu definition and the accelerator table, and remove the inclusion of resource.h.
3. Edit hello.h to remove the declaration of *CHelloWindow*.
4. Edit hello.cpp to remove the *CHelloWindow* members and message map, and remove the inclusion of resource.h.
5. Edit the makefile to remove the references to resource.h.
6. Edit the caption text in hello.dlg to indicate that this application is HelloDialog, not Hello (optional).
7. In hello.cpp, replace the Hello program's *InitInstance()* member function with this *InitInstance()*:

```
BOOL CTheApp::InitInstance()
{
    TRACE( "HELLO WORLD\" );

    m_pMainWnd=0;

    CModalDialog about( "AboutBox", NULL );
    about.DoModal();

    return TRUE;
}
```

8. If you are feeling ambitious, rename all the hello.* files hellodlg, and change the file name references (in makefile, hellodlg.cpp, and hellodlg.rc) accordingly (optional).

MFC Naming Conventions

One important aspect of the MFC library is its naming conventions. Naming conventions help you understand programs more easily by providing clues.

Here are the most important rules of the MFC naming conventions:

- A class name starts with a capital *C*, followed by a capitalized, mixed-case class name. For example, *CFrameWnd*, *CWnd*. The *C* stands for *Class*.
- A member function name starts with a capital letter and is in mixed case. For example, *InitInstance()*.
- A member variable name starts with *m_*, followed by the Hungarian notation for the data type, followed by a capitalized, mixed-case name. For example, *m_pMainWnd*. The *m_* part stands for *member*. Static data members don't have the *m_* prefix.
- A class enumeration constant is often in mixed case but starts with a lowercase letter. For example, the *CFileException* class in the MFC library defines the *fileNotFound* and *badPath* enumeration values.

- Other than the _ (underscore) in *m_*, avoid underscores in your program element names. Instead use mixed case to show word boundaries. *SetDigit()* is preferable to *set_digit()*.

These naming conventions aren't mandatory, but they are sensible and helpful. I recommend that you follow them when you create your own extensions of the classes in the MFC library.

Hungarian Notation

Hungarian notation, which is used in many data member names, will be familiar to anyone who has written programs for Windows. Hungarian is a naming convention that helps the human reader discover data types without having to refer back to the original declaration. In Hungarian notation, a character or two is prefixed to the variable name to indicate its type. For example, *h* in the name *m_hInstance* indicates a HANDLE. Figure 13-9 contains most of the commonly used Hungarian prefixes.

Prefix	***Built-In Data Type***	***Prefix***	***MFC Data Type***	***Prefix***	***Windows Data Type***
p	pointer	*by*	BYTE	*h*	HANDLE
lp	far pointer				
r	reference	*n*	UINT		
fn	function	*w*	WORD		
c	char	*l*	LONG		
n	int	*dw*	DWORD		
sz	string[1]	*b*	BOOL		

1. Null (zero) terminated string.

Figure 13-9.
Common Hungarian notation prefixes.

Hungarian notation, widely used in C programs for Windows, doesn't scale well to C++ class types because C++ contains far too many types. And C++ has stricter type checking than C, which reduces the need for Hungarian notation. You might retain some Hungarian flavor, though—by adopting the convention of declaring *CString* objects using the *str* prefix, for instance. And even when the use of C++ objects makes it hard to create enough short, memorable Hungarian prefixes, the *p* (pointer), *r* (reference), and *fn* (function) prefixes are often useful, and the prefixes for the built-in and MFC data types are always useful.

14

MFC Library Windows Menus and Dialog Boxes

That it's "graphical" is only part of the appeal of the Windows Graphical User Interface. What's equally appealing is that it is a consistent interface. Nearly all Windows applications have menu bars in which an application's major functionality is presented. Similarly, most Windows applications have dialog boxes that let you make several related choices regarding some aspect of a program.

Creating and managing menus and dialog boxes has always been one of the more straightforward aspects of programming for Windows. From the earliest days, there have been tools that help you create menu and dialog box resources, and the formats of the Windows resource files (with the extensions .rc, .dlg, .ico, .bmp, .cur, and so on) have always been relatively simple. The consensus among programmers is that Windows menus and dialog boxes are easier to manage than the equivalent features in MS-DOS applications are.

The chief problem with traditional C routines that manage complex menus and dialog boxes is that the code is bulky and clumsy. It's not unusual for a menu to have 50 choices; many have far more. This means that a 50-case C switch statement will be nested inside an already large switch statement that handles other Windows messages. Yes, it's mostly boilerplate. And yes, it's unpleasant, tedious, and error prone.

The MFC library provides an object-oriented framework for managing menus and dialog boxes. This is more sensible and convenient than the traditional C approach. Each menu selection, group of menu selections, dialog box control, or group of dialog box controls is hooked up to a class member function. This is software as it should be—one requirement, and one procedure to tend to that requirement.

The MFC library is compatible with the extensive set of Windows design tools that help you create menu and dialog box resource files. You can create menu and dialog resources with any of these tools and then use MFC library classes to manage the resources. In this chapter, we'll see in some detail exactly how this works. However, we won't review Windows basics—the idea of program resources, the individual resource files, and the mechanics of creating a menu or dialog box resource. These fundamentals are fully covered in the usual sources: the Windows SDK reference manuals and Charles Petzold's *Programming Windows*.

The *CMenu* Class

The MFC library's *CMenu* class encapsulates most of the functionality of the Windows procedures that use *HMENU* handles. *CMenu* is a light wrapper; most *CMenu* functions are implemented as calls to native Windows functions with little or no true "work" being done by the class functions themselves. But being a wrapper doesn't mean having little value. *CMenu* imposes much tighter type checking on your code, lets you omit the explicit *HMENU* parameter that is passed to most Windows menu functions, and is an important organizational framework.

As in most other MFC classes, a *CMenu* object is constructed in two phases. The first is the ordinary C++ construction phase, in which not very much goes on. In the second phase, the process is completed with the invocation of one of several functions to finish the initialization. These second-tier construction helpers let you initialize a *CMenu* object for which you already have an *HMENU* handle, load a menu from a resource, or create a brand-new menu.

Menu destruction comes in two flavors. If you own a menu object, you can simply delete it. This will free up any system resources associated with the menu, and it will also delete the object itself. But you have to be careful about deleting most *CMenu* objects. You can't delete *CMenu* objects that you have acquired from the system, and you can't delete *CMenu* objects that you have attached to a menu bar. But even when you can't delete a *CMenu* object, you can call *DestroyMenu()* to free the menu's system resources. This is necessary, for instance, after you have replaced a menu in a menu bar.

The *CWnd* Class's Menu Functions

The *CWnd* class, which as we've already seen is at the center of the window aspects of the Windows interface, also has a set of facilities for menus. These facilities let you get handles to menus and change menus, and they provide other operations that relate specific *CMenu* objects to specific menu bars.

The two fundamental *CWnd* member functions for menus are *GetMenu()* and *GetSystemMenu()*, which retrieve pointers to an application's top-level and system menu objects. The complement of *GetMenu()* is *SetMenu()*, which replaces an application's top-level menu. When an application's top-level menu has been changed, you probably need to call *CWnd*'s *DrawMenuBar()* function so that the menu bar will be redrawn.

Two other aspects of *CWnd* relate to menus. First are the message handlers for menu-related messages: the *OnMenuChar()*, *OnMenuSelect()*, *OnInitMenu()*, and

OnInitMenuPopup() functions. The *OnMenuChar()* handler gives you control when the user has opened a menu and typed an accelerator but the typed character doesn't match any of the specified text menu item accelerators. It is used primarily so that an accelerator can be used for a bitmap menu item. The *OnMenuSelect()* member function notifies you that a menu selection has been made, giving you additional control over menu selections. The *OnInitMenu()* and *OnInitMenuPopup()* member functions notify the program when a menu is about to be accessed for the first time, giving the program time to modify the menu before it is made visible.

The other role for *CWnd* in the menu system is related to the multiple document interface (MDI). The *CMDIFrameWnd* class, which is derived from *CWnd*, contains a member function called *MDISetMenu* that plays a big role in the special menu management of MDI applications.

The Chinese Restaurant Menu Example

Using menus to make choices in programs for Windows comes from our experiences with traditional menus, so I decided to devise an MFC menu example program that mimics a few of the selections on a traditional, printed restaurant menu. It might be a long time before a Windows program will be able to replace a printed menu in a Chinese restaurant, but the hLucky application[1] is one small step in that direction.

The basic appearance of the hLucky program is shown in Figure 14-1. Its principal source files appear in Figure 14-2 on the next page.

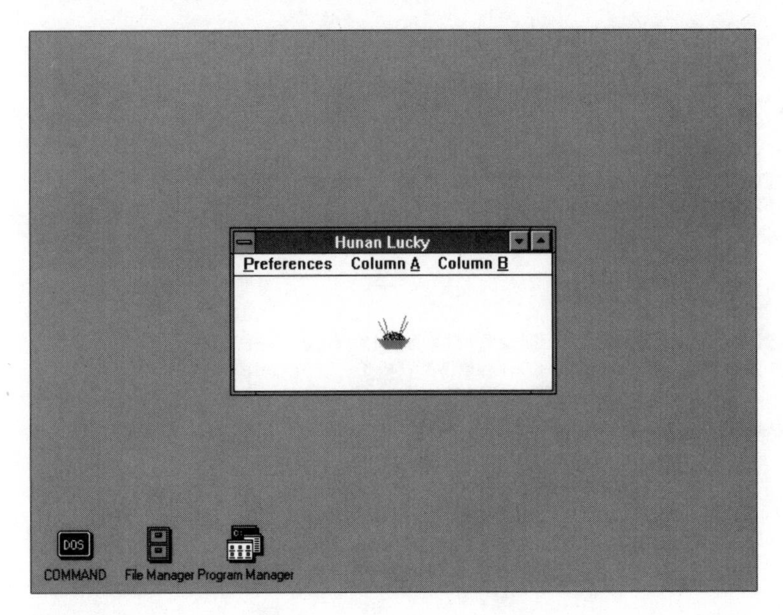

Figure 14-1.
The basic hLucky program screen.

1. My children's favorite Chinese restaurant is named Hunan Lucky.

resource.h

```
#define IDM_NoMeat        101
#define IDM_NoVeggies     102
#define IDM_Short         103
#define IDM_Long          104

#define IDM_ShrimpRice    111
#define IDM_TsoChicken    112
#define IDM_Dumplings     113
#define IDM_SzechFish     114

#define IDM_Delight       121
#define IDM_Scallions     122
#define IDM_Pork          123
#define IDM_Eggplant      124

#define IDM_Shark         131
#define IDM_EggDrop       132
#define IDM_Wonton        133
#define IDM_HouseSpecial 134
```

hlucky.rc

```
#include <windows.h>
#include <afxres.h>
#include "resource.h"

MainMenu MENU
BEGIN
    POPUP "&Preferences"
    BEGIN
        MENUITEM "No &Meat\tAlt+M", IDM_NoMeat
        MENUITEM "No &Veggies\tAlt+V", IDM_NoVeggies
        MENUITEM "&Short Menus\tAlt+S", IDM_Short
    END

    POPUP "Column &A"
    BEGIN
        MENUITEM "&Shrimp Fried Rice", IDM_ShrimpRice, CHECKED
        MENUITEM "General Tso's &Chicken", IDM_TsoChicken
        MENUITEM "Steamed &Dumplings", IDM_Dumplings
        MENUITEM "Szechuan &Fish", IDM_SzechFish
    END
```

Figure 14-2. *(continued)*

The principal source files for the hLucky program: resource.h, hlucky.rc, hlucky.h, and hlucky.cpp.

Figure 14-2. *continued*

```
    POPUP "Column &B"
    BEGIN
        MENUITEM "Triple &Delight", IDM_Delight, CHECKED
        MENUITEM "Ginger &Scallions", IDM_Scallions
        MENUITEM "Sweet and Sour &Pork", IDM_Pork
        MENUITEM "Eggplant with &Garlic", IDM_Eggplant
    END

END

ShortMenu MENU
BEGIN
    POPUP "&Preferences"
    BEGIN
        MENUITEM "&Long Menus\tAlt+L", IDM_Long
    END

    POPUP "Column &A"
    BEGIN
        MENUITEM "&Shrimp Fried Rice", IDM_ShrimpRice, CHECKED
    END

    POPUP "Column &B"
    BEGIN
        MENUITEM "Triple &Delight", IDM_Delight, CHECKED
    END

END

AFX_IDI_STD_FRAME ICON hlucky.ico

AccelTable ACCELERATORS
BEGIN
    "m", IDM_NoMeat, ASCII, ALT
    "v", IDM_NoVeggies, ASCII, ALT
    "s", IDM_Short, ASCII, ALT
    "l", IDM_Long, ASCII, ALT
END
```

hlucky.h

```
//
// The Top Window
//
class CMainWindow : public CFrameWnd
{public:
    CMainWindow();
```

(continued)

Figure 14-2. *continued*

```
    afx_msg void OnNoMeat();
    afx_msg void OnNoVeggies();
    afx_msg void OnShort();
    afx_msg void OnLong();
    afx_msg void OnColumnA();
    afx_msg void OnColumnB();
    afx_msg void OnSoup();

    afx_msg void OnPaint();
    afx_msg void OnRButtonDown(UINT nFlags, CPoint point);

    DECLARE_MESSAGE_MAP()
};

//
// The Application
//
class CTheApp : public CWinApp
{
public:
    BOOL InitInstance();
};
```

hlucky.cpp

```
#include <afxwin.h>
#include "resource.h"
#include "hlucky.h"

//
// Play with Menus (c) 1992 by Kaare Christian
//

// Build application object
CTheApp theApp;

#define GSM GetSystemMetrics
static const CRect smallrect(
    GSM(SM_CXSCREEN)/2 - 8 * GSM(SM_CYMENU),    // left
    GSM(SM_CYSCREEN)/2 - 4 * GSM(SM_CYMENU),    // top
    GSM(SM_CXSCREEN)/2 + 8 * GSM(SM_CYMENU),    // right
    GSM(SM_CYSCREEN)/2 + 4 * GSM(SM_CYMENU)     // bottom
);

// Main window
CMainWindow::CMainWindow()
{
```

(continued)

Figure 14-2. *continued*

```
    LoadAccelTable("AccelTable");
    Create(NULL, "Hunan Lucky",
        WS_OVERLAPPEDWINDOW, smallrect, NULL, "MainMenu");
}

// CMainWindow message map:
BEGIN_MESSAGE_MAP(CMainWindow, CFrameWnd)
    ON_WM_PAINT()
    ON_WM_RBUTTONDOWN()
    // preferences
    ON_COMMAND(IDM_NoMeat, OnNoMeat)
    ON_COMMAND(IDM_NoVeggies, OnNoVeggies)
    ON_COMMAND(IDM_Short, OnShort)
    ON_COMMAND(IDM_Long, OnLong)
    // column a
    ON_COMMAND(IDM_ShrimpRice, OnColumnA)
    ON_COMMAND(IDM_TsoChicken, OnColumnA)
    ON_COMMAND(IDM_Dumplings, OnColumnA)
    ON_COMMAND(IDM_SzechFish, OnColumnA)
    // column b
    ON_COMMAND(IDM_Pork, OnColumnB)
    ON_COMMAND(IDM_Scallions, OnColumnB)
    ON_COMMAND(IDM_Eggplant, OnColumnB)
    ON_COMMAND(IDM_Delight, OnColumnB)
    // soup popup
    ON_COMMAND(IDM_Shark, OnSoup)
    ON_COMMAND(IDM_EggDrop, OnSoup)
    ON_COMMAND(IDM_Wonton, OnSoup)
    ON_COMMAND(IDM_HouseSpecial, OnSoup)
END_MESSAGE_MAP()

inline match(int id1, int id2)
{ return id1 == id2 ? MF_CHECKED : MF_UNCHECKED; }

//
// Menu handlers
//
void CMainWindow::OnColumnA()
{
    WORD id = GetCurrentMessage()->wParam;
    CMenu* menu = GetMenu();
    menu->CheckMenuItem(IDM_ShrimpRice, match(id, IDM_ShrimpRice));
    menu->CheckMenuItem(IDM_TsoChicken, match(id, IDM_TsoChicken));
    menu->CheckMenuItem(IDM_Dumplings, match(id, IDM_Dumplings));
    menu->CheckMenuItem(IDM_SzechFish, match(id, IDM_SzechFish));
}
```

(continued)

Figure 14-2. *continued*

```
void CMainWindow::OnColumnB()
{   WORD id = GetCurrentMessage()->wParam;
    CMenu *menu = GetMenu();
    menu->CheckMenuItem(IDM_Pork, match(id, IDM_Pork));
    menu->CheckMenuItem(IDM_Scallions, match(id, IDM_Scallions));
    menu->CheckMenuItem(IDM_Eggplant, match(id, IDM_Eggplant));
    menu->CheckMenuItem(IDM_Delight, match(id, IDM_Delight));
}

void CMainWindow::OnNoMeat()
{
    CMenu *menu = GetMenu();
    WORD checked = menu->GetMenuState(IDM_NoMeat, MF_BYCOMMAND)
        & MF_CHECKED;
    checked = !checked;
    menu->CheckMenuItem(IDM_NoMeat, checked ? MF_CHECKED : MF_UNCHECKED);
    // a relaxed definition of "meat"
    WORD enable = MF_BYCOMMAND;
    enable |= checked ? MF_GRAYED : MF_ENABLED;
    menu->EnableMenuItem(IDM_TsoChicken, enable);
    menu->EnableMenuItem(IDM_Dumplings, enable);
    menu->EnableMenuItem(IDM_Pork, enable);
    menu->EnableMenuItem(IDM_SzechFish, enable);
}

void CMainWindow::OnNoVeggies()
{
    CMenu *menu = GetMenu();
    WORD checked = menu->GetMenuState(IDM_NoVeggies, MF_BYCOMMAND)
        & MF_CHECKED;
    checked = !checked;
    menu->CheckMenuItem(IDM_NoVeggies, checked ? MF_CHECKED : MF_UNCHECKED);
    WORD enable = MF_BYCOMMAND;
    enable |= checked ? MF_GRAYED : MF_ENABLED;
    menu->EnableMenuItem(IDM_Scallions, enable);
    menu->EnableMenuItem(IDM_Eggplant, enable);
}

void CMainWindow::OnSoup()
{
    WORD id = GetCurrentMessage()->wParam - IDM_Shark;
    static char *SoupName[] = {
        "Shark Soup",
        "Egg Drop Soup",
        "Wonton Soup",
        "House Special Soup" };

    MessageBox(SoupName[id],
        "Soup Choice", MB_ICONINFORMATION | MB_OK);
}
```

(continued)

Figure 14-2. *continued*

```
void CMainWindow::OnShort()
{
    CMenu *pMenu = GetMenu();
    pMenu->DestroyMenu();              // discard old resources
    pMenu->LoadMenu("ShortMenu");      // careful: automatic attach()
    SetMenu(pMenu);
    pMenu->Detach();                   // remove from map; pMenu is a temp
}

void CMainWindow::OnLong()
{
    CMenu *m_pMenu = GetMenu();
    m_pMenu->DestroyMenu();            // discard old
    m_pMenu->LoadMenu("MainMenu");
    SetMenu(m_pMenu);
    m_pMenu->Detach();
}

void CMainWindow::OnPaint()
{
    CPaintDC dc(this);
    CRect rect;

    GetClientRect(rect);

    dc.DrawIcon(
        (rect.right-GSM(SM_CXICON))/2, (rect.bottom-GSM(SM_CYICON))/2,
        ::GetClassWord(m_hWnd, GCW_HICON));
}

void CMainWindow::OnRButtonDown(UINT nFlags, CPoint point)
{
    CMenu popup;
    popup.CreatePopupMenu();
    popup.AppendMenu(MF_STRING, IDM_Shark, "Shark Soup");
    popup.AppendMenu(MF_STRING, IDM_EggDrop, "Egg Drop Soup");
    popup.AppendMenu(MF_STRING, IDM_Wonton, "Wonton Soup");
    popup.AppendMenu(MF_STRING, IDM_HouseSpecial, "House Special Soup");
    ClientToScreen(&point);
    popup.TrackPopupMenu(0, point.x, point.y, this);
}

//
// The Application's initialization code
//
```

(continued)

Figure 14-2. *continued*

```
BOOL CTheApp::InitInstance()
{
    m_pMainWnd = new CMainWindow();
    m_pMainWnd->ShowWindow(m_nCmdShow);
    m_pMainWnd->UpdateWindow();
    return TRUE;

}
```

Unlike my hLucky application, the real Hunan Lucky restaurant has never featured a menu urging you to choose one item from Column A and one from Column B. But while writing this whimsical menu application, I found the Column A, Column B stereotype to be irresistible.

In Chapter 13, we looked at the idea of using a message map and message-handler member functions. You can use a handler function to manage one specific menu selection, but sometimes you want a handler to service a group of related items. In the hLucky example, all of the Preference menu items have individual handlers, but all of the Column A menu items are handled by the *OnColumnA()* handler and all of the Column B items are handled by *OnColumnB()*.

Menu Item Selection

Let's start our detailed examination of hLucky with the *OnColumnA()* message handler. Like all menu message handlers, it doesn't have any parameters and it doesn't return a value. The *OnColumnA()* handler is used to service all the selections in the Column A menu. This fact is reflected in the message map in hLucky.cpp, which specifies *OnColumnA* for all four Column A menu identifiers.

When a handler responds to several menu selections, it usually needs to know which menu item was actually selected. In a menu handler, you can get the actual menu selection ID number with this code, which we looked at in Chapter 13:

```
WORD id = GetCurrentMessage()->wParam;
```

In *OnColumnA()*, the variable name *id* should have the value *IDM_ShrimpRice*, *IDM_TsoChicken*, *IDM_Dumplings*, or *IDM_SzechFish* because these are the only menu selections that are attached to the *OnColumnA()* handler in the message map.

The other standard expression in a menu handler creates a pointer to a *CMenu* object and initializes it to point at the window's menu:

```
CMenu *menu = GetMenu();
```

The major role of the *OnColumnA()* handler is to place a check mark next to the current menu selection. Thus, *OnColumnA()* must enforce the "choose one from column A" rule. When a menu item is selected, it is checked and the check mark for the old selection must be removed. We might employ any of several strategies for this, but the simplest is to set all the check marks either on or off each time a selection is made, using the *CheckMenuItem()* function.

The *CMenu* class's *CheckMenuItem()* member function takes two parameters:

```
BOOL CMenu::CheckMenuItem(WORD wIDCheckItem, WORD wCheck);
```

The first specifies the menu item, and it can be either the menu item ID or the ordinal position of the menu item. The second parameter has two roles: to specify whether the menu selection should be checked or unchecked and to specify whether the first parameter refers to a menu ID code or to an ordinal position. The four defined constants that we need to supply for the *wCheck* parameter are

```
MF_CHECKED            MF_BYCOMMAND
MF_UNCHECKED          MF_BYPOSITION
```

Your *wCheck* value should be the OR of one defined constant from Column A and one defined constant from Column B, although you can omit *MF_BYCOMMAND* because it is the default.

Graying Menu Items

Most programs have menu selections that are inappropriate at least some of the time. On the typical Edit menu, for example, the Cut, Copy, and Paste selections are usually grayed if nothing in the main window is selected. This ability to disable menu items is shown in the *OnNoMeat()* and *OnNoVeggies()* member functions, which use *CMenu*'s *EnableMenuItem()* member function to do the enabling and graying. Like *CheckMenuItem()*, *EnableMenuItem()* takes two parameters—the menu item and the operation that should be performed:

```
BOOL CMenu::EnableMenuItem(WORD wIDEnableItem, WORD wEnable);
```

The second parameter for *EnableMenuItem()* should be the OR of *MF_BYCOMMAND* or *MF_BYPOSITION* and one of the following:

```
MF_DISABLED
MF_ENABLED
MF_GRAYED
```

Toggling Menu Items

Another chore demonstrated in *OnNoMeat()* and *OnNoVeggies()* is toggling a menu selection. The relevant code is on the next page.

```
WORD checked = menu->GetMenuState(IDM_NoMeat, MF_BYCOMMAND) & MF_CHECKED;
checked = !checked;
menu->CheckMenuItem(IDM_NoMeat, checked ? MF_CHECKED : MF_UNCHECKED);
```

The *GetMenuState()* function returns a *WORD* whose bits represent the status of the menu selection. Combining the result of *GetMenuState()* with *MF_CHECKED* produces a value that indicates whether the *IDM_NoMeat* menu item is currently checked. In the code above, the flag is inverted and then used to specify the new status by means of the *CheckMenuItem()* function. The hLucky application with the Column B menu pulled down is shown in Figure 14-3, after the No Meat option has been selected and the names of the meat dishes have therefore been grayed out.

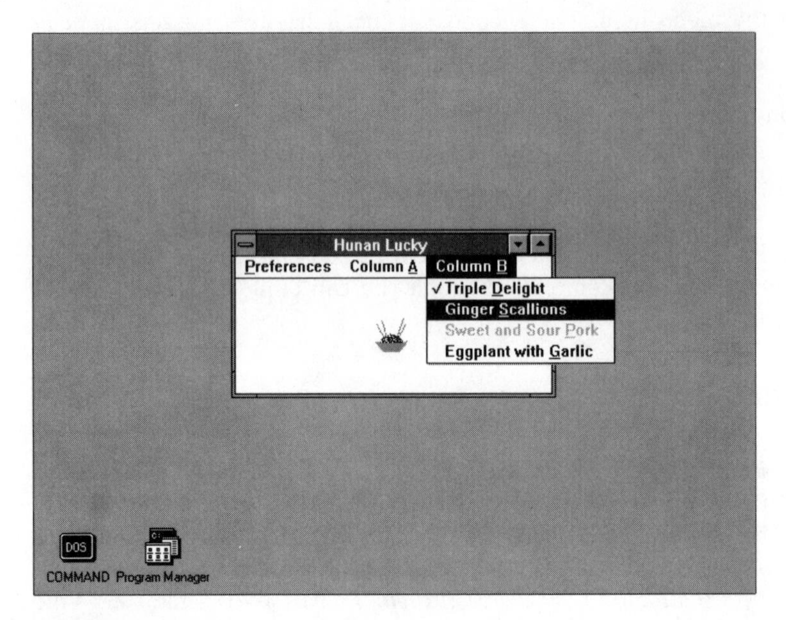

Figure 14-3.
hLucky's Column B menu with No Meat selected.

Short and Long Menus

Many programs have short and long menu options so that less experienced users are exposed to only a fraction of an application's complexity. Although the complexity of the hLucky application isn't too daunting, the application nevertheless has both short and long menus so that we can look at the switching mechanism.

But before we look at the details, we need a little background information. In the menu code that we've already looked at for graying and checking menu items, I used the *GetMenu()* member function of the *CWnd* class to retrieve a pointer to a *CMenu* object for the current window's menu. You might have noticed that in the hLucky application I never explicitly created a *CMenu* object, yet *GetMenu()* is able to return a pointer to a *CMenu* object. Here's how this works: If you use a *CMenu* object to initialize the application's menu, *GetMenu()* returns a pointer to that object. But if you simply use *Create()* to create the window and specify a menu ID in the last parameter of *Create()*, which is what happens in hLucky, *GetMenu()* returns a pointer to a temporary *CMenu* object that has been created for you by the MFC library. This gives you a uniform way to access Windows menus using *CMenu* objects.

As we gray and toggle menu items, it isn't important to know whether we are using a temporary *CMenu* object or a permanent *CMenu* object. In these cases, the menu object is simply used to help convey menu information to Windows. But changing menus is more profound, and then we have to distinguish between temporary *CMenu* objects and permanent *CMenu* objects.

The approach taken in hLucky is to use the MFC library's temporary *CMenu* objects—but with care. Here is the *OnShort()* member function from hLucky:

```
void CMainWindow::OnShort()
{
        CMenu *pMenu = GetMenu();          // get pointer to temporary
                                           //  CMenu object
        pMenu->DestroyMenu();              // discard Windows resources
        pMenu->LoadMenu("ShortMenu");      // careful: automatic attach()
        SetMenu(pMenu);                    // install menu
        pMenu->Detach();                   // remove from map; *pMenu is a
                                           //  temporary object
}
```

The first four statements in *OnShort()* should harbor no surprises. To change a Windows menu, first you get a pointer to the *CMenu* object, next you free the Windows resources consumed by the current menu, then you load a new menu from the resource file, and finally you call *SetMenu()* (from the *CWnd* class) to install the new menu. The only surprise in *OnShort()* is the last line, the call to *Detach()*. *Detach()* is called because *Attach()* was automatically invoked during the call to *LoadMenu()*. *Attach()* should be used only with permanent *CMenu* objects because it makes a permanent record of the current *CMenu* object's association with the current menu handle. But the current *CMenu* object is a temporary object created on the fly by the MFC library, so it is vital to erase that permanent record with a call to *Detach()*. Be careful when you call any of the *CMenu* class's constructor helpers—*CreateMenu()*, *CreatePopupMenu()*, *LoadMenu()*, or *LoadMenuIndirect()*—because they all invoke *Attach()*.

Another approach is to create your own *CMenu* objects, so that *GetMenu()* always returns a pointer to your permanent menu object. Here's how hLucky could be modified for this approach: In the *CMainWindow* constructor, you would use *NULL* as the last parameter for *Create()*, which would signify that you were doing your own menu management. Then in the constructor you would create a *CMenu* object and initialize menus manually.

```
CMenu *pMenu = new CMenu;           // create permanent CMenu objects
pMenu->LoadMenu("MainMenu");        // load menu from resource
SetMenu(pMenu();                    // install
```

You could store the *pMenu* pointer in the *CMainWindow* object, but that's not necessary because you can always get at the window's *CMenu* object by calling *GetMenu()*.

Given a permanent *CMenu* object, here's how we would code the *OnShort()* member function:

```
void CMainWindow::OnShort()
{
      CMenu *pMenu = GetMenu();
      pMenu->DestroyMenu();    // free Windows resources
      pMenu->LoadMenu("ShortMenu");
      SetMenu(pMenu);
}
```

The *OnLong()* function would be written similarly. If we followed this approach and used permanent *CMenu* objects, we'd have a few more cleanup chores when the window was destroyed. This cleanup would be best accomplished from within *OnDestroy()*. (Don't forget to mention ON_WM_DESTROY() in the *CMainWindow* message map.)

```
void CMainWindow::OnDestroy()
{
      CMenu *pMenu = GetMenu();
      pMenu->Detach()          // remove from MFC map before deletion
      delete pMenu;
      CFrameWnd::OnDestroy();  // invoke base class OnDestroy()
}
```

Floating Menus

If you love Chinese food, you might have noticed that none of the menu selections let the user choose a soup. In the hLucky application, the user picks a soup by means of a floating menu. Floating menus were first introduced in Windows 3 and are also called "menus on demand" or "popup menus." There isn't a formal standard for how or when floating menus are brought up, but in hLucky, as in most apps for Windows, the floating menu is brought up by a click of the right mouse button. Figure 14-4 shows the application screen just after the floating menu has appeared.

Using the MFC library to program a floating menu involves several steps. The easiest part is having the application respond to the right mouse button, which is accom-

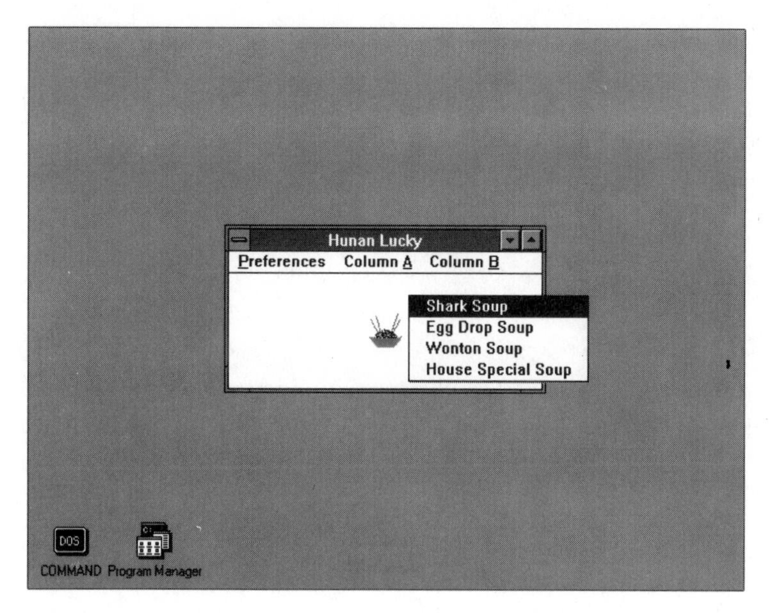

Figure 14-4.
hLucky's soup-selection popup menu.

plished by means of the *OnRButtonDown()* member function. Inside *OnRButtonDown()* is the logic for creating the floating menu:

```
void CMainWindow::OnRButtonDown(UINT nFlags, CPoint point)
{
    CMenu popup;
    popup.CreatePopupMenu();
    popup.AppendMenu(MF_STRING, IDM_Shark, "Shark Soup");
    popup.AppendMenu(MF_STRING, IDM_EggDrop, "Egg Drop Soup");
    popup.AppendMenu(MF_STRING, IDM_Wonton, "Wonton Soup");
    popup.AppendMenu(MF_STRING, IDM_HouseSpecial, "House Special Soup");
    ClientToScreen(&point);
    popup.TrackPopupMenu(0, point.x, point.y, this);
}
```

The popup menu object is created on the stack, so it will be deallocated automatically when *OnRButtonDown()* returns. This is appropriate because by then the menu is no longer needed and should be fully deallocated. Note that the *CMenu* destructor, which will be invoked automatically, will perform the *DestroyMenu()* chore to ensure that system resources are freed. As usual, the *CMenu* object is built in a two-step process, first by means of the constructor and then by means of the constructor's helper—in this case, using *CreatePopupMenu()*. In *OnRButtonDown()*, the soup-selection popup menu is created dynamically; *CreatePopupMenu()* is followed by several *AppendMenu()* calls. Alternatively, the soup menu could have been loaded from a resource by means of *LoadMenu()*.

The floating menu is displayed and managed by means of the *TrackPopupMenu()* function. *TrackPopupMenu()* must be told, in terms of screen coordinates, where to place the menu. The *OnRButtonDown()* function is invoked with the mouse cursor address in its second parameter, but the address is specified in client area coordinates. The client area coordinates must be converted to screen coordinates by *CWnd*'s *ClientToScreen()* function before they can be used with *TrackPopupMenu()*. When one of the soup-selection menu's items is selected, the *OnSoup()* handler is invoked, and it displays a message box confirming the selection.

The MFC Dialog Classes

Object-oriented programming is more useful in some programming domains than in others. Object-oriented programming is particularly suitable for GUI environments such as Windows. The environment itself is objectlike, which encourages and supports the use of an object-oriented approach. And the complexity of a GUI environment is best managed by means of a hierarchical approach. But when you want to come up with a task that really shows off object-oriented techniques, don't just think GUI; think GUI dialogs. The dialog box is the most object-appropriate domain that I've encountered.

The MFC library contains two principal classes for controlling dialog boxes: *CDialog* for modeless dialog boxes and *CModalDialog* for modal dialog boxes. The *CDialog* class is derived from *CWnd*, and *CModalDialog* is derived from *CDialog*. For a simple modal dialog, such as a typical About dialog, you can use *CModalDialog* directly. But for most modal dialogs, and for all modeless dialogs, you will derive your own class from either *CModalDialog* or *CDialog*.

These two classes manage the process of dialog box creation. The *CDialog* and *CModalDialog* classes don't reduce the role of a good dialog box editor in designing a dialog box. The two dialog classes provide ways to create a dialog box object, ways to initialize the controls just before the dialog box is first displayed, and ways to move the focus from one control to another.

Your derived dialog box class will usually contain a set of message-handler functions that respond to control messages. This lets you give a dialog box its unique personality. Derived dialog box classes also usually contain data members that relate to the controls. Sometimes data members are static so that they can be accessed even when the dialog box object has been deleted.

Dialog boxes are usually populated with controls. Each control is a type of window that already "knows" how to do much of its job. The MFC library contains six control classes, each derived from *CWnd*, that provide an object-oriented interface for a dialog box: *CStatic*, *CEdit*, *CButton*, *CListBox*, *CComboBox*, and *CScrollBar*. Figure 14-5 shows the MFC library dialog and control classes in their relationship to the *CWnd* base class.

You might expect each of your specialized dialog box classes to contain control objects. You might expect, for example, that an About dialog box would contain a

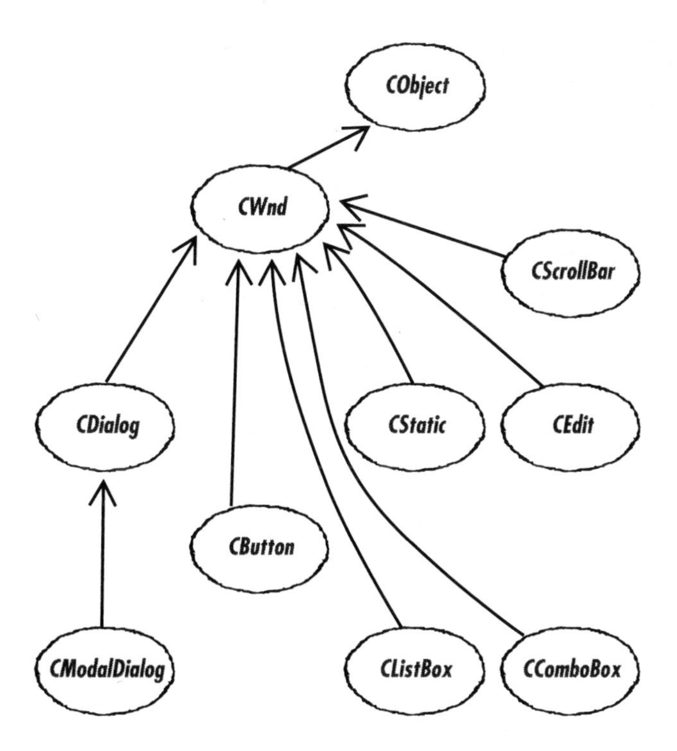

Figure 14-5.
The MFC library dialog and control classes.

CButton object to manage the OK button. But what actually happens is that Windows creates the dialog box controls based on your dialog box template, and then you dynamically construct objects to manage the controls. For example, if you need a *CListBox* object to interact with a list box control, you can create it on the fly by calling *CWnd*'s *GetDlgItem()*.

A dialog box is special in a few ways, such as in the way it can grab the focus. But in many other ways, it is just a standard window that contains child control windows. Thus, *CWnd* contains about a dozen member functions that let you interact with a dialog box's controls. They often give you two ways to do many tasks. For example, if a dialog box contains a button control, you can use *CWnd*'s *CheckDlgButton()* member function to check the button, or you can use *GetDlgItem()* to create a *CButton* object to manage the button control and then use the *CButton* object's *SetCheck()* member function.

The Food Dialog Example

The Food program whose screen is shown in Figure 14-6 on the next page contains both a modal Food Choices dialog box and a modeless Drink Choices dialog box.

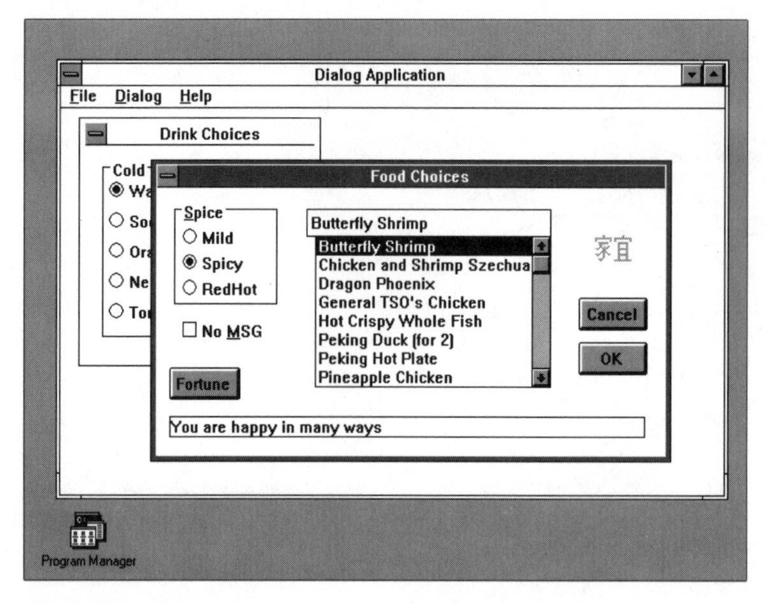

Figure 14-6.
The Food Choices and Drink Choices dialog boxes.

(Actually, the Food program contains two modal dialog boxes, but the second is a relatively trivial About box we won't go into.) The modeless Drink Choices dialog box lets the user select hot or cold drinks by means of radio buttons. It's of interest to us because it has much to teach us about the management of modeless dialog boxes, but we won't dwell on its radio button controls. The modal Food Choices dialog box is interesting both because it shows us how to manage a modal dialog and because it has an interesting set of controls that warrant discussion. The source code for the Food program is shown in Figure 14-7. The module definition file and the makefile are standard, so we won't look at them.

dialog.h

```
//
// CMainWindow:
//
class CMainWindow : public CFrameWnd
{
public:
    CMainWindow();
```

Figure 14-7. *(continued)*
The chief source files for the Food program: dialog.h, dialog.ccp, food.ccp, drink.ccp, about.dlg, food.dlg, drink.dlg, resource.h, and dialog.rc.

Figure 14-7. *continued*

```
    afx_msg void OnAbout();
    afx_msg void OnFood();
    afx_msg void OnDrink();
    afx_msg void OnExit();

    DECLARE_MESSAGE_MAP()
};
//
// CTheApp:
//
class CTheApp : public CWinApp
{
public:
    BOOL InitInstance();
};

//
// FoodDialog
//
class CFoodDialog : public CModalDialog
{
public:
    // constructor
    CFoodDialog(CWnd* pWndParent = NULL)
        : CModalDialog("FoodDialog", pWndParent)
    { }

    BOOL OnInitDialog();

    // Message handlers
    //
    afx_msg void OnBtnMSG();        // No MonoSodiumGlutamate check button
    afx_msg void OnBtnFortune();    // Pick a fortune
    afx_msg void OnBtnSeasoning();  // Seasoning radio buttons
    afx_msg void OnLbnFood();       // Food list box change
    afx_msg void OnOK();            // OK button

    // build a ComboBox object
    CComboBox& ComboBox() {return *(CComboBox*)GetDlgItem(IDC_FOOD);}

    DECLARE_MESSAGE_MAP()

    // member variables
    static BOOL m_bMsg;
    static WORD m_wSeasoning;
    static WORD m_wFood;
};
```

(continued)

Figure 14-7. *continued*

```
//
// DrinkDialog
//
class CDrinkDialog : public CDialog
{
public:
    // constructor
    CDrinkDialog(CWnd* pWndParent)
    {
        Create("DrinkDialog", pWndParent);
    }

    BOOL OnInitDialog();

    // Message handlers
    //
    afx_msg void OnClose();
    afx_msg void OnDone();
    afx_msg void OnHotDrink();
    afx_msg void OnColdDrink();

    DECLARE_MESSAGE_MAP()
};
```

dialog.cpp

```
#include <afxwin.h>
#include "resource.h"
#include "dialog.h"

//
// Dialog example program
// (c) 1992 by Kaare Christian
//

// Create the application object
CTheApp theApp;

//
// CMainWindow message map:
//
BEGIN_MESSAGE_MAP(CMainWindow, CFrameWnd)
    ON_COMMAND(IDM_ABOUT, OnAbout)
    ON_COMMAND(IDM_FOOD, OnFood)
    ON_COMMAND(IDM_DRINK, OnDrink)
    ON_COMMAND(IDM_EXIT, OnExit)
END_MESSAGE_MAP()
```

(continued)

Figure 14-7. *continued*

```
//
// The main window
//
CMainWindow::CMainWindow()
{
    LoadAccelTable("MainAccelTable");
    Create(NULL, "Dialog Application",
        WS_OVERLAPPEDWINDOW, rectDefault, NULL, "MainMenu");}

//
// OnAbout
//
void CMainWindow::OnAbout()
{
    CModalDialog about("AboutBox", this);
    about.DoModal();
}

//
// Food menu choice
//
void CMainWindow::OnFood()
{
    CFoodDialog food( this );
    food.DoModal();
}

//
// Drink menu choice
//
void CMainWindow::OnDrink()
{
    CMenu *menu = GetMenu();
    menu->EnableMenuItem(IDM_DRINK, MF_BYCOMMAND | MF_GRAYED);
    CDrinkDialog *drink = new CDrinkDialog(this);
}

//
// Exit menu choice
//
void CMainWindow::OnExit()
{
    SendMessage(WM_CLOSE, 0, 0L);
}

//
// CTheApp::InitInstance
//
BOOL CTheApp::InitInstance()
{
```

(continued)

Figure 14-7. *continued*

```
    m_pMainWnd = new CMainWindow();
    m_pMainWnd->ShowWindow(m_nCmdShow);
    m_pMainWnd->UpdateWindow();

    return TRUE;
}
```

food.cpp

```
#include <afxwin.h>
#include "resource.h"
#include "dialog.h"

//
// Management of the Food Choices dialog box
//

static CString Fortunes[] = {
    "You will be fortunate in everything",
    "The time is right to make new friends",
    "The will of the people is the best law",
    "Many a short question is evaded by a long answer",
    "Everything has beauty, but not everyone sees it",
    "Second thoughts are often wiser than first impressions",
    "You are gifted in many ways",
    "There is no great genius without some touch of madness",
    "Age is like love; it cannot be hidden",
    "A good home is happiness",
    "You are beautiful in many ways",
    "Rascals are always sociable",
    "You will have a comfortable old age",
    "You have the uncommon gift of common sense",
    "You are wild in many ways",
    "What's learnt in the cradle lasts till the tomb",
    "Your happiness is intertwined with your outlook",
    "A true friend walks in when others exit",
    "Friends long absent are coming back",
    "You are happy in many ways",
    "You have a friendly heart and are well admired",
    "A friend asks only for your time, not your money"
};

static CString Foods[] = {
    "Chicken and Shrimp Szechuan",
    "Triple Delight",
    "Peking Duck (for 2)",
    "Dragon Phoenix",
    "Peking Hot Plate",
    "Three Kings of the Sea",
```

(continued)

Figure 14-7. *continued*

```
    "Hot Crispy Whole Fish",
    "Subgum Wonton",
    "General TSO's Chicken",
    "Butterfly Shrimp",
    "Szechuan Sesame Beef",    "Seven Stars and Moon",
    "Tung Ting Shrimp",
    "Pineapple Chicken"
};

//
// The Food Choices dialog box message map
//
BEGIN_MESSAGE_MAP(CFoodDialog, CModalDialog)
    ON_BN_CLICKED(IDC_FOOD_MSG, OnBtnMSG)
    ON_BN_CLICKED(IDC_FOOD_MILD, OnBtnSeasoning)
    ON_BN_CLICKED(IDC_FOOD_SPICY, OnBtnSeasoning)
    ON_BN_CLICKED(IDC_FOOD_HOT, OnBtnSeasoning)
    ON_BN_CLICKED(IDC_FOOD, OnBtnFortune)
    ON_LBN_SELCHANGE(IDC_FOOD, OnLbnFood)
    ON_COMMAND(IDOK, OnOK)
END_MESSAGE_MAP()

// initialize static member variables
BOOL CFoodDialog::m_bMsg = FALSE;
WORD CFoodDialog::m_wSeasoning = IDC_FOOD_MILD;
WORD CFoodDialog::m_wFood = 0;

//
// Initialize the Food Choices dialog box
//
BOOL CFoodDialog::OnInitDialog()
{
    if (!CModalDialog::OnInitDialog())
        return FALSE;
    SetCtlBkColor(::GetSysColor(COLOR_WINDOW));

    // initialize Food Choices dialog radio buttons
    CheckDlgButton(IDC_FOOD_MSG, m_bMsg);
    CheckRadioButton(IDC_FOOD_MILD, IDC_FOOD_HOT, m_wSeasoning);

    // initialize list of fortunes
    OnBtnFortune();

    for(int i = 0; i < sizeof(Foods)/sizeof(CString); i++)
        ComboBox().AddString(Foods[i]);
    ComboBox().SetCurSel(m_wFood);

    return TRUE;
}
```

(continued)

Figure 14-7. *continued*

```
//
// Message handlers
//
void CFoodDialog::OnOK(){
    m_bMsg = IsDlgButtonChecked(IDC_FOOD_MSG);
    m_wSeasoning = GetCheckedRadioButton(IDC_FOOD_MILD, IDC_FOOD_HOT);
    m_wFortune = ComboBox().GetCurSel();
    CModalDialog::OnOK();
}

void CFoodDialog::OnBtnMSG()
{
    CheckDlgButton(IDC_FOOD_MSG, !IsDlgButtonChecked(IDC_FOOD_MSG));
}

void CFoodDialog::OnBtnSeasoning()
{
    WORD button = GetCurrentMessage()->wParam;
    CheckRadioButton(IDC_FOOD_MILD, IDC_FOOD_HOT, button);
}

afx_msg void CFoodDialog::OnBtnFortune()
{
    const int nFortunes = sizeof(Fortunes)/sizeof(CString);
    SetDlgItemText(IDC_FOOD_CUR_FORTUNE, Fortunes[rand() % nFortunes]);
}

afx_msg void CFoodDialog::OnLbnFood()      // Food combo box change
{
}
```

drink.cpp

```
#include <afxwin.h>
#include "resource.h"
#include "dialog.h"

//
// Management of the Drink Choices dialog box
//

BEGIN_MESSAGE_MAP(CDrinkDialog, CDialog)
    ON_WM_CLOSE()
    ON_BN_CLICKED(IDC_DONE, OnDone)
    ON_BN_CLICKED(IDC_WATER, OnColdDrink)
    ON_BN_CLICKED(IDC_SODA, OnColdDrink)
    ON_BN_CLICKED(IDC_ORANGE, OnColdDrink)
    ON_BN_CLICKED(IDC_NECTAR, OnColdDrink)
    ON_BN_CLICKED(IDC_TOMATO, OnColdDrink)
    ON_BN_CLICKED(IDC_TEA, OnHotDrink)
```

(continued)

Figure 14-7. *continued*

```
    ON_BN_CLICKED(IDC_COFFEE, OnHotDrink)
    ON_BN_CLICKED(IDC_NONE, OnHotDrink)
END_MESSAGE_MAP()

//
// Initialize the Drink Choices dialog box
//
BOOL CDrinkDialog::OnInitDialog()
{
    if (!CDialog::OnInitDialog())
        return FALSE;

    CheckRadioButton(IDC_TEA, IDC_NONE, IDC_NONE);
    CheckRadioButton(IDC_WATER, IDC_TOMATO, IDC_WATER);

    return TRUE;
}

// Message handlers
//
void CDrinkDialog::OnClose()
{
    OnDone();
}

void CDrinkDialog::OnDone()
{
    CMenu *menu = GetParent()->GetMenu();
    menu->EnableMenuItem(IDM_DRINK, MF_BYCOMMAND | MF_ENABLED);
    delete this;
}

void CDrinkDialog::OnHotDrink()
{
    WORD button = GetCurrentMessage()->wParam;
    CheckRadioButton(IDC_TEA, IDC_NONE, button);
}

void CDrinkDialog::OnColdDrink()
{
    WORD button = GetCurrentMessage()->wParam;
    CheckRadioButton(IDC_WATER, IDC_TOMATO, button);
}
```

about.dlg

```
DLGINCLUDE RCDATA DISCARDABLE
BEGIN
    "RESOURCE.H\0"
END
```

(continued)

Figure 14-7. *continued*

```
ABOUTBOX DIALOG 34, 22, 144, 75
CAPTION "Dialog Example"
STYLE DS_MODALFRAME | WS_CAPTION | WS_SYSMENU
BEGIN
    CTEXT "Dialog Box Example Program", -1, 0, 19, 144, 8
    CTEXT "Copyright (c) 1992 by Kaare Christian", -1, 0, 34, 144, 8
    CONTROL "OK", IDOK, "BUTTON", WS_GROUP, 56, 53, 32, 14
END
```

food.dlg

```
FOODDIALOG DIALOG 36, 32, 226, 115
CAPTION "Food Choices"
STYLE DS_MODALFRAME | WS_POPUP | WS_CAPTION | WS_SYSMENU
BEGIN
    GROUPBOX "&Spice",       -1,                     8,  5,  46, 45
    RADIOBUTTON "Mild",      IDC_FOOD_MILD,         12, 15,  37, 12
    RADIOBUTTON "Spicy",     IDC_FOOD_SPICY,        12, 26,  37, 12
    RADIOBUTTON "RedHot",    IDC_FOOD_HOT,          12, 37,  37, 12
    CHECKBOX "No &MSG",      IDC_FOOD_MSG,          12, 55,  44, 12
    PUSHBUTTON "Fortune",    IDC_FORTUNE,            6, 77,  32, 14
    LTEXT "CurrentFortune", IDC_FOOD_CUR_FORTUNE, 6, 98, 211,  9,
        WS_BORDER
    COMBOBOX                 IDC_FOOD,              67,  9, 109, 80,
        WS_VSCROLL
    ICON AFX_IDI_STD_FRAME, -1,                   195, 17,  16, 16
    DEFPUSHBUTTON "OK",      IDOK,                 188, 47,  30, 14
    PUSHBUTTON "Cancel",     IDCANCEL,             188, 66,  30, 14
END
```

drink.dlg

```
DRINKDIALOG DIALOG 20, 30, 103, 92
CAPTION "Drink Choices"
STYLE WS_POPUP | WS_CAPTION | WS_SYSMENU | WS_VISIBLEBEGIN
    GROUPBOX "Cold", -1,                  8,  5, 40, 77
    RADIOBUTTON "Water", IDC_WATER,      11, 13, 32, 12
    RADIOBUTTON "Soda", IDC_SODA,        11, 26, 30, 12
    RADIOBUTTON "Orange", IDC_ORANGE,    11, 39, 34, 12
    RADIOBUTTON "Nectar", IDC_NECTAR,    11, 52, 34, 12
    RADIOBUTTON "Tomato", IDC_TOMATO,    11, 65, 34, 12
    GROUPBOX "Hot", -1,                  53,  5, 42, 49
    RADIOBUTTON "Tea", IDC_TEA,          57, 13, 31, 12
    RADIOBUTTON "Coffee", IDC_COFFEE,    57, 27, 32, 12
    RADIOBUTTON "None", IDC_NONE,        57, 41, 28, 12
    PUSHBUTTON "Done", IDC_DONE,         60, 65, 32, 14
END
```

resource.h

```
#define IDM_ABOUT   100
#define IDM_FOOD    101
```

(continued)

Figure 14-7. *continued*

```
#define IDM_DRINK   102
#define IDM_EXIT    103

#define IDC_DONE    120

#define IDC_WATER   141
#define IDC_SODA    142
#define IDC_ORANGE  143
#define IDC_NECTAR  144
#define IDC_TOMATO  145

#define IDC_TEA     151
#define IDC_COFFEE  152
#define IDC_NONE    153

#define IDC_FOOD_MSG          200
#define IDC_FOOD_MILD         201
#define IDC_FOOD_SPICY        202
#define IDC_FOOD_HOT          203
#define IDC_FOOD_CUR_FORTUNE  204
#define IDC_FOOD              205
#define IDC_FORTUNE           206
```

dialog.rc

```
#include <windows.h>
#include <afxres.h>#include "resource.h"

AFX_IDI_STD_FRAME ICON dialog.ico

MainMenu MENU
BEGIN
    POPUP "&File"
    BEGIN
        MENUITEM "E&xit", IDM_EXIT
    END

    POPUP "&Dialog"
    BEGIN
        MENUITEM "&Food...", IDM_FOOD
        MENUITEM "&Drink...", IDM_DRINK
    END

    POPUP "&Help"
    BEGIN
        MENUITEM "&About...", IDM_ABOUT
    END

END
```

(continued)

Figure 14-7. *continued*

```
MainAccelTable ACCELERATORS
BEGIN
    VK_F1, IDM_ABOUT, VIRTKEY
END

rcinclude about.dlg
rcinclude food.dlg
rcinclude drink.dlg
```

The *CDialog* Class

CDialog is the MFC library class for managing modeless dialog boxes. In the Food example program, the modeless Drink Choices dialog is implemented by the *CDrinkDialog* class, which is derived from *CDialog*. *CDrinkDialog* is declared in dialog.h. The Drink Choices dialog is shown in Figure 14-8.

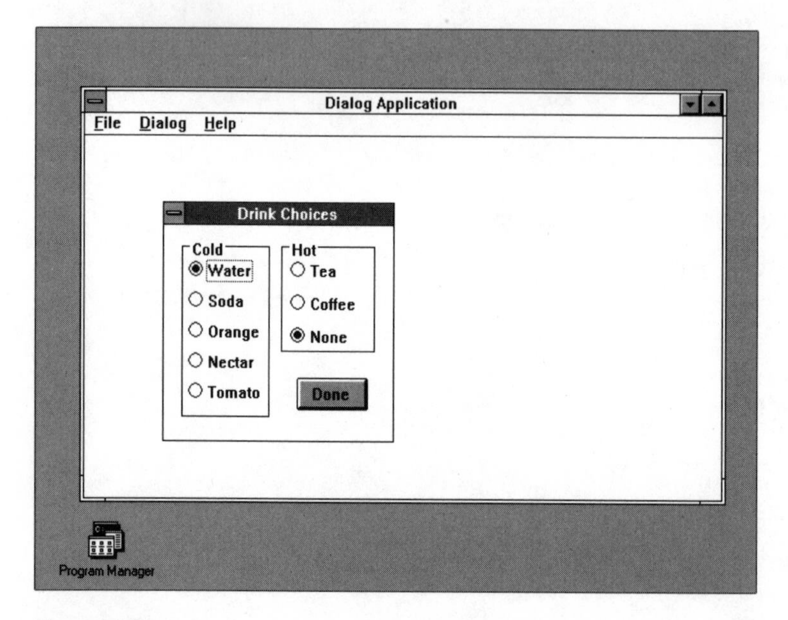

Figure 14-8.
The modeless Drink Choices dialog box.

The Drink Choices dialog box is created in the *OnDrink()* member function of the main window. The *OnDrink()* function first grays the Drink menu choice, so that it is clear that another Drink Choices dialog can't be started. Then it dynamically allocates a *CDrinkDialog* object:

```
void CMainWindow::OnDrink()
{
    CMenu *menu = GetMenu();
    menu->EnableMenuItem(IDM_DRINK, MF_BYCOMMAND | MF_GRAYED);
    new CDrinkDialog(this);
}
```

Note that dynamic allocation is required. If the dialog box were allocated on the stack, by writing

```
CDrinkDialog drink = CDrinkDialog(this);
```

we would be providing for automatic deletion when the *OnDrink()* handler returns. This would destroy the dialog an instant after creation, which is not polite behavior.

Creating a *CDrinkDialog* object

Like most MFC objects, a *CDialog* object is assembled in two phases: a deliberately do-little construction phase followed by a call to either *Create()* or *CreateIndirect()*. In the *CDialog* class, both the constructor and *Create()* are protected, so we can create a *CDialog* object only by deriving our own specialized dialog class from *CDialog*. Often the constructor of your derived class will automatically invoke the *CDialog* class *Create()*. That's what happens in the *CDrinkDialog* class:

```
CDrinkDialog(CWnd* pWndParent)
{
    Create("DrinkDialog", pWndParent);
}
```

The *"DrinkDialog"* argument to *Create()* is the name of the dialog resource, which is mentioned at the beginning of the file drink.dlg.

Note that during construction of a dialog object, the individual controls are not yet created and can't be initialized. Thus the constructor above can't initialize the radio buttons in the Drink Choices dialog.

The other important step in dialog initialization is the call to the *CDialog* class's overridable *OnInitDialog()* member function. This function is called immediately before the dialog box is displayed but after all the components are functional. Unlike most of the *OnXxx()* functions in the *CWnd* and *CDialog* classes, *OnInitDialog()* isn't a message handler and must not be mentioned in a message map. Instead, *OnInitDialog()* is a virtual member function that is invoked from the virtual function table. *OnInitDialog()* is used to initialize dialog box controls and perform other last-minute chores:

```
BOOL CDrinkDialog::OnInitDialog()
{
    if (!CDialog::OnInitDialog())
        return FALSE;
    SetCtlBkColor(::GetSysColor(COLOR_WINDOW));
```

```
        // initialize controls
        CheckRadioButton(IDC_TEA, IDC_NONE, IDC_NONE);
        CheckRadioButton(IDC_WATER, IDC_TOMATO, IDC_WATER);

        return TRUE;
    }
```

As must all classes that handle window messages, a class derived from *CDialog* must have a message map. Entries in the message map usually specify which handlers will respond to Windows control notification messages, although you can also provide message handlers for any of the more general functions that are usually managed by *CWnd* handlers. The *CDrinkDialog* class contains three such handlers: *OnDone()*, *OnHotDrink()*, and *OnColdDrink()*. The two drink handlers manage the radio buttons; we'll look later at similar handlers for the Food Choices dialog.

Deleting the *CDrinkDialog* object

OnDone() is the most interesting handler for the Drink Choices dialog box. It is called when the Done button of the Food Choices dialog is clicked, and its job is to remove the Drink Choices dialog box from the screen. Remember that the Drink Choices dialog is modeless; it remains on the screen either until the *DestroyWindow()* member function is invoked or until the dialog object is deleted. The *OnDone()* member function has two chores. First, it must enable the Drink menu choice of the main window, so that the dialog box can be redisplayed. Second, it must delete the *CDrinkDialog* object, which has the side effect of removing the dialog window from the screen:

```
    void CDrinkDialog::OnDone()
    {
        CMenu *menu = GetParent()->GetMenu();
        menu->EnableMenuItem(IDM_DRINK, MF_BYCOMMAND | MF_ENABLED);
        delete this;
    }
```

Graying the menu is straightforward, although you must remember that the menu is in the dialog box's parent, not in the dialog box itself. The C++ idiom to delete the *CDrinkDialog* object, the *delete this;* statement, can be a little startling. It might seem analogous to sawing off the tree limb you're sitting on. But that analogy would be flawed. In C++, it's acceptable for a member function to delete its object—you just have to be sure not to directly or indirectly use any class members following the deletion. To be safe, make *delete this;* the last statement in the member function.

And remember that most modeless dialog boxes have a system menu, which allows the user to select Move or Close. If you specify the WS_SYSMENU style for a modeless dialog box, you should install a handler for the WM_CLOSE message. In the *CDrinkDialog* class, the *OnClose()* handler simply calls *OnDone()* so that the code isn't duplicated.

The *CModalDialog* Class

Modal dialog boxes are far more common than modeless dialogs. They get the user to make a selection immediately, before continuing with other operations. We've already seen one simple modal dialog, the About dialog in the Hello application in Chapter 13. A *CModalDialog* object was created, and then the *DoModal()* member function was called. This simple approach is fine for dialogs that have only OK and Cancel buttons because the *CModalDialog* class contains the *OnOK()* and *OnCancel()* handlers for those two buttons. Of course, these two handlers get activated only if you use the standard control IDs for these buttons, *IDOK* and *IDCANCEL*.

But most modal dialogs are created by deriving a specialized dialog class from the *CModalDialog* class. The Food Choices dialog in the Food application is managed, for example, by the *CFoodDialog* class, which is defined in dialog.h. Unlike a modeless dialog box, a modal dialog box is usually constructed with a resource name and a parent window handle. This allows you to construct a fully initialized dialog, which can then be displayed and executed by a call to the *DoModal()* member function. Here's the *CFoodDialog* class's constructor:

```
CFoodDialog(CWnd* pWndParent = NULL)
    : CModalDialog("FoodDialog", pWndParent)
{ }
```

The *CFoodDialog* constructor, which should be handed a pointer to the parent window, simply invokes the *CModalDialog* base class's constructor to build the object.

Many derived dialog box classes contain data members that represent the states of some of the controls. There are several strategies that you can adopt to manage dialog data. The only clearly wrong strategy is the C strategy, that is, storing the dialog status information in global variables. One strategy for storing control status information is to make the dialog object exist for the lifetime of the program, so that the dialog object member variables are always available. Another strategy is to make the dialog member variables static, so that the member variables will be available even when no dialog object exists. You can see in dialog.h that the *CFoodDialog* class employs the second strategy.

Because the *CModalDialog* class is derived from *CDialog*, it has an *OnInitDialog()* virtual member function that is used to initialize the controls just before the dialog is displayed. Here is the *OnInitDialog()* function from the *CFoodDialog* class:

```
BOOL CFoodDialog::OnInitDialog()
{
    if (!CModalDialog::OnInitDialog())
        return FALSE;
    SetCtlBkColor(::GetSysColor(COLOR_WINDOW));

    // initialize Food Choices dialog radio buttons
    CheckDlgButton(IDC_FOOD_MSG, m_bMsg);
    CheckRadioButton(IDC_FOOD_MILD, IDC_FOOD_HOT, m_wSeasoning);
```

```
        // initialize list of fortunes
        OnBtnFortune();

        for(int i = 0; i < sizeof(Foods)/sizeof(CString); i++)
            ComboBox().AddString(Foods[i]);
        ComboBox().SetCurSel(m_wFood);

        return TRUE;
    }
```

In *OnInitDialog()*, the three static member variables (*m_bMsg*, *m_wSeasoning*, and *m_wFortune*) are used to initialize the dialog controls. If the modal dialog is terminated by a click of the Cancel button, these member variables needn't be updated. However, when OK is clicked, the status of the dialog controls must be preserved in these three variables. That's the job of the *OnOK()* member function:

```
    afx_msg void CFoodDialog::OnOK()
    {
        m_bMsg = IsDlgButtonChecked(IDC_FOOD_MSG);
        m_wSeasoning = GetCheckedRadioButton(IDC_FOOD_MILD, IDC_FOOD_HOT);
        m_wFood = ComboBox().GetCurSel();
        CModalDialog::OnOK();      // now do normal terminate actions
    }
```

The first three lines in the *OnOK()* body simply save the state of the controls. Then, in the last line, the *CModalDialog* base class's *OnOK()* is called to perform the standard cleanup of a modal dialog.

MFC Control Classes

The MFC library has six classes that encapsulate the functionality of standard Windows controls: *CStatic*, *CButton*, *CListBox*, *CComboBox*, *CEdit*, and *CScrollBar*. The main use of these control classes is to interact with windows controls in dialog boxes, although many other uses are possible. As we've already observed, you don't place a *CButton* object in your dialog class just because you want to manage a BUTTON control. Instead, you create the control objects on the fly by means of the *CWnd* base class's *GetDlgItem()* member function.

GetDlgItem() returns a pointer to a *CWnd* object that is associated with a specific control. For example, the following statement will return a pointer to the *CWnd* object associated with the OK button:

```
    CWnd *pOKButtonWnd = GetDlgItem(IDOK);
```

We're close, but what we really want is a pointer to a *CButton* object, not a pointer to a *CWnd*. Because *CButton* is derived from *CWnd*, we can trivially convert a *CButton** pointer into a *CWnd** pointer. But going in the other direction, which is often called "casting up," is problematic. Remember that a base class object doesn't have an *is a* relationship to its derived classes. However, in this specific case, the MFC control classes and the *GetDlgItem()* function have been designed so that casting up is acceptable:

```
CButton *pOKButton = (CButton *)GetDlgItem(IDOK);
```

Another way to create and access a control object is to use an inline member function. In the *CFoodDialog* class, for example, there is an inline member function that returns a reference to the dialog's *CComboBox* object:

```
CComboBox& ComboBox() {return *(CComboBox*)GetDlgItem(IDC_FOOD);}
```

It's the *ComboBox()* member function that makes it possible to write statements such as the following, which appeared in the *OnInitDialog()* function we saw earlier:

```
ComboBox().AddString(Foods[i]);
```

You should build access functions such as *ComboBox()* to make it easier to manage frequently referenced controls.

15

MFC Library Windows Graphics Device Interface

Before the Windows environment burst onto the PC scene, each program had to include drivers for the display and drivers for printing. One major advance offered by Windows is that it lets programs work with whatever display and print devices are available. The low-level hardware support is bundled into Windows. At the lowest level are the drivers, which perform the actual I/O operations. One step up from the drivers is the programmable interface, the Windows Graphical Device Interface (GDI).

The GDI is primarily a raster graphics programming language because it lets programs perform low-level raster operations, such as bit block transfers (BitBlts) and individual bit operations. Of course, the GDI also contains slightly higher level functionality, such as line drawing, area filling, and text output. The GDI does not provide for many of the more specialized operations, such as drawing Bézier curves, drawing text on paths, warping, and using graded area fills.

The central concept in the GDI is that of the device context. A device context is an entry to some specific graphics device, such as the screen or a printer. It contains information about the device so that a program can adjust its operation to suit the needs and abilities of the device. The device context also contains information specified by the program at runtime, such as the currently selected drawing color, the current pen shape, and the like.

Device contexts are allocated by Windows whenever a program needs to do graphical operations. They are, in essence, the currency of the graphical realm. When your program has a device context, it can perform graphical operations; without a device context, your software is silenced.

The *CDC* Class Family

In tacit acknowledgment of the importance of the device context, the MFC library has as its principal class for graphics the *CDC* class. Like *CWnd*, *CDC* is a vast class, comprising scores of member functions. *CDC* doesn't have as many offspring as *CWnd*, and the *CDC* offspring offer only small increments of functionality. Another difference between *CWnd* and *CDC* is that you will rarely, if ever, derive a class from *CDC*, whereas you routinely derive classes from *CWnd* or *CWnd* descendants. As a general and useful rule, a Windows function that takes an *HWND* handle as its first argument usually has analogs in the *CWnd* class; a Windows function that takes an *HDC* handle as its first argument usually has analogs in the *CDC* class.

Many programmers are surprised by, and initially confused by, Windows' handling of windows. It is within the windowing part of Windows that we find the messaging paradigm, and that imparts a somewhat upside-down flavor to our programs. The windowing interface also interacts heavily with the .rc file, and the idea of resources can be a foreign concept to a PC programmer. But the basic concepts of the GDI are familiar to anyone who has done some graphical programming. The chief surprise and major difficulty of the GDI is its size.

The descendants of the MFC library's *CDC* that we'll deal with are *CPaintDC*, *CWindowDC*, and *CClientDC*. *CPaintDC* is a device context class that responds to the WM_PAINT message. Its chief advantage is that it encapsulates *::BeginPaint()* and *::EndPaint()* calls. The other two device context classes are for the window—*CWindowDC* for an entire window, and *CClientDC* for the client part of a window. They are called into play when you need the window's device context for purposes other than responding to a WM_PAINT message.

The *CGdiObject* Class Family

In addition to the *CDC* class family, the MFC library contains a group of classes that represent elements of the GDI environment. The base class for these GDI classes is *CGdiObject*, which contains several primitive operations for connecting Windows' object handles to GDI object classes. The derived GDI object classes are *CBitmap*, *CBrush*, *CFont*, *CPalette*, *CPen*, and *CRgn*. These classes encapsulate Windows bitmaps, brushes, fonts, palettes, pens, and regions. Figure 15-1 shows all the classes with which we'll be concerned in this GDI chapter.

The *CDC* class has been present in many of the earlier examples in this book. The Hello program in Chapter 13, for instance, contains this *OnPaint()* message handler:

```
void CMainWindow::OnPaint()
{
    CString s = "Hello, Windows!";
    CPaintDC dc(this);
    CRect rect;
```

```
    GetClientRect(rect);
    dc.SetTextAlign(TA_BASELINE | TA_CENTER);
    dc.SetBkMode(TRANSPARENT);
    dc.TextOut((rect.right / 2), (rect.bottom / 2), s, s.GetLength());
}
```

With the statement

```
CPaintDC dc(this);
```

OnPaint() creates a device context. The creation of a *CPaintDC* object automatically calls *CWnd*'s *BeginPaint()* function to notify Windows that the painting is under way. At the end of *OnPaint()*, the *CPaintDC* class's destructor is invoked automatically, and the destructor automatically issues the necessary *EndPaint()* call to signal the completion of the painting operation. In the body of *OnPaint()*, the *dc* device context object is used three times: once to specify the text alignment, once to specify how the background will be handled, and once to write a text message at the center of the client area.

The Hello application's *OnPaint()* is typical, and most MFC library device context operations follow its model:

1. Creation and initialization of a device context object

MFC Library Graphics Device Interface Classes

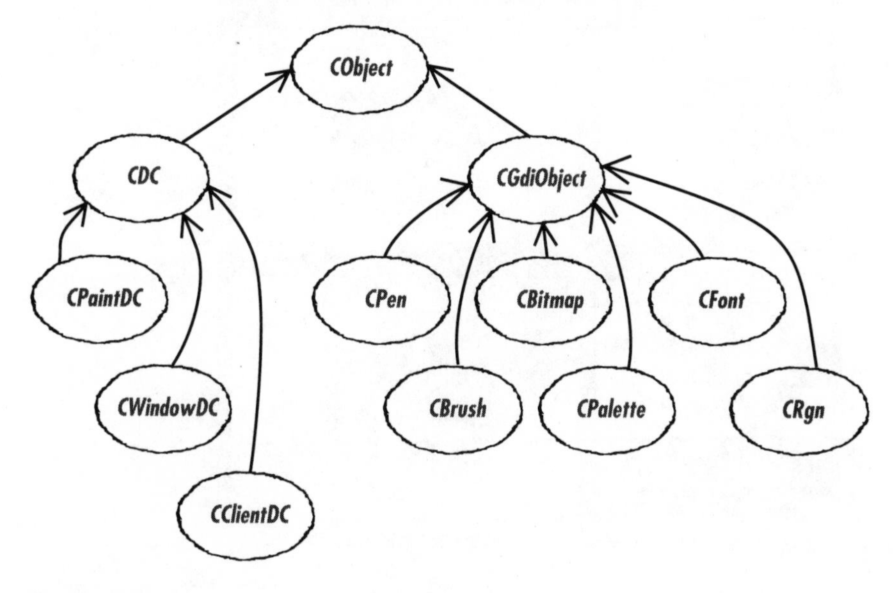

Figure 15-1.
The CDC *and* CGdiObject *class hierarchies derived from the* CObject *ultimate base class.*

2. Setup of the device context
3. Output operations
4. Cleanup of the device context

Some of these tasks often contain many subtasks. Setup of the device context, for instance, often involves creation of *CBrush* and *CPen* objects that are then selected into the device context.

The Quilt Example

The Quilt program we looked at briefly in Chapter 4 is a small MFC application that draws several interesting shapes by means of recursion. The program name comes from the resemblance of some of the shapes to geometric patterns in patchwork quilts. Figure 15-2 shows some of the whimsical patchwork effects the Quilt program can achieve.

The Quilt program is organized into two major files, quilt.cpp and shapes.cpp. The quilt.cpp file contains the by now familiar MFC library framework for a simple Windows application. We'll delve into some of the *CDC* class parts in detail but will touch only lightly on the class's message-handling, menu, and dialog box capabilities. The Quilt program source code appears in Figure 15-3. Its standard .def file and makefile are omitted here.

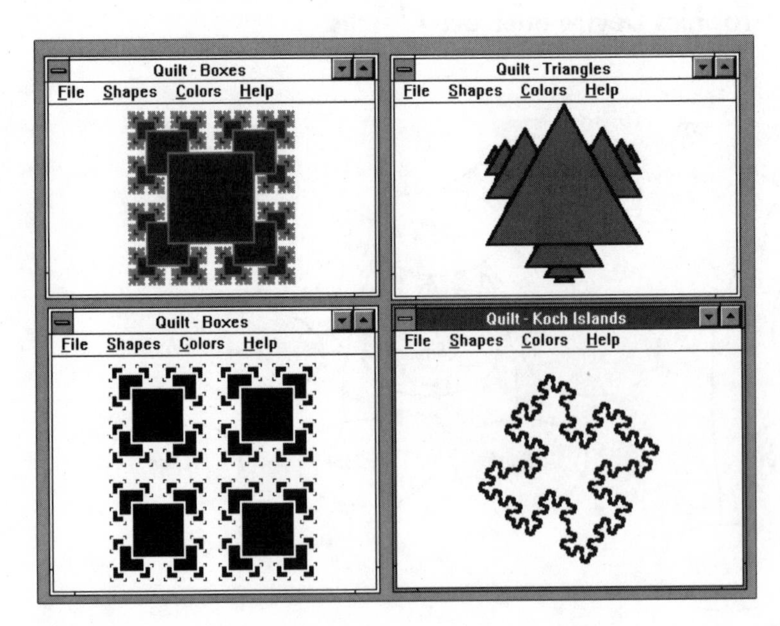

Figure 15-2.
Four of the shape patterns produced by the Quilt program.

quilt.h

```
//
// CTheApp
//
class CTheApp : public CWinApp
{
public:
    BOOL InitInstance();
};

//
// CMainWindow
//
class CMainWindow : public CFrameWnd
{
public:
    CMainWindow();
    ~CMainWindow();

    afx_msg int OnCreate(LPCREATESTRUCT p);
    afx_msg void OnPaint();
    afx_msg void OnAbout();
    afx_msg void OnExit();
    afx_msg void OnColor();
    afx_msg void OnShape();

    UINT m_nColor;
    UINT m_nShape;

    DECLARE_MESSAGE_MAP()
};
```

quilt.cpp

```
#include <afxwin.h>
#include "quilt.h"
#include "resource.h"
#include "shapes.h"

//
// Quilt application--draws patterns
// Copyright (c) 1992 by Kaare Christian
//

//
// The application object
//
```

Figure 15-3.
The Quilt program source files: quilt.h, quilt.cpp, shapes.h, shapes.cpp, resource.h, about.dlg, and quilt.rc.

(continued)

Figure 15-3. *continued*

```
CTheApp theApp;

//
// The application--InitInstance
//
BOOL CTheApp::InitInstance()
{
    m_pMainWnd = new CMainWindow();
    m_pMainWnd->ShowWindow(m_nCmdShow);
    m_pMainWnd->UpdateWindow();

    return TRUE;
}

// colors
static tagRGBTRIPLE clrArray[] = {
    {   0,   0,   0 },   // black
    {   0,   0, 255 },   // red
    {   0, 255,   0 },   // green
    { 255,   0,   0 },   // blue
    { 255, 255, 255 }    // white
};

// main window titles
static CString csTitles[] = {
    "Quilt - Triangles", "Quilt - Triangles",
    "Quilt - Boxes", "Quilt - Boxes",
    "Quilt - Koch Islands", "Quilt - Koch Islands", "Quilt - Koch Islands"
};

BEGIN_MESSAGE_MAP(CMainWindow, CFrameWnd)
    ON_WM_CREATE()
    ON_WM_PAINT()
    ON_WM_TIMER()
    ON_COMMAND(IDM_EXIT, OnExit)
    ON_COMMAND(IDM_ABOUT, OnAbout)
    ON_COMMAND(IDM_RED, OnColor)
    ON_COMMAND(IDM_GREEN, OnColor)
    ON_COMMAND(IDM_BLUE, OnColor)
    ON_COMMAND(IDM_WHITE, OnColor)
    ON_COMMAND(IDM_TRIA, OnShape)
    ON_COMMAND(IDM_TRIB, OnShape)
    ON_COMMAND(IDM_BOXESA, OnShape)
    ON_COMMAND(IDM_BOXESB, OnShape)
    ON_COMMAND(IDM_KOCH1, OnShape)
    ON_COMMAND(IDM_KOCH2, OnShape)
    ON_COMMAND(IDM_KOCH3, OnShape)
END_MESSAGE_MAP()
```

(continued)

Figure 15-3. *continued*

```
//
// Constructor
//
CMainWindow::CMainWindow()
{
    m_wColor = IDM_WHITE;
    m_wShape = IDM_BOXESA;
    LoadAccelTable("MainAccelTable");
    Create(NULL, "Quilt", WS_OVERLAPPEDWINDOW,
        rectDefault, NULL, "MainMenu");
}

//
// Destructor
//
CMainWindow::~CMainWindow()
{
}

//
// OnCreate:
//
int CMainWindow::OnCreate(LPCREATESTRUCT /* p */)
{
    CMenu *pMenu = GetMenu();
    pMenu->CheckMenuItem(m_wColor, MF_CHECKED);
    pMenu->CheckMenuItem(m_wShape, MF_CHECKED);
    SetWindowText(csTitles[m_wShape - IDM_TRIA]);

    return 0;
}

//
// OnShape
//
void CMainWindow::OnShape()
{
    CMenu *pMenu = GetMenu();
    pMenu->CheckMenuItem(m_wShape, MF_UNCHECKED);

    m_wShape = GetCurrentMessage()->wParam;
    pMenu->CheckMenuItem(m_wShape, MF_CHECKED);

    SetWindowText(csTitles[m_wShape - IDM_TRIA]);

    Invalidate(TRUE);
}
```

(continued)

Figure 15-3. *continued*

```
//
// OnColor
//
void CMainWindow::OnColor()
{
    CMenu *pMenu = GetMenu();
    pMenu->CheckMenuItem(m_wColor, MF_UNCHECKED);

    m_wColor = GetCurrentMessage()->wParam;
    pMenu->CheckMenuItem(m_wColor, MF_CHECKED);

    Invalidate(TRUE);
}

//
// OnAbout
//
void CMainWindow::OnAbout()
{
    CModalDialog about("aboutbox", this);
    about.DoModal();
}

//
// OnExit
//
void CMainWindow::OnExit()
{
    DestroyWindow();
}

//
// OnPaint
//
void CMainWindow::OnPaint()
{
    CPaintDC paintDC(this);
    CRect rect;
    GetClientRect(&rect);

    int clr = m_wColor - IDM_BLACK;
    int r = clrArray[clr].rgbtRed;
    int g = clrArray[clr].rgbtGreen;
    int b = clrArray[clr].rgbtBlue;

    DWORD rgbPen = RBG(r, g, b);
    if (rgbPen == paintDC.GetBkColor())
        rgbPen = RGB(3*r/4, 3*g/4, 3*b/4);
    CPen Pen(PS_SOLID, 2, rgbPen);
    CPen *oldPen = paintDC.SelectObject(&Pen);
```

(continued)

Figure 15-3. *continued*

```
    DWORD rgbBrush = RGB(r/2, g/2, b/2);
    if (rgbBrush == paintDC.GetBkColor())
        rgbBrush = RGB(3*r/4, 3*g/4, 3*b/4);
    CBrush Brush(rgbBrush);
    CBrush *oldBrush = paintDC.SelectObject(&Brush);

    switch(m_wShape) {
        case IDM_TRIA:
            shape = new CTriangle(&paintDC, &rect, 4, TRUE);
            break;
        case IDM_TRIB:
            shape = new CTriangle(&paintDC, &rect, 4, FALSE);
            break;
        case IDM_BOXESA:
            shape = new CBox(&paintDC, &rect, 6);
            break;
        case IDM_BOXESB:
            shape = new CQBox(&paintDC, &rect, 5);
            break;
        case IDM_KOCH1:
            shape = new CKochIsle(&paintDC, &rect, 1);
            break;
        case IDM_KOCH2:
            shape = new CKochIsle(&paintDC, &rect, 2);
            break;
        case IDM_KOCH3:
            shape = new CKochIsle(&paintDC, &rect, 3);
            break;
    }

    if (shape) {
        shape->Draw();
        delete shape;
    }
    paintDC.SelectObject(oldPen);
    paintDC.SelectObject(oldBrush);
}
```

shapes.h

```
//
// The basic shape class--stores drawing information
//
class CShape {
public:
    virtual void Draw() = 0;
    virtual ~CShape() {}
protected:
    CDC *m_pDC;
    CRect *m_pRect;
```

(continued)

Figure 15-3. *continued*

```
    UINT m_nDepth;
    CShape(CDC *dc, CRect *rect, UINT nDepth);
};

//
// A box shape--other boxes appear below . . .
//
class CBox : public CShape {
public:
    CBox(CDC *dc, CRect *rect, int nDepth);
    virtual void Draw();
protected:
    void Draw(int nRadius, CPoint pt, UINT nDepth);
};

//
// A quad box shape--four CBox patterns
//
class CQBox : public CBox {
public:
    CQBox(CDC *dc, CRect *rect, UINT nDepth);
    virtual void Draw();
};

//
// A triangle shape--on top of other triangles . . .
//
class CTriangle : public CShape {
public:
    CTriangle(CDC *dc, CRect *rect, UINT nDepth, BOOL front);
    virtual void Draw();
protected:
    void Draw(int nRadius, CPoint pt, UINT nDepth);
    void Drawone(CPoint pt, int nRadius);
    BOOL m_bFront;
    static const double dSin30;        // some useful angles
    static const double dCos30;
    static const double dSin30Cos30;
    static const double dSin30Sin30;
};

//
// A Koch Islands shape
//
class CKochIsle : public CShape {
public:
    CKochIsle(CDC *dc, CRect *rect, UINT nDepth);
    virtual void Draw();
```

(continued)

Figure 15-3. *continued*

```
protected:
    void Line(CPoint from, CPoint to, UINT nDepth);
};
```

shapes.cpp

```
#include <afxwin.h>
#include <math.h>
#include "shapes.h"

//
// CShape constructor
//
CShape::CShape(CDC *dc, CRect *rect, UINT nDepth) :
    m_pDC(dc),
    m_pRect(rect),
    m_nDepth(nDepth)
{
}

//
// CBox constructor
//
CBox::CBox(CDC *dc, CRect *rect, UINT nDepth) :
    CShape(dc, rect, nDepth)
{
}

//
// CBox Draw()--starts the drawing process
//
void CBox::Draw()
{
    if (m_pRect->Height() < 4 || m_pRect->Width() < 4) return;
    m_pRect->InflateRect(-2, -2);
    int min = m_pRect->Height();
    if (m_pRect->Width() < min)
        min = m_pRect->Width();
    int side = min/4;
    CPoint midPt(m_pRect->left + m_pRect->Width()/2,
        m_pRect->top + m_pRect->Height()/2);
    Draw(side, midPt, m_nDepth);
}

//
// CBox Draw()--recursively draws four smaller boxes at the midpoint of
//  each side and then draws the current box on top
//
void CBox::Draw(int nRadius, CPoint pt, UINT nDepth)
{
```

(continued)

Figure 15-3. *continued*

```
    if (!nDepth-- || nRadius < 1) return;
    int r = nRadius;
    Draw(r/2, CPoint(pt.x-r, pt.y-r), nDepth);
    Draw(r/2, CPoint(pt.x+r, pt.y-r), nDepth);
    Draw(r/2, CPoint(pt.x-r, pt.y+r), nDepth);
    Draw(r/2, CPoint(pt.x+r, pt.y+r), nDepth);
    m_pDC->Rectangle(pt.x-r, pt.y-r, pt.x+r, pt.y+r);
}

//
// CQBox constructor
//
CQBox::CQBox(CDC *dc, CRect *rect, UINT nDepth) :
    CBox(dc, rect, nDepth)
{
}

//
// CQBox Draw()--starts the drawing process
//
void CQBox::Draw()
{
    if (m_pRect->Height() < 4 || m_pRect->Width() < 4) return;
    m_pRect->InflateRect(-2, -2);
    int min = m_pRect->Height();
    if (m_pRect->Width() < min)
        min = m_pRect->Width();
    int side = min/4;
    int midX = m_pRect->left + m_pRect->Width()/2;
    int midY = m_pRect->top + m_pRect->Height()/2;
    CBox::Draw(side/2, CPoint(midX-side, midY-side), m_nDepth);
    CBox::Draw(side/2, CPoint(midX+side, midY-side), m_nDepth);
    CBox::Draw(side/2, CPoint(midX-side, midY+side), m_nDepth);
    CBox::Draw(side/2, CPoint(midX+side, midY+side), m_nDepth);
}

//
// CTriangle helpers
//
inline double Sin(double deg) { return sin(deg * 3.14159 / 180.0); }
inline double Cos(double deg) { return cos(deg * 3.14159 / 180.0); }

//
// CTriangle static members
//
const double CTriangle::dSin30 = Sin(30.0);
const double CTriangle::dCos30 = Cos(30.0);
const double CTriangle::dSin30Cos30 = Sin(30) * Cos(30.0);
const double CTriangle::dSin30Sin30 = Sin(30) * Sin(30.0);
```

(continued)

Figure 15-3. *continued*

```
//
// CTriangle constructor
//
CTriangle::CTriangle(CDC *dc, CRect *rect, int nDepth, BOOL front) :
    CShape(dc, rect, nDepth),
    m_bFront(front)
{
}

//
// CTriangle Draw()--starts the drawing process
//
void CTriangle::Draw()
{
    if (m_pRect->Height() < 4 || m_pRect->Width() < 4) return;
    m_pRect->InflateRect(-2, -2);
    int min = m_pRect->Height();
    if (m_pRect->Width() < min)
        min = m_pRect->Width();
    int radius = min/2;
    CPoint midPt(m_pRect->left + m_pRect->Width()/2,
        m_pRect->top + m_pRect->Height()/2);
    Draw(radius, midPt, m_nDepth);
}

//
// CTriangle Drawone()--draws a single triangle
//
void CTriangle::Drawone(CPoint pt, int nRadius)
{
    CPoint vertices[3];
    vertices[0].x = pt.x;
    vertices[0].y = pt.y - nRadius;
    vertices[1].x = pt.x + nRadius * dCos30;
    vertices[1].y = pt.y + nRadius * dSin30;
    vertices[2].x = pt.x - nRadius * dCos30;
    vertices[2].y = pt.y + nRadius * dSin30;
    m_pDC->Polygon(vertices, 3);
}

//
// CTriangle Draw()--does the real work; draws one triangle
//  and recursively calls Draw() to draw other triangles
//  at the middle of each side
//
void CTriangle::Draw(int nRadius, CPoint pt, UINT nDepth)
{
    if (!nDepth-- || nRadius < 5) return;
    int r = nRadius;
    nRadius /= 2;
```

(continued)

Figure 15-3. *continued*

```
    if (m_bFront)
        Drawone(pt, r);
    Draw(nRadius,
        CPoint(pt.x+r*dSin30Cos30, pt.y-r*dSin30Sin30), nDepth);
    Draw(nRadius,
        CPoint(pt.x-r*dSin30Cos30, pt.y-r*dSin30Sin30), nDepth);
    Draw(nRadius, CPoint(pt.x, pt.y+r*dSin30), nDepth);
    if (!m_bFront)
        Drawone(pt, r);
}

//
// CKochIsle constructor
//
CKochIsle::CKochIsle(CDC *dc, CRect *rect, UINT nDepth) :
    CShape(dc, rect, nDepth)
{
}

//
// CKochIsle Draw()--starts the drawing process
//
void CKochIsle::Draw()
{
    if (m_pRect->Height() < 4 || m_pRect->Width() < 4) return;
    m_pRect->InflateRect(-2, -2);
    int min = m_pRect->Height();
    if (m_pRect->Width() < min)
        min = m_pRect->Width();
    int side = min/4;
    int midX = m_pRect->left + m_pRect->Width()/2;
    int midY = m_pRect->top + m_pRect->Height()/2;
    // an initial square
    Line(CPoint(midX-side, midY-side),
        CPoint(midX+side, midY-side), m_nDepth);
    Line(CPoint(midX+side, midY-side),
        CPoint(midX+side, midY+side), m_nDepth);
    Line(CPoint(midX+side, midY+side),
        CPoint(midX-side, midY+side), m_nDepth);
    Line(CPoint(midX-side, midY+side),
        CPoint(midX-side, midY-side), m_nDepth);
}

//
// CKochIsle Line()--divides line into segments, up to limit of recursion
//
void CKochIsle::Line(CPoint from, CPoint to, UINT nDepth)
{
    if (!nDepth--) { // recursion depth reached; actually draws something
        m_pDC->MoveTo(from);
```

(continued)

Figure 15-3. *continued*

```
        m_pDC->LineTo(to);
        return;
    }

    if (from.x == to.x) {     // vertical
        int yTwo = (from.y + to.y) / 2;
        int yOne = (yTwo + from.y) / 2;
        int yThree = (to.y + yTwo) / 2;
        int dX = (to.y - from.y) / 4;
        Line(from, CPoint(from.x, yOne), nDepth);
        Line(CPoint(from.x, yOne), CPoint(from.x+dX, yOne), nDepth);
        Line(CPoint(from.x+dX, yOne), CPoint(from.x+dX, yTwo), nDepth);
        Line(CPoint(from.x+dX, yTwo), CPoint(from.x, yTwo), nDepth);
        Line(CPoint(from.x, yTwo), CPoint(from.x-dX, yTwo), nDepth);
        Line(CPoint(from.x-dX, yTwo), CPoint(from.x-dX, yThree), nDepth);
        Line(CPoint(from.x-dX, yThree), CPoint(from.x, yThree), nDepth);
        Line(CPoint(from.x, yThree), to, nDepth);
    } else {                  // horizontal
        int xTwo = (from.x + to.x) / 2;
        int xOne = (xTwo + from.x) / 2;
        int xThree = (to.x + xTwo) / 2;
        int dY = (to.x - from.x) / 4;
        Line(from, CPoint(xOne, from.y), nDepth);
        Line(CPoint(xOne, from.y), CPoint(xOne, from.y-dY), nDepth);
        Line(CPoint(xOne, from.y-dY), CPoint(xTwo, from.y-dY), nDepth);
        Line(CPoint(xTwo, from.y-dY), CPoint(xTwo, from.y), nDepth);
        Line(CPoint(xTwo, from.y), CPoint(xTwo, from.y+dY), nDepth);
        Line(CPoint(xTwo, from.y+dY), CPoint(xThree, from.y+dY), nDepth);
        Line(CPoint(xThree, from.y+dY), CPoint(xThree, from.y), nDepth);
        Line(CPoint(xThree, from.y), to, nDepth);
    }
}
```

resource.h

```
#define IDM_ABOUT   100
#define IDM_EXIT    101

#define IDM_BLACK   150
#define IDM_RED     151
#define IDM_GREEN   152
#define IDM_BLUE    153
#define IDM_WHITE   154

#define IDM_TRIA    200
#define IDM_TRIB    201
#define IDM_BOXESA  202
#define IDM_BOXESB  203
#define IDM_KOCH1   204
#define IDM_KOCH2   205
#define IDM_KOCH3   206
```

(continued)

Figure 15-3. *continued*

about.dlg

```
DLGINCLUDE RCDATA DISCARDABLE
BEGIN
    "RESOURCE.H\0"
END

ABOUTBOX DIALOG 71, 46, 144, 75
CAPTION "About Quilt"
STYLE DS_MODALFRAME | WS_CAPTION | WS_SYSMENU
BEGIN
    CTEXT "Quilt Application", -1, 49, 18, 68, 8
    CTEXT "Copyright (c) 1992 by Kaare Christian", -1, 9, 38, 126, 8
    CONTROL "OK", IDOK, "BUTTON", WS_GROUP, 56, 53, 32, 14
    ICON AFX_IDI_STD_FRAME, -1, 26, 14, 16, 16
END
```

quilt.rc

```
#include <windows.h>
#include <afxres.h>
#include "resource.h"

AFX_IDI_STD_FRAME ICON quilt.ico
rcinclude about.dlg

MainMenu MENU
BEGIN
    POPUP "&File"
    BEGIN
        MENUITEM "E&xit", IDM_EXIT
    END

    POPUP "&Shapes"
    BEGIN
        MENUITEM "&1. Triangles A", IDM_TRIA
        MENUITEM "&2. Triangles B", IDM_TRIB
        MENUITEM "&3. Boxes A", IDM_BOXESA
        MENUITEM "&4. Boxes B", IDM_BOXESB
        MENUITEM "&5. Koch Islands 1", IDM_KOCH1
        MENUITEM "&6. Koch Islands 2", IDM_KOCH2
        MENUITEM "&7. Koch Islands 3", IDM_KOCH3
    END

    POPUP "&Colors"
    BEGIN
        MENUITEM "&Red", IDM_RED
        MENUITEM "&Green", IDM_GREEN
        MENUITEM "&Blue", IDM_BLUE
        MENUITEM "&White", IDM_WHITE
    END
```

(continued)

Figure 15-3. *continued*

```
    POPUP "&Help"
    BEGIN
        MENUITEM "&About Quilt...\tF1", IDM_ABOUT
    END

END

MainAccelTable ACCELERATORS
{
    VK_F1, IDM_ABOUT, VIRTKEY
}
```

The Quilt Graphics Routines

Let's look first at the shapes.cpp file, which contains the actual graphics routines. Not surprisingly, there is little Windows user interface programming in shapes.cpp. Instead, shapes.cpp contains programming that tackles geometric and algebraic problems using GDI. The file contains a hierarchy of classes derived from a *CShape* base class. *CShape* houses a pointer to a device context object and stores a pointer to a *CRect* object that denotes the size of the device context. The *m_pDC* member is used to call the *CDC* class's drawing member functions, such as *LineTo()*, and the *m_pRect* member is used to scale the graphic to the size of the window.

The *CShape* class contains a virtual *Draw()* function that is used in derived classes to start the drawing process. Note that *Draw()* is a pure virtual function, which implies that *CShape* is an abstract class. *CShape* contains a public, virtual destructor, and it contains a protected constructor that guarantees that the data members are initialized.

The classes derived from *CShape* are *CBox*, *CTriangle*, *CKochIsle*, and *CQBox*. You've seen their corresponding four shapes starting clockwise from the upper left corner of Figure 15-2 on page 332. *CBox* is the simplest offspring of *CShape*. The basic idea of the pattern is to draw four half-size boxes in the middle of each quadrant and then to draw the current box on top of them. Repeated recursively to a depth of four or five, this produces interesting patterns. *CBox* has two *Draw()* member functions: *Draw()* without parameters starts the drawing, using information stored in the object by the constructor to find the size and center of the drawing area and then invoking the workaholic *Draw()* with parameters; *Draw()*'s three parameters do the real work. The actual "drawing" is performed by *CDC*'s *Rectangle()* member function.

The idea of the *CTriangle* class is the same as the idea for *CBox* except that the geometry is more difficult. The *Drawone()* member of *CTriangle* is responsible for drawing a single triangle, and *Draw()* is the recursive function that invokes *Drawone()* for the current triangle and calls itself to draw smaller triangles at the midpoint of each side of the current triangle. The geometrical explanation for the formulas used in *Drawone()* and *Draw()* appears in Figure 15-4 on the next page.

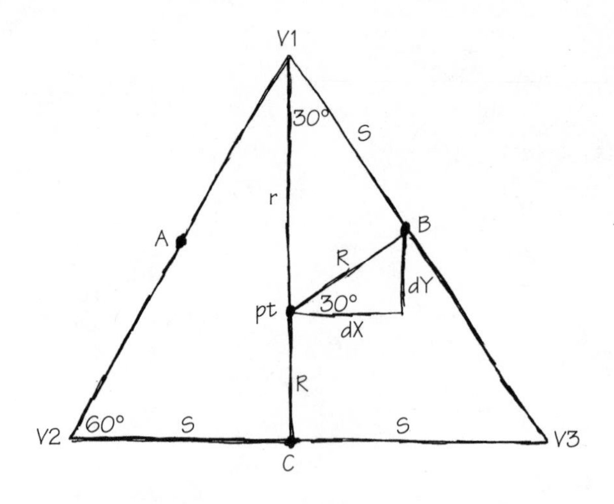

Distances
$$R = r * \sin 30$$
$$S = r * \cos 30$$
$$dX = R * \cos 30 = r * \sin 30 * \cos 30$$
$$dY = R * \sin 30 = r * \sin 30 * \sin 30$$

Midpoint positions
A = CPoint (pt.x − dX, pt.y − dY)
B = CPoint (pt.x + dX, pt.y − dY)
C = CPoint (pt.x , pt.y + R)

Vertex positions
V1 = CPoint (pt.x, pt.y − r)
V2 = CPoint (pt.x − S, pt.y + R)
V3 = CPoint (pt.x + S, pt.y + R)

Figure 15-4.
The geometric basis for the operations of CTriangle's Drawone() *and* Draw() *member functions.*

One other interesting aspect of the *Draw()* function is that the current triangle can be drawn either before or after the trio of smaller triangles, as dictated by the *m_bFront* boolean value.

A quadratic Koch Islands shape is based on a square. Each line segment is repeatedly replaced with a series of shorter wiggly line segments that span the same distance. If the process were repeated forever, the result would be a shape with a fractal dimension. But the *CKochIsle* class is careful not to draw forever; that would be impolite. A recursion depth of one clearly shows the replacement operation, but depths of two and three produce more interesting patterns.[1] Figure 15-5 shows three recursion depths, starting at the upper left.

1. The approach I've used here for drawing a quadratic Koch Islands shape is not my favorite because it is too bulky and lacks generality. A more elegant solution, based on L-systems, is presented in the first chapter of *The Algorithmic Beauty of Plants,* by Prusinkiewicz and Lindenmayer (Springer-Verlag, 1990).

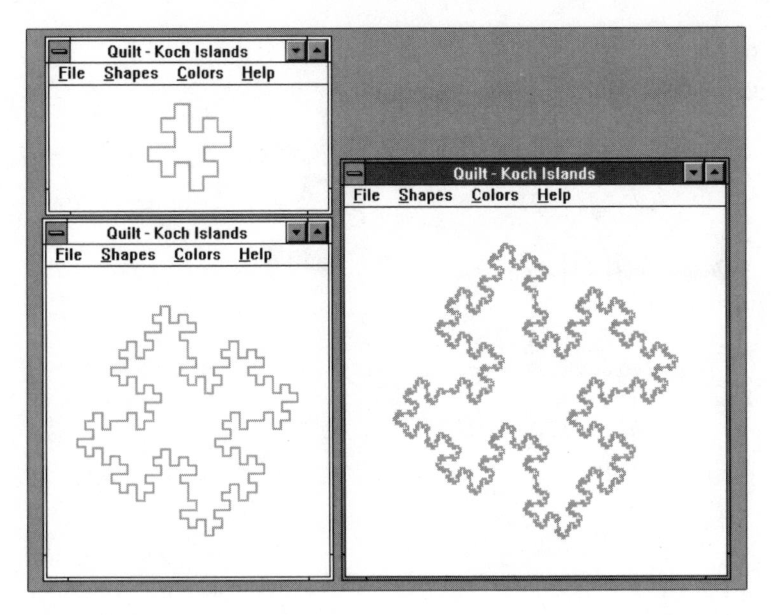

Figure 15-5.
The Koch Islands shape moving through three recursion depths.

Recursion past a fourth depth wouldn't add detail to the screen display because of the screen's resolution limits. Fourth and fifth recursion depths might be interesting on a high-resolution printer.

Each recursion replaces all the original line segments in the drawing with eight new line segments. The replacement logic appears in the *CKochIsle* class's *Line()* member function, which also does the actual drawing once the specified recursion depth is reached. Figure 15-6 on the next page shows the geometry programmed in the *CKochIsle* class's *Line()* function.

Each point in the replacement line segment can be determined from *dX*, *yOne*, *yTwo*, and *yThree*, plus the original endpoints. For example, point *E* is at *X* position *from.x–dX*, and at *Y* position *yTwo*. One slight complication, which is evident in the *Line()* member function, is that horizontal and vertical lines need slightly different treatment. Figure 15-6 shows a vertical example; the horizontal version is analogous. The actual drawing is done by *CDC*'s *MoveTo()* and *LineTo()* member functions.

The *CQBox* class draws four *CBox* patterns, which explains why it is derived from *CBox*. The motivation for *CQBox* came from one of my children, who didn't like the *CBox* pattern because the large central box obscured too much of the pattern. *CQBox* has its own virtual *Draw()* (no parameters) member function to initiate the drawing process, but it uses the *CBox* class's *Draw()* (with parameters) to do the actual drawing.

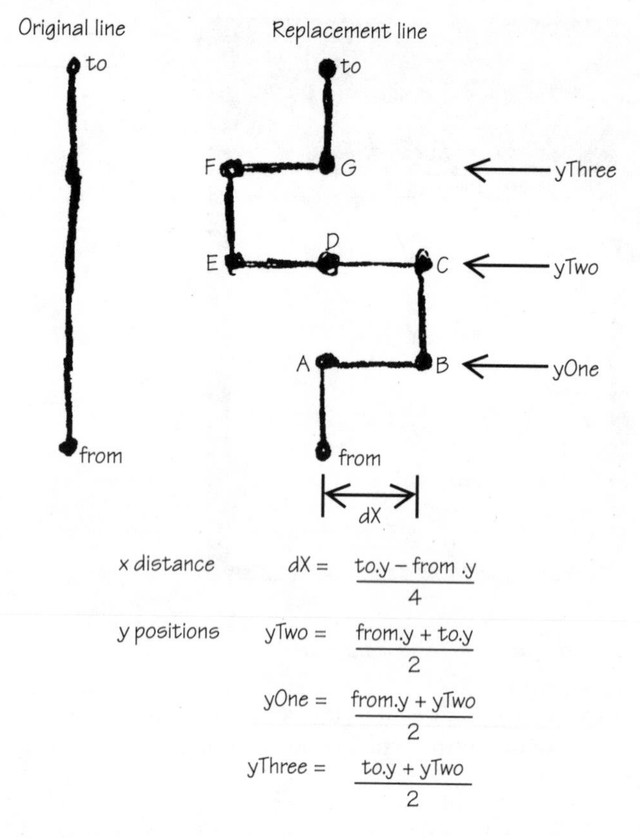

Figure 15-6.
The geometric basis for the operation of CKochIsle's Line() *member function.*

The GDI Object Classes

Each device context object maintains status information about how things should be drawn. For example, each device context has a current pen that is used to draw lines. The pen has a size, a color, and a drawing pattern such as solid, dotted, or dashed. The connection between a specific pen and a device context object is made by the *CDC* class's *SelectObject()* function. The native Windows *::SelectObject()* function, which is invoked by *CDC*'s *SelectObject()*, is just one indication of the object-based thinking that went into Windows even before object-oriented languages were available for programming for Windows.

The *OnPaint()* member function of the *CMainWindow* class contains this code, which creates a *CPen* object and selects it into the current *paintDC* object:

```
CPen Pen(PS_SOLID, 2, rgbPen);
CPen *oldPen = paintDC.SelectObject(&Pen);
```

The *CPen* object, named *Pen*, is constructed in the first statement. It has the *PS_SOLID* style, is 2 pixels in size, and is the color specified by the *r*, *g*, and *b* variables. (*RGB* is a macro defined in windows.h that builds a color from individual red, green, and blue components.) When an object is selected by means of *SelectObject()*, a pointer to the previous object (of the same type) is returned. In the code we've just looked at, this pointer is stored in the *oldPen* pointer.

Readers of Charles Petzold's *Programming Windows* might recall his rules governing the use of GDI objects:

- Delete all GDI objects that you create.
- Don't delete GDI objects while they are selected into a valid device context.

At the end of *OnPaint()*, the *Pen* object's destructor[2] will be invoked automatically. This takes care of the first rule, because the destructor will free the *Pen* GDI object. The second rule is a bit harder to observe because the *Pen* object has been selected into the *paintDC* device context. We could argue and speculate about what gets destroyed first and what order of declarations won't lead to a problem, but the far simpler and more reliable technique is to deselect the pen before leaving *OnPaint()*. That's why the *oldPen* pointer was saved at the beginning of *OnPaint()*, and here is how it is used at the end of *OnPaint()*:

```
paintDC.SelectObject(oldPen);
```

Note that in *OnPaint()*, the *CBrush* object is treated similarly; it is created and selected into the *paintDC* device context at the beginning of *OnPaint()* and then deselected before *OnPaint()* completes execution.

The Zette Example

A "zette" is a legendary creature known for darting rapidly from one place to another. Various sizes, shapes, and colors have been reported, but nothing is reliably known about zettes. The zettes in this example are small shapes that wander across a window. They are careful not to wander off the edge, but otherwise they move randomly.

The Zette application creates a tribe of moving zettes. The Zette application window is shown in Figure 15-7 on the next page, although this frozen screen shot doesn't convey the slow, wandering motion of the zettes.

---

2. From looking at the *CPen* class definition, you might think that the *CPen* class doesn't have a destructor. But remember that *CPen* is derived from *CGdiObject*. It is the *CGdiObject* destructor that actually frees the GDI resources.

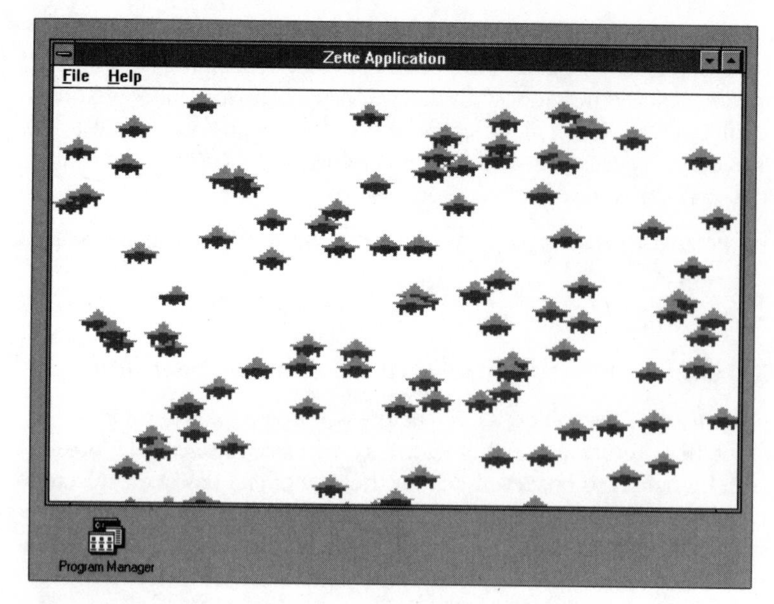

Figure 15-7.
The zette tribe on the move across a window.

The Zette application source code appears in Figure 15-8.

zette.h

```
//
// CTheApp
//
class CTheApp : public CWinApp
{
public:
    BOOL InitInstance();
    BOOL OnIdle(long cnt);
};

//
// zette modeless dialog box--allows zettes to continue to wander
//  while dialog is displayed
//
class CZetteDialog : public CDialog
{
```

Figure 15-8. *(continued)*
The Zette program source files: zette.h, zette.cpp, resource.h, about.dlg, and zette.rc.

Figure 15-8. *continued*

```
public:
    // constructor
    CZetteDialog(CWnd* pWndParent)
    {
        Create("AboutBox", pWndParent);
    }

    afx_msg void OnDone();
    afx_msg void OnClose();

    DECLARE_MESSAGE_MAP()
};

//
// CMainWindow
//
class CMainWindow : public CFrameWnd
{
public:
    CMainWindow();
    ~CMainWindow();

    afx_msg void OnPaint();
    afx_msg void OnAbout();
    afx_msg void OnExit();
    afx_msg int  OnCreate(LPCREATESTRUCT lpCreateStruct);
    afx_msg void OnTimer(UINT nIDEvent);

    void Draw(CDC *dc, CRect *rect);

    BOOL m_bNeedRedraw;

    enum {
        nZettes = 100,      // number of moving zettes
        drawXsize = 200,    // size of the drawing bitmap
        drawYsize = 200,
        wanderX   = 5,      // distance traveled each time
        wanderY   = 5       //  (should be odd)
    };

protected:

    CBitmap *m_pBitmap;
    CBitmap *m_pBitmask;
    CPoint *m_pLocations;

    DECLARE_MESSAGE_MAP()
};
```

(continued)

Figure 15-8. *continued*

zette.cpp

```
#include <afxwin.h>
#include "resource.h"
#include "zette.h"

//
// Zette application--draw patterns
// Copyright (c) 1992 by Kaare Christian
//

const TimerID = 1;

// theApp application object
CTheApp theApp;

// CTheApp
// InitInstance
BOOL CTheApp::InitInstance()
{
    m_pMainWnd = new CMainWindow();
    m_pMainWnd->ShowWindow(m_nCmdShow);
    m_pMainWnd->UpdateWindow();

    return TRUE;
}

//
// force screen redraw when needed and there is nothing else to do
//
BOOL CTheApp::OnIdle(LONG)
{
    if (((CMainWindow *)m_pMainWnd)->m_bNeedRedraw) {
        m_pMainWnd->Invalidate(FALSE);
        ((CMainWindow*)m_pMainWnd)->m_bNeedRedraw = FALSE;
    }

    return TRUE;
}

//
// CMainWindow message map
//
BEGIN_MESSAGE_MAP(CMainWindow, CFrameWnd)
    ON_WM_PAINT()
    ON_WM_CREATE()
    ON_WM_TIMER()
    ON_COMMAND(IDM_ABOUT, OnAbout)
    ON_COMMAND(IDM_EXIT, OnExit)
END_MESSAGE_MAP()
```

(continued)

Figure 15-8. *continued*

```
//
// CMainWindow constructor
//
CMainWindow::CMainWindow()
{
    m_pBitmap = NULL;
    m_pBitmask = NULL;
    m_pLocations = new CPoint[100];    // list of zette locations
    m_bNeedRedraw = FALSE;
    for(int i = 0; i < nZettes; i++)
        m_pLocations[i] = CPoint(rand() % drawXsize,
            rand() % drawYsize);

    LoadAccelTable("MainAccelTable");
    Create(NULL, "Zette Application",
        WS_OVERLAPPEDWINDOW, rectDefault, NULL, "MainMenu");
}

CMainWindow::~CMainWindow()
{
    delete m_pBitmap;
    delete m_pBitmask;
    delete m_pLocations;
    KillTimer(TimerID);
}

//
// OnCreate
//
int CMainWindow::OnCreate(LPCREATESTRUCT /* p */)
{
    if (!SetTimer(TimerID, 200, NULL))
        MessageBox("Not enough timers available.",
                  "Zette", MB_ICONEXCLAMATION | MB_OK);

    if (!m_pBitmap)
        m_pBitmap = new CBitmap;
    m_pBitmap->LoadBitmap("zette");

    if (!m_pBitmask)
        m_pBitmask = new CBitmap;
    m_pBitmask->LoadBitmap("zettem");
    return 0;
}

//
// OnTimer--ask OnIdle to invalidate rectangle to force a redraw
//
afx_msg void CMainWindow::OnTimer(UINT nIDEvent)
{
```

(continued)

Figure 15-8. *continued*

```
    if (!IsIconic())
        m_bNeedRedraw = TRUE;
}

//
// OnPaint
//
void CMainWindow::OnPaint()
{
    CPaintDC paintDC(this);
    CRect rect;

    GetClientRect(&rect);
    Draw(&paintDC, &rect);
}

//
// draw the zettes into a memory DC; then stretchblt to the screen
//
void CMainWindow::Draw(CDC *clientDC, CRect *rect)
{
    CDC dcZette;              // the zette image (colored)
    CDC dcMask;               // the zette image outline (monochrome)
    CDC memDC;                // a memory device context
    CBitmap Bitmap;           // a memory bitmap
    CBitmap* pOldMapZ = NULL;
    CBitmap* pOldMapM = NULL;
    CBitmap* pOldBitmap = NULL;

    dcZette.CreateCompatibleDC(clientDC);
    dcMask.CreateCompatibleDC(clientDC);
    memDC.CreateCompatibleDC(clientDC);

    Bitmap.CreateCompatibleBitmap(clientDC, drawXsize, drawYsize);

    pOldMapZ = dcZette.SelectObject(m_pBitmap);
    pOldMapM = dcMask.SelectObject(m_pBitmask);
    pOldBitmap = memDC.SelectObject(&Bitmap);

    memDC.Rectangle(-1, -1, drawXsize+2, drawYsize+2);     // clear memDC

    for(int i = 0; i < nZettes; i++) {
        int x = m_pLocations[i].x + (rand() % wanderX - wanderX/2);
        int y = m_pLocations[i].y + (rand() % wanderY - wanderY/2);
        if (x < 0) x = -x;
        if (x > drawXsize) x -= wanderX;
        if (y < 0) m_pLocations[i].y = -y;
        if (y > drawYsize) y -= wanderY;
```

(continued)

Figure 15-8. *continued*

```
        memDC.BitBlt(x, y, 12, 12, &dcMask, 0, 0, SRCAND);
        memDC.BitBlt(x, y, 12, 12, &dcZette, 0, 0, SRCPAINT);

        m_pLocations[i].x = x;
        m_pLocations[i].y = y;
    }

    // copy to screen
    clientDC->StretchBlt(rect->left, rect->top,
        rect->right, rect->bottom,
        &memDC, 0, 0, drawXsize, drawYsize, SRCCOPY);

    dcZette.SelectObject(pOldMapZ);
    dcMask.SelectObject(pOldMapM);
    memDC.SelectObject(pOldBitmap);
}

//
// OnAbout
//
void CMainWindow::OnAbout()
{
    CMenu *menu = GetMenu();
    menu->EnableMenuItem(IDM_ABOUT, MF_BYCOMMAND | MF_GRAYED);
    CZetteDialog *about = new CZetteDialog(this);
}

//
// OnExit
//
void CMainWindow::OnExit()
{
    SendMessage(WM_CLOSE, 0, 0L);
}

//
// zette modeless dialog box
//

BEGIN_MESSAGE_MAP(CZetteDialog, CDialog)
    ON_WM_CLOSE()
    ON_COMMAND(IDOK, OnDone)
END_MESSAGE_MAP()

void CZetteDialog::OnDone()
{
    CMenu *menu = GetParent()->GetMenu();
    menu->EnableMenuItem(IDM_ABOUT, MF_BYCOMMAND | MF_ENABLED);
    delete this;
}
```

(continued)

Figure 15-8. *continued*

```
void CZetteDialog::OnClose()
{
    OnDone();
}
```

resource.h

```
#define IDM_ABOUT   100
#define IDM_EXIT    110
```

about.dlg

```
DLGINCLUDE RCDATA DISCARDABLE
BEGIN
    "RESOURCE.H\0"
END

ABOUTBOX DIALOG 34, 22, 144, 75
CAPTION "About Zette"
STYLE DS_MODALFRAME | WS_CAPTION | WS_SYSMENU | WS_VISIBLE
BEGIN
    CTEXT "Zette Wandering Shapes", -1, 0, 14, 144, 8
    CTEXT "Copyright (c) 1992 by Kaare Christian", -1, 0, 36, 144, 8
    CONTROL "OK", IDOK, "BUTTON", WS_GROUP, 56, 53, 32, 14
END
```

zette.rc

```
#include <windows.h>
#include <afxres.h>
#include "resource.h"

MainMenu MENU
{
    POPUP "&File"
    {
        MENUITEM "E&xit", IDM_EXIT
    }
    POPUP "&Help"
    {
        MENUITEM "&About Zette...\tF1", IDM_ABOUT
    }
}

MainAccelTable ACCELERATORS
{
    VK_F1, IDM_ABOUT, VIRTKEY
}

rcinclude about.dlg

zette BITMAP zette.bmp
zettem BITMAP zettem.bmp
AFX_IDI_STD_FRAME ICON zette.ico
```

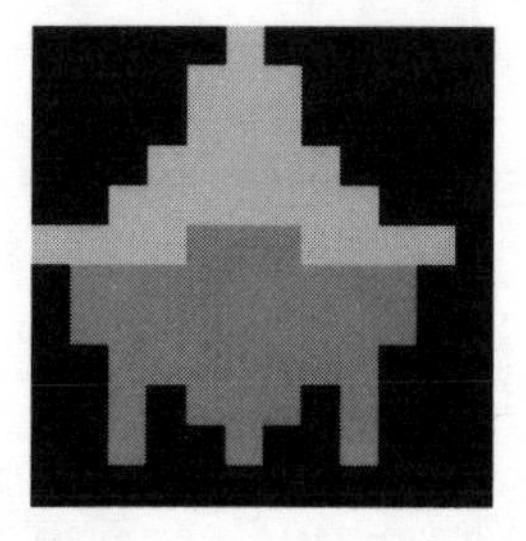

Zette is like many animated Windows programs in that it runs continuously. As most programmers of applications for Windows know, it's just not acceptable to write an infinite-loop Windows-based application. Being a good citizen in Windows means letting other applications have a chance. In traditional Windows programs you can use *::PeekMessage()* to discover idle time. When *::PeekMessage()* indicates that no messages are pending, you can safely do other chores for a short time.

In MFC library programming, you shouldn't use the native Windows *::PeekMessage()* because there is a better way. In the *CWinApp* class is a virtual member function called *OnIdle()* that is invoked continually when idle time is available. The Zette application defines a *CTheApp OnIdle()* member function in conjunction with a timer so that refreshing the Zette window doesn't shut out other activities. The first half of the solution is to use a *CMainWindow OnTimer()* message handler to respond to timer events specified to occur every 200 milliseconds. Here is the *OnTimer()* member function of the Zette application:

```
afx_msg void CMainWindow::OnTimer(UINT nIDEvent)
{
    if (!IsIconic())
        m_bNeedRedraw = TRUE;
}
```

The Windows timer is started in the *OnCreate()* member function and killed in the *CMainWindow* destructor. The *m_bNeedRedraw* member variable is a BOOL flag that is sensed by the *OnIdle()* function of the *CTheApp* application class. When it is set, the *OnIdle()* routine invalidates the main window's client area, which leads to a window redrawing. Here is the *OnIdle()* member function of the *CTheApp* class:

```
BOOL CTheApp::OnIdle(LONG)
{
    if (((CMainWindow *)m_pMainWnd)->m_bNeedRedraw) {
        m_pMainWnd->Invalidate(FALSE);
        ((CMainWindow *)m_pMainWnd)->m_bNeedRedraw = FALSE;
    }

    return TRUE;
}
```

Remember that *OnIdle()* belongs to the *CTheApp* class, not to the *CMainWindow* class. It thus has to work hard, using its *m_pMainWnd* pointer, to access the main window object. Each time the *m_bNeedRedraw* flag is *TRUE*, the *OnIdle()* routine invalidates the main window and resets the flag.

The *CBitmap* Class

Bitmaps are central to the Windows graphical environment because Windows is essentially a raster graphics system. In one narrow sense, a bitmap can be said to behave just as a pen or a brush does: A bitmap is a GDI object that must be selected into a device context. But a bitmap is also much more complex than other kinds of GDI objects, and that's why we'll look at bitmaps separately.

When you get a device context for something that already exists, such as the screen or the client area of a window, it comes complete with a bitmap and can be used for drawing immediately. But often you want to do graphical operations in memory, so that the resultant image can be pumped out to the screen or a printer in a single operation. The basic technique is to create a memory DC that is compatible with the physical device, create a memory bitmap that is compatible with the DC, and then associate the two using *SelectObject()*. Once a memory DC and a compatible memory bitmap have been combined, you can use the device context for graphical operations, just as if it were associated with a physical display.

The Zette application demonstrates using a memory device context and hand-built bitmaps. The Zette application actually has three bitmaps: one bitmap that contains the painted image (picture) of a zette, one bitmap that contains a monochrome silhouette of the zette, and a third, destination, bitmap in which each frame of the zette animation is produced. The zette picture and zette silhouette bitmaps are created and loaded from resources when the *OnCreate()* member function is invoked. Here is the *CMainWindow* class's *OnCreate()* member function:

```
int CMainWindow::OnCreate(LPCREATESTRUCT /* p */)
{
    if (!SetTimer(TimerID, 200, NULL))
        MessageBox("Not enough timers available.",
            "Zette", MB_ICONEXCLAMATION | MB_OK);

    if (!m_pBitmap)
        m_pBitmap = new CBitmap;
    m_pBitmap->LoadBitmap("zette");

    if (!m_pBitmask)
        m_pBitmask = new CBitmap;
    m_pBitmask->LoadBitmap("zettem");

    return 0;
}
```

The *zette* and *zettem* names used in the *LoadBitmap()* function calls are the bitmap resource names from zette.rc.

The Zette application's purpose is to create the illusion that a group of small graphical objects move about on the screen. Our first inclination might be to paint the objects directly on the screen, but this will result in our sometimes seeing half-drawn figures, and it can also cause performance problems because most display adapters are accessed much more slowly than main memory is. Most Windows animation programs resort to building bitmap images in memory and then sending them to the screen by means of *CDC*'s *BitBlt()* function. Thus, the *Draw()* function, which does most of the work in the Zette application, produces each frame of the animation by allocating a 200-by-200 bitmap in memory, writing the zette images into that bitmap, and then copying that bitmap to the screen.

The Zette application addresses another problem common in graphics programs, background transparency. Bitmaps are rectangular, but images are usually irregularly shaped. When I mentioned "writing the zette images into that bitmap" in the previous paragraph, you probably visualized copying an irregularly shaped zette image, not a rectangular bitmap. Yes, it's possible to copy an irregularly shaped image, but it takes a little work. The basic idea is to use two bitmaps, not one. That's why the Zette application has both a colored zette bitmap and a silhouette zette bitmap. First the silhouette bitmap is *AND*ed into the destination bitmap, which clears the destination underneath the silhouette of the image. Then the colored image is *OR*'d into the destination. This is a lot of work, but it is the only way to copy an irregularly shaped image.

Now that we've looked at the general approach, let's take a look at some code from the *Draw()* member function body. For the complete function definition, see zette.cpp in Figure 15-8. *Draw()* is passed two parameters: a pointer to the window's device context and a pointer to a *CRect*. The *Draw()* function declares three *CDC* objects and then initializes them:

```
dcZette.CreateCompatibleDC(clientDC);
dcMask.CreateCompatibleDC(clientDC);
memDC.CreateCompatibleDC(clientDC);
```

A "compatible" DC is simply a device context that is not already associated with a physical device but that is intended to be used with the specified device. In this case, the three new device contexts will be used with the application's window because *clientDC*, a pointer to the window's device context, is passed to the *CreateCompatibleDC()* function. The Zette application already has the bitmaps that will be selected into the *dcZette* and *dcMask* device contexts, but the large drawing surface must be created:

```
Bitmap.CreateCompatibleBitmap(clientDC, drawXsize, drawYsize);
```

The *drawXsize* and *drawYsize* identifiers are enumeration constants defined in the *CMainWindow* class. They each have the value *200*, so the newly minted bitmap will measure 200 by 200 and will have the pixel resolution of the screen.

Each of the three newly built memory device contexts we've just initialized has a one-pixel monochrome bitmap. Clearly, the next step is to use *SelectObject()* to associate our trio of bitmaps with the trio of waiting device contexts:

```
pOldMapZ = dcZette.SelectObject(m_pBitmap);
pOldMapM = dcMask.SelectObject(m_pBitmask);
pOldBitmap = memDC.SelectObject(&Bitmap);
```

As we've already noted, pointers to the current objects are saved so that the device contexts can be restored to their initial states before they are deleted. The next step is to clear the memory bitmap by drawing a rectangle:

```
memDC.Rectangle(-1, -1, drawXsize+2, drawYsize+2);      // clear memDC
```

The next part of the *Draw()* function is a loop that repeatedly updates the position of each zette and then draws each zette image into the *memDC* device context. Let's skip the code that updates the positions and move right to the drawing:

```
memDC.BitBlt(x, y, 12, 12, &dcMask, 0, 0, SRCAND);
memDC.BitBlt(x, y, 12, 12, &dcZette, 0, 0, SRCPAINT);
```

First the silhouette zette bitmap is *AND*ed into the destination bitmap. This creates a hole into which the color image zette is *OR*'d. (The *BitBlt() OR* operation is called *SRCPAINT*.)

Once all the zette images have been written to the *memDC*, the *CDC* class's *StretchBlt()* member function can copy them to the screen:

```
clientDC->StretchBlt(rect->left, rect->top, rect->right, rect->bottom,
    &memDC, 0, 0, drawXsize, drawYsize, SRCCOPY);
```

The final chore in *Draw()* is cleanup. The three memory device context objects and the bitmap object all have destructors that will be called as *Draw()* terminates execution. But before the destructors clean up, it is crucial to return the device contexts to their initial states:

```
dcZette.SelectObject(pOldMapZ);
dcMask.SelectObject(pOldMapM);
memDC.SelectObject(pOldBitmap);
```

The GDI object classes are very thin wrappers of the native Windows operations. Unlike the classes in the *CWnd* family, which seem to markedly increase my productivity by catching many of my mistakes during compilation, the *CDC* and *CGdiObject* classes are like Windows itself in that they are unforgiving. You must bear in mind that destructors are automatically cleaning things up, because cleanup operations have consequences. Often you need to pave the way for the destructors; other times, you need to clean up manually.

The TestBed Example

When you're writing a true Windows-based application, the muss and fuss of the Windows interface is acceptable. But when all you want to do is display a few lines of text, the bulky Windows interface, even enabled by MFC, is an unpalatable undertaking. Several programmers have implemented solutions to this problem, but none of those solutions have taken advantage of the MFC library, and none have tried to provide a type-safe output solution similar to iostream library output.

The TestBed application we'll look at next is a truly simple program. It uses a *CStringArray* collection to store the output text and borrows the scroll bar and paint logic from Microsoft C7's FileList example program. The basic idea of TestBed is to call a user-supplied subroutine, named *tbMain()*, to fill up the *CStringArray* collection. This strategy doesn't make any provisions for user input, and it requires that all the text be input at the outset instead of allowing text to accumulate. We could address these shortcomings, but they don't impede the simple display of text, which is the simple purpose of the TestBed application. The source code for TestBed appears in Figure 15-9.

testbed.h

```
//
// TestBed application
//

// the user-supplied routine that should fill CStringArray
extern void tbMain(CStringArray& a, CString& title);

class CTestDialog;

//
// CTheApp--the application object
//
class CTheApp : public CWinApp
{
public:
    BOOL InitInstance();
};

//
// CMainWindow
//
class CMainWindow : public CFrameWnd
{
    friend class CTheApp;
    friend class CTestDialog;
```

Figure 15-9. *(continued)*
The TestBed source files: testbed.h, testbed.cpp, testbed.dlg, and testbed.rc.

Figure 15-9. *continued*

```
public:
    CMainWindow();
    ~CMainWindow();

    afx_msg int  OnCreate(LPCREATESTRUCT lpcs);
    afx_msg void OnPaint();
    afx_msg void OnAbout();
    afx_msg void OnExit();
    afx_msg void OnVScroll(UINT nSBCode, UINT nPos, CScrollBar* pScrollBar);
    afx_msg void OnHScroll(UINT nSBCode, UINT nPos, CScrollBar* pScrollBar);
    afx_msg void OnKeyDown(UINT nChar, UINT nRepCnt, UINT nFlags);

    DECLARE_MESSAGE_MAP()

protected:
    short m_nVScrollPos;
    short m_nHScrollPos;

    short m_nTopLine;

    CStringArray m_StringArray;
    CString m_csTitle;

    UINT m_nCxChar;
    UINT m_nCyChar;
    UINT m_nLinesPainted;
};

class CTestDialog : public CModalDialog {
public:
    CTestDialog(CWnd* pWndParent, CString& title) :
        CModalDialog("AboutBox", pWndParent),
        m_csTitle(title)
    { }
    BOOL OnInitDialog();
protected:
    CString m_csTitle;
};
```

testbed.cpp

```
#include <afxwin.h>
#include <afxcoll.h>
#include "resource.h"
#include "testbed.h"

//
// Testbed application--displays a CStringArray
// Link these routines to a tbMain(CStringArray&, CString&) that fills
```

(continued)

Figure 15-9. *continued*

```
//  the array
// Also see the CIOString class for an iostreamlike interface
//
// Copyright (c) 1992 by Kaare Christian
//

#define MAXSTRING  256        // maximum number of characters in string

//
// The application object
//
CTheApp theApp;

//
// InitInstance
//
BOOL CTheApp::InitInstance()
{
    m_pMainWnd = new CMainWindow;
    m_pMainWnd->ShowWindow(m_nCmdShow);
    m_pMainWnd->UpdateWindow();

    return TRUE;
}

//
// CMainWindow message map
//
BEGIN_MESSAGE_MAP(CMainWindow, CFrameWnd)
    ON_WM_CREATE()
    ON_WM_PAINT()
    ON_WM_HSCROLL()
    ON_WM_VSCROLL()
    ON_WM_KEYDOWN()
    ON_COMMAND(IDM_ABOUT, OnAbout)
    ON_COMMAND(IDM_EXIT, OnExit)
END_MESSAGE_MAP()

//
// CMainWindow constructor
//
CMainWindow::CMainWindow()
{
    m_csTitle = "TestBed";
    LoadAccelTable("MainAccel");
    Create(NULL, m_csTitle,
        WS_OVERLAPPEDWINDOW | WS_VSCROLL | WS_HSCROLL,
        rectDefault, NULL, "MainMenu");
}
```

(continued)

Figure 15-9. *continued*

```
CMainWindow::~CMainWindow()
{
}

//
// OnCreate
//
int CMainWindow::OnCreate(LPCREATESTRUCT /* lpcs */)
{
    // call tbMain() to fill the m_StringArray object
    tbMain(m_StringArray, m_csTitle);

    SetWindowText(m_csTitle);      // retitle main window

    CMenu *menu = GetMenu();       // rebuild About menu

CString about = "About ";
    about += m_csTitle;
    about += " ...\tF1";
    menu->ModifyMenu(IDM_ABOUT, MF_BYCOMMAND | MF_ENABLED,
        IDM_ABOUT, about);

    // attend to scroll bar settings
    TEXTMETRIC tm;
    CWindowDC dc(this);

    dc.SelectStockObject(SYSTEM_FIXED_FONT);
    dc.GetTextMetrics(&tm);

    m_nCxChar = tm.tmAveCharWidth;
    m_nCyChar = tm.tmHeight + tm.tmExternalLeading;

    m_nHScrollPos = 0;
    m_nTopLine = 0;

    SetScrollRange(SB_VERT, 0, m_StringArray.GetUpperBound(), FALSE);
    SetScrollRange(SB_HORZ, 0, MAXSTRING, FALSE);

    return 0;
}

//
// OnAbout
//
void CMainWindow::OnAbout()
{
    CTestDialog about(this, m_csTitle);
    about.DoModal();
}
```

(continued)

Figure 15-9. *continued*

```
//
// OnInitDialog
//
BOOL CTestDialog::OnInitDialog()
{
    if (!CModalDialog::OnInitDialog())
        return FALSE;

    SetCtlBkColor(::GetSysColor(COLOR_WINDOW));

    CString title;
    title += m_csTitle;
    title += " Application";
    SetDlgItemText(IDD_APPNAME, title);

    return TRUE;
}

//
// OnExit
//
void CMainWindow::OnExit()
{
    DestroyWindow();
}

//
// OnPaint
//
void CMainWindow::OnPaint()
{
    char szNullLine[] = "";
    const char* pszCurLine;
    CPaintDC paintDC(this);
    CRect rectClient, rectLine;
    int y;

    GetClientRect(&rectClient);
    rectLine.left = rectClient.left;
    rectLine.right = rectClient.right;

    paintDC.SetTextAlign(TA_LEFT);
    paintDC.SelectStockObject(SYSTEM_FIXED_FONT);

    m_nLinesPainted = 0;
    for (y = m_nCxChar/2; y < rectClient.bottom; y += m_nCyChar)
    {
```

(continued)

Figure 15-9. *continued*

```
        int line = m_nTopLine + m_nLinesPainted;
        if (line > m_StringArray.GetUpperBound())
            pszCurLine = szNullLine;
        else
            pszCurLine = m_StringArray[line];

        if ((int)strlen(pszCurLine) < m_nHScrollPos)
            pszCurLine = szNullLine;
        else
            pszCurLine += m_nHScrollPos;

        rectLine.top = y;
        rectLine.bottom = y + m_nCyChar;
        paintDC.ExtTextOut(m_nCyChar/2, y, ETO_OPAQUE, &rectLine,
            pszCurLine, strlen(pszCurLine), NULL);
        m_nLinesPainted++;
    }
}

//
// OnVScroll
//
void CMainWindow::OnVScroll(UINT nSBCode, UINT nPos,
    CScrollBar* /*pScrollBar*/)
{
    short oldLine = m_nTopLine;

    switch (nSBCode) {
        case SB_LINEUP:
            m_nTopLine--;
            break;

        case SB_LINEDOWN:
            m_nTopLine++;
            break;

        case SB_PAGEUP:
            m_nTopLine -= m_nLinesPainted;
            break;

        case SB_PAGEDOWN:
            m_nTopLine += m_nLinesPainted;
            break;

        case SB_BOTTOM:
        case SB_TOP:
            nPos = (nSBCode == SB_TOP) ?
                0 : m_StringArray.GetUpperBound();
            // fall through
        case SB_THUMBPOSITION:
```

(continued)

Figure 15-9. *continued*

```
            m_nTopLine = nPos;
            break;

        default:
            return;
        }

    // range checking
    if (m_nTopLine < 0)
        m_nTopLine = 0;
    if (m_nTopLine > m_StringArray.GetUpperBound())
        m_nTopLine = m_StringArray.GetUpperBound();

    SetScrollPos(SB_VERT, m_nTopLine, TRUE);

    if (m_nTopLine != oldLine)
        Invalidate(FALSE);
}

//
// OnHScroll
//
void CMainWindow::OnHScroll(UINT nSBCode, UINT nPos,
    CScrollBar* /*pScrollBar*/)
{
    switch (nSBCode) {
        case SB_LINEUP:
            m_nHScrollPos -= 1;
            break;

        case SB_LINEDOWN:
            m_nHScrollPos += 1;
            break;

        case SB_PAGEUP:
            m_nHScrollPos -= 10;
            break;

        case SB_PAGEDOWN:
            m_nHScrollPos += 10;
            break;

        case SB_TOP:
            nPos = 0;
            // fall through
        case SB_THUMBPOSITION:
            m_nHScrollPos = nPos;
            break;

        default:
            return;
    }
```

(continued)

Figure 15-9. *continued*

```
    if (m_nHScrollPos < 0)
        m_nHScrollPos = 0;
    if (m_nHScrollPos > MAXSTRING)
        m_nHScrollPos = MAXSTRING;

    SetScrollPos(SB_HORZ, m_nHScrollPos, TRUE);
    Invalidate(FALSE);
}

//
// catch arrow keys and simulate touching scroll bars
//
void CMainWindow::OnKeyDown(UINT wChar, UINT /*nRepCnt*/, UINT /*wFlags*/)
{
    switch(wChar)
    {
    case VK_HOME:
        SendMessage(WM_VSCROLL, SB_TOP, 0L);
        SendMessage(WM_HSCROLL, SB_TOP, 0L);
        break;

    case VK_END:
        SendMessage(WM_VSCROLL, SB_BOTTOM, 0L);
        break;

    case VK_PRIOR: // page up
        SendMessage(WM_VSCROLL, SB_PAGEUP, 0L);
        break;

    case VK_NEXT:  // page down
        SendMessage(WM_VSCROLL, SB_PAGEDOWN, 0L);
        break;

    case VK_UP:
        SendMessage(WM_VSCROLL, SB_LINEUP, 0L);
        break;

    case VK_DOWN:
        SendMessage(WM_VSCROLL, SB_LINEDOWN, 0L);
        break;

    case VK_RIGHT:
        SendMessage(WM_HSCROLL, SB_LINEDOWN, 0L);
        break;

    case VK_LEFT:
        SendMessage(WM_HSCROLL, SB_LINEUP, 0L);
        break;
    }
}
```

(continued)

Figure 15-9. *continued*

testbed.dlg

```
DLGINCLUDE RCDATA DISCARDABLE
BEGIN
    "RESOURCE.H\0"
END

ABOUTBOX DIALOG 34, 22, 144, 75
CAPTION "About"
STYLE DS_MODALFRAME | WS_CAPTION | WS_SYSMENU
BEGIN
    CTEXT "NAMEHERE", IDD_APPNAME, 0, 12, 144, 8
    CTEXT "Copyright (c) 1992 by Kaare Christian", -1, 0, 25, 144, 8
    CTEXT "Version 1.0", -1, 0, 36, 144, 8
    CONTROL "OK", IDOK, "BUTTON", WS_GROUP, 56, 53, 32, 14
END
```

testbed.rc

```
#include <windows.h>
#include <afxres.h>
#include "resource.h"

AFX_IDI_STD_FRAME ICON testbed.ico
rcinclude testbed.dlg

MainMenu MENU
{
    POPUP "&File"
    {
        MENUITEM "E&xit", IDM_EXIT
    }
    POPUP "&Help"
    {
        MENUITEM "&About TestBed...\tF1", IDM_ABOUT
    }
}

MainAccel ACCELERATORS
{
    VK_F1, IDM_ABOUT, VIRTKEY
}
```

Our *CMainWindow* class's *OnCreate()* member function starts the process by calling the *tbMain()* function. It passes *tbMain()* a reference to its *CStringArray* object and a reference to an ordinary *CString*. Any text placed in the *CStringArray* collection will be displayed on the screen, and any text placed in the *CString* will be used as the main window title, the About menu item text, and one of the legends in the About dialog box.

The tbHello Test

The tbHello application shown in Figure 15-10 is a simple example of a program that consists of a *tbMain()* routine.

tbhello.cpp

```
#include <afx.h>
#include <afxcoll.h>

//
// tbHello, a test for TestBed
//
void tbMain(CStringArray& strArray, CString& strAppTitle)
{
    CString strA;
    CString strB = "Hello, TestBed!";
    CString strC;

    strAppTitle = "Hello, TestBed";

    for(int i = 0; i < 30; i++) {
        strC = strA + strB;
        strArray.Add(strC);
        strA += ' ';
    }
}
```

Figure 15-10.
The tbHello application.

When tbHello is linked with TestBed, they form a complete program; tbHello generates text information, and then TestBed manages its display, as shown in Figure 15-11.

In tbhello.cpp, the application title is set to "Hello, TestBed," and the *CStringArray* object is filled with 30 increasingly long messages. (To fully understand tbHello, you need to understand MFC strings and collections, which we'll get to in Chapter 18.)

Scroll Bars

Programming a scroll bar for the first time can bring back memories of writing your first program for Windows. Objectively, it isn't that difficult, but there are several pieces that need to fit together smoothly. Once you move to a scrolling environment, you must be prepared to handle a flock of new messages, and you have to account for scrolling in your *OnPaint()* routine.

The first key to using scroll bars is to specify the *WS_HSCROLL* and *WS_VSCROLL* scroll bar styles when you create your window. Here is the *Create()* call that creates TestBed's main window:

```
Create(NULL, m_csTitle,
    WS_OVERLAPPEDWINDOW | WS_VSCROLL | WS_HSCROLL,
    rectDefault, NULL, "MainMenu");
```

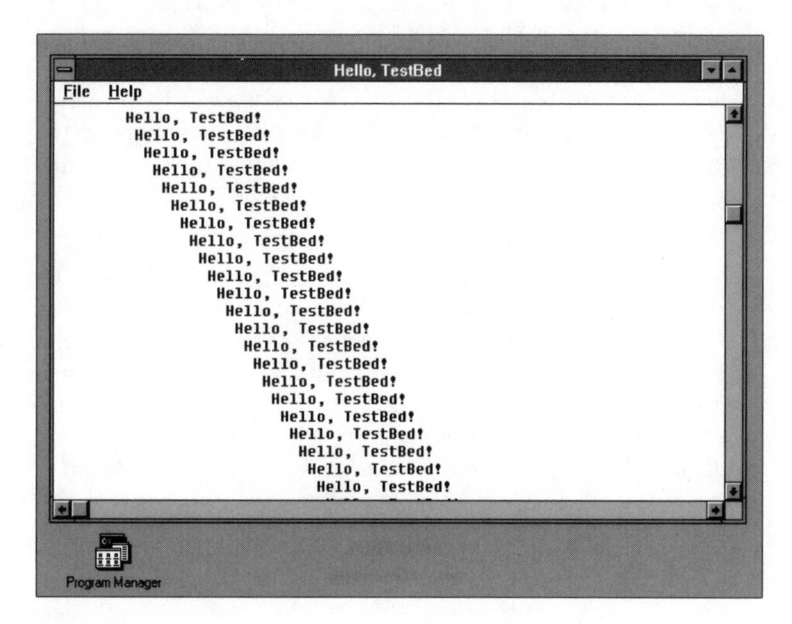

Figure 15-11.
TestBed's display of the text generated by the tbHello application.

The next step is usually to initialize the scrolling ranges in the *OnCreate()* function. In the TestBed application, I arbitrarily decided that horizontal scrolling would accommodate strings of as many as 255 characters, and I set the vertical scrolling range to correspond to the number of elements (lines) in the *CStringArray* object, which is easily obtained by calling the *GetUpperBound()* member of the *CStringArray* class. Here is the code in *OnCreate()* that initializes the scrolling ranges:

```
SetScrollRange(SB_VERT, 0, m_StringArray.GetUpperBound(), FALSE);
SetScrollRange(SB_HORZ, 0, MAXSTRING, FALSE);
```

Using these settings is convenient because the scroll bar values correspond directly to the displayed text. For example, when the vertical scroll bar is at position 10, line 10 (the tenth element of *CStringArray*) should be at the top of the screen.

The scrolling logic in testbed.cpp is found in three places. First, *OnPaint()* must be aware of scroll bar settings and paint the windows accordingly. Second, the *OnVScroll()* and *OnHScroll()* message handlers must respond to the WM_VSCROLL and WM_HSCROLL messages. These message handlers must leave behind enough status information for *OnPaint()* to do its job, and they must set the position of the scroll bar thumb using the *SetScrollPos()* function. The third place in testbed.cpp that contains scrolling logic is in the *OnKeyDown()* handler, which provides a keyboard interface to the scrolling function. *OnKeyDown()* simply maps keystrokes to Windows messages, thereby passing the buck to *OnVScroll()* and *OnHScroll()*.

Let's look at the *OnVScroll()* function in some detail. Notice that *OnVScroll()* is invoked with three parameters: the WM_VSCROLL message subcode, the current scroll bar position, and a pointer to the scroll bar *CScrollBar* object. Inside *OnVScroll()* is a switch statement based on the message subcodes. Each case is simple. For example, the SB_LINEDOWN subcode is handled by incrementing the *m_nTopLine* member variable. At the end of *OnVScroll()* is some range checking, so that repetitive range checking can be omitted from the switch statement. The *OnHScroll()* logic is similar.

The *OnPaint()* function is moderately complex. The basic idea is quite simple: The current top string is painted at the top of the client area, the next below, and so forth, until the bottom of the client area is reached. But the details add some obscurity. Because strings are of varying length, we must be careful to fully cover the client area. That's why the *ExtTextOut()* function is used to draw the text, and why the *rectLine* object is used to refer to the total client area of the current line. Near the beginning of *OnPaint()*, the *rectLine* object's left and right boundaries are set to correspond to the width of the client area:

```
rectLine.left = rectClient.left;
rectLine.right = rectClient.right;
```

Then, at the bottom of the loop, the *rectLine* top and bottom members are specified, and *ExtTextOut()* outputs the string:

```
rectLine.top = y;
rectLine.bottom = y + m_nCyChar;
paintDC.ExtTextOut(m_nCyChar/2, y, ETO_OPAQUE, &rectLine,
    pszCurLine, strlen(pszCurLine), NULL);
```

One other interesting aspect of *OnPaint()* is its treatment of the *paintDC* device context. At the beginning of the *OnPaint()* function, the *SYSTEM_FIXED_FONT* stock object is selected into the *paintDC* context but never deselected. This works because the *SYSTEM_FIXED_FONT* object itself is never deleted. It's fine for a device context to be deleted while it contains a reference to a stock object; what we must avoid is deleting any object selected into an active device context. The rules are simple:

- When you use *SelectObject()*, save the returned pointer and deselect the object before the selected object or the device context is deleted.
- When you use *SelectStockObject()*, don't worry about deselection.

The scrolling in TestBed is slightly simpler than in some programs because what's being scrolled is an array of strings presented in a single font. In more complex applications, you must attend to more details, but the basic idea applies to all scrollable applications.

The *CIOString* Class

Earlier in this book, I commented favorably on the iostream library because it provides a convenient and type-safe text input/output system. After using iostream for several years, I find it hard to revert to using *printf()*. Yet in Windows, *sprintf()* is the main tool for formatting text. Somewhat surprisingly, this deficiency isn't addressed by the MFC library. The first solution that springs to mind is using *strstreams* (string iostreams) from the iostream library. In a technical sense, this might work, but the huge iostream library is better suited to other environments, such as Unix or character mode MS-DOS. At some point, a more Windows-compatible variant of the iostream library might be developed, but such a version doesn't exist right now.

In working with early versions of the MFC library, I often wanted a simple way to create simple text-based (tty model) applications. To meet that need, I developed TestBed. But it further occurred to me that it would be easy to write a small set of routines that would pour text into a *CStringArray* object using iostreamlike notation. Figure 15-12 shows these routines.

iostring.h

```
#include <afx.h>
#include <afxcoll.h>

//
// A CStringArray managed similarly to an iostream (ostream)
//
class CIOString : public CObject {
    DECLARE_DYNAMIC(CIOString)
    public:
        CIOString(CStringArray& stringArray) :
            m_nWidth(nullWidth),
            m_cFillChar(stdFillChar),
            m_StringArray(stringArray)
        { }
        enum IOWidth { nullWidth };
        enum IOFillChar { stdFillChar = ' ' };
inline  CIOString& operator<<(IOWidth);
inline  CIOString& operator<<(IOFillChar);
        CIOString& operator<<(const char*);
inline  CIOString& operator<<(const unsigned char*);
inline  CIOString& operator<<(const signed char*);
inline  CIOString& operator<<(char);
        CIOString& operator<<(unsigned char);
inline  CIOString& operator<<(signed char);
        CIOString& operator<<(short);
        CIOString& operator<<(unsigned short);
```

Figure 15-12. *(continued)*
Routines for simple text output based on the CIOString *class.*

Figure 15-12. *continued*

```
        CIOString& operator<<(int);
        CIOString& operator<<(unsigned int);
        CIOString& operator<<(long);
        CIOString& operator<<(unsigned long);
        CIOString& operator<<(void*);
    protected:
            void pad(int n);
            CStringArray& m_StringArray;
            CString m_CurString;
            IOWidth m_nWidth;
            IOFillChar m_cFillChar;
};

const char endl = '\n';

// manipulators
extern CIOString::IOWidth setw(int n);
extern CIOString::IOFillChar setfill(char c);
inline CIOString& CIOString::operator<<(IOWidth n)
    { m_nWidth = n; return *this; }
inline CIOString& CIOString::operator<<(IOFillChar c)
    { m_cFillChar = c; return *this; }

// char inserters
inline  CIOString& CIOString::operator<<(char c)
    { return operator<<((unsigned char) c); }
inline  CIOString& CIOString::operator<<(signed char c)
    { return operator<<((unsigned char) c); }

// string inserters
inline  CIOString& CIOString::operator<<(const unsigned char* s)
    { return operator<<((const char*) s); }
inline  CIOString& CIOString::operator<<(const signed char* s)
    { return operator<<((const char*) s); }
```

iostring.cpp

```
#include "iostring.h"

IMPLEMENT_DYNAMIC(CIOString, CObject)

CIOString::IOWidth setw(int n)
{
    return (CIOString::IOWidth)n;
}

CIOString::IOFillChar setfill(char ch)
{
    return (CIOString::IOFillChar)ch;
}
```

(continued)

Figure 15-12. *continued*

```
void CIOString::pad(int n)
{
    while (n < m_nWidth) {
        m_CurString += m_cFillChar;
        n++;
    }
    m_nWidth = nullWidth;
}

CIOString& CIOString::operator<<(unsigned char c)
{
    if (c == '\n') {
        m_StringArray.Add(m_CurString);
        m_CurString = "";
    } else
        m_CurString += c;
    pad(1);
    return *this;
}

CIOString& CIOString::operator<<(const char* s)
{
    if (strchr(s,'\n')) {
        CString str = s;
        int n = str.Find('\n');
        if (n == -1)
            return *this;
        m_CurString += str.Left(n);
        m_StringArray.Add(m_CurString);
        m_CurString = "";
        if (n != str.GetLength()) {
            n++;
            return operator<<(str.Right(str.GetLength() - n));
        }
    } else
        m_CurString += s;
    pad(strlen(s));
    return *this;
}

CIOString& CIOString::operator<<(short s)
{
    char buf[10];
    _itoa(s, buf, 10);
    pad(strlen(buf));
    m_CurString += buf;
    return *this;
}
```

(continued)

Figure 15-12. *continued*

```
CIOString& CIOString::operator<<(unsigned short us)
{
    char buf[10];
    _ultoa((unsigned long)us, buf, 10);
    pad(strlen(buf));
    m_CurString += buf;
    return *this;
}

CIOString& CIOString::operator<<(int i)
{
    char buf[10];
    _itoa(i, buf, 10);
    pad(strlen(buf));
    m_CurString += buf;
    return *this;
}

CIOString& CIOString::operator<<(unsigned int ui)
{
    char buf[10];
    _ultoa((unsigned long)ui, buf, 10);
    pad(strlen(buf));
    m_CurString += buf;
    return *this;
}

CIOString& CIOString::operator<<(long l)
{
    char buf[10];
    _ltoa(l, buf, 10);
    pad(strlen(buf));
    m_CurString += buf;
    return *this;
}
```

A *CIOString* object is an *ostream*-inspired text output stream. It has insertion routines modeled on *ostream*'s that let you output text to the array. The iostring library is far less general than the iostream libary, but it is also far less bulky and complex. The iostring library isn't meant to be the last word in Windows I/O; rather, it is meant to make it easy to write programs like *DevCaps*, which we'll look at a little later, that need to output numbers and text as if to a tty application.

The *CIOString* constructor, which is defined in Figure 15-12, must be given a reference to a *CStringArray* object that will be used for all output operations. The *CIOString* class defines just over a dozen insertion functions, which convert basic types, such as *int*, to text. The class also contains a *CString* object called *m_CurString*, which accumulates text until a newline is inserted. The text and string inserters must watch for newlines. When a newline is inserted, the *m_CurString* object is appended to the array by the *Add()* function, and then the *m_CurString* object is reset to the null string so that it is ready for further insertions.

The tbHello1 Application

The tbHello1 application is a simple demonstration of the *CIOString* facility. The source code for tbHello1 is shown in Figure 15-13.

tbhello1.cpp

```
#include "iostring.h"

//
// tbhello1--exercises the iostring library
//
void tbMain(CStringArray& a, CString& title)
{
    CIOString cout(a);          // construct an iostring object
    title = "Hello";            // specify the application title

    cout << "Hello" << endl;
    cout << "     World!" << endl;
    cout << endl;
    cout << setw(12) << "Characters:" << 'a' << 'b' << 'c' << endl;
    cout << setw(12) << "Integers:" << setw(3) << 7 << endl;
    cout << setw(12) << "Unsigned:" << setw(3) << (unsigned)7 << endl;
    cout << setw(12) << "Long:" << setw(3) << (long)7 << endl;
}
```

Figure 15-13.
The source code for the tbHello1 application.

The tbHello1 application has a simple *tbMain()* routine that uses its *CStringArray* argument to create a *CIOString* object called *cout.* Then *cout* is filled with a few items of text by means of insertion operations. The onscreen appearance of the tbHello1 application is shown in Figure 15-14 on the next page.

The DevCaps Example

The DevCaps example shown in Figure 15-15 on pages 378–79 is a more practical example of using the iostring facility.

In the second edition of *Programming Windows,* Charles Petzold presents in Chapter 11 an example called DevCaps1 that displays a variety of information about devices. The application is pretty complete, displaying detailed information and covering printer devices. But the Petzold application is a full Windows program with menus, message loops, and the like. My own version of DevCaps presents only the basic information about the display device. This version of DevCaps is more traditional in that it retrieves information from the system and then displays it, without much ado or obvious complexity. The DevCaps application screen is shown in Figure 15-16 on page 379.

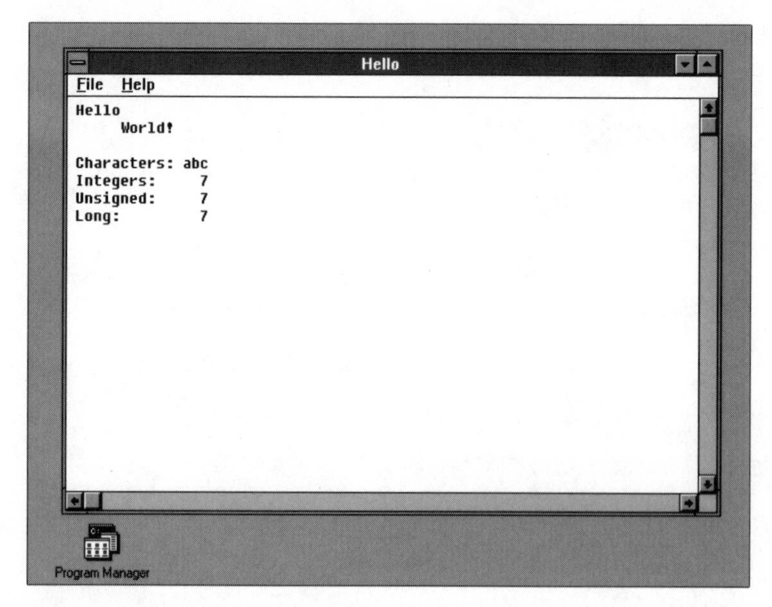

Figure 15-14.
The tbHello1 application screen.

devcaps.cpp

```
#include <afxwin.h>
#include "iostring.h"

struct Info {
    int index;
    char *name;
    char *description;
};

#define Entry(nm, desc) { nm, #nm, desc },
static Info info[] = {
    Entry(HORZSIZE, "Width in millimeters:")
    Entry(VERTSIZE, "Height in millimeters:")
    Entry(HORZRES, "Width in pixels:")
    Entry(VERTRES, "Height in pixels:")
    Entry(BITSPIXEL, "Color bits per pixel:")
    Entry(PLANES, "Number of color planes:")
    Entry(NUMBRUSHES, "Number of device brushes:")
    Entry(NUMPENS, "Number of device pens:")
    Entry(NUMMARKERS, "Number of device markers:")
    Entry(NUMFONTS, "Number of device fonts:")
    Entry(NUMCOLORS, "Number of device colors:")
    Entry(PDEVICESIZE, "Size of device structure:")
    Entry(ASPECTX, "Relative width of pixel:")
```

Figure 15-15.
The DevCaps application source code.

(continued)

Figure 15-15. *continued*

```
    Entry(ASPECTY, "Relative height of pixel:")
    Entry(ASPECTXY, "Relative diagonal of pixel:")
    Entry(LOGPIXELSX, "Horizontal dots per inch:")
    Entry(LOGPIXELSY, "Vertical dots per inch:")
    Entry(SIZEPALETTE, "Number of palette entries:")
    Entry(NUMRESERVED, "Reserved palette entries:")
    Entry(COLORRES, "Actual color resolution:")
};

void putOne(CIOString& cout, Info *i, CDC &dc)
{
    cout << setw(12) << i->name <<
        setw(30) << i->description <<
        setw(8) << dc.GetDeviceCaps(i->index) << endl;
}

void tbMain(CStringArray& a, CString& title)
{
    CIOString cout(a);                  // build an iostring
    title = "Device Capabilities";      // application title

    CDC hdcDisplay;
    hdcDisplay.CreateIC("DISPLAY", NULL, NULL, NULL);

    for(int i = 0; i < sizeof(info) / sizeof(Info); i++)
        putOne(cout, info+i, hdcDisplay);
}
```

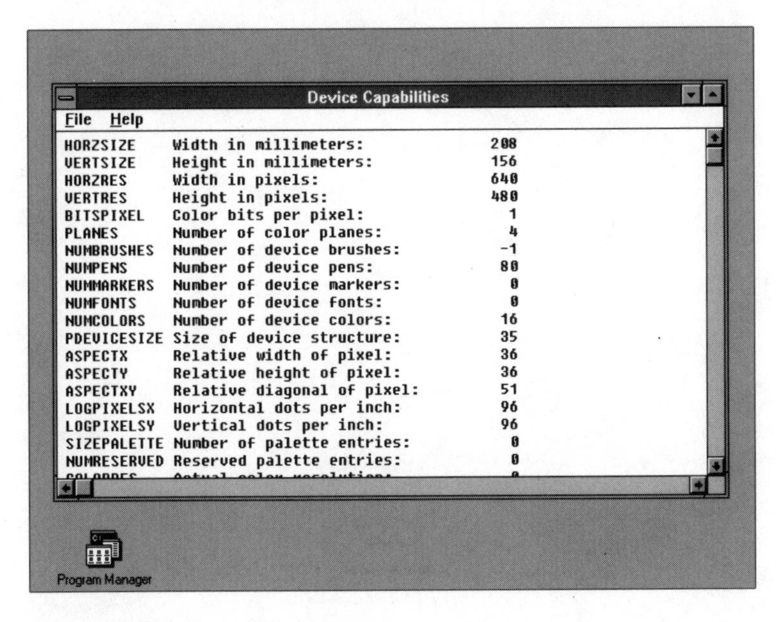

Figure 15-16.
The DevCaps application screen.

16

MFC Library Windows Multiple Document Interface

Most sophisticated applications for the Windows environment need to manage more than a single main window. Some, like the Microsoft Word for Windows word processor, need to manage several document windows so that the user can work on multiple documents simultaneously. Others, like the Microsoft Excel spreadsheet, need several types of windows. (Microsoft Excel uses, for instance, worksheet windows, graph windows, and macro windows.) The Windows Multiple Document Interface, usually called the MDI, meets all of these needs.

The MDI provides a wealth of functionality that would be difficult to build from scratch. But using this functionality requires commitment on your part because it presents yet another set of interlocking capabilities that must be tracked and coordinated. The MFC library classes take care of some MDI chores, and the MFC library message map architecture simplifies the remaining chores.

The individual document windows in an MDI application are called child windows. The MDI's complexity stems in part from the need to change interface features automatically as the user switches from one child window to the next. Windows can already handle some of these changes, such as switching from one kind of cursor to another, by registering individual window classes for each type of child window. Other changes, such as modifying the main window's menu, are accomplished by means of standard facilities, but the changes are instigated in response to the WM_MDI_ACTIVATE messages that occur when the user switches from one child window to another. Still other MDI facilities, such as the merging of the main window's menu bar with the child window's title bar when a child window is maximized, are accomplished mostly by Windows functions that aren't MDI specific.

Other aspects of the MDI are merely conventional, but the conventions should be maintained. For example, most MDI applications have a popup menu named Window on the main menu bar, and each time a new child window is created, a new menu item is added to the popup, so that you can easily switch to each child, even to one that is hidden. Other conventional aspects of MDI applications are the ability to tile or cascade the child windows, the ability to switch to the next child window, the ability to iconize child windows, the provision of separate icons for each type of child window, and the ability to arrange a set of child window icons appearing in the main window.

The ViewData Application

The Microsoft C/C++ 7.0 compiler comes with three example programs that use the multiple document interface: MinMDI, MDI, and MultiPad. The simplest is MinMDI, which is to the MDI as HelloApp is to Windows. The next most complicated is MDI, which is also called the MDI Sample application. MDI (the program) is a combination of Charles Petzold's MDIDemo program from Chapter 18 of *Programming Windows* and the Bounce program from Chapter 13 of that book. The MDI program is a realistic demonstration of MDI techniques, but its more than 1100 lines of code make it too large to discuss in detail in this book. The third MDI application in the C7 distribution is MultiPad. This multiple window text editor is a valuable resource because it is the most realistic program in the C7 samples collection. But at 2400 lines of code, it is far too long and complex to discuss here.

We'll look instead at my much smaller demonstration of MDI programming, the ViewData application. In complexity, ViewData falls somewhere between the C7 MinMDI application and the MDI Sample application. It contains about 450 lines of code, which certainly makes it a long example for a book, but it is nonetheless a tractable example for our purposes here.

The ViewData program presents as many as eight child windows for displaying live data, oscilloscope-style. In a real-world implementation, the data might come from a stock quotation service, an industrial process, laboratory instrumentation, or some other source. In this chapter's ViewData, the data actually comes from a random number generator, but that's just because I wanted to focus on the Windows MDI, not on data acquisition. A snapshot of the ViewData application, with two active child windows and one iconized child, is shown in Figure 16-1.

The MFC Library *CFrameWnd* Class

In ordinary (non-MDI) MFC application programming, you create the application by creating your own application and main window classes from the supplied *CWinApp* and *CFrameWnd* classes. MDI applications also use an application class derived from *CWinApp*, but the window class changes. In an MDI application, the application's main window is derived from *CMDIFrameWnd* and child windows are derived from *CMDIChildWnd*. Both *CMDIFrameWnd* and *CMDIChildWnd* are derived from *CFrameWnd*, the single document MFC library class. Also note that each type of child window should be implemented as a separate class.

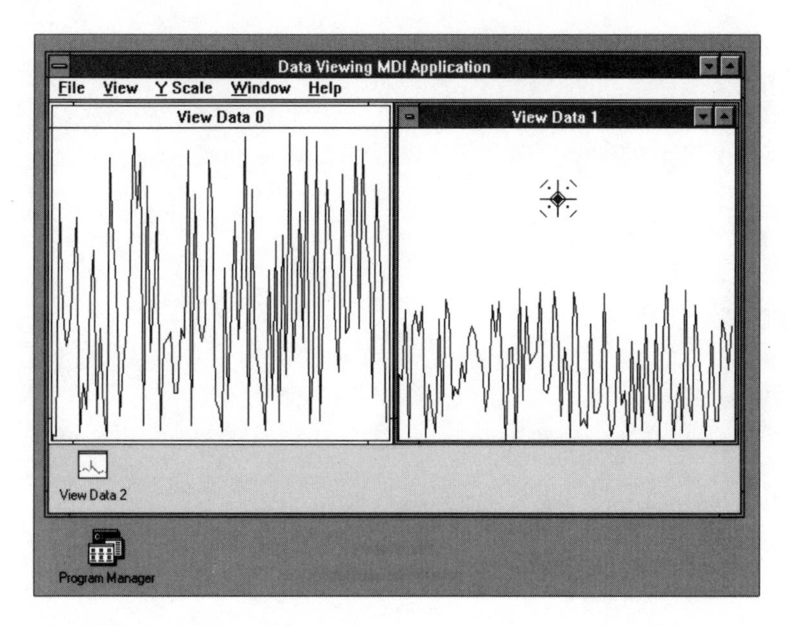

Figure 16-1.
The ViewData application screen, showing the two active child windows View Data 0 and View Data 1 and the iconized child window View Data 2.

The MFC library's *CMDIFrameWnd* class contains member functions that implement an interface between MDI capabilities and Windows. The *MDICascade()* function sees that child windows are arranged in a cascade. Similar capabilities in *CMDIFrameWnd* come from the *MDIIconArrange()* function that arranges the child icons, the *MDITile()* function that tiles the child windows, the *MDINext()* function that switches to the next child window, the *MDIMaximize()* function that maximizes a child window, and the *MDIRestore()* function that restores a child window after maximization or iconization. *CMDIFrameWnd* also contains *MDIGetActive()*, which gets a pointer to the active child window object, and *MDISetMenu()*, which helps manage automatic menu operations. The other important *CMDIFrameWnd* member function is *CreateClient()*, which you call to create a child window.

Both *CMDIFrameWnd* objects and *CMDIChildWnd* objects are created in a two-part process. First the constructor creates the object, and then the *Create()* member function carries out further initialization. Often the derived class's constructor will both construct and then *Create()* the base class object, which is the approach of the ViewData application's *CMainWindow* class.

Much of the ViewData program, which is shown in Figure 16-2, is standard MFC library programming.

viewdata.h

```
//
// view multiple data streams
//

//
// The application class
//
class CTheApp : public CWinApp
{
public:
    BOOL InitInstance();
};

//
// The main window class
//
class CMainWindow : public CMDIFrameWnd
{
public:
    CMainWindow();                  // constructor

    // necessary for menus to work correctly
    OnCreate(LPCREATESTRUCT lpCreateStruct);

    // message handlers.
    afx_msg void OnAbout();
    afx_msg void OnExit();
    afx_msg void OnNewWindow();

    DECLARE_MESSAGE_MAP();
};

//
// The child window class
//
class CChildWindow : public CMDIChildWnd
{
public:
    CChildWindow(int n) :           // constructor
        m_nChildID(n),
        m_nYScale(IDM_Gain_1)
    { /**/ }

    // message handlers
    afx_msg int OnCreate(LPCREATESTRUCT s);
```

Figure 16-2. *(continued)*

The source files for the ViewData multiple document interface application: viewdata.h, viewdata.cpp, child.cpp, data.h, data.cpp, resource.h, about.dlg, and viewdata.rc.

Figure 16-2. *continued*

```
    afx_msg void OnClose();
    afx_msg void OnPaint();
    afx_msg void OnYscale();
    afx_msg void OnSize(UINT type, int x, int y);
    afx_msg void OnTimer(UINT token);
    afx_msg void OnMDIActivate(BOOL, CWnd*, CWnd*);
    DECLARE_MESSAGE_MAP();

protected:
    // utility
    void ChangeMenu(char *pszMenuName, int iWinMenuPos);
    // member variables
    int m_nChildID;          // child win id num 0..7
    int m_cxClient;          // child window x size
    int m_cyClient;          // child window y size
    int m_nYScale;           // y scale: IDM_Gain_1 .. IDM_Gain_10
    CDataTrace m_Data;       // the data
    // static member variables
    static CMenu *pCurMenu;  // current menu object
    static int iChildCount;  // keeps track of the number of child windows
};
```

viewdata.cpp

```
#include <afxwin.h>
#include "resource.h"
#include "data.h"
#include "viewdata.h"
//
// ViewData example MDI application
// Copyright (c) 1992 by Kaare Christian
//
// frame window routines
//

//
// The application object
//
CTheApp theApp;

//
// InitInstance
//
BOOL CTheApp::InitInstance()
{
    m_pMainWnd = new CMainWindow();
    m_pMainWnd->ShowWindow(m_nCmdShow);
    m_pMainWnd->UpdateWindow();
    return TRUE;
}
```

(continued)

Figure 16-2. *continued*

```
//
// CMainWindow message map
//
BEGIN_MESSAGE_MAP(CMainWindow, CMDIFrameWnd)
    ON_WM_CREATE()
    ON_COMMAND(IDM_ABOUT, OnAbout)
    ON_COMMAND(IDM_EXIT, OnExit)
    ON_COMMAND(IDM_CHILD0, OnNewWindow)
    ON_COMMAND(IDM_CHILD1, OnNewWindow)
    ON_COMMAND(IDM_CHILD2, OnNewWindow)
    ON_COMMAND(IDM_CHILD3, OnNewWindow)
    ON_COMMAND(IDM_CHILD4, OnNewWindow)
    ON_COMMAND(IDM_CHILD5, OnNewWindow)
    ON_COMMAND(IDM_CHILD6, OnNewWindow)
    ON_COMMAND(IDM_CHILD7, OnNewWindow)
    ON_COMMAND(IDM_CASCADE, MDICascade)
    ON_COMMAND(IDM_TILE, MDITile)
    ON_COMMAND(IDM_NEXT, MDINext)
    ON_COMMAND(IDM_ARRANGE, MDIIconArrange)
END_MESSAGE_MAP()

//
// CMainWindow
//
CMainWindow::CMainWindow()
{
    LoadAccelTable("MainAccelTable");
    Create(NULL, "Data Viewing MDI Application",
         WS_OVERLAPPEDWINDOW, rectDefault, NULL, "MainMenu");
}

//
// OnCreate--loads application's initial MDI frame menu
//  and creates an MDI client
//
int CMainWindow::OnCreate(LPCREATESTRUCT lpCreateStruct)
{
    CMenu menu;
    menu.LoadMenu("MainMenu");
    CreateClient(lpCreateStruct, menu.GetSubMenu(0));
    return 0;
}

//
// menu handlers
//
void CMainWindow::OnAbout()
{
```

(continued)

Figure 16-2. *continued*

```
    CModalDialog about("AboutBox", this);
    about.DoModal();
}
void CMainWindow::OnExit()
{
    SendMessage(WM_CLOSE, 0, 0L);
}

// keep pointers to the child windows
static CChildWindow *pChildWnd[8];

//
// OnNewWindow--creates and shows a new CMDIChildWnd object and window
//
void CMainWindow::OnNewWindow()
{
    int wMenuID = GetCurrentMessage()->wParam;
    int iChild = wMenuID - IDM_CHILD0;
    char title[20];
    lstrcpy(title, "View Data X");
    title[lstrlen(title)-1] = '0' + iChild;

    CMenu *menu = GetMenu();
    if (menu->GetMenuState(wMenuID, MF_BYCOMMAND) & MF_CHECKED) {
        // already active; close window
        pChildWnd[iChild]->SendMessage(WM_CLOSE, 0, 0L);
    } else {
        // not active; create a new child window
        const char* pszViewClass =
            AfxRegisterWndClass(CS_HREDRAW | CS_VREDRAW,
                 theApp.LoadCursor(BombSight),
                 COLOR_WINDOW+1,
                 theApp.LoadIcon(AFX_IDI_STD_FRAME));

        pChildWnd[iChild] = new CChildWindow(iChild);
    if (pChildWnd[iChild]->Create(pszViewClass, title, 0,
        rectDefault, this))
        pChildWnd[iChild]->ShowWindow(SW_SHOW);
    else
        MessageBox("Child window creation problem.",
            "ViewData", MB_ICONEXCLAMATION | MB_OK);
    }
}
```

child.cpp

```
#include <afxwin.h>
#include "resource.h"
#include "data.h"
#include "viewdata.h"
```

(continued)

Figure 16-2. *continued*

```
//
// ViewData example MDI Application
// Copyright (c) 1992 by Kaare Christian
//
// child window routines

//
// child window message map
//
BEGIN_MESSAGE_MAP(CChildWindow, CMDIChildWnd)
    ON_COMMAND(IDM_Gain_1, OnYscale)
    ON_COMMAND(IDM_Gain_2, OnYscale)
    ON_COMMAND(IDM_Gain_5, OnYscale)
    ON_COMMAND(IDM_Gain_10, OnYscale)
    ON_WM_CLOSE()
    ON_WM_CREATE()
    ON_WM_PAINT()
    ON_WM_SIZE()
    ON_WM_MDIACTIVATE()
    ON_WM_TIMER()
END_MESSAGE_MAP();

// CChildWindow static members
int CChildWindow::iChildCount = 0;
CMenu *CChildWindow::pCurMenu = NULL;

//
// OnCreate--starts timers and possibly adjusts main menu
//
int CChildWindow::OnCreate(LPCREATESTRUCT s)
{
    if (!SetTimer(IDM_CHILD0+m_nChildID, 200, NULL)) {
        MessageBox("No timers for this window.",
            "ViewData", MB_ICONEXCLAMATION | MB_OK);
        return -1;
    }

    if (iChildCount++ == 0)
        ChangeMenu("ViewMenu", ViewMenu_WindowPos);

    CMenu *pMenu = GetParentFrame()->GetMenu();
    pMenu->CheckMenuItem(IDM_CHILD0+m_nChildID, MF_CHECKED);
    return CMDIChildWnd::OnCreate(s);
}

//
// OnClose
//
void CChildWindow::OnClose()
{
```

(continued)

Figure 16-2. *continued*

```
    CMenu *menu = GetParentFrame()->GetMenu();
    menu->CheckMenuItem(IDM_CHILD0+m_nChildID, MF_UNCHECKED);
    KillTimer(IDM_CHILD0+m_nChildID);

    if (--iChildCount == 0)
        ChangeMenu("MainMenu", 0);

    CMDIChildWnd::OnClose();
}

//
// ChangeMenu--switches to a different main menu
//
void CChildWindow::ChangeMenu(char *pszMenuName, int iWinMenuPos)
{
    CMenu *pNewMenu = new CMenu;
    CMenu *pWinPopupMenu = NULL;
    CMDIFrameWnd* pFrame = (CMDIFrameWnd*)GetParentFrame();

    pNewMenu->LoadMenu(pszMenuName);
    pWinPopupMenu = pNewMenu->GetSubMenu(iWinMenuPos);

    CMenu *pLastMenu = pFrame->MDISetMenu(pNewMenu, pWinPopupMenu);
    pLastMenu->DestroyMenu();     // discards old menu's Windows resources

    delete pCurMenu;              // deletes old object
    pCurMenu = pNewMenu;

    pFrame->DrawMenuBar();
}

//
// OnYscale handler--unchecks old selection, records current selection,
//  and checks new selection
//
void CChildWindow::OnYscale()
{
    CMenu *menu = GetParentFrame()->GetMenu();
    menu->CheckMenuItem(m_nYScale, MF_UNCHECKED);
    m_nYScale = GetCurrentMessage()->wParam;
    menu->CheckMenuItem(m_nYScale, MF_CHECKED);
    Invalidate();
}

//
// OnSize handler--records window size
//
void CChildWindow::OnSize(UINT nType, int x, int y)
{
```

(continued)

Figure 16-2. *continued*

```
    m_cxClient = x;
    m_cyClient = y;
    CMDIChildWnd::OnSize(nType, x, y);
}

//
// OnPaint
//
void CChildWindow::OnPaint()
{
    CPaintDC dc(this);
    int iyExt;

    dc.SetMapMode(MM_ANISOTROPIC);
    switch(m_nYScale) {
        case IDM_Gain_1: iyExt = 2000; break;
        case IDM_Gain_2: iyExt = 1000; break;
        case IDM_Gain_5: iyExt = 400; break;
        case IDM_Gain_10: iyExt = 200; break;
    }

    dc.SetWindowExt(CDataTrace::TraceLen - 1, iyExt);
    dc.SetViewportExt(m_cxClient, -m_cyClient);
    dc.SetViewportOrg(0, m_cyClient);

    dc.MoveTo(0,0);
    for(int i = 0; i < CDataTrace::TraceLen; i++)
        dc.LineTo(i, m_Data[i]);
}

//
// OnTimer
//
void CChildWindow::OnTimer(UINT)
{
    if (IsIconic()) return;
    m_Data.Randomize();
    Invalidate(TRUE);
}

//
// OnMDIActivate--activates/deactivates menu chores
//
void CChildWindow::OnMDIActivate(BOOL bActivate, CWnd* /* pActive */,
                                 CWnd* /* pDeActive */)
{
    CMenu *pMenu = GetParentFrame()->GetMenu();
    pMenu->CheckMenuItem(m_nYScale,
        bActivate ? MF_CHECKED : MF_UNCHECKED);
}
```

(continued)

Figure 16-2. *continued*

data.h

```
//
// class for storing data traces (random data for now)
//
class CDataTrace {
public:
    enum { TraceLen = 100 };
    void Randomize();
    CDataTrace() { Randomize(); }
    int operator[](int n) { return m_nYvalues[n]; }
protected:
    int m_nYvalues[TraceLen];
};
```

data.cpp

```
//
// class for storing data traces (random data for now)
//
#include <stdlib.h>
#include "data.h"

void CDataTrace::Randomize()
{
    int i;
    for(i=0;i<TraceLen;i++)
        m_nYvalues[i] = rand() % 200;
}
```

resource.h

```
/* menu stuff */

#define IDM_ABOUT   100

#define IDM_CHILD0  101
#define IDM_CHILD1  102
#define IDM_CHILD2  103
#define IDM_CHILD3  104
#define IDM_CHILD4  105
#define IDM_CHILD5  106
#define IDM_CHILD6  107
#define IDM_CHILD7  108

#define IDM_QUIT    110

#define IDM_TILE    140
#define IDM_CASCADE 141
#define IDM_NEXT    142
```

(continued)

Figure 16-2. *continued*

```
#define IDM_ARRANGE 143

#define IDM_Gain_1  200
#define IDM_Gain_2  201
#define IDM_Gain_5  202
#define IDM_Gain_10 203

/* cursor */
#define BombSight   300

// position of the &Window submenu of ViewMenu
#define ViewMenu_WindowPos 3
```

about.dlg

```
AboutBox DIALOG 63, 40, 124, 65
CAPTION "About ViewData"
STYLE DS_MODALFRAME | WS_CAPTION | WS_SYSMENU
BEGIN
    CTEXT "View Data", -1, 0, 6, 124, 8
    CTEXT "Example MDI Application", -1, 0, 17, 124, 8
    CTEXT "Copyright (c) 1992 by Kaare Christian", -1, 0, 30, 124, 8
    CONTROL "OK", IDOK, "BUTTON", WS_GROUP, 45, 45, 33, 14
END
```

viewdata.rc

```
#include <windows.h>
#include <afxres.h>
#include "resource.h"

rcinclude about.dlg

AFX_IDI_STD_MDIFRAME ICON frame.ico
AFX_IDI_STD_FRAME ICON child.ico
BombSight CURSOR bombsght.cur

MainMenu MENU
BEGIN
    POPUP "&File"
    BEGIN
        MENUITEM "&Exit", IDM_EXIT
    END

    POPUP "&View"
    BEGIN
        MENUITEM "Channel &0", IDM_CHILD0
        MENUITEM "Channel &1", IDM_CHILD1
        MENUITEM "Channel &2", IDM_CHILD2
        MENUITEM "Channel &3", IDM_CHILD3
```

(continued)

Figure 16-2. *continued*

```
        MENUITEM "Channel &4", IDM_CHILD4
        MENUITEM "Channel &5", IDM_CHILD5
        MENUITEM "Channel &6", IDM_CHILD6
        MENUITEM "Channel &7", IDM_CHILD7
    END

    POPUP "&Help"
    BEGIN
        MENUITEM "&About ViewData . . . ", IDM_ABOUT
    END

END
ViewMenu MENU
BEGIN
    POPUP "&File"
    BEGIN
        MENUITEM "&Exit", IDM_EXIT
    END

    POPUP "&View"
    BEGIN
        MENUITEM "Channel &0", IDM_CHILD0
        MENUITEM "Channel &1", IDM_CHILD1
        MENUITEM "Channel &2", IDM_CHILD2
        MENUITEM "Channel &3", IDM_CHILD3
        MENUITEM "Channel &4", IDM_CHILD4
        MENUITEM "Channel &5", IDM_CHILD5
        MENUITEM "Channel &6", IDM_CHILD6
        MENUITEM "Channel &7", IDM_CHILD7
    END

    POPUP "&Y Scale"
    BEGIN
        MENUITEM "&One", IDM_Gain_1
        MENUITEM "&Two", IDM_Gain_2
        MENUITEM "&Five", IDM_Gain_5
        MENUITEM "Te&n", IDM_Gain_10
    END

    POPUP "&Window"
    BEGIN
        MENUITEM "&Cascade Windows\tShift+F5", IDM_CASCADE
        MENUITEM "&Tile Windows\tShift+F4", IDM_TILE
        MENUITEM "&Arrange Icons", IDM_ARRANGE
        MENUITEM "&Next Window", IDM_NEXT
    END

    POPUP "&Help"
    BEGIN
```

(continued)

Figure 16-2. *continued*

```
        MENUITEM "&About ViewData . . . ", IDM_ABOUT
    END

END


MainAccelTable ACCELERATORS
{
    VK_F1, IDM_ABOUT, VIRTKEY,
    VK_F5, IDM_CASCADE, VIRTKEY, SHIFT
    VK_F4, IDM_TILE, VIRTKEY, SHIFT
}
```

In viewdata.h, the *CTheApp* and *CMainWindow* classes look just like the application and main window classes for single document interface applications we've seen earlier in this book. The only substantive difference is that the *CMainWindow* class is derived from *CMDIFrameWnd* instead of from *CFrameWnd. CTheApp* and *CMainWindow* are implemented in the viewdata.cpp file.

In much of viewdata.cpp, you'll find little trace of the multiple document interface. You'll find the first indication of the ViewData application's MDI involvement in the *CMainWindow* message map, which specifies that the *CMDIFrameWnd* class's *MDICascade()*, *MDITile()*, *MDINext()*, and *MDIIconArrange()* member functions should be invoked by the corresponding *CMainWindow* menu options. The second aspect of the MDI interface that's visible in viewdata.cpp is the *OnNewWindow()* message-handler member function, which is called to create a new child window in response to a menu selection. *OnNewWindow()* contains code related to child window creation, main window menu management, and child window class registration. We'll dissect each of these aspects of *OnNewWindow()* individually later in this chapter.

Another sign of MDI activity appears in the names of the icons. An MDI program customarily has one icon for the application as a whole and one icon for each type of child window. In an MDI application, it's customary to use the name *AFX_IDI_STD_MDIFRAME* for the application icon, and *AFX_IDI_STD_FRAME* for the child window icons.

The MFC Library *CMDIChildWnd* Class

Child windows in the ViewData application are implemented by members of the *CChildWindow* class, which is derived from *CMDIChildWnd.* The *CChildWindow* class's declaration is in viewdata.h, but its implementation is in child.cpp. In some ways the *CChildWindow* class is like an ordinary main window class—it contains a message map, it contains handlers that are called in response to menu selections, and it has handlers such as the *OnPaint()* and *OnSize()* handlers for standard Windows messages.

One indication that *CChildWindow* is an MDI child window is its use of the main window's menu bar. As in any Windows application window, many of the member functions in the *CChildWindow* class need to access the menu bar. But the menu bar belongs to the MDI frame window, not to the child itself. Thus the following idiom is often used:

```
CMenu *pMenu = GetParentFrame()->GetMenu();
```

GetParentFrame() is a *CMDIChildWnd* member function that returns a *CFrameWnd** pointer to the application's frame window, which contains the menu bar.

Window class registration

You've probably noticed that we've come a long way in our treatment of programming for Windows with the MFC library without mentioning window class registration. That's because the MFC library handles window class registration automatically, and often you don't need to intervene. But in MDI applications, it is often useful to have a separate class for each type of child window, which means that you have to step in and register the window class manually.

The MFC interface to window class registration is more convenient than the native Windows support for window type registration. The MFC interface is a global procedure named *AfxRegisterWndClass()* that takes four arguments:

- The class style, which is formed by *OR*'ing the *CS_* constants in windows.h. The most common class style is probably *CS_HREDRAW | CS_VREDRAW* for redrawing the window whenever its size changes.
- A handle to the window's cursor; or *NULL* to indicate that the application will handle the cursor manually.
- A handle to the window's background brush, or to one of the *COLOR_* constants from windows.h; or NULL to indicate that the application will paint its own background. If you use a *COLOR_* constant, you must add 1, thus writing

  ```
  (COLOR_WINDOW+1)
  ```

  when you want the window to be painted using the standard color for windows.
- A handle to the window's icon; or NULL to indicate that the application will paint its own icon.

The native Windows *::RegisterClass()* function requires that you specify a class name, but *AfxRegisterWndClass()* does the opposite; it synthesizes a class name and returns it to you. As with *::RegisterClass()*, duplicate registrations with *AfxRegisterWndClass()* are harmless.

Each child window is created within the *CMainWindow* class's *OnNewWindow()* member function. The code from *OnNewWindow()*, in which the child window class is registered, is on the next page.

```
const char* pszViewClass =
    AfxRegisterWndClass(CS_HREDRAW | CS_VREDRAW,
        theApp.LoadCursor(BombSight),
        COLOR_WINDOW+1,
        theApp.LoadIcon(AFX_IDI_STD_FRAME));
```

Once the child window class is registered and a *CChildWindow* object has been constructed, you can call *Create()* to finish the process:

```
if (pChildWnd[iChild]->Create(pszViewClass,
     title, 0, rectDefault, this))
    pChildWnd[iChild]->ShowWindow(SW_SHOW);
else
    MessageBox("Child window creation problem.",
        "ViewData", MB_ICONEXCLAMATION | MB_OK);
```

Note that after a successful creation, the *ShowWindow()* function (from the *CWnd* class) is used to display the window. This is the same procedure *InitInstance()* follows when a normal frame window is created.

The code we've looked at shows how to create a child window with its own class, but the same approach can be used in *InitInstance()* to create a main window that has a nonstandard class.

Closing child windows

A child window in the ViewData application can be closed in two ways. The user can activate the Close option from the child window's system menu, or the user can deselect the child window using the View menu on the ViewData menu bar. In either case, the child window will receive the WM_CLOSE message. Selecting Close on the child's system menu automatically issues the WM_CLOSE message; deselecting the child using the View menu activates the *OnNewWindow()* function, which explicitly sends the WM_CLOSE message.

The *CChildWindow* class has an *OnClose()* handler that responds to the WM_CLOSE message. *OnClose()* has several roles. First, it takes care of unchecking the application's View menu, to indicate that the child is no longer active. *OnClose()* also stops the timer used by the child and keeps track of the number of active child windows by decrementing the *iChildCount* static member. Finally, the *OnClose()* function of the last active child switches the application back to the main menu.

Notice that the ViewData application never deletes its *CChildWindow* objects. This is not a memory leak. The MFC library deletes them automatically during the final stages of closing a window.

Because the deletion of the child window objects is automatic, be careful that you don't try to use a child window object after it has been closed. In the ViewData application, I keep track of child window status by means of checkmarks next to the View menu. The *CChildWindow* class's *OnCreate()* function places checkmarks next to the View menu items, and the *OnClose()* procedure removes them.

MDI Menu Modifications

An important requirement of a user interface is that it seem natural. Surprises aren't a good idea. One appeal of the multiple document interface is that it dovetails with the way we often work. It is natural for us to work on several related items within a single, larger environment. The application's menu bar is an important part of the total application environment, and usually there is only one menu bar even though there might be many child windows. The MDI relies on sharing the menu bar, so that it accurately shows the choices that are available to someone using the current child window.

First let's review ways in which menus adapt to the current task in an MDI application.

- When no child windows are present, the main menu usually omits or grays menu choices that are appropriate only when a child is active. Figure 16-3 shows the ViewData application after it has been launched but before any child windows have been opened.

Figure 16-3.
ViewData after startup but before any windows other than the main window have been opened.

- When child windows are present, the main menu usually expands to include child window choices. In Figure 16-4 on the next page, Y Scale and Window popup menus have been added to the ViewData menu upon activation of a child window.

- When a child window is maximized, its title bar merges into the frame window's menu and title bars. In Figure 16-5 on the next page, the child window's title is appended to the main window's title, the child window's system menu button is prepended to the frame window's menu bar, and the child window's minimize/maximize control is appended to the right end of the frame's menu bar.

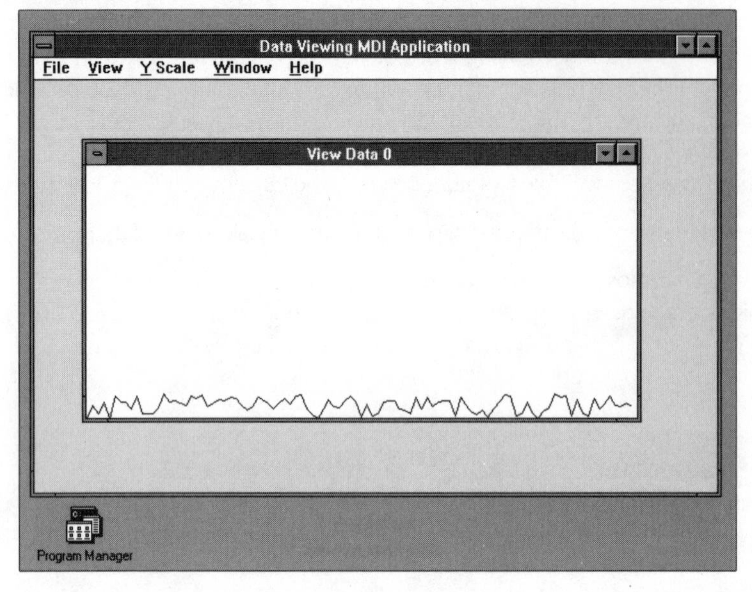

Figure 16-4.
Upon activation of a child window, new choices are added to the main window's menu bar.

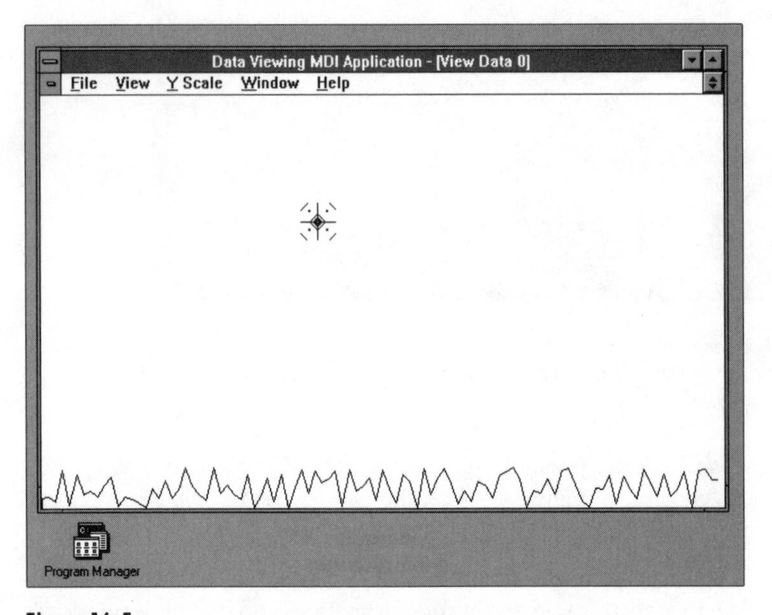

Figure 16-5.
Upon maximization of a child window, its title bar and controls merge with the main window's.

- When a child window is created, its title is automatically added to the Window popup menu. This provides a useful list of all the child windows and makes it easy for the user to switch to an obscured child window. As shown in Figure 16-6, the current child window's title is checked in the Window menu at all times.

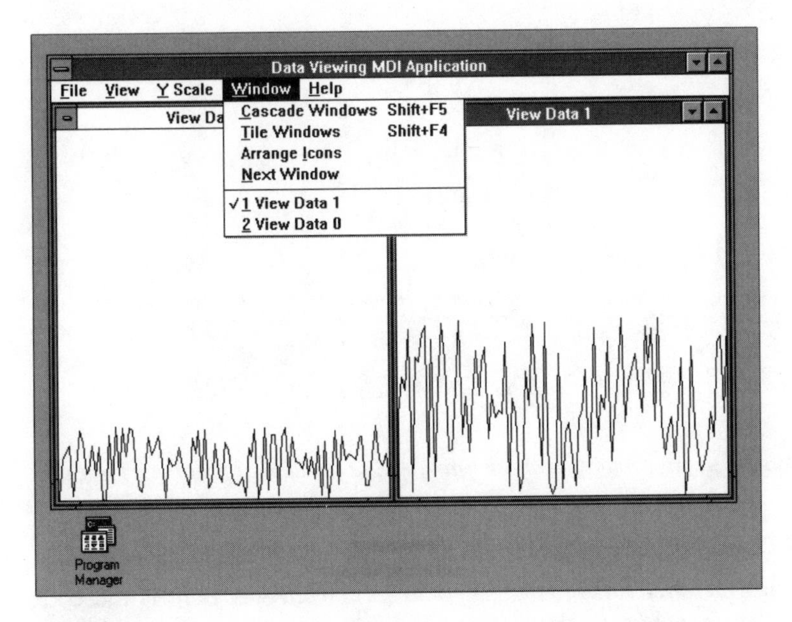

Figure 16-6.
The Window popup menu showing a list of all child window titles with a check mark beside the title of the current window.

- Checked child menu choices must correspond to the characteristics of the current child window. In Figure 16-7 on the next page, the child window on the left, View Data 0, has a Y Scale of Two, and the child window on the right, View Data 1, has a Y Scale of Five. The Y Scale popup menu correctly shows a check mark beside the Five item. If the user were to switch to the other child window, the Y Scale check mark would have to move to the Two item.

Now let's look at the code in ViewData that accomplishes these menu tasks. We'll skip around because that's the way the system works. MDI menu control isn't hard, but the code is scattered throughout an MDI application.

First we'll look at switching from one menu to another. We've already seen this technique in Chapter 14's hLucky application, but the details are different in an MDI application. In the *CChildWindow* class declaration in viewdata.h (Figure 16-2) is a static member variable named *iChildCount*. Each time a child window is created, this count is incremented in the *OnCreate()* member function; and each time a child window is destroyed, this count is decremented in the *OnClose()* member function.

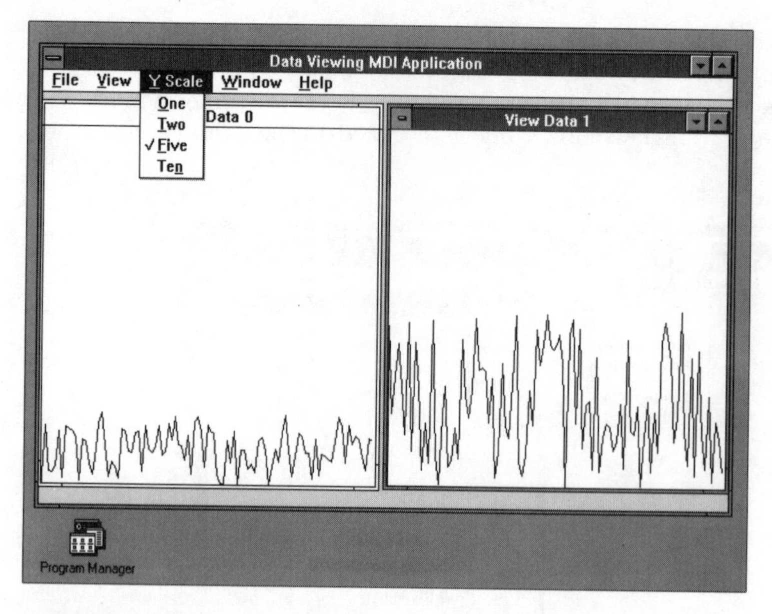

Figure 16-7.
The Y Scale popup menu showing a check mark beside the item appropriate for the current window.

When the first child window is created, or when the last is closed, *CChildWindow*'s *ChangeMenu()* member function is called to switch menus. Here is the code in *OnCreate()* that switches to the larger menu that contains the child window selections:

```
if (iChildCount++ == 0)
    ChangeMenu("ViewMenu", ViewMenu_WindowPos);
```

And here is the code in *OnClose()* that switches back to the short menu:

```
if (--iChildCount == 0)
    ChangeMenu("MainMenu", 0);
```

The first parameter of *ChangeMenu()* is obvious; it is the name of a menu resource defined in viewdata.rc. The second parameter indicates the location on the menu bar of the Window popup menu—necessary because the system handles part of the Window popup menu. It automatically appends the child window title to the Window popup, automatically puts a check mark by the item corresponding to the current child window, and automatically switches to one of the child windows when the user makes a window selection from the Window menu. If you look in viewdata.rc, you'll see that the Window menu is popup number 3, counting from 0, on the ViewMenu menu; and if you look in resource.h, you'll see that the *ViewMenu_WindowPos* symbol is defined as 3.

Here is the *CChildWindow*'s *ChangeMenu()* member function:

```
void CChildWindow::ChangeMenu(char *pszMenuName, int iWinMenuPos)
{
    CMenu *pNewMenu = new CMenu;
    CMenu *pWinPopupMenu = NULL;
    CMDIFrameWnd* pFrame = (CMDIFrameWnd*)GetParentFrame();

    pNewMenu->LoadMenu(pszMenuName);
    pWinPopupMenu = pNewMenu->GetSubMenu(iWinMenuPos);

    CMenu *pLastMenu = pFrame->MDISetMenu(pNewMenu, pWinPopupMenu);
    pLastMenu->DestroyMenu();     // discards old menu's Windows resources

    delete pCurMenu;              // deletes old object
    pCurMenu = pNewMenu;

    pFrame->DrawMenuBar();
}
```

The *ChangeMenu()* function illustrates several subtle but important techniques. First, notice that *ChangeMenu()* immediately fetches a pointer to the parent frame window because that's where the menu is, not in the current (child) window. Second, notice that the *CMenu* object **pCurMenu* is not created on the stack; instead, it is dynamically allocated by means of *new*. Stack allocation would imply deallocation on function return, which would be a disaster because the **pCurMenu* object becomes the application menu before *ChangeMenu()* returns.

In *ChangeMenu()*, the *CMDIFrameWnd* class's *MDISetMenu()* function is used to change the menu. It requires two arguments: a pointer to the full menu, and a pointer to the popup menu that is used to record child windows, as we saw in Figure 16-6. Recording child windows is handled automatically, but only if Windows knows which popup menu to use.

MDIActivate()

The last menu chore is to ensure that the positions of menu check marks and the dimmed menu items are appropriate for the current child window. In a single document program, you can use menu selections as a sort of database and simply query the database when you want to know what choice has been made. But in MDI programs, this technique is impractical; you must record all menu selections in the child window class object. In the ViewData application, only one popup contains items that pertain to child windows, the Y Scale popup menu. Thus, the child window object needs only one menu status variable, the *m_mYScale* member variable of the *CChildWindow* class.

Each time a selection is made from the Y Scale menu, the old menu selection is unchecked, the current selection is recorded in *m_mYScale*, and the new selection is checked. These standard chores are handled in the simple member function

OnYscale(). The more interesting task is handling the Y Scale menu when the user switches from one child menu to another.

When the user switches to another child window, each of the child windows receives a *WM_MDIACTIVATE* message. The first child is informed that it is no longer active, and the second is informed of the activation. The child windows can define an *OnMDIActivate()* handler so that they can handle necessary chores, such as menu management. Here is the *CChildWindow* class's *OnMDIActivate()* member function:

```
void CChildWindow::OnMDIActivate(BOOL bActivate,
     CWnd* /* pActive */, CWnd* /* pDeActive */)
{
    CMenu *pMenu = GetParentFrame()->GetMenu();
    pMenu->CheckMenuItem(m_nYScale,
         bActivate ? MF_CHECKED : MF_UNCHECKED);
}
```

The logic is simple; the deactivated window unsets the check mark for its own Y Scale item, and the activated window sets the check mark for its Y Scale item.

Multiple Child Window Types

Having several child window types changes many details, but the basic approach shown in ViewData holds. I don't want to go too deeply into the details but will mention some of the considerations. For more detail, look at the C7 distribution's MDI Sample application, which has both Bounce and Hello child windows.

Perhaps what changes least when you have several child window types is the way you create a child window with its own style, color, icon, and cursor. Simply register a window class for each type of child window, and let Windows take care of those details.

What changes the most in an application with several types of child windows is the difficulty of switching from one child to another. In the ViewData application, *OnMDIActivate()* needed only to check and uncheck menu selections because that was the only difference between one child and another. But in applications with several child window types, switching to a new child window is likely to mean switching to a new type of child, which involves changing the application's main menu. In the ViewData application, this would mean moving the *ChangeMenu()* logic into the *OnMDIActivate()* member functions.

17

MFC Library General Purpose Classes

In the preceding four chapters, we've looked at some of the Windows classes in the MFC library. Roughly the other half of the library contains facilities for runtime typing, serialization, file I/O, exception handling, strings, dates, and collections.

The ultimate base class in the MFC library hierarchy and the source of many of these services is *CObject*. *CObject* is a framework that provides for access to class information at runtime and for "object persistence," the storage and subsequent retrieval of objects after they have been deleted from memory. You need to be familiar with *CObject*, both so that you can understand the supplied MFC library classes and so that you can integrate your own classes into the MFC family. Figure 17-1 on the next page shows the relationship of *CObject* to the "non-Windows" classes derived from it.

In addition to the simple value types we've already looked at in our consideration of MFC library programming for Windows—*CPoint*, *CRect*, and *CSize*—the simple value classes *CString*, *CTime*, and *CTimeSpan* are not derived from *CObject*. Neither are the runtime object modal support classes *CArchive* and *CDumpContext*. Nor are the runtime structures *CRuntimeClass* (more of which soon), *CMemoryState*, and *CFileStatus*. All other MFC library classes are derived from *CObject*.

CObject and *CRuntimeClass*

CObject contains a small set of virtual member functions, which are typically overridden in derived classes, and a static *CRuntimeClass* structure. The *CObject* member functions address object destruction and optional runtime class information and object persistence facilities.

CObject's destructor is virtual, which makes the destructors of all objects derived from *CObject* virtual. Virtual destructors ensure that the correct destructor is always activated. The vtables carry overhead, as do *CObject*'s optional runtime typing and object persistence facilities.

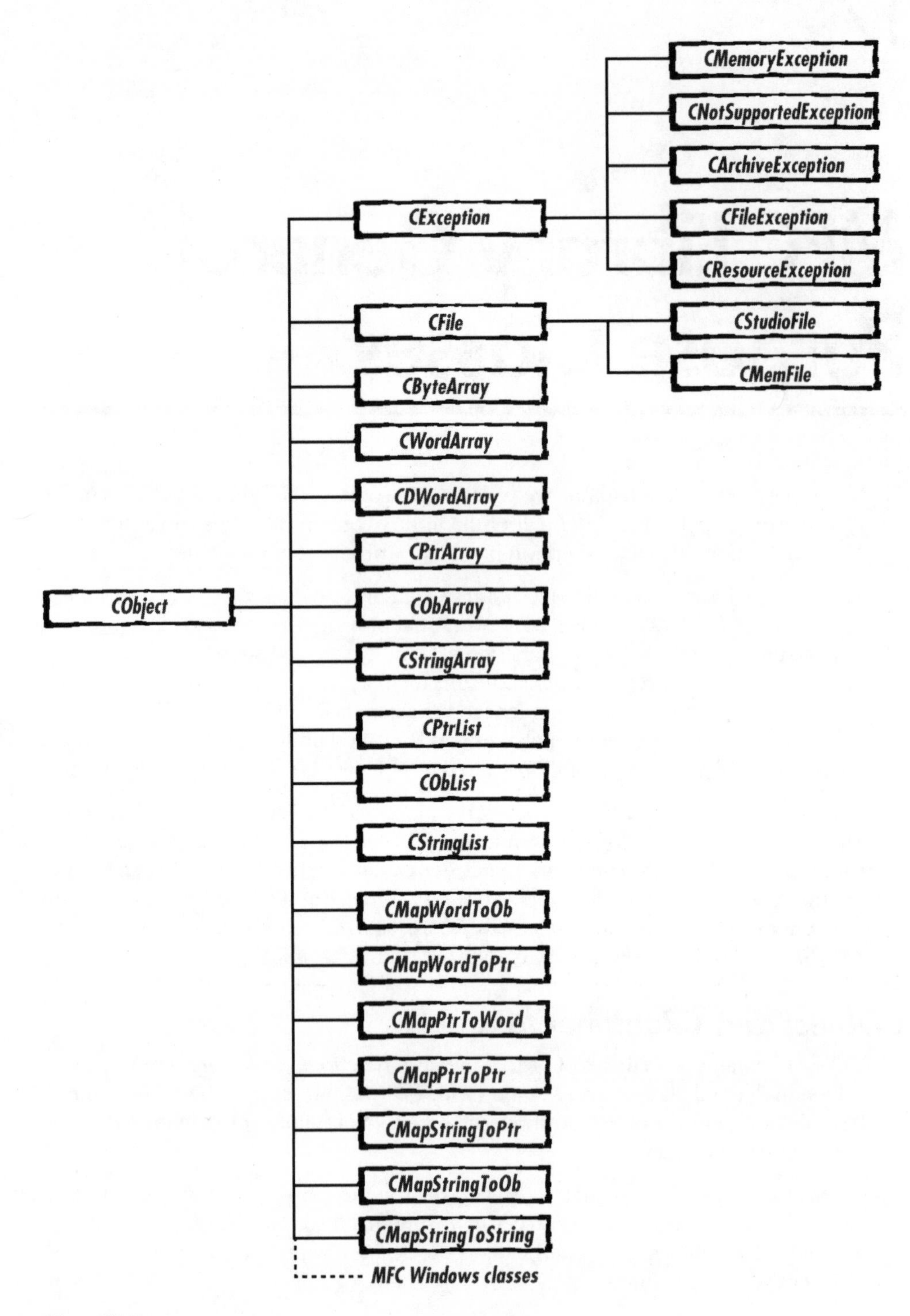

Figure 17-1.
The "non-Windows" half of the MFC library classes derived from CObject.

CObject's optional facilities for runtime class information help with several safeguarding chores. They allow a routine to check to be sure that an object that it has been handed is of the proper class. They also allow a routine to behave differently for different classes, although the primary mechanism for class-specific behavior in C++ is the virtual function.

But perhaps the most important role of *CObject*'s runtime class information facilities is as an aid to object persistence. An object is stored to disk along with its runtime class information. When it is reloaded from disk, the runtime class information informs the object's reconstitution.

An excerpt, shown in Figure 17-2, from Microsoft's header file afx.h shows several of the *CObject* public members that are involved in runtime class information services.

```
virtual CRuntimeClass* GetRuntimeClass() const;

BOOL IsSerializable() const;

virtual void Serialize(CArchive& ar);

virtual void AssertValid() const;

virtual void Dump(CDumpContext& dc) const;

BOOL IsKindOf(const CRuntimeClass* pClass) const;

static CRuntimeClass NEAR classCObject;
```

Figure 17-2.
Important public members of the CObject *class (excerpts from Microsoft's header file afx.h).*

For the complete definition of *CObject*, see the afx.h header file and consult your Microsoft C/C++ 7.0 *Class Libraries Reference.*

The most important of *CObject*'s runtime class information member functions is *GetRuntimeClass()*, which returns a pointer to a *CRuntimeClass* struct. The MFC library's *CRuntimeClass* struct, whose definition is shown in Figure 17-3 on the next page, is the heart of the MFC runtime type system.

Yes, *CRuntimeClass* is a struct, not a class, despite its name. For each class derived from *CObject*, there is one *CRuntimeClass* struct—not one per object but one for each class derived from *CObject*. *CRuntimeClass* stores the name of the class, several pointers to functions used for implementing persistence if persistence is specified, a pointer to the *CRuntimeClass* struct of the class's base class, and some pointers used to create a singly linked list of *CRuntimeClass* structs.

```
struct CRuntimeClass
{
// attributes
    const char* m_pszClassName;
    int m_nObjectSize;
    WORD m_wSchema; // schema number of the loaded class
    void (PASCAL *m_pfnConstruct)(void* p); // NULL => abstract class
    CRuntimeClass* m_pBaseClass;

// operations
    CObject* CreateObject();
    BOOL ConstructObject(void* pThis);
    void Store(CArchive& ar);
    static CRuntimeClass* Load(CArchive& ar, WORD* pwSchema);

// implementation
    static CRuntimeClass* pFirstClass; // start of class list
    CRuntimeClass* m_pNextClass;    // linked list of registered classes
};
```

Figure 17-3.
The CRuntimeClass *struct definition (excerpted from Microsoft's header file afx.h).*

To find out an object's class, you can use *CObject*'s *GetRuntimeClass()* member function to get a pointer to the class's *CRuntimeClass* struct, and then you can use the *CRuntimeClass m_pszClassName* member variable to find out the class name. These features of *CObject* are illustrated in the Dyna1 program shown in Figure 17-4.

dyna1.cpp

```
#include <afxwin.h>
#include <afxcoll.h>
#include "../testbed/testbed.h"
#include "../testbed/iostring.h"

CByteArray bytearray;
CPtrList ptrlist;
CWordArray words;

CIOString& operator<<(CIOString& cout, CRuntimeClass *p)
{
    CRuntimeClass *b = p->m_pBaseClass;
    cout << setw(30) << p->m_pszClassName
        << setw(4) << p->m_nObjectSize << "  "
```

Figure 17-4. *(continued)*
The Dyna1 program, illustrating simple CObject *runtime class information facilities.*

Figure 17-4. *continued*

```
        << b->m_pszClassName;
    return cout;
}

void tbMain(CStringArray& s, CString& title)
{
    title = "Dyna 1";
    CIOString cout(s);

    cout << setw(30) << "Class"
        << setw(4) << "Size" << "  "
        << "Base"
        << endl;

    cout << bytearray.GetRuntimeClass() << endl;
    cout << ptrlist.GetRuntimeClass() << endl;
    cout << words.GetRuntimeClass() << endl;
}
```

Dyna1 declares several collection classes and then prints their names using the MFC library runtime facilities. (Don't worry for now about the *CByteArray*, *CPtrList*, and *CWordArray* objects declared in Figure 17-4. We'll take them up in the section of Chapter 18 on collections.) The output of the Dyna1 program is shown in Figure 17-5.

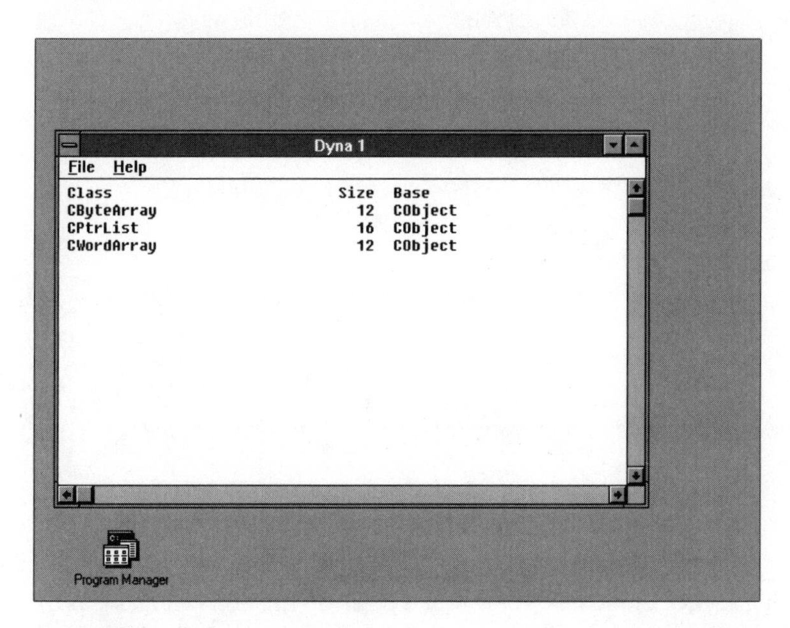

Figure 17-5.
Sample of the Dyna1 program's output.

Another task of the *CRuntimeClass* struct is to maintain a singly linked list of all the known descendants of *CObject*. The list is created when you derive classes from *CObject* and use the *IMPLEMENT_SERIAL* macro or the *IMPLEMENT_DYNAMIC* macro to register your classes. The Dyna2 program, shown in Figure 17-6, illustrates using the singly linked list maintained by the *CRuntimeClass* struct to print a list of all the descendants of *CObject* that exist in your program.

dyna2.cpp

```
#include <afxwin.h>
#include <afxcoll.h>
#include "../testbed/testbed.h"
#include "../testbed/iostring.h"

CIOString& operator<<(CIOString& cout, CRuntimeClass *p)
{
    CRuntimeClass *b = p->m_pBaseClass;
    cout << setw(30) << p->m_pszClassName
        << setw(4) << p->m_nObjectSize << "  "
        << b->m_pszClassName;
    return cout;
}

void tbMain(CStringArray& s, CString& title)
{
    title = "Dyna 2";
    CIOString cout(s);

    cout << setw(30) << "Class"
        << setw(4) << "Size" << "  "
        << "Base" << endl;

    CRuntimeClass *runtime = CObject::classCObject.pFirstClass;
    while(runtime) {
        cout << runtime << endl;
        runtime = runtime->m_pNextClass;
    }
}
```

Figure 17-6.
The Dyna2 program, illustrating use of the singly linked list maintained by the CRuntimeClass *struct.*

The output of the Dyna2 program is shown in Figure 17-7. Because of reordering, the output items might not exactly match those shown in Figure 17-7.

Another interesting service of the *CObject* runtime class information facilities is provided by the *IsKindOf()* member function that appears in all *CObject*-derived classes. *IsKindOf()* tests whether a given object is related to a particular class. "Relation" can mean either that the object belongs to the specified class or that the object

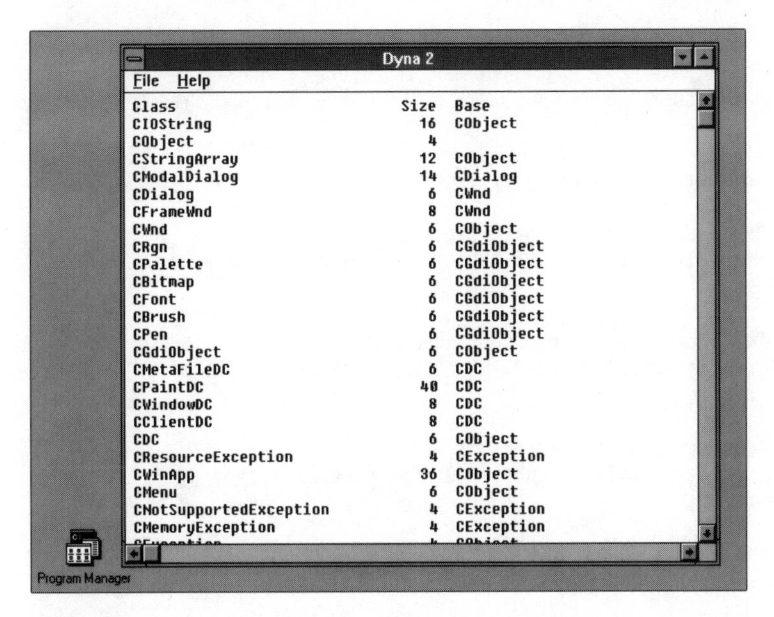

Figure 17-7.
Sample Dyna2 output, a list of all object classes in a program that have been derived from CObject.

belongs to a class directly or indirectly derived from that class. The KindOf program shown in Figure 17-8 illustrates *IsKindOf()* testing, in which the *RUNTIME_CLASS* macro converts a class name to a pointer to that class's *CRuntimeClass* object.

kindof.cpp

```
#include <afxwin.h>
#include <afxcoll.h>
#include "../testbed/testbed.h"
#include "../testbed/iostring.h"

CMemoryException memExcept;

char *truth(BOOL b)
{
    return b ? "TRUE" : "FALSE";
}

void tbMain(CStringArray& s, CString& title)
{
```

Figure 17-8. *(continued)*
The KindOf program, illustrating use of the RUNTIME_CLASS *macro to test an object's class membership.*

Figure 17-8. *continued*

```
    title = "IsKindOf";
    CIOString cout(s);

    CObject *ptr = &memExcept;    // lose compile time class information

    cout << "memExcept is a CMemoryException: "
        << truth(ptr->IsKindOf(RUNTIME_CLASS(CMemoryException)))
        << endl;

    cout << "memExcept is a CNotSupportedException: "
        << truth(ptr->IsKindOf(RUNTIME_CLASS(CNotSupportedException)))
        << endl;

    cout << "memExcept is a CException: "
        << truth(ptr->IsKindOf(RUNTIME_CLASS(CException)))
        << endl;

    cout << "memExcept is a CObject: "
        << truth(ptr->IsKindOf(RUNTIME_CLASS(CObject)))
        << endl;
}
```

Our sample output of the KindOf program, shown in Figure 17-9, indicates that *CMemoryException*, *CException*, and *CObject* are related. The *memExcept* object is a *kind of CException* and also a *kind of CObject.*

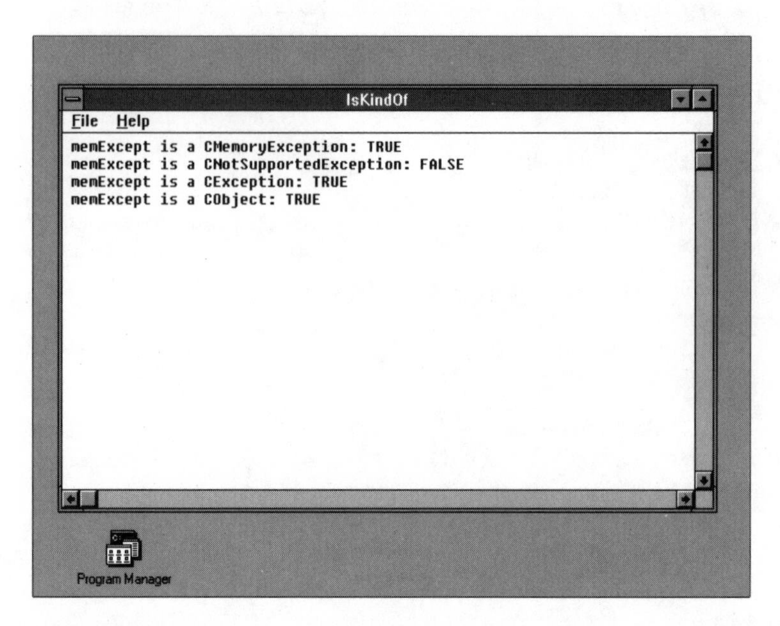

Figure 17-9.
Sample KindOf output, showing memExcept*'s relationship to various related classes.*

A diagram of the relationships among the *CObject* class and the exception classes in our *memExcept* example appears in Figure 17-10 on the next page.

Deriving Classes from *CObject*

Deriving a class from *CObject* is more complex than you might expect because you need to think about how your class is going to be used. Objects of your class might not need to use all of the *CObject* services. There are three levels of exploiting *CObject* facilities, which I am arbitrarily going to call levels Q, R, and S.

- At level Q, your derived class doesn't take advantage of *CObject*'s dynamic (runtime) class information and serialization facilities. Level Q compliance allows only the use of objects of your class in the *CObject* collections.
- At level R, your derived class uses *CObject*'s dynamic (runtime) class information services but no serialization. This allows the use of objects of your class in the *CObject* collections, and it allows you to determine the class of each object that you have collected. In a derived class, runtime typing is implemented by using MFC's *DECLARE_DYNAMIC* macro in the class definition and then using the *IMPLEMENT_DYNAMIC* macro in the class implementation (.cpp) module.
- At level S, your derived class exploits all of *CObject*'s services, including both runtime class information services and serialization. This allows use of objects of your class in the *CObject* collections, and it also provides for object persistence in the serialized storage of objects of the class on disk. Serialization requires that all members of your class also support serialization. You must use the *DECLARE_SERIAL* macro in your class definition, and you must use the *IMPLEMENT_SERIAL* macro in the class implementation module. You must supply a *Serialize()* member function to perform the serialization, and you must have a default constructor.

You must give some thought to your data types when you design classes that will be derived from *CObject*. In the first decade of PC programming, we could safely assume that an *int* was 16 bits, but that assumption is dated. Today we must strive to create classes that will behave identically in both 16-bit and 32-bit environments, and that means that *int* variables should be banished from our key classes. And if we intend to serialize our classes derived from *CObject*, avoiding the *int* type isn't just a strong suggestion; it is a requirement. The afx.h header file defines these portable data types: BYTE, WORD, LONG, and DWORD. Use them in your own classes.

For a level Q class, all you need to do is derive your class from *CObject*. If you use public derivation, all of *CObject*'s public facilities will be available, but few will be of any use. You will, however, be able to use your objects in situations that require *CObject* compliance—in some of the MFC collections, for instance.

Dynamic Class Information

For a level R class, you must derive your class from *CObject* and you must also use the *DECLARE_DYNAMIC* and *IMPLEMENT_DYNAMIC* macros to implement

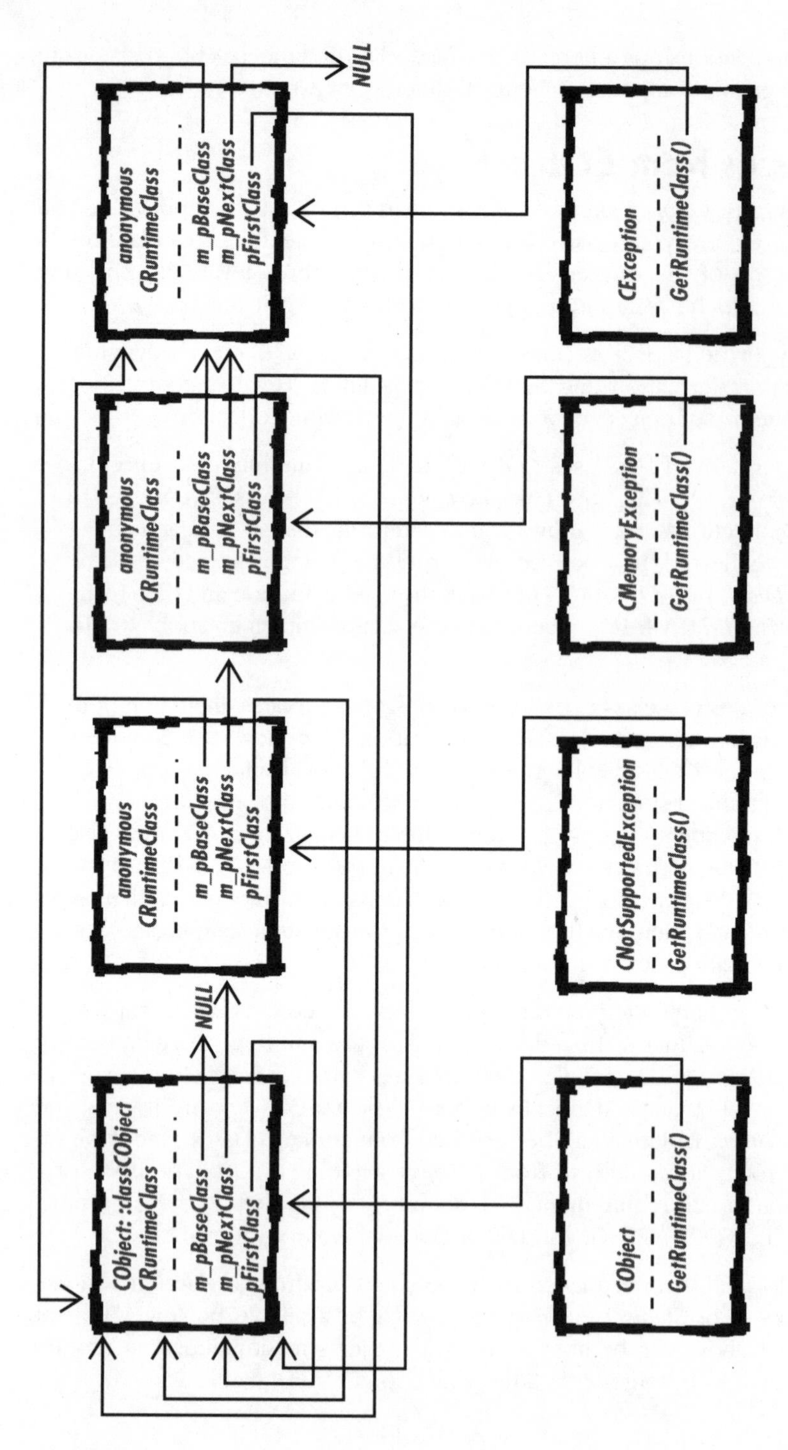

Figure 17-10.
CObject*'s relationships to the exception classes in the KindOf program.*

dynamic, runtime class information services. These macros add capability to your class, but they also add a small overhead. The MFC library implements runtime typing by means of optional macros so that you pay for the feature only if you need it. The *CIOString* class we looked at in Chapter 15 illustrates use of these macros. *DECLARE_DYNAMIC* is placed inside the class definition and requires the class name as its argument. *IMPLEMENT_DYNAMIC* is in the implementation module, in global scope, and requires both the class name and the base class name as arguments. Keep in mind that *DECLARE_DYNAMIC* is a macro and that it declares two public members. By convention, you should place *DECLARE_DYNAMIC* at the beginning of the class definition, and you should follow it with the *public*, *private*, or *protected* access specifier. Any access specifier placed before *DECLARE_DYNAMIC* is ineffective because the *DECLARE_DYNAMIC* macro contains the *public* specifier:

```
class CMistaken : public CObject {
    private:
        DECLARE_DYNAMIC(CMistaken)
        WORD m_wPrivateKey;      // public, but looks like private
};
```

To a human reader, the intention is clear: The programmer intends *m_wPrivateKey* to be private. But it is actually public because the *DECLARE_DYNAMIC* macro contains the *public* keyword. Here's the correct implementation of the idea:

```
class COkay : public CObject {
        DECLARE_DYNAMIC(COkay)
    private:
        WORD m_wPrivateKey;
};
```

Serialization

What I've called a level S class, with serialization, requires some effort on your part. First you must implement a *Serialize()* member function whose job is the actual saving and restoring of information. Second you must see that your class contains a default constructor so that it will create the empty object that will be initialized by the *Serialize()* member function. Finally you need to use the *DECLARE_SERIAL* and *IMPLEMENT_SERIAL* macros to mark the class for serialization. Note that serialization support includes dynamic, runtime class information services. Thus the serial macros (*DECLARE_SERIAL* and *IMPLEMENT_SERIAL*) include all the functionality of the dynamic macros (*DECLARE_DYNAMIC* and *IMPLEMENT_DYNAMIC*). Don't use both sets of macros in a single class. Use the dynamic macros if you want only runtime typing; use the serial macros if you want runtime typing plus serialization support.

The excerpts from iostring.h and iostring.cpp shown in Figure 17-11 on the next page illustrate ways in which the *CIOString* class can be changed to support serialization with the addition of a default constructor, the replacement of the dynamic macros with the serial macros, and the addition of the *Serialize()* member function. The unchanged parts of the *CIOString* class aren't shown.

iostring.h

```
class CIOString : public CObject {
    DECLARE_SERIAL(CIOString)
public:
    CIOString() :                   // default constructor
        m_nWidth(nullWidth),
        m_cFillChar(stdFillChar),
        m_StringArray(m_DefaultStringArray)
    { }
    void Serialize(CArchive& ar);
private:
    CStringArray m_DefaultStringArray;
public:

    //
    // CIOString inserters and other members
    //
};
```

iostring.cpp

```
IMPLEMENT_SERIAL(CIOString, CObject, 0)

void CIOString::Serialize(CArchive& ar)
{
    CObject::Serialize(ar);         // base part
    m_StringArray.Serialize(ar);
}
```

Figure 17-11.
The iostring.h and iostring.cpp files altered to include serialization support.

The *Serialize()* member function of the *CIOString* class is simple because the only thing that needs to be serialized is the *CStringArray* member, and the MFC library's *CStringArray* class contains a *Serialize()* member function. The other member variables of a *CIOString* object are temporary and needn't be saved when the object is stored. However, you do need to be careful to serialize the base class part of a *CIOString*, which is what is accomplished by invoking the first *Serialize()* function inside the *CIOString* class's *Serialize()* function.

The *CFile* Class

The *CFile* class contains the MFC library's file operations—both for I/O operations (reading/writing) and for file maintenance operations such as renaming and removing. *CFile* takes advantage of the MFC exception mechanism. This mechanism, which we'll look at later in this chapter, lets you give a program an error-handling framework without laboriously checking the error status of every procedure call.

CFile is required for MFC library facilities that call for I/O, such as serialization and dumping. *CFile* is fast and responsive, which means that I/O will be done at the speed of the underlying system and hardware.

Microsoft will make *CFile* available on all platforms that support the MFC library, so if you are taking advantage of the MFC library, you might want to recode your existing file operations to use *CFile*. This will ensure that your I/O is exactly as portable as the rest of your MFC code, which means portable to MFC platforms and out of contention elsewhere. If all you are using of the MFC library is *CFile*, you're probably making a mistake because *CFile* isn't portable to non-MFC computing platforms without a lot of work.

CFile isn't the only low-level file I/O mechanism in Microsoft C. One alternative is the *read()/write()/lseek()* set of functions. These functions originated in early Unix C compilers, and they have been supplied in most subsequent C compilers. Microsoft C supplies the *read()/write()/lseek()* troika, but I don't recommend them. They have been implemented in too many ways in different platforms and present too many chances for subtle failure.

Another possibility for low-level file I/O is the *fread()/fwrite()/fseek()* trio. These routines behave consistently on all platforms, and they are part of the ANSI C standard, but they pull in the entire C standard I/O library, which is undesirable in most MFC library software. The third choice is *_dos_read()/_dos_write()*, which I don't recommend both because it is MS-DOS specific and because it lacks a *seek()* component. *CFile* is not universally available, but it works consistently and efficiently on all MFC platforms.

CFile is solely a binary file I/O mechanism. It won't perform the CR/LF translation that is convenient for reading and writing MS-DOS text files, and it doesn't pay any attention to the archaic Ctrl-Z character, which was once used to indicate end of file in MS-DOS text files. If you want to access MS-DOS text files, you should use *CStdioFile*, which is derived from *CFile*. *CStdioFile* uses a STDIO stream for I/O, and it offers both text (translated CR/LF) and binary operation. *CFile* uses your buffer, not its own, so you don't need to worry about extra copy operations. I/O goes directly to (or from) the underlying operating system from (or to) your application's buffers. *CFile's* enumeration constants are listed in Figure 17-12.

***CFile* open flags enumeration constants**		
`modeRead`	`shareCompat`	`typeText`
`modeWrite`	`shareExclusive`	`typeBinary`
`modeReadWrite`	`shareDenyWrite`	
`modeNoInherit`	`shareDenyRead`	
`modeCreate`	`shareDenyNone`	

Figure 17-12.
CFile *enumeration constants.*

(continued)

Figure 17-12. *continued*

***CFile* attribute enumeration constants**

```
normal          readOnly
hidden          system
volume          directory
archive
```

***CFile* seek-position enumeration constants**

```
begin
current
end
```

***CFile* null file handle constant**

```
hFileNull
```

Even though the *CFile* class defines *typeText* and *typeBinary* constants, they are placeholders for use in classes derived from *CFile*, such as *CStdioFile*. The *typeText* and *typeBinary* constants have no meaning to *CFile*.

Figure 17-13 shows *CFile*'s nonstatic member functions, and Figure 17-14 shows the *CFile* static member functions. The first step in using a *CFile* object is to create the object. Usually, you first use the *CFile* default constructor to create a *CFile* object that is not yet attached to a specific file. Next you use *CFile*'s *Open()* to attach the *CFile* object to a specific file. The advantage of this two-step approach is control; constructing a default *CFile* object and then calling *Open()* gives you more error-handling opportunities than using either of the two more automatic *CFile* constructors.

```
// constructors
CFile();
CFile(int hFile);
CFile(const char* pszFileName, UINT nOpenFlags);

// operations
virtual BOOL   Open(const char* pszFileName, UINT nOpenFlags,
    CFileException *pError = NULL);
virtual UINT   Read(void FAR* lpBuf, UINT nCount);
virtual void   Write(const void FAR* lpBuf, UINT nCount);
virtual CFile* Duplicate() const;
virtual DWORD  GetPosition() const;
virtual BOOL   GetStatus(CFileStatus& rStatus) const;
virtual void   Flush();
virtual void   Close();
// seek functions
virtual LONG   Seek(LONG lOff, UINT nFrom);
        DWORD  SeekToEnd();
        void   SeekToBegin();
```

Figure 17-13.
CFile *nonstatic member functions.*

(continued)

Figure 17-13. *continued*

```
// length functions
virtual void   SetLength(DWORD dwNewLen);
virtual DWORD  GetLength() const;

// locking functions
virtual void   LockRange(DWORD dwPos, DWORD dwCount);
virtual void   UnlockRange(DWORD dwPos, DWORD dwCount);
```

When you want one-step object creation, or when you are given an open-file descriptor from existing C code, you should use one of the argument-taking *CFile* constructors shown in Figure 17-13. Note that the *CFile* constructor that takes a file handle argument assumes that the handle references a valid, open file. No error checking is done and no exception will be thrown. The *CFile* constructor that takes a file name and an *nOpenFlags* argument actually opens the named file by calling *Open()*, in the specified mode, and does error checking. If an error occurs, the *CFileException* will be thrown. If you use this constructor, either you must install an exception CATCH block or you must be prepared for your program to terminate on construction failure.

If you create a *CFile* object using the default constructor, you must then complete the process by calling *Open()* to attach the *CFile* object to a file. *CFile*'s *Open()* member function requires an *nOpenFlags* parameter that should be created by *OR*'ing the open flags constants shown in Figure 17-12. The *Open()* member function also can take a pointer to a *CFileException* object. If a pointer is supplied, the exception object will be filled in with status information about the success or failure of the file open operation. But *Open()* will never throw an exception; its only action is to fill in the *m_cause* and *m_IOsError* fields of the exception object. Actually throwing the exception is the invoker's choice. It is perfectly reasonable to invoke *Open()* with a pointer to a *CFileException* object for the sole purpose of getting the extended failure information stored in the object.

```
static void Rename(const char* pszOldName, const char* pszNewName);
static void Remove(const char* pszFileName);
static BOOL GetStatus(const char* pszFileName, CFileStatus& rStatus);
static void SetStatus(const char* pszFileName, const CFileStatus& status);
```

Figure 17-14.
CFile *static member functions.*

The *CArchive* Class

An archive is a repository, a place to store things. The MFC library's *CArchive* class helps you create an archive so that you can conveniently store objects in files. Usually the objects will be from classes derived (directly or indirectly) from *CObject*, although it is also possible to use the *CArchive* facilities with non-*CObject* classes.

CArchive is just the tip of the serialization iceberg. The framework for MFC library serialization is in the *CObject* class, and the actual code that implements serialization is in the individual derived classes. Almost any class that you serialize

- Will be derived from *CObject*
- Will be declared and implemented using the *DECLARE_SERIAL* and *IMPLEMENT_SERIAL* macros we've talked about
- Will have a default constructor
- Will have a *Serialize()* member function that implements serialization

Once these facilities are in place, as they are for the *CIOString* class, all you need to do is create an archive object and archive the class.

The Dyna3 program creates a *CIOString* object, fills it with runtime class information (just as Dyna2 does), and then archives that object in a file. Upon success, a status message is output to the application window. The code for Dyna3 is shown in Figure 17-15.

dyna3.cpp

```
#include <afxwin.h>
#include <afxcoll.h>
#include "../testbed/testbed.h"
#include "../testbed/iostring.h"

CIOString& operator<<(CIOString& cout, CRuntimeClass *p)
{
    CRuntimeClass *b = p->m_pBaseClass;
    cout << setw(30) << p->m_pszClassName
        << setw(4) << p->m_nObjectSize << "  "
        << b->m_pszClassName;
    return cout;
}

void tbMain(CStringArray& s, CString& title)
{
    // create a local CIOString and fill it with runtime information
    CStringArray local;
    CIOString filestream(local);

    filestream << setw(30) << "Class"
        << setw(4) << "Size" << "  "
        << "Base" << endl;

    CRuntimeClass *runtime = CObject::classCObject.pFirstClass;
    while(runtime) {
```

Figure 17-15. *(continued)*
The Dyna3 program, for storing an object in an archive.

Figure 17-15. *continued*

```
        filestream << runtime << endl;
        runtime = runtime->m_pNextClass;
    }

    CFile file;
    CString fileName = "info.win";
    file.Open(fileName, CFile::modeCreate | CFile::modeWrite);
    CArchive ar(&file, CArchive::store);
    filestream.Serialize(ar);
    ar.Close();
    file.Close();

    title = "Dyna 3 - Store RuntimeInfo to a File";
    CIOString cout(s);
    cout << local.GetSize() << " records written to " << fileName
        << endl;
}
```

The complementary operation is loading an object from an archive, which is shown in the Dyna4 code in Figure 17-16.

dyna4.cpp

```
#include <afxwin.h>
#include <afxcoll.h>
#include "../testbed/testbed.h"
#include "../testbed/iostring.h"

void tbMain(CStringArray& s, CString& title)
{
    title = "Dyna 4 - Load RuntimeInfo from a File";
    CIOString cout(s);

    CFile file;
    CString fileName = "info.win";
    file.Open(fileName, CFile::modeRead);
    CArchive ar(&file, CArchive::load);
    cout.Serialize(ar);
    ar.Close();
    file.Close();
}
```

Figure 17-16.
The Dyna4 program, for loading an object from an archive.

The output of both applications is shown in Figure 17-17 on the next page.

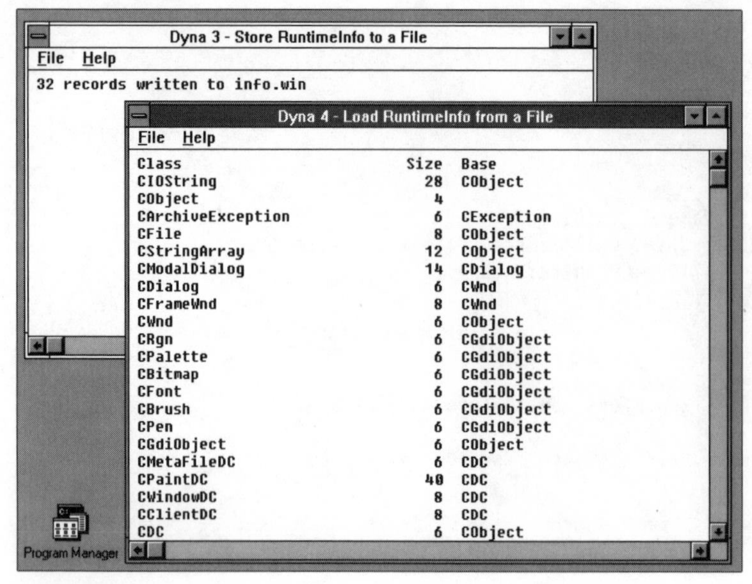

Figure 17-17.
Sample Dyna3 and Dyna4 program output.

The *CDumpContext* Class

The *CDumpContext* class is used to perform a "dump," that is, a plain text output, of an object. Like *CArchive*, *CDumpContext* doesn't do much of the work; rather, it facilitates the process. The framework for object dumping is established by *CObject*, which contains a virtual *Dump()* member function. Classes derived from *CObject* should override *Dump()* so that their significant members will be dumped. Most MFC library classes define a *Dump()* member function, and the *CDumpContext* class contains a set of *operator<<()* insertion functions for inserting the standard types (*BYTE*, *WORD*, *DWORD*, *LONG*, *CObject**, *int*, and *void**). So usually the job of a *Dump()* function is to determine which objects of the class should be dumped and which (few) can be ignored.

Dumping is considered a diagnostic feature of an MFC library application, not a standard runtime feature. Dumping is enabled only when you compile with the *_DEBUG* symbol defined. Thus, in your own classes, you should bracket your *Dump()* member function with *#ifdef* conditionals. Here is what is added to the *CIOString* class declaration to enable diagnostic dumping:

```
#ifdef _DEBUG
void Dump(CDumpContext& dc) const
{
    CObject::Dump(dc);
    m_StringArray.Dump(dc);
}
#endif
```

The MFC library includes a predefined *CDumpContext* class object called *afxDump*. In an application for Windows, *afxDump* is connected to either the debugger or the AUX output port, or it is disabled.

The other option is to create your own *CDumpContext* class object so that dump information will be routed to a file. This approach is shown in the Whitman program in Figure 17-18.

whitman.cpp

```
#include <afxwin.h>
#include <afxcoll.h>
#include "../testbed/testbed.h"
#include "../testbed/iostring.h"

//
// Dump an object
//
void tbMain(CStringArray& s, CString& title)
{
    afxTraceEnabled = TRUE;
    title = "Whitman - Dump RuntimeInfo to a File";
    CIOString cout(s);

    // create a local CIOString
    CStringArray csaArray;
    CIOString ciosWalt(csaArray);

    ciosWalt << "Centre of equal daughters, equal sons," << endl
        << "All, all alike endear'd, grown, ungrown, young or old," << endl
        << "Strong, ample, fair, enduring, capable, rich," << endl
        << "Perennial with the Earth, with Freedom, Law and Love." << endl
        << "   -- Walt Whitman, America" << endl;

    // now dump ciosWalt
    CFile file;
    CString dumpFileName = "info.dmp";
    file.Open(dumpFileName, CFile::modeCreate | CFile::modeWrite);
    CDumpContext dump(&file);
    dump.SetDepth(1);
    ciosWalt.Dump(dump);
    dump.Flush();
    file.Close();

    cout << csaArray.GetSize() << " records in ciosWalt" << endl;
    cout << "ciosWalt successfully dumped to " << dumpFileName << endl;
}
```

Figure 17-18.
The Whitman program, illustrating creation of a CDumpContext *object for dumping information to a file.*

The Whitman program first initializes a *CIOString* object named ciosWalt using text from Whitman's poem "America," and then it dumps that *CIOString* object to a file. Here is the info.dmp dump file:

```
a CIOString at $2D0C a CStringArray with 5 elements

    [0] = Centre of equal daughters, equal sons,
    [1] = All, all alike endear'd, grown, ungrown, young or old,
    [2] = Strong, ample, fair, enduring, capable, rich,
    [3] = Perennial with the Earth, with Freedom, Law and Love.
    [4] =     -- Walt Whitman, America
```

The first line of the file is produced by the *CObject* class's *Dump()* member function, which prints class names by means of *CObject*'s runtime class information facility. The remainder of the file is produced by the *CStringArray* class's *Dump()* member function, which prints each *CString* in the array preceded by the [*n*] = notation, which suggests the assignment of array members.

Tracing and Assertions

The MFC library contains several macros that can help you during development.

The *TRACE()* Macro

The simplest is *TRACE()*, which outputs its message argument to the debug window, or to the AUX port if you aren't using a debugger. *TRACE()* accepts a series of *printf()*-like arguments, so you can use it to output built-in types. To use *TRACE()*, you must compile your program with the *_DEBUG* symbol defined, and you must link to the debug versions of the MFC library classes. Details on generating debug versions of your software are best gleaned from the MFC library sample source files.

The *ASSERT()* Macro

The *ASSERT()* macro is used to state your assertions. *ASSERT()* requires a single *booleanExpression* argument, which should be *TRUE.* If the argument is *FALSE,* an assertion is generated that will stop your program and display a message showing the file name and the number of the line that contains the error. *ASSERT()*, like *TRACE()*, is active only when your program is compiled and linked for debugging. *ASSERT()* is a no-op in a nondebugging version of the executable file.

You have to be careful that your *ASSERT()* expressions don't have important side effects. The following, for example, would be a terrible assertion:

```
char *p;
ASSERT((p = (char *)malloc(100)) != NULL);
```

In the debug version of the program, the code would test the pointer returned by *malloc()*, but in the release version, *malloc()* would be skipped entirely.

There are two solutions to the problem of side effects in *ASSERT()* expressions. The first solution, the one I favor, is to avoid side effects altogether in your assertions. Here is the code rewritten in a more prudent style:

```
char *p;
p = (char *)malloc(100);
ASSERT(p != NULL);
```

The *VERIFY()* Macro

The other solution is to use the *VERIFY()* macro. *VERIFY()* is identical to *ASSERT()* during debugging, but in the release version of the program, the expression is performed even though its result is ignored. Here's how the code would be rewritten to use the *VERIFY()* macro:

```
char *p;
VERIFY((p = (char *)malloc(100)) != NULL);
```

The MFC Exception Mechanism

One of the hard parts of software development is learning to anticipate and handle all the possibilities. At all times, you have to be alert to the myriad of "what ifs" potential in the code at hand. The possibility of failure always looms: memory that cannot be allocated, files that cannot be opened, disk drives whose doors pop open, printers that wander off line.

Defensive programming is an important approach to handling failure. All the C guides have always stressed, for instance, that every return value from *malloc()* should be tested to ensure that memory has actually been allocated. But in your own work, how faithfully have you followed this advice? How often have you seen lapses in the code of your friends and coworkers? Clearly, one problem with the defensive programming approach is that it requires constant vigilance.

Defensive programming is also difficult because error indications are inconsistent. Routines that return pointers usually signal failure by returning *NULL.* Other routines signal failure by returning negative values, and still others return *TRUE* or *FALSE* on failure—but *TRUE* sometimes means OK and sometimes means failure.

Exception handling is meant to alleviate these difficulties by providing a way to specify how failures should be managed in a given region of a program. Exception handling lets you make statements such as "If there is a memory allocation failure in this part of my program, this is how it should be handled."

Exception handling is becoming a standard part of C++, but during the development of Microsoft C/C++ 7.0, the standard wasn't fully defined and finalized. The MFC library's exception scheme is thus similar to the broad outline of the proposed C++ mechanism, but it isn't identical to the final standard version of that mechanism.

The MFC exception mechanism is based on a *TRY()/CATCH()/THROW()* paradigm that uses the *CException* classes shown in Figure 17-1 on page 404. The *TRY()* macro, which is defined in the Microsoft afx.h header file, marks the start of an exception-handling block. The end of the block is marked by a series of *CATCH()* macros, each of which is used to catch a different type of exception. Here's a schematic expression of exception macro usage:

```
TRY {
    // exception block--application code goes here
} CATCH some exception type {
    // exception handler here
} AND_CATCH another exception type {
    // exception handler goes here
}
END_CATCH
```

Each *CATCH()* or *AND_CATCH()* macro requires two parameters: the name of an exception class and the name of a pointer variable. For example, this *CATCH()* statement would catch a file exception:

```
CATCH(CFileException, pFileException);
```

The parameter *CFileException* specifies the type of exception to be caught, and the *pFileException* identifier is a pointer, declared by the *CATCH()* macro, that can be used inside the handler block to get more information about the exception.

If an exception of the given type is thrown, the body of the first matching *CATCH()* will be executed. Exception matching is accomplished by means of the *CObject* class's *IsKindOf()* function. This means that catching a *CException* will catch any exception because the six specialized MFC library exception classes are "kinds of" (which means derived from) *CExceptions*. So if you catch a *CException*, be sure it will be the last catch in the chain.

The C/C++ 7.0 exception facility uses the *setjmp()/longjmp()* subroutines from the C library. Thus, whenever an exception occurs, a transfer of control bypasses the usual flow-of-control structures. This means that the usual object cleanup that is automatically wired into your program by the compiler is bypassed. If you are counting on destructors to perform vital tasks, or if you are building an application that must be leakproof (no loss of dynamically allocated memory), you must be careful with exceptions. Basically, you need to have an exception handler for every context that creates local or heap objects whose destructors must be called on procedure exit. This is illustrated by the *leaky()* procedure:

```
leaky()
{
    char *p = new char[100];
    risky();
    delete p;
}
```

leaky() tries to be a well-behaved function by deallocating its dynamically allocated memory. But if *risky()* triggers an exception, the last statement in *leaky()* will be bypassed and 100 bytes of memory will never be released. The solution is to place a *TRY()* block around *risky()* to catch any exception it generates. If an exception is caught, the handler can perform the cleanup and then pass the exception along:

```
leaky()
{
    char *p = new char[100];
    TRY {
        risky();
    } CATCH(CException, pExcept) {
        delete p;
        THROW(pExcept);
    } END_CATCH
    delete p;
}
```

Figure 17-19 shows a version of the Whitman application, Whitman2, that has been enhanced with exception handling.

whitman2.cpp

```
#include <afxwin.h>
#include <afxcoll.h>
#include "../testbed/testbed.h"
#include "../testbed/iostring.h"

//
// dump an object
//
void tbMain(CStringArray& s, CString& title)
{
    title = "Whitman - Dump RuntimeInfo to a File";
    CIOString cout(s);
    CString dumpFileName = "info.dmp";

    TRY {
        // create a local CIOString
        CStringArray csaArray;
        CIOString ciosWalt(csaArray);

        ciosWalt
            << "Centre of equal daughters, equal sons," << endl
            << "All, all alike endear'd, grown, ungrown, young or
               old," << endl
            << "Strong, ample, fair, enduring, capable, rich," << endl
            << "Perennial with the Earth, with Freedom, Law and Love."
               << endl
            << "   -- Walt Whitman, America" << endl;
```

Figure 17-19. *(continued)*
The Whitman2 program, illustrating exception handling.

Figure 17-19. *continued*

```
        // now dump ciosWalt
        CFile file;
        CFileException e;
        if (!file.Open(dumpFileName, CFile::modeCreate | CFile::modeWrite,
            &e)) THROW(&e);
        CDumpContext dump(&file);
        dump.SetDepth(1);
        ciosWalt.Dump(dump);
        dump.Flush();
        file.Close();

        cout << csaArray.GetSize() << " records in ciosWalt" << endl;
        cout << "ciosWalt successfully dumped to " << dumpFileName << endl;
    }
    CATCH(CFileException, theException) {
        cout << "File Exception: Can't open " << dumpFileName << endl;
        cout << "Error code " << theException->m_cause << endl;
    }
    AND_CATCH(CMemoryException, theException) {
        cout << "Memory Exception: Out of memory" << endl;
    }
    AND_CATCH(CException, theException) {
        cout << "Unexpected, unknown exception" << endl;
    }
    END_CATCH
}
```

One unusual aspect of this example is that the most likely exception is generated manually after a file open failure. Unlike many MFC library classes, which will automatically generate exceptions when errors occur, the *CFile* class has been designed to allow more manual control. If you pass a *CFileException* pointer to *Open()* and an open failure occurs, *Open()* will fill in the exception information but will refrain from throwing the exception. You are free to use the exception object solely for acquiring status information from *Open()*, or you can throw the exception object as the Whitman2 application does.

In a small program such as Whitman2, exception handling is more bother than ordinary runtime error checking would be, but in larger works, exception handling provides a good return on investment.

18

MFC Library String, Time, and Collection Classes

The MFC library facilities we looked at in the previous chapter are powerful and useful, but they probably aren't what springs to mind when you think of using a C++ class library. My guess is that you think about how a class library might save you from writing your own string class or about how you don't want to face another doubly linked list implementation. Such topics are the subject of this chapter.

The *CString* Class

Programmers who migrate to C from more protective languages such as Pascal can feel let down by C's handling of character strings. Part of the disappointment probably comes from how little C does for strings. For example, C doesn't automatically maintain the storage for a string.

But the shock migrating programmers often feel comes from the sheer danger. C doesn't provide any safeguards. Strings overflow routinely in C programs, causing mysterious crashes in MS-DOS and UAEs in Windows. C's cavalier string handling even played a central role in the Internet worm fiasco. Native C++ isn't any better than C when it comes to string handling—but C++ does let you create a string class to address the shortcomings of the native string support.

The MFC library contains a safe, reliable, and convenient string class called *CString*. It lets you compare strings using standard comparison operators and concatenate or lengthen strings without worrying about memory allocation; and *CString* contains some substring functions that remind me of the convenient substring operations found in Basic.

The declarations in Figure 18-1, which is a condensed excerpt from the Microsoft afx.h header file, give you an idea of the major facilities of the *CString* class.

```
// construction
CString();
CString(const CString& stringSrc);
CString(char ch, int nRepeat = 1);
CString(const char* psz);
CString(const char* pch, int nLength);

// single character access
char GetAt(int nIndex) const;                  // 0-based indexing
char operator[](int nIndex) const;             // same as GetAt
void SetAt(int nIndex, char ch);

// char* access
operator const char*() const;                  // as a C string

// utilities
void Empty();                                  // empty the buffer
BOOL IsEmpty() const;                          // true if empty

// assignment and concatenation operator member functions
const CString& operator=(CompatType);          // assignment
const CString& operator+=(CompatType);         // concatenation

// substring extraction
CString Mid(int nFirst, int nCount) const;
CString Mid(int nFirst) const;
CString Left(int nCount) const;
CString Right(int nCount) const;

// conventional "C" string library analogs
int GetLength() const;                                  // like "C" strlen
int Compare(const char* psz) const;                     // like "C" strcmp
int CompareNoCase(const char* psz) const;               // like "C" stricmp
int Collate(const char* psz) const;                     // like "C" strcoll
CString SpanIncluding(const char* pszCharSet) const;    // like "C" strspn
CString SpanExcluding(const char* pszCharSet) const;    // like "C" strcspn
void MakeUpper();                                       // like "C" strupr
void MakeLower();                                       // like "C" strlwr
void MakeReverse();                                     // like "C" strrev
int Find(char ch) const;                                // like "C" strchr
int ReverseFind(char ch) const;                         // like "C" strrchr
int FindOneOf(const char* pszCharSet) const;            // like "C" strpbrk
int Find(const char* pszSub) const;                     // like "C" strstr

// Windows support (available only in programs for Windows)
BOOL LoadString(UINT nID);   // load from string resource
```

Figure 18-1.
Major facilities of the MFC library's CString *class.*

(continued)

Figure 18-1. *continued*

```
void AnsiToOem();
void OemToAnsi();

// see afx.h for other allowed operands
CString operator+(CompatType, CompatType);
BOOL operator==(CompareType, CompareType);
BOOL operator!=(CompareType, CompareType);
BOOL operator<(CompareType, CompareType);
BOOL operator>(CompareType, CompareType);
BOOL operator<=(CompareType, CompareType);
BOOL operator>=(CompareType, CompareType);
friend CArchive& operator<<(CArchive& ar, const CString& string);
friend CArchive& operator>>(CArchive& ar, CString& string);
friend CDumpContext& operator<<(CDumpContext&, const CString& string);
```

CompatType means either a *const CString&*, a *const char **, or a *char type*, and *CompareType* means either a *const CString&* or a *const char **. For the *operator+()* function, at least one operand must be a *const CString&*.

You'll find more detailed information on the MFC library's *CString* class in the afx.h header file and in the MFC library documentation. In the condensed version above, you'll notice that most of the *CString* facilities are member functions, except for the addition, comparison, and I/O operator functions at the end of the list.

Unlike most MFC library classes, *CString* isn't derived from *CObject*—primarily because *CString* is designed, first and foremost, for performance. It contains no virtual functions and no overhead members such as the *CObject* members that manage run-time class information facilities. This is a trade-off that most performance-minded programmers will appreciate. *CString* performance not only equals or exceeds the performance of the conventional C string library but does it with the safety and convenience of C++. Exceeds? Yes, sometimes. The *CString* class maintains the string's length in a member variable. This makes some *CString* operations more efficient than equivalent C string operations. For example, the C library's *strcat()* requires a call to *strlen()* whereas the equivalent *CString operator+=(const char *)* operator function can simply use the stored lengths.

It's easy to use a *CString* object with a traditional function that expects a character pointer because the *CString* class contains an *operator const char *() const* member function. This implies that *CString* objects can be used only with functions that don't modify the strings they use, and it also implies that you might need to do some work to make such functions "*const* correct." For example, you can use a *CString* to hold the name of a directory that you plan to pass to *chdir()* because *chdir()*'s prototype (from direct.h) is

```
int __cdecl chdir(const char *); // const char*--OK for CString
```

However, you can't use a *CString* object to store a directory name returned by *getcwd()* because *getcwd()* modifies its string. You can easily tell that *getcwd()* can't use a *CString* argument because its function prototype in direct.h is

```
char * __cdecl getcwd(char *, int); // char* parameter--no good
                                    //  for CString
```

Note that the C 7.0 header files are *const* correct for *char** arguments; C library routines that don't modify their *char** string arguments are always declared to have a *const char ** parameter.

We can use *CString* objects with the iostream library, but that requires a modicum of effort and understanding, particularly for extraction. Insertion is easy. Because *CString* contains a built-in conversion to *const char **, we can easily output *CString* objects using the iostream library:

```
include <iostream.h>
#define _DOS
#include <afx.h>

void main()
{
    CString S("Hello IOstreams!");
    cout << S << endl;
}
```

Extraction is a bit harder. Because the iostream library doesn't contain an extraction operator for a *CString*, we need to build our own. The key is to temporarily take over the buffer of a *CString* object. Then we can use standard iostream extraction operators to fill the *CString* object's buffer, subsequently returning the buffer to the *CString* object.

```
istream& operator>>(istream& is, CString& s)
{
    // extract safely into at least 255-character buffer
    is >> setw(255) >> s.GetBuffer(255);
    s.ReleaseBuffer();
    return is;
}
```

Notice that the low-level buffering facilities of the *CString* class, which are used in our iostream extraction operator above, are not mentioned in Figure 18-1. If you need to use *CString*'s low-level buffering facilities in your own code, study the MFC library reference manual and the MFC library source code to learn, in detail, how these facilities work.

Although the MFC library's *CString* class contains more facilities and features than I would have designed into a string class for my own needs, it lacks one feature I consider fundamental—sequential character-by-character access. When I am using strings in my own work, I often simply want to get the next unread character. To meet this need, I derived the *CStringStream* class from *CString*. Its only innovations are the *Get()*, *Put()*, and *Rewind()* member functions. And *Put()* is just a synonym for the existing *operator+=(char ch)* member function, which adds a character to the end of a *CString*.

Figure 18-2 shows the code for the *CStringStream* class.

```
//
// a CString with serial Get() and Put() routines
//
class CStringStream : public CString {
    public:
        // repeat the CString constructors to retain full flexibility
        CStringStream() :
            m_nGetIndex(0) {}
        CStringStream(const CString& stringSrc) :
            m_nGetIndex(0), CString(stringSrc) {}
        CStringStream(char ch, int nRepeat = 1) :
            m_nGetIndex(0), CString(ch, nRepeat) {}
        CStringStream(const char* psz) :
            m_nGetIndex(0), CString(psz) {}
        CStringStream(const char* pch, int nLength) :
            m_nGetIndex(0), CString(pch, nLength) {}
#ifdef _NEARDATA
        // Additional versions for far string data
        CStringStream(const char FAR* lpsz) :
            m_nGetIndex(0), CString(lpsz) {}
        CStringStream(const char FAR* lpch, int nLength) :
            m_nGetIndex(0), CString(lpch, nLength) {}
#endif
        char Get();                                  // get next character
        void Rewind() { m_nGetIndex = 0; }           // reset Get() index
        void Put(char ch) { *this += ch; }           // add to end of string
    protected:
        int m_nGetIndex;                             // Get() index
};

char CStringStream::Get()
{
    if (m_nGetIndex < m_nDataLength)
        return m_pchData[m_nGetIndex++];
    else
        return 0;
}
```

Figure 18-2.
The CStringStream *class derived from* CString.

In order to retain the flexibility of the *CString* class, I had to repeat all of its constructors. This is easy because you can simply pick up the text of the constructors from afx.h and then make small editing changes. In order to create the *CStringStream* class, I needed to browse through the *CString* source so that I understood how its *m_nDataLength* member variable was used. I noted that *m_nDataLength* was protected, which meant that it was fair game for use in a derived class, but I needed to investigate the base class source to be sure that I used the member variable properly in *CStringStream*.

CTime and CTimeSpan

Certain difficult features of the standard C library, such as its notorious *printf()* routine, eventually become good friends, but other capabilities are forever strangers. Actually, "acquaintances" is probably a better word for the C library's time and date facilities: I've encountered them many times, but we've never become friends. The C library's time and date facilities remain unfamiliar to most of us, partly because we don't find many occasions for their routine use but mostly because there are so many of them. C/C++ 7.0's C library contains all the time- and date-related data structures and subroutines shown in this by no means complete list.

Typedef	**Procedures**	**Procedures**
time_t	*time()*	*clock()*
	difftime()	*asctime()*
Structs	*ctime()*	*mktime()*
tm	*localtime()*	*gmtime()*
_dosdate_t	*strftime()*	*_dos_getftime()*
_dostime_t	*_tzset()*	*_dos_setftime()*
	_strdate()	*_strtime()*
	_dos_getdate()	*_dos_gettime()*
	_dos_setdate()	*_dos_settime()*
	_utime()	*_ftime()*

The MFC library has collected most of this list's functionality into the single, coherent *CTime* class whose constructors and member functions are shown in Figure 18-3.

```
// constructors
CTime();
CTime(time_t time);
CTime(int nYear, int nMonth, int nDay, int nHour, int nMin, int nSec);
CTime(WORD wDosDate, WORD wDosTime);
CTime(const CTime& timeSrc);

// assignment
const CTime& operator=(const CTime& timeSrc);
const CTime& operator=(time_t t);
```

Figure 18-3.
CTime *constructors and other member functions.*

(continued)

Figure 18-3. *continued*

```
// output functions
time_t GetTime() const;
int GetYear() const;              // 1900 ...
int GetMonth() const;             // month of year (1 = Jan)
int GetDay() const;               // day of month 1..31
int GetHour() const;              // 0..23
int GetMinute() const;            // 0..59
int GetSecond() const;            // 0..59
int GetDayOfWeek() const;         // 1=Sun, 2=Mon, ..., 7=Sat

// math operations
CTimeSpan operator-(CTime time) const;
CTime operator-(CTimeSpan timeSpan) const;
CTime operator+(CTimeSpan timeSpan) const;
const CTime& operator+=(CTimeSpan timeSpan);
const CTime& operator-=(CTimeSpan timeSpan);

// comparison operators ==, !=, <, >, <=, >=

// formatting using "C" strftime
CString   Format(const char* pFormat);
CString   FormatGmt(const char* pFormat);
```

The *CTime* comparison operators require two *CTime* operands and return a *BOOL*.

CTime lets you manage time and date information in an orderly and convenient format. You can easily use the *CTime* constructors to create *CTime* objects from *time_t* values (in Microsoft C 7.0, *time_t* is the number of elapsed seconds since midnight, December 31, 1899); from individual year, month, day, hour, minute, and second values; and from the format used to time- and date-stamp MS-DOS files. *CTime* has member functions that return the individual elements (hours, minutes, and so forth) in a *CTime* object and operator functions for comparison and arithmetic.

It's a good idea to use one of the argument-taking constructors to create a *CTime* object that is initialized to a specific time. Somewhat surprisingly, there isn't a *CTime* constructor that initializes the *CTime* object to the current time. However, such an initialization is easy to come up with:

```
CTime now(CTime::GetCurrentTime());
```

The *CTimeSpan* Class

Adding two *CTime* objects or subtracting one from another produces a *CTimeSpan* object. A *CTimeSpan* object stores intervals, not absolute times, so it doesn't have member functions that speak to absolute time. *CTimeSpan* makes it easy to calculate how many days apart two dates are. The major facilities of the *CTimeSpan* class are shown in Figure 18-4 on the next page.

```
// constructors
CTimeSpan();
CTimeSpan(time_t time);
CTimeSpan(LONG lDays, int nHours, int nMins, int nSecs);
CTimeSpan(const CTimeSpan& timeSpanSrc);

// assignment
const CTimeSpan& operator=(const CTimeSpan& timeSpanSrc);

// output functions
LONG GetDays() const;                    // total number of days
LONG GetTotalHours() const;
int  GetHours() const;                   // 0..23
LONG GetTotalMinutes() const;
int  GetMinutes() const;                 // 0..59
LONG GetTotalSeconds() const;
int  GetSeconds() const;                 // 0..59

// math operators -, +, +=, -=

// comparison operators ==, !=, <, >, <=, >=

// formatting using "C" strftime
CString   Format(const char* pFormat);
```

Figure 18-4.
CTimeSpan *constructors and output member functions, with math, comparison, and formatting functions sketched in.*

The *CTimeSpan* math operator functions require two *CTimeSpan* operands. The add and subtract operator functions return a *CTimeSpan* object; the assign sum and assign difference operator functions return a *const CTimeSpan&*.

Example: The Kids Program

Both *CTime* and *CTimeSpan* objects are illustrated by the Kids program shown in Figure 18-5.

```
#include <afxwin.h>
#include <afxcoll.h>
#include "../testbed/testbed.h"
#include "../testbed/iostring.h"

CIOString& operator<<(CIOString& cout, CTime& t);
```

Figure 18-5. *(continued)*
The Kids program shows the birthdates of Kari and Arli, followed by the difference in their ages.

Figure 18-5. *continued*

```
void tbMain(CStringArray &s, CString& title)
{
    title = "Kari and Arli";
    CIOString cout(s);

    CTime Kari(1980, 2, 13, 3, 30, 0); // Born Feb 13, 1980 at 3:30 am
    CTime Arli(1982, 4, 26, 14, 35, 0);// Born Apr 26, 1982 at 2:35 pm

    cout << "Kari was born " << Kari << endl;
    cout << "Arli was born " << Arli << endl;
    cout << endl;

    // note that Arli-Kari is a CTimeSpan object, not a CTime object
    cout << "Kari is "
        << (Arli-Kari).GetDays()
        << " days older than Arli."
        << endl;
}

//
// CTime inserter
//
CIOString& operator<<(CIOString& cout, CTime& t)
{
    static char *Days[8] = {
        "xxx", "Mon", "Tue", "Wed",
        "Thu", "Fri", "Sat", "Sun" };
    static char *Months[13] = {
        "yyy", "Jan", "Feb", "Mar", "Apr", "May", "Jun",
        "Jul", "Aug", "Sep", "Oct", "Nov", "Dec" };

    cout << setw(2) << t.GetHour() << ":"
        << setfill('0')
        << setw(2) << t.GetMinute() << ":"
        << setw(2) << t.GetSecond() << " "
        << setfill(' ')       << Days[t.GetDayOfWeek()] << " "
        << Months[t.GetMonth()] << " "
        << setw(2) << t.GetDay() << ", "
        << t.GetYear();
    return cout;
}
```

Kids creates two *CTime* objects that are initialized with the birthdates of my daughters. The program uses a *CTime* inserter to print the birthdates, and then it subtracts one *CTime* object from the other to produce a *CTimeSpan* object representing the age difference. (Kari, by the way, is very proud of the difference, 803 days.) The Kids application output is shown in Figure 18-6 on the next page.

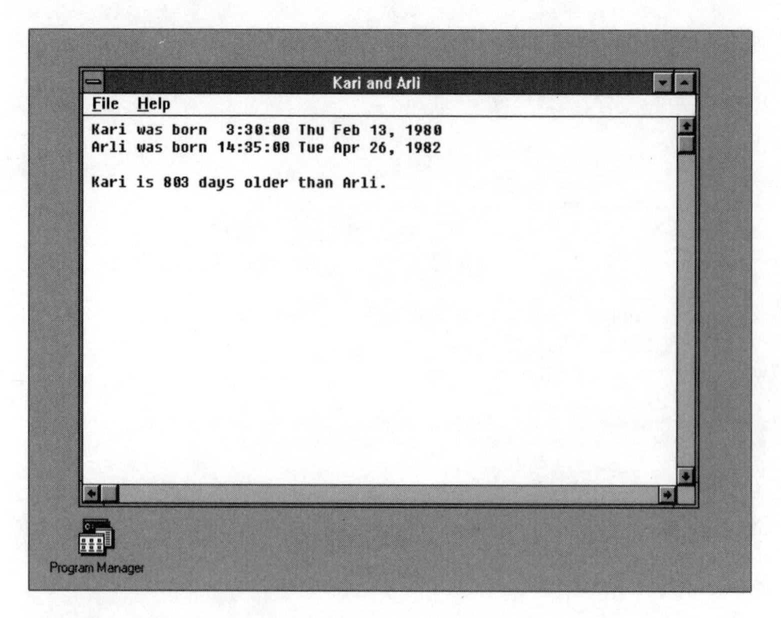

Figure 18-6.
The Kids program output screen.

Collections

Autographs, baseball cards, shocking-pink ponies, marbles, stamps, albums, recipes, CDs, dreams. We all collect things, and sometimes we need to use a computer to keep track of our collections. It's hard to manage collections in C because the language doesn't encourage us to separate code for managing the collection from code that addresses the things that are in the collection. But C++ objects make it easy to separate operations pertaining to a collection from operations that pertain to the individual elements of the collection. If we have a list of stamps in a stamp collection, list operations would be activities such as adding and removing items and searching for a particular item. Operations on individual stamps might include printing the value of a stamp and showing its place of origin.

The MFC class library has a number of useful collection facilities. Its simple but effective classes don't try to address all of your needs; instead, they serve as bases for further specialization. If you need a stack, for example, you can easily construct one from the supplied collection classes.

Figure 18-7 lists the MFC library collection classes by types.

The arrays are similar to but more flexible than the built-in array type. The lists are doubly linked lists. The maps relate one value to another. All programs that use MFC library collection classes should include the file afxcoll.h. See afxcoll.h and the MFC library reference manuals for detail beyond the summaries excerpted here.

Arrays	*Lists*	*Maps*
CByteArray	*CObList*	*CMapWordToPtr*
CWordArray	*CPtrList*	*CMapPtrToWord*
CDWordArray	*CStringList*	*CMapWordToOb*
CObArray		*CMapPtrToPtr* *CMapStringToPtr*
CPtrArray		*CMapStringToOb*
CStringArray		*CMapStringToString*

Figure 18-7.
The MFC library collection classes.

In the collection class names, *Byte*, *Word*, and *DWord* refer to the MFC library *BYTE*, *WORD*, and *DWORD* data types, *Ob* refers to a *CObject** pointer, *Ptr* refers to a *void** pointer, and *String* refers to a *CString* object. All collections except those that store *void** pointers are serializable.

MFC Library Array Collection Classes

The MFC library array collection classes let you create array data structures that are more flexible than the built-in array type. An MFC library array easily grows and shrinks, you can insert and delete items from the array, you can easily serialize it (unless it's a *CPtrArray*), and you can merge it with another MFC library array. If none of these advanced features are helpful to you, you should probably stick to ordinary C/C++ arrays.

MFC library arrays support the operations shown for the *CByteArray* class in Figure 18-8. Substitute *CObject**, *void**, *CString*, *WORD*, or *DWORD* for *BYTE* to see the operations for the other MFC library array collection classes.

```
// accessing elements
BYTE     GetAt(int nIndex) const;
void     SetAt(int nIndex, BYTE newElement);
BYTE&    ElementAt(int nIndex);

// accessing elements using subscript notation
BYTE     operator[](int nIndex) const;
BYTE&    operator[](int nIndex);

// adding and removing elements
int      Add(BYTE newElement);
void     SetAtGrow(int nIndex, BYTE newElement);
```

Figure 18-8.
MFC library CByteArray *class operations.*

(continued)

Figure 18-8. *continued*

```
void        InsertAt(int nIndex, BYTE newElement, int nCount = 1);
void        InsertAt(int nStartIndex, CByteArray* pNewArray);
void        RemoveAt(int nIndex, int nCount = 1);

// attributes and operations
int         GetSize() const;
int         GetUpperBound() const;
void        SetSize(int nNewSize, int nGrowBy = -1);
void        FreeExtra();
void        RemoveAll();
```

You can access elements of an array using the *GetAt()* and *SetAt()* member functions or using convenient *operator[]()* member functions. You can add items to an array by means of the *Add()*, *SetAtGrow()*, or *InsertAt()* member functions. *Add()* adds an element at the end, *SetAtGrow()* assigns a value to a specific element of the array, growing the array if necessary, and *InsertAt()* makes room for a new element by moving the others up one position before adding the new element.

The *CIOString* class we saw in Chapter 15 provides us with a good example of building upon an MFC library array class. The most important member of the *CIOString* class is a *CStringArray* object. Because the *CStringArray* object takes care of all the storage concerns, the *CIOString* class is relatively simple and able to provide a significant amount of functionality in little more than 100 lines of code. That density of expression is achieved by subcontracting the job, primarily to the *CStringArray* class.

MFC Library List Collection Classes

The MFC library's three list collection classes let you create doubly linked list data structures. The list members are either generic (*void**) pointers, *CObject** pointers, or *CString*s. The MFC library lists support the operations shown for the *CObList* class in Figure 18-9. Substitute *void** or *CString* for *CObject** to see the operations for the other MFC library list collection classes.

```
// accessing elements
CObject*& GetHead();
CObject*  GetHead() const;
CObject*& GetTail();
CObject*  GetTail() const;
CObject*& GetAt(POSITION position);
CObject*  GetAt(POSITION position) const;
void      SetAt(POSITION pos, CObject* pNewElement);
```

Figure 18-9. (continued)
MFC library CObList *class operations.*

Figure 18-9. *continued*

```
// adding elements
POSITION  AddHead(CObject* pNewElement);
POSITION  AddTail(CObject* pNewElement);
void      AddHead(CObList* pNewList);
void      AddTail(CObList* pNewList);
POSITION  InsertBefore(POSITION position, CObject* pNewElement);
POSITION  InsertAfter(POSITION position, CObject* pNewElement);

// removing elements
CObject*  RemoveHead();
CObject*  RemoveTail();
void      RemoveAll();
void      RemoveAt(POSITION position);

// iteration
POSITION  GetHeadPosition() const;
POSITION  GetTailPosition() const;
CObject*& GetNext(POSITION& rPosition);       // return *Position++
CObject*  GetNext(POSITION& rPosition) const; // return *Position++
CObject*& GetPrev(POSITION& rPosition);       // return *Position--
CObject*  GetPrev(POSITION& rPosition) const; // return *Position--

// helper functions (note: O(n) speed);
POSITION  Find(CObject* searchValue, POSITION startAfter = NULL) const;
POSITION  FindIndex(int nIndex) const;

// attributes
int       GetCount() const;
BOOL      IsEmpty() const;
```

Many of the list access functions use the *POSITION* data type, which is defined in afx.h as a *void** pointer. Treat *POSITION*s as you would Windows HANDLEs; don't pass a *POSITION* to a list function unless you have previously been handed that position by a list function.

List serialization

Serialization often has an impact on class design because it breaks class initialization into two phases. In the first phase, an empty object is created by invocation of the default constructor. In the second, the contents of the object are loaded from disk. Because support for serialization requires that construction not do very much, we're forced to delay much of the work that construction might do until after the constructor has terminated.

All of the MFC library collection classes have constructors that create empty collection objects. This is often what you want, and it works well with the demands of serialization, but sometimes it is nice to be able to create a collection object that is ready to use. To gratify that occasional wish, I created the *CIStringList* class, an initialized string list class. It has a constructor that accepts a pointer to an array of C strings that are used to initialize the list:

```
class CIStringList : public CStringList {
    DECLARE_SERIAL(CIStringList);
public:
    CIStringList() { }                    // default constructor
    CIStringList(char *p[], int n);
};
```

The only new member of the *CIStringList* class is the initializing constructor:

```
CIStringList::CIStringList(char *p[], int n)
{
    while(n--)
        AddHead(p[n]);
}
```

The constructor works backward through the list of C strings, but adding them to the head of the list preserves the order. Here's one way in which you might use a *CIStringList*:

```
char *s[] = {
    "First", "Second", "Third" };

CIStringList islCounts(s, sizeof(s)/sizeof(char*));
```

Lists are designed for sequential access. Usually you start at either the head or the tail and move through the list one element at a time. The basic technique with an MFC list is to use the *GetHeadPosition()* or *GetTailPosition()* member function to get a pointer to one end and then use *GetNext()* or *GetPrev()* to move through the list. Both the *GetNext()* and the *GetPrev()* member functions require a *POSITION* pointer, which is updated at each invocation to point at the next or the previous element of the list. The *GetNext()* member function's job is to "Get the object at the current position, and then move the position pointer to the Next object in the list." Similarly, *GetPrev()* means "Get the object at the current position, and then move to the Previous object." Here is a way to use *GetHeadPosition()* and *GetNext()* to print all the members of a *CIStringList* object:

```
POSITION pos = islCounts.GetHeadPosition();
while(pos)
    puts(islCounts.GetNext(pos));
```

The key to understanding this idiom is remembering that *GetNext()* performs two chores. One chore is returning a reference to the *CString* that *pos* initially points at; the other is changing *pos* (a reference argument) to point at the next element in the list. *GetNext()* assigns the value *NULL* to *pos* when the end of the list is encountered, which terminates the loop.

MFC Library Map Collection Classes

The MFC library's map collection classes let you create various types of associations between keys and values. In an employee database, for instance, you might have a map between an employee identification number and an employee record. In a hypertext system, you might have a map that associates a word with its definition. If you have a mathematics or computer science background, you might think of a map as a sparse array, an array in which only the occupied elements are allocated.

The MFC library maps support the fundamental operations shown for the *CMapWordToOb* class in Figure 18-10. Substitute the appropriate data type for *WORD* and *CObject** to see the operations for the other MFC map collection classes.

```
// looking up
BOOL       Lookup(WORD key, CObject*& rValue) const;

// adding a new (key and value) pair
void       SetAt(WORD key, CObject* newValue);

// looking up and adding if not there
CObject*& operator[](WORD key);

// removing existing (key and value) pair
BOOL       RemoveKey(WORD key);
void       RemoveAll();

// iterating all (key and value) pairs
POSITION  GetStartPosition() const;
void       GetNextAssoc(POSITION& rNxt, WORD& rKey, CObject*& rVal) const;

// attributes
int        GetCount() const;
BOOL       IsEmpty() const;
```

Figure 18-10.
MFC library CMapWordToOb class operations.

Once a map has been created, associations can be added using either the *AddAt()* or the *operator[]()* member function. You can follow (look up) an association using the *Lookup()* or the *operator[]()* member function. Although the customary use of a map is to follow a single association, you can also browse through an entire map using the *GetStartPosition()* and *GetNextAssoc()* member functions, which are analogous to the *GetHeadPosition()* and *GetNext()* member functions of the list collection classes. The main difference between a list and a map is sequence. You can control the order of elements in a list, but the key-value associations in a map don't have a specified order.

A simple program named Map that demonstrates use of a *CMapStringToOb* map class is shown in Figure 18-11. The program outlines how you might use a map object to implement a flexible command interpreter. When you type in a command name, the map is used to look up a command object, and then the *Execute()* member function of the specified command object is invoked. In this example program, all the command objects are of the same class, but you could alternatively use a hierarchy of derived types and polymorphism to create a more powerful system.

map.h

```
// CTheApp:
class CTheApp : public CWinApp
{
public:
    BOOL InitInstance();
};

//
// The main window, a dialog box
//

class CMapDialog : public CModalDialog {
    class CCmdDialog;
    friend CCmdDialog;
public:
    CMapDialog(CWnd* pWndParent)
        : CModalDialog("MapDialog", pWndParent)
    { }

    BOOL OnInitDialog();
    afx_msg void OnCMD();          // a command has been entered
    afx_msg void OnShowCmds();     // the "Cmds..." button has been pressed

    // build an edit box object for the command-entry edit control
    CEdit& EditBox() { return *(CEdit*)GetDlgItem(IDC_CMD); }

    DECLARE_MESSAGE_MAP()

protected:
    CMapStringToOb m_Map;
};

//
// Dialog box to list the commands
//

class CCmdDialog : public CModalDialog {
public:
    CCmdDialog(CMapDialog* pWndParent) :
```

Figure 18-11. *(continued)*

The Map program source files: map.h, map.cpp, resource.h, and map.rc.

Figure 18-11. *continued*

```
        CModalDialog("CmdDialog", pWndParent),
        m_pMapDialog(pWndParent)
    { }

    BOOL OnInitDialog();
    afx_msg void OnOK();

    CListBox& ListBox() { return *(CListBox*)GetDlgItem(IDC_CMDLIST); }

    DECLARE_MESSAGE_MAP()

protected:
    CMapDialog *m_pMapDialog;
};

//
// 'Action' objects
//
class CAction : public CObject {
    DECLARE_DYNAMIC(CAction)
    public:
        CAction(const char *s) : m_Str(s) {}
        const char* Execute() { return m_Str; }
    protected:
        CString m_Str;
};
```

map.cpp

```
#include <afxwin.h>
#include <afxcoll.h>

#include "resource.h"
#include "map.h"

// various weather reports
CAction Forecast("Milder tomorrow.");
CAction Rain("None in the forecast.");
CAction Snow("None in the forecast.");
CAction FiveDays("Mild and dry.");
CAction Wind("NNW at 5 miles per hour.");
CAction Pressure("30.15 and falling.");
CAction Temp("84 Fahrenheit.");
CAction SunRise("6:18 A.M.");
CAction SunSet("8:40 P.M.");
CAction Waves("Swells below normal.");
CAction Default("Unrecognized command.");
```

(continued)

Figure 18-11. *continued*

```
// CTheApp

CTheApp theApp;

// InitInstance:
BOOL CTheApp::InitInstance()
{
    m_pMainWnd=0;

    CMapDialog mapdlg(NULL);
    mapdlg.DoModal();

    ::PostQuitMessage(0);
    return TRUE;
}

BEGIN_MESSAGE_MAP(CMapDialog, CModalDialog)
    ON_COMMAND(IDOK, OnCMD)
    ON_COMMAND(IDC_SHOWCMDS, OnShowCmds)
    ON_COMMAND(IDC_QUIT, OnOK)
END_MESSAGE_MAP()

IMPLEMENT_DYNAMIC(CAction, CObject)

BOOL CMapDialog::OnInitDialog()
{
    if (!CModalDialog::OnInitDialog())
        return FALSE;

    SetCtlBkColor(::GetSysColor(COLOR_WINDOW));

    // map commands to CAction objects
    m_Map.SetAt("forecast", &Forecast);
    m_Map.SetAt("rain", &Rain);
    m_Map.SetAt("snow", &Snow);
    m_Map.SetAt("5 days", &FiveDays);
    m_Map.SetAt("five days", &FiveDays);
    m_Map.SetAt("wind", &Wind);
    m_Map.SetAt("pressure", &Pressure);
    m_Map.SetAt("temp", &Temp);
    m_Map.SetAt("temperature", &Temp);
    m_Map.SetAt("sunrise", &SunRise);
    m_Map.SetAt("sunset", &SunSet);
    m_Map.SetAt("waves", &Waves);
    m_Map.SetAt("ocean", &Waves);

    EditBox().SetSel(0, -1);      // select all
    EditBox().Clear();            // clear selection
    SetDlgItemText(IDC_ACTION, "");
    return TRUE;
}
```

(continued)

Figure 18-11. *continued*

```
void CMapDialog::OnCMD()
{
    char buf[128];
    CObject *pAction;

    buf[EditBox().GetLine(0, buf, sizeof(buf))] = 0;
    EditBox().SetSel(0, -1);        // select all
    EditBox().Clear();              // clear selection

    if (m_Map.Lookup(buf, pAction))
        SetDlgItemText(IDC_ACTION, ((CAction *)pAction)->Execute());
    else
        SetDlgItemText(IDC_ACTION, ::Default.Execute());
}

void CMapDialog::OnShowCmds()
{
    CCmdDialog cmddialog(this);
    cmddialog.DoModal();
    GotoDlgCtrl(GetDlgItem(IDC_CMD));
}

BEGIN_MESSAGE_MAP(CCmdDialog, CModalDialog)
    ON_COMMAND(IDOK, OnOK)
    ON_LBN_DBLCLK(IDC_CMDLIST, OnOK)
END_MESSAGE_MAP()

void CCmdDialog::OnOK()
{
    int i = ListBox().GetCurSel();
    if (i != LB_ERR) {
        char *s = new char[ListBox().GetTextLen(i)+1];
        ListBox().GetText(i, s);
        m_pMapDialog->EditBox().SetWindowText(s);
        delete s;
    }
    CModalDialog::OnOK();
}

BOOL CCmdDialog::OnInitDialog()
{
    if (!CModalDialog::OnInitDialog())
        return FALSE;

    SetCtlBkColor(::GetSysColor(COLOR_WINDOW));

    POSITION pos;
    CString key;
    CObject *val;
```

(continued)

Figure 18-11. *continued*

```
    for(pos = m_pMapDialog->m_Map.GetStartPosition(); pos != NULL; ) {
        m_pMapDialog->m_Map.GetNextAssoc(pos, key, val);
        ListBox().AddString(key);
    }

    return TRUE;
}
```

resource.h

```
// MapDialog IDs
#define IDC_CMD          101  // command entry edit control
#define IDC_ACTION       102  // command display static control
#define IDC_SHOWCMDS     103  // button to invoke CmdDialog
#define IDC_QUIT         104  // Quit button

// CmdDialog IDs
#define IDC_CMDLIST      201  // list box control
```

map.rc

```
#include <windows.h>
#include <afxres.h>
#include "resource.h"

AFX_IDI_STD_FRAME ICON map.ico

MapDialog DIALOG 47, 59, 157, 70
CAPTION "M  A  P"
STYLE DS_MODALFRAME | WS_CAPTION | WS_SYSMENU
BEGIN
    EDITTEXT IDC_CMD,        8, 16, 100, 12
    LTEXT "", IDC_ACTION,    9, 50,  99, 11
    GROUPBOX "Command", -1, 4,  4, 110, 28
    GROUPBOX "Action", -1,  4, 38, 109, 28
    PUSHBUTTON "Cmds...", IDC_SHOWCMDS, 121, 31, 32, 14
    PUSHBUTTON "Quit",    IDC_QUIT,     121, 51, 32, 14
END

CmdDialog DIALOG 18, 18, 142, 92
CAPTION "Commands"
STYLE DS_MODALFRAME | WS_POPUP | WS_CAPTION | WS_SYSMENU
BEGIN
    LISTBOX IDC_CMDLIST,   13, 10, 114, 61, WS_VSCROLL | LBS_SORT
    PUSHBUTTON "OK", IDOK, 92, 72,  35, 14, WS_TABSTOP
END
```

At the bottom of the map.h file is the declaration of the *CAction* class, a repository for a weather message stored in a *CString* object. In the map.cpp file, the program declares a set of *CAction* objects, and then the *OnInitDialog()* function associates each *CAction* object with a text string using a *CMapStringToOb* map object. The edit box (titled "Command") in the MAP dialog box allows the user to type in command names. Each input string is looked up in the map. If an association is found, the *Execute()* member function of that command object is invoked and the resulting text is placed in the static text control; if an association is not found, the *Default* object's *Execute()* is invoked. Figure 18-12 shows the application screen just after the "wind" command has been entered. Yes, this is a very simplistic command interpreter, but it is flexible, extensible during runtime, and simple to build.

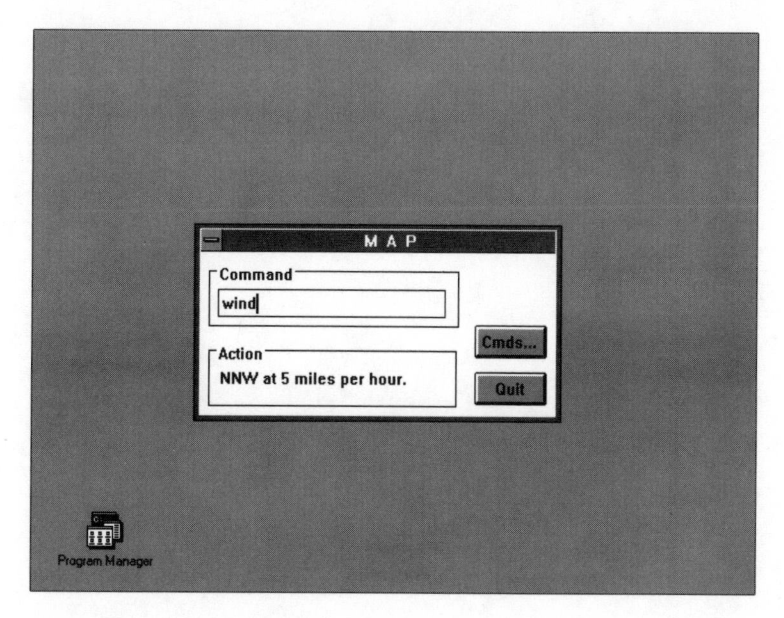

Figure 18-12.
The Map application screen just after the user has typed in the "wind" command. The "Action" box shows the result.

Appendix A

C++ Rules for Special Member Functions

	Can Be Inherited	*Can Be Virtual*	*Can Be a Friend*	*Can Be Overloaded*	*Return Type*	*Generated by Default*
default constructor	no[1]	no	no	no	none	yes[2]
copy constructor	no[1]	no	no	yes	none	yes[3]
other constructors	no[1]	no	no	yes	none	no
destructor	no[1]	yes	no	no	none	yes[4]
operator=()	no	yes	no	yes	any	yes[5]
operator type	yes	yes	no	no	none[6]	no
operator() *operator[]* *operator–>*	yes	yes	no	yes	any	no
operator new()[7]	yes	no	no	yes	*void**	no
operator delete()[8]	yes	no	no	no	*void*	no
other operators	yes	yes	yes	yes	any	no

1. Constructors and destructors aren't inherited, although they are invoked by derived classes.

2. A default constructor will be generated only when no constructor for the class has been defined. It will be public, and its only action will be to invoke default constructors for base and member classes.

3. An *X(X&)* copy constructor will be generated only if no other copy constructors have been defined. It will be public, and it will perform memberwise initialization.

4. A default destructor will be generated only when no destructor for the class has been defined and when the class has base class or member objects that have destructors. It will be public, and its only action will be to invoke default destructors for base class and member object classes.

5. An *operator=()* will be generated automatically only if no *operator=()* has been defined. It will be public, and it will perform memberwise assignment.

6. The implicit return type is the type of the conversion, but it cannot be specified explicitly.

7. *operator new()* is always a static member function, although the *static* keyword need not be mentioned explicitly. It takes a *size_t* first argument and optional user-defined placement arguments.

8. *operator delete()* is a static member function, even if it is not explicitly declared so with the *static* keyword. It can take a single *void** argument or both a *void** and a *size_t* argument; only one of these two forms should be defined.

Appendix B

C++ Constructors and Destructors

C++ Constructor Activation Order

Creation of an object can require activating four separate sets of constructors invoked in this order:

1. The constructors of any virtual base classes are activated first, in the order in which they are encountered in a left-to-right, depth-first traversal of the class hierarchy.
2. Base class constructors are activated second, in the left-to-right order in which the base classes are mentioned in the header of the class definition.
3. Constructors for member objects are activated third, in the order in which the members are declared in the class definition.
4. The constructor for the class itself is activated last. It can rely on the activation of the earlier constructors. It might invoke ordinary or virtual member functions. When virtual member functions are invoked, the class's own versions (its own member functions) are activated.

The order of a constructor's initialization list is irrelevant, having nothing to do with the actual order in which constructors are invoked. This is counterintuitive, but the order of construction is determined by the rules above and by the order in which base and member classes appear in a class definition. This forces the same order of initialization to be used in all of a class's constructors.

Destructors are activated in the opposite order.

C++ Constructor Rules and Exceptions

- A constructor can be invoked for a *const* or *volatile* object. An ordinary member function must be specifically declared as *const* or *volatile* in order to work with a *const* or *volatile* object.

- A constructor cannot be declared as *const* or *volatile*. It is hard to imagine what role a *const* constructor would have if it couldn't modify its object.
- A constructor cannot be declared as *static*. Constructors exist to initialize member variables, which would be inaccessible to a static constructor. Static member variables can be initialized by means of ordinary initializations.
- A constructor cannot initialize static member variables in its initialization list. It can of course assign values to static member variables in its body.
- A constructor cannot be virtual. C++ sees that all relevant constructors are invoked for every object.
- A constructor cannot be inherited. C++ will write its own trivial constructor when a class without a constructor is derived from a class with a constructor.
- A constructor cannot have a return type, not even *void*. A constructor can signal an error only by means of member variables or the like.
- A class that has constructors can't be a member of a union, but a union can be a member of a class regardless of whether the class has constructors.
- The declaration for a class must explicitly specify all the constructors it needs except copy constructors and default constructors.

C++ Destructor Rules and Exceptions

- Each class can have only a single destructor.
- A destructor cannot have arguments.
- A destructor cannot have a return type, not even *void*.
- Destructors can be virtual, and in general should be virtual.
- A destructor cannot be inherited. However, C++ ensures that the base class destructor is invoked when a derived class object is destroyed.
- A destructor can be invoked explicitly. The destructor for an object named *o* whose class is named *OBJ* is invoked by writing

  ```
  o.~OBJ();
  ```

  Similarly, if *po* points at an *OBJ* object, its destructor can be explicitly invoked by writing

  ```
  po->~OBJ();
  ```

- A class with a destructor can't be a member of a union.
- A destructor can be called for a *const* or *volatile* object.

- A destructor cannot be declared as *const* or *volatile*.
- A destructor cannot be static.

C++ Constructor Usage Summary

In this summary, you'll find a compendium of information about using constructors that can serve as a convenient reference.

Ordinary Declarations

Ordinary declarations are used in the global scope or in the function scope to create objects. Ordinary declarations are distinct from member declarations, function argument declarations, and function return value declarations, which are considered separately.

```
OBJ o;
```

Create an object named *o* using the default constructor.

```
OBJ o[n];
```

Create an array of objects named *o* using the default constructor once for each element of the array.

```
OBJ o(args);
OBJ o = OBJ(args);
```

Create an object named *o* using a constructor that is selected according to argument type. The selection is governed by the usual rules for selecting an overloaded function.

```
OBJ o = existing_obj;
OBJ o(existing_obj);
```

Create an object named *o* using a copy constructor, which will be generated if none is supplied in the class definition. The copy constructor will use a reference to an *existing_obj* to create the new object.

```
OBJ o[n] = {
    init1,
    init2,
    . . .
    initm
};
```

Create an array of objects named *o* using *init1* through *initm* for the initial values. The *init* clauses can be simple values or constructor expressions. The types of the *init* clauses determine which constructor is invoked. If *m* is fewer than *n*, array elements *m* through *n–1* are initialized using the default constructor. In the following example, *o[0]* is initialized by the *OBJ(int)* constructor, *o[1]* is initialized by the *OBJ(double)* constructor, *o[2]* is initialized by the *OBJ(char *)* constructor, *o[3]* is initialized by the *OBJ(int, int)* constructor, and *o[4]* is initialized by the default constructor:

```
OBJ o[5] = {
   1, 2.0, "three", OBJ(1,2) };
```

Dynamically Allocated Objects

The *new* operator is used to create objects dynamically. All dynamically allocated objects persist until they are explicitly deleted.

`OBJ *po = new OBJ;` — Dynamically allocate a new object, accessible by means of *po*, using the default constructor.

`OBJ *po = new OBJ(args);` — Dynamically allocate a new object, accessible by means of *po*, using a constructor that is selected according to argument type.

`OBJ *pao = new OBJ[n];` — Dynamically allocate an array of *n* objects, accessible by means of *pao*, using the default constructor to initialize each element. Note that dynamically allocated arrays are always initialized using the default constructor; other constructors are not available.

Base Class Objects

```
class X : OBJ {
    . . .
    // no X constructor
};
```

If a class that lacks a constructor is derived from a class that does have a constructor, the compiler generates a default constructor for the derived class that activates the default constructor for the base class. In such a case, the base class must of course have a default constructor.

```
class X : OBJ {
    . . .
    // X constructors
    X();
    . . .
};
```

If both the base class and the derived class contain constructors, the derived class's constructor initialization lists are used to pass arguments to the base class constructors. If all of *X*'s constructors explicitly initialize their *OBJ* part in their initialization lists, *OBJ* might not need a default constructor. If any *X* constructors fail to mention *OBJ*, *OBJ* must have a default constructor.

```
X::X(void) :
    // initialize base class
    OBJ(1, 2.0),
    // other initializations
{ /* body */ }
```

This derived class's constructor explicitly initializes the derived class's base class component using the *OBJ(int, double)* constructor. If this explicit initialization were missing, the compiler would automatically invoke the base class's default constructor.

Member Objects

```
class X {
    . . .
    OBJ o;
    // no X constructor
    . . .
};
```

If a class that lacks a constructor contains a member of a class that does have a constructor, the compiler generates a default constructor for the containing class that activates the default constructor for the member objects. In such a case, the member's class must of course have a default constructor.

```
class X {
    . . .
    OBJ o;
    // X constructor
    X();
    . . .
};
```

If a class has a constructor, the constructor's initialization lists are used to specify arguments for member object constructors. Any member object that isn't explicitly initialized in one of the initialization lists must have a default constructor. The compiler will ensure that every member object is initialized whenever the containing class's object is initialized.

```
X::X(void) :
    // initialize member object
    o(1, 2.0),
    // other initializations
{ /* body */ }
```

The *X* constructor explicitly initializes the *o* member object using the *OBJ(int, double)* constructor. If this explicit initialization were missing, the compiler would automatically invoke the default constructor for *o*.

Function Value Parameters and Function Return Values

An object's constructors are automatically invoked when an object is passed by value (not by pointer or by reference) to a function and when an object (not a pointer to an object or a reference to an object) is returned from a function.

```
void fn(OBJ o);
```

Each time an object is passed to *fn()*, a copy constructor is invoked to initialize *o*. The copy constructor receives a reference to an *OBJ*, and its *this* pointer indicates the space reserved for *o*. The copy constructor will be generated automatically if it is not supplied by the class designer.

```
OBJ fn(declarations)
{
    OBJ o;
    . . .
    return o;
}
```

When an object is returned by a function, a copy constructor is called to create the return value. In the function shown on the left, a default constructor is invoked first to construct *o*, then *o* is used inside the function, and then a copy constructor is called to create a copy of *o*, which is returned as the value of *fn()*.

It is easy to confuse declarations of functions that return objects with declarations of objects that pass parameters to the object constructors. The following example shows both:

```
void v()
{
    OBJ fn(double);// fn() is a function that takes a double argument
                   // and returns an OBJ
    OBJ var(1.2);  // var is an OBJ that is constructed using the
                   // OBJ(double) constructor
    var = fn(1.2); // the value returned by fn() will be assigned to var
}
```

The declaration of *fn()* mentions its argument types in the argument header, but the declaration of the *var* object mentions actual values that are passed to its class *OBJ*'s constructor. To avoid ambiguity, declare an object that is to be constructed by the default constructor as

```
OBJ o;
```

not as

```
OBJ o();
```

The second declaration is legal, but it doesn't create an object named *o* using the default constructor. Instead, the parentheses specify that *o* is a function that doesn't take any arguments and returns an *OBJ*.

Constructor Bypassing

There are two leaks in C++'s object construction system. Both "features" have few if any legitimate uses, but they are aspects of C++ that you should understand.

```
OBJ *po = (OBJ *)
  malloc(sizeof(OBJ));
```

The *malloc()* routine from the C library can be used to allocate a region of storage that is the same size as an object. However, not only will base classes and ordinary members be uninitialized, but also a class with virtual member functions will find that its *vptr*, which is supposed to point at a virtual function dispatch table, will also be uninitialized. Attempts to invoke virtual functions will therefore fail.

```
void v(void)
{
    OBJ o;
    void fn( . . . );
    fn(o);
}
```

When the *o* object is passed to the *fn()* function, a simple copy of *o*'s bits is made. A copy constructor is not used. Inside *fn()*, the argument should be treated as a block of memory, not as an object.

Index

Page number references to figures and illustrations are in italics.

D

E

F

G

H

I

P

U

V

W

Z

About the Author

Kaare Christian is a research associate at the Rockefeller University, in the laboratory of Nobel prize–winning scientist and University president Torsten Wiesel. He constructs instrumentation used in studies of the human visual system. Kaare's C experience dates back to the mid-1970s. In the early 1980s, he became interested in alternatives to C's rough-and-tumble style and spent several years working with Modula-2, which lead eventually to a well-received book on Modula-2. In the mid-1980s, Kaare turned his attention to the then little-known C++, and he has been using it ever since. Kaare is an occasional contributor to *PC Magazine,* and he has often reviewed C and C++ compilers for the PC.

The manuscript for this book was prepared and submitted to Microsoft Press in electronic form. Text files were processed and formatted using Microsoft Word.

Principal editorial compositor: Debbie Kem
Principal proofreader/copy editor: Shawn Peck
Principal typographer: Carolyn Magruder
Interior text designer: Kim Eggleston
Principal illustrators: Christine Castigliano and Lisa Sandburg
Cover designer: Tom Draper
Cover color separator: Color Control

Text composition by Microsoft Press in Garamond Light with display type in Futura Heavy, using the Magna composition system and the Linotronic 300 laser imagesetter.

Printed on recycled paper stock.

SPECIAL OFFER

Companion Disk for THE MICROSOFT® GUIDE TO C++ PROGRAMMING

Microsoft Press has created a companion disk for *The Microsoft Guide to C++ Programming*. This disk, available in 3.5-inch format (720-KB) and 5.25-inch format (360-KB), contains over 100 programs presented in this book. You can create programs that include code fragments from the companion disk for commercial or personal purposes without infringing on the copyright of the book.

Domestic Ordering Information:
To order, use the special reply card in the back of the book. If the card has already been used, please send **$19.95**, plus sales tax in the following states if applicable: AZ, CA, CO, CT, DC, FL, GA, HI, ID, IL, IN, IA, KS, KY, ME, MD, MA, MI, MN, MS, MO, NE, NV, NJ, NM, NY, NC, OH, OK, PA, RI, SC, TN, TX, UT, VA, WA, WV, WI. Microsoft reserves the right to correct tax rates and/or collect the sales tax assessed by additional states as required by law, without notice. Please add $5.00 per disk set for domestic postage and handling charges. Mail your order to: **Microsoft Press, Attn: Companion Disk Offer, 21919 20th Ave. SE, Box 3011, Bothell, WA 98041-3011**. Specify 3.5-inch format (item number 097-000-721) or 5.25-inch format (item number 097-000-718). Payment must be in U.S. funds. You may pay by check or money order (payable to Microsoft Press) or by American Express, VISA, or MasterCard; please include credit card number, expiration date, and cardholder signature. Allow 2–3 weeks for delivery upon receipt of order.

Foreign Ordering Information (within the U.K. and Canada, see below):
Follow procedures for domestic ordering. Add $15.00 per disk set for foreign postage and handling.

U.K. Ordering Information:
Send your order in writing along with £17.95 (includes VAT) to: Microsoft Press, 27 Wrights Lane, London W8 5TZ. You may pay by check or money order (payable to Microsoft Press) or by American Express, VISA, MasterCard, or Diners Club; please include credit card number, expiration date, and cardholder signature. Specify 3.5-inch format (item number 097-000-721) or 5.25-inch format (item number 097-000-718).

Canadian Ordering Information:
Send your order in writing along with $26.95 (includes GST) to: Macmillan Canada, Attn: Microsoft Press Department, 164 Commander Blvd., Agincourt, Ontario, Canada M1S 3C7. You may pay by check or money order (payable to Microsoft Press) or by VISA or MasterCard; please include credit card number, expiration date, and cardholder signature. Specify 3.5-inch format (item number 097-000-721) or 5.25-inch format (item number 097-000-718).

Microsoft Press Companion Disk Guarantee:
If a disk is defective, a replacement disk will be sent. Please send the defective disk and your packing slip (or copy) to: Microsoft Press, Consumer Sales, One Microsoft Way, Redmond, WA 98052-6399.